THE HISTORY OF THAT INIMITABLE MONARCH TIBERIUS

THE HISTORY OF THAT INIMITABLE MONARCH TIBERIUS

John Rendle

www.General-Books.net

Publication Data:

Title: The history of that inimitable monarch Tiberius
Subtitle: who, in the XIV year of his reign, requested the Senate to permit the worship of Jesus Christ; and who, in the XVI and three following years ... suppressed all opposition to it
Author: John Rendle
General Books publication date: 2010
Original publication date: 1813
Original Publisher: Printed for Longman, Hurst, Rees, Orme, and Brown
Subject:
Rome
Fiction / Classics
History / Ancient / Rome
Literary Collections / General
Literary Criticism / General

How We Made This Book
We automated the typing, proof reading and design of this book using Optical Character Recognition (OCR) software on a scanned copy of the original rare book. That allowed us to keep your cost as low as possible.
If the book is very old, worn and the type is faded, this can result in a lot of typos or missing text. This is also why our books don't have illustrations; the OCR software can't distinguish between an illustration and a smudge.
We understand how annoying typos, missing text or illustrations can be. That's why we provide a free digital copy of most books exactly as they were originally published. Simply go to our website (www.general-books.net) to check availability. And we provide a free trial membership in our book club so you can get free copies of other editions or related books.
OCR is not a perfect solution but we feel it's more important to make the book available for a low price than not at all. So we warn readers on our website and in the descriptions we provide to book sellers that our books don't have illustrations and may have typos or missing text. We also provide excerpts from each book to book sellers and on our website so you can preview the quality of the book before buying it.
If you would prefer that we manually type, proof read and design your book so that it's perfect, we are happy to do that. Simply contact us via our website for the cost.

Limit of Liability/Disclaimer of Warranty:
The publisher and author make no representations or warranties with respect to the accuracy or completeness of the book. The advice and strategies in the book may not be suitable for your situation. You should consult with a professional where appropriate. The publisher is not liable for any damages resulting from the book.
Please keep in mind that the book was written long ago; the information is not current. Furthermore, there may be typos, missing text or illustration and explained above.

CONTENTS

Section 1	1
Section 2	9
Section 3	11
Section 4	19
Section 5	43
Section 6	69
Section 7	81
Section 8	97
Section 9	111
Section 10	125
Section 11	131
Section 12	141
Section 13	159
Section 14	173
Section 15	183

Section 16	205
Section 17	227
Section 18	241
Section 19	249
Section 20	257
Section 21	281
Section 22	293

1

SECTION 1

HISTORY
 OF
 THAT INIMITABLE JfOJVJRCH
 TIBERIUS,
 WHO,
 IN THE XIV YEAR OF HIS REIGN,
 REQUESTED THE SEJVATE
 TO PERMIT THE WORSHIP OF JESUS CHRIST;
 AND WHO,
 IN THE XVI AND THREE FOLLOWING YEARS,
 Or,
 BEFORE THE COJVfERSIOJV OF CORJVELIUS BY PETER,
 SUPPRESSED ALL OPPOSITION TO IT.
 The Rev. JOHN RENDLE, M. A.
 LATELY MATH. LECT. OF SID. SUSsTcOLL. CAMBRIDGE,
 AND SINCE FELLOW OF THAT SOCIETY,
 BUT NOW VICAR OF WIDECOMBE IN THE MOOR, DEVON.
 Ut quibus initiis, *quunttt arte Tiberii* gravissimum exitium irrepserit,

dein repressum sit, postremo arserit, cunctaque c. trripueric,
noscatur. Tac. Ann. i. 73.
Repressaque in praesens exitiabilis superstitio rursus erumpebat, non
modo per Judsam originem ejus mali, sed per urbem etiam.
Ann. xv. 44.
Cum interim usque eo *sceleratittimre gentit* consuetudo conraluit ut
per omncs *jam* terras recepta sit: *victi victoribus leges dedsrunt.*
Sen. de Superstition?.
: Pb-. nteu BY Trewman And Son, HICH-STRttr.

THE HISTORY
'. T J B E B I IT S :
Who, as seven cotemporory and other writers say, was
VERY STUDIOUS OF EVERY LIBERAL AND USEFUL SCIENCE.
As long as he lived
THE FRIEND OF NONE BUT VIRTUOUS AND LEARNED MEN.
When commander in chief
MOST CORDIALLY BELOVED BY ALL HIS OFFICERS AND MEN.
During the Pannonian and German wars
THE SOLE SUPPORTER OF THE ROMAN SUPER-EMINENCE.
Five years before he became a Monarch
BY THE SENATE MADE EQUAL IN POWER TO AUGUSTUS.
Long after he was a Monarch
A DETESTER OF FLATTERY AND OF ALL POMPOUS TITLES.
In the tenth year of his Monarchy
THE ABHORRENT OPPOSER OF HIS OWN DEIFICATION.
Long after the disaster at Fidenae
MOST EMINENTLY EXEMPLARY, GREAT, JUST, AND HUMANE.
After he was so very txemplaiy, &c.
AN EATER OF HUMAN FLESH AND A DRINKER OF HUMAN BLOOD. .
During most of his reign
THE UNIVERSAL DISPENSER OF THE BLESSINGS OF PEACE.
From the fourteenth to the nineteenth of his reign
PERMITTED THE WORST OF ALL CIVIL WARS TO RAGE AT ROME.
During the three first years of the same period
OVERCOME BY THE PRESSURE OF FAMILY AFFLICTIONS.
In the decline of life
NEGLIGENT OF THE GODS, BUT ATTENTIVE TO SOME ONE GOD.
Always
A FRIEND OF JEWS AND THE MAINTAINER OF JEWISH RITES.
From the time he went to Rhodes
A HEARER OF THE LAW AND A PARTIAL DOER OF IT.
Sometime before he died
REMARKABLY INQUISITIVE ABOUT FUTURITY.
In the fourteenth year of his reign
A BELIEVER IN THE DIVINITY OF JESUS CHRIST.

After the Jews had preferred Barobbas to Jefus
THE, ABOLJSHER OF ALL SANCTUARY PROTECTIONS.
Before the death of Sejanus
THE FIRST PROHIBITOR OF IMMEDIATE EXECUTIONS.
During the last eight years of his reign
THE NURSING FATHER OF THE INFANT CATHOLIC CHURCH.
In the sixteenth year of his reign
THE PROTECTOR OF JEWISH CHRISTIANS AS NOT BLASPHEMERS.
When old
OF ALL KINGS OR AUTOCRATS THE MOST VENERABLE.
Whose death was
AS SOME AFFIRMED, PREFIGURED BY THAT OF A PHCENIX.
Whose funerol was
SOLEMNIZED WITH DUE POMP AND AT THE PUBLIC EXPEHCE.
And, laftly, who, at his death
FOLLOWED AUGUSTUS TO THE RESIDENCE OF THE GODS. ORIGINAL QUOTATIONS
FROM
The works 'of the ancient Authors,
Alluded to in the preceding TITLE PAGE,
IN SUPPORT OP THE
SEVERAL PARTICULARS THEREIN ASSERTED OF
Very studious of every liberal and useful Science. Augustus. – Vale jucundiffimc Tiberi, et rem gere feliciter –

i xai rait Mso-ais- *cfariyxv,* . Suet. Hi. 21,

Horace. – Legentis honefta Neronis. *Eflifl.* i. 9. /. 4.

Paterculus. – Innutritus *cteleftlum pr1eceptorttm difci/ilinis,* ju- venis genere, forma, celfitudine corporis, *optimis jlud'ris* maximoque ingenio inftruftiffimus. ii. 94.

Tut Xt' avrot ax/uiiravTaiv; p. 7 "3' '- 8 *Ii.-m* aXXa xaj *en vsos vv, o irfto-Gunis* sXtyero Si iSw *rm mifi rm ayinuH.* p. 783. F.

tgtiSn *irfos* To o-E/voTrfot Te *v. ai avrvfoTif* o *o-xfSor at* riii *irfurrts yiaiat* Suetonius. – Artcs liberates utriufque generis ftudiofiffime coluit iii. 70.

DlON C. – Evffi'/xfltu sv Vmctos *irift avru, ircttras ras ra roiavra axfiGwras avru* Ts xXw SiaXE7Eyflasj.

L. 57. p. 613. E.

The friend of none but virtuous and learned Men.

Paterculus. – Honorantur refta, prava puniuntur – honor dignis paratiffimus – nam facere refte cives fuos Princeps optimus faciendo docet. ii. 126.

V. Maximus. – Te igitur huic caepto, penes quem hominum Deorumque confenfus, maris ac terrae regimen efle voluit, certiffima falus patriae Caefar invoco : cujus coelefti prudentia, virtutes de quibus difturus fum benigniffime foventur : vitia feveriffime vindicantur.

Prel. ad Tib.

PHI I/O. – EXtxtuv *aKtytvo-atro Tut tyxvxtu Krat Qtl. tny. txv ra trfaref to-smra, as avrm tSuftnraro TtGtftu Kxnrotft rare Im* av *Hhj. ius trvyyan lafonlttas, oo-x fAttfaxtun afntn&y. ar TtGffta* Sttf/icntxt)Tsf *tmitn trfos Tv ftptorefot* Ti Xoh acs-Dfortfot o-tSov en vfuTtts vtKtets artxttm "Xfv-
p. 786. F.

CLEMENS OF R. - *Stxaannos It* o Kar/i Tov Ti *trartfat xat* mv *xat nrtytss ourus* tl ern *tn -rorw. xa-t vefttyvs avru ra Tfanu, Qcfpus*

Se *ra 'fnv&as, trfos rov avyytrot* (MrofXtar, *mtyxafnn pot, tifin Ut* Kojwiv *tof rm mtntnapcQa, Ttst tmvfw'n Qvre Kvi tAar&tltas , on vcxf0! anno-att, xat* TToXotXorss *tvfuQtmu, DegejJtsP. f.* 143.

Tacitus. – Caeteri liberalibus ftudiis praediti, ferme Graeci, quorum fermonibus levaretur. *Ann.* iv. 58.

– – – – – Cocceius Nerva continuus Principis omnis divini humanique juris fciens. *Ann.* vi. 26.

Turn complexus eum (Thrafyllum) Tiberius inter inti-
mos amicorum tenet. *Ann.* vi. 21.

N. B. Julian fays of Thrafyllus that he would have been equally famous if he never had been acquainted with Tiberius.

DION C. – Ou Ss *fy tn,* ttpt), *al-tos upt, ttyt xt* AtvrtXov *pt*
L. 57.

§E $i *ffaQifv: aura Mxpxos 'S. iaios, aff
irtiot) fixpvs avru Vtto Tt fyjs aptTys uat vffo Tys yvyyevtias yv xai oix faro inpitGfiiro, laiTM xarcfyfaro.* o / yap *TiGipios urus aunt* Iti/iiv., *Usti p. yri* txxXiiTot *wore air avru Sixatrsti tQrt.'i-jxv,* XX' *iatita ttatroc $vQis rtt roiavrx lyxfipurai.* JL. 59. P- 45- f . 646. A.

JVLost cordially beloved by all his Officers and Men.

Paterculus. – Neque *illi* fpeftaculo, quo fruftus fum, fimile conditio mortalis recipere videtur mihi : cum per celeberrimam Italise pattem, traftam omnem Galliae provinciarum veterem im- peratorem, et ante meritis ac virtutibus quam nomine, Caefarem revifentes, fibi quifque quam illi, gratularentur plenius. At vero militum confpeftu ejus elicita e gaudio lacrymae, alacritafque et falu- tationes novaquaedam exultatio, et contingendi manus cupiditas, non continentium protinus, quin adjecerant – Videmus te, Imperator? falvum recepimus ? – ac deinde – Ego tecum, Imperator, in Armenia, ego in Pannonia, ego in Germania donatus fum. ii. 104.

Quauta cum quiete hominum, rem perpetui praecipuique
timoris, fupplementum, fine trepidatione deleftus providet ? ii. 130.

Tacitus. – Ire ipfum, et opponere majeftatem imperatoriam de- buifle, cefluris, ubi principem longa experientia, eundemque feveri- tatis et munificentiae fummum vidiflent. A. i. 46.

The sole supporter of the Roman super-eminence.

Augustus Ad Tib. – Teque rogo ut parcas tibi: ne fi te lan- guere audierimus, et ego et mater tua exfpiremus et de fumma im- perii p. R. periclitetur. *Suet.* iii. 21.

N. B. Suetonius had before faid of Auguftus – et epiftolis aliquot, (Tib.)   ut paritiffimum rei militaris, atque *unicum prajtd'aun* P. R- profequebatur.

Paterculus. – Laetitiam illius diei, concurfumque civitatis, ct; vota pene inferentium coelo manus fpemque conceptae *perpetuce*
tatis aternitatifque R. I., vix in illo jufto opere abunde perfequi pote- rimus, nedum hie implere tentemus. Id unum dixifle [juvat] quam ille omnibus fuerit [carus] turn refulfit certa fpes liberorum paren- tibus, viris matrimoniorum, dominis patrimonii; omnibus hominibus falutis, quietis, pacis, tranquillitatis: adco, ut nee plus fperari potuerit, nee fpei refponderi felicius. ii. 103.

V. Maximus. – Princeps parenfque nofter auftor ct tutela
incolumitatis noftra. ix. ii.

By the Senate made equal in power to Augustus.

Paterculus. – Autumno (that is in autumn of the year u. c. 761, and immediately after the peace with Pannonia, as Dion fays in the end of 55 book) viftor in hyberna reducitur exercitus, cujus omnibus copiis a Caefare (a Caefaribas, no doubt, fays the Oxf. Ed.) M. Lepidus praefeftus eft, vir nominis et fortunae *eorum* proximus.

ii. 114.

Initio aetatis Lepidus, edufto hybernis exercitvi, &c. –
pervenit ad Caefarem; et ob ea, quae, fi propriis geffiflet aufpiciis, triumphare debuerat, ornamentis triumphalibus, confentiente prin- cipum voluntate donatus eft. – . 115.

N. B. By the former of thofe two extrafts it appears that Lepidus was, early in the year u. c. 762, made, by Auguftus and Tiberius, commander in chief. And by the other, that he, in the fame year, and by confent of the fame princes, was invefted with triumphal ornaments.

Eadem, et virtus et fortuna fubfequenti tempore ingreflk
animum imperatoris Tiberii fuit, quae initio fuerat, qui .... cum .... molliflct, et fenatus populufque Romanus (poftulante patre ejus) ut lequum ei jus in omnibus provinciis exercitibufque eflet, quam erat ipfi, decreto complexus eflet (etenim ab- furdum erat ....) *in urbcm reverfus,* jam pridem debitum, fed continuatione bellorum dilatum, ex Pannonicis Dalmatifque egit triumphum. ii- i2i-

N. B. By this we learn that Tiberius was, before he returned to Rome and triumphed over the Pannonians and Dalmatians, by the Senate, invefted with power equal to that of Auguftus.

Quibus,/KWta;
nejusexaggeravithonoribus, refpondente
cultu triumphi rerum quas geflerat magnitudini ? ii. 129.

Thofe honors appear, by what Dion fays L. 56. p. 582. B., to have been conferred on Germanicus in the year u. c. 763, and before the news arrived of the defeat of Varus.

Suetonius. – Data rurfus poteftas Tribunitia in quinquennium: delegate pacandae Germaniae flatus: Parthorum legati, mandatis Augufto Romae redditis, cum quoque adire in Provinciam juffi.

' ' ' j'
in. 16.

Nihilominus urbem praetextatus, et laurea coronatus intravk, pofi- tumque in Septis tribunal, Senatu adftante, confcendit: ac medius inter duos Cofs. *cum Augufto Jimul fedit:* unde, populo confalutato, circum templa deductus eft. iii. 17.

N. B. This triumphant entrance into the city muft, according to Dion, L. 56, init., have happened in the year u. c. 762. And, therefore, the Parthian ambafladors muft, before that entrance, have been fent to Tiberius in Germany.

- ' Ac non multo poft Lege per Cofs. lata, ut Provincial cum Augufto communiter adminiftraret, *Jimulque cenfum ageret,* con- dito luftro in lllyricum profeftus eft. iii. 21.

N. B. By this it appears that this law enabling Tiberius, with Auguftus, to govern the provinces and to make a cenfus, was. pafled before the laft cenfus was begun, and as every cenfus lafted five years, and that here fpoken of ended a little before the death of Auguftus, this law muft have been pafled u. c. 762.

B. ... .'

Tacitds. – Drufoque pridem exftinfio, Nero foluse privignis erat: iliac cuafta verge re: filius, collega imperil, confers tribooitke potes- tatis adfumitur, omoifque per ezercitos oftentatur: non, &c. A. L 3.

N. B. By the order in which Tacitus has mentioned thofe three degrees of promotion, it mould feem that Tiberias was made colleague in the empire before he was made partner in the tribunitial authority.

. ... .., t Etenim Auguftus, *ftouch ante anna,* cum Tiberio tribu- nitiam poteftatem a patribus *rurfian* poftularet, qaamquam, &c.

A. L 10.

Query – How many yean before the death of Augnftus was the ! r; bunitial authority *again* conferred on Tiberius ? – Dion fays L 55. p. 556. E. that in 757 the tribunitial power was conferred on Tiberias for ten years. Confequently, if that power was given to him in the year u. c. 757, it muft have ended in the year u. c. 767, the year in which Auguftus died. That it was then given to him, Paterculus fays. ii. 103. But could Tacitus have here meant by *fuutcis annis* the year 757, when Auguftus adopted Tiberius ? Would Auguftus then have expofed his defefts? Did he not then fay – Hoc reip. cauffa facio ? Surely Tacitus muft have here meant the fame year, as he had before done, i. 3. when Tiberius was made collega imperii. – And the fame as Suetonius does, iii, 16. where he fays the Parthian am- bafladors were fent into Germany to attend Tiberius.

Ut verfa Cacfarum fobole, imperium adeptus eft.

Ann. ii. 42.

Now what does he mean by this ? That he could not have meant by it to allude to the commencement of Tiberius' monarchy is plain, from what he fays, i. 6. – primum facinus *novi imperii* fuit Agrippx Pofthumi cacdes. Does he then mean that Tiberius obtained a mare in the government foon after the death of Caius ? At that time Agrippa Pofthumus was alive and in favor. Muft he notthen have meant by it the difgrace of Agrippa Pofthumus ? If he does, Tiberius muft have been admitted to a fhare in the government after u. c. 760, for Dion fays, 1. 55. p. 570. A. that Agrippa was in that year banifhed to Planafia, near Corfica.

– Fine anni (u. c. 788. T. 22.) Poppaeus Sabinus conceffit

vita principum amicitia, confulatum et triumphale decus adcp-
tus: maximifque provinciis per quatuor et viginti annps impofitus.
Ann. vi. 39.

Now P. Sabinus was, we know, conful u. c. 762, feveral years after the deaths of Caius and Lucius, and, more than one after the banifhment of Agrippa. – Confequently, by – principum amicitia – can only be underftood that of Auguftus and Tiberius.

DlON C. – *tTntn* St o AttyBjov *xatt rZ fn(f xat rn ra TUf. atrv! aStntp txayuta, tft fMt* ouvaffS' *TTS. ft fats* Sfoutou T/ *ura xfnpxntytv, rat ij. tt* XXa; *tttros /j. stx. ron mntyut xat tso-xc–aro, Kxl* ftxatv, cv Tar *llftana lvt ffmjatns* 7Tfo *ras* Se *vftcGttaft toK re tratfat Tut SnlAuv, xxt Tas trxfa rut ftaunfaut* art

T$v *wrrnvxorvI* ttnTftv, *us uras yufts* fxrov *xat taxacH ntuv, xat* t, ? rXt)v *Tut east* rayxv *'nt rvv n* /3aXnv *Kcci txttvn*

1. 55- P- 57- -

– – O Jt St) *TtGtfws ts Tm fufun turn tn yftyfata, tv u Kvnlros ZaivtKtos tuct Teuos* ZCrts *vnarwmtf etttxo/lf-Qn. xt avru xat o Avyafos ts r0 vfoattot xv mrnxras, nQt re fur avra ts rot Zutfra,* xvTavfl *rn fmttret ret* SS/vv *tavataat. ro. ,* 1. j|6. p. 572- "

An Ancient PANEGYRtst. – Quoufque hoc Maiminiarte, parialr, me quad, te quiefcere, mihi libertatem adimi, te ufurpare tibi illi- citam miffionem? An quod Divo Augufto, poft feptuaginta aetatis, quinquaginta imperil, non licuit annos, tam cito licuit tibi ?

Pagius – Critic. A. C.. num. iii.

2

SECTION 2

A detester of flattery and of all pompous Titles:
 Suetonius. – Interceffit et quo minus in afta fua juraretur: et ne- mcnfis September, Tiberius; Oftober, Livius vocaretur. Praenomen quoque Imperatoris, cognomenque Patris Patriae, et civicam in vefti- bulo coronam recufavit. Ac ne Augufti quidem nomen, quanquam haereditarium, ullis nifi ad Reges ac dynaftas epiftolis addidit.
 iii. 26.
 – – – – Adulationes adeo averfatus eft, ut neminem Senatorum aut officii aut negotii cauf a ad lefticam fuam admiferit: confularem vero fatisfacientem fibi, ac per genua orare conantem ita fuffugerit, ut caderet fupinus: atque etiam fi quid in fermone; vel in continua oratione blandius de fe diceretur, non dubitaret interpellare ac re- prehendere, et commutare continue. Dominns appellatus a quodam, tjenuntiavit, ne fe amplius contumeliae cauf a nominaret. iii. 27.
 Tacitus. – Nomen patris patriae Tiberius a populo faepins in- geftum repudiavit: neque in afta fua jurari, quamquam cenfente fenatu, permifit: cunfta mortalium incerta, quantoque plus adeptus foret, tanto fe magis in lubrico diftans. *Ann.* . 72.'
 DlON. C. – *vat i ari Sttntorm to. vrot rois civQifois, ari atinxfurofa, fXTiurair,* xaXtiv *ityut: To, re ra itarfos riis irarfi$os irf* SftiiaaTO. *rifoxpiros* St Tr *yipayias xarot ro apaio* ii0eXtii *ttcffoxis* tXtyev Oti – AtOTToTDi fcsv *rut* JaXw, *auroxfarvp* Ss

rut rfanuruv, fut ee fanruli trpaxpms tifti, nvtro re ria-uro xoti fyaai xai apl-ai yy/vwi, oa-ot as Tu SniMyiu orftpipi). *nal aria* ye 5ia *irxtrvt Cft. oius &ilMrmos y x. T. ..*
1. 57. p. 607. A.
' *ro* SE *TiGtfiu -ns* /3aXr *tyxtiiams, xai rot yat pma rot tiotpSftn, et a ry earv vat* Stxa *lyeymro, T&ifiot* xaXtio-OasJ al i8o-)i-Kaj *ri, ttyn, iryimrv, ti yetutrtti.*
J. *$j.* p. 614. E.

3

SECTION 3

Tlte abhorrent opposer of his own Deification.
Suetonius. – Templa, Flamines, Sacerdotes decerni fibi prohibuit: ctiam ftatuas, atque imagines, nifi permittente fe poni : permifitque, ea fola conditione, ne inter fimulacra Deorum, fed inter ornamenta aedium ponerentur. Interceffit et quo minus in afta fua juraretur.
iii. 26.
Dommus appellatus a quodam, denuntiavit, ne fe am-
plius contumeliae caufa nominaret. Alium dicentem facras ejus occupationes, &c. pro facris laboriofas dicere coegit. iii. 27.
Tacitus. – Ego me P. C. mortalem efle, et hominum officia fungi, fatifque habere, fi locum principem impleam, et vos teftor, et memi- nifle pofteros velo, &c. – Tiberius to the Senate. – To which Tacitus fubjoins – Perftititque pofthoc, fecretis etiam fermonibus, afpernari talem fui cultum. *Ann.* iv. 38.
DlON C. – Taura n at Sx/xorfxair *ottaxtt. xatt on an retf. svlo-px eatru fj uQatt(tnv,* XX' vS' atAAwr Toti yf tn/xtno-fl *an ttxotx tnt avra aSttt (trufafriu. at atmyoftttn, fam tnn* it' iSiTt *varv yatf rn atrofftHru,* ori, – *ea pn tya ratrffiu* – *Vfatmrtnn* St *on* – *ax*

u – Fttf/ To *yt vfnrQizt trfvs nms xat To vi7tGno-Qat Vfos Ttnt (&at(3ct&v* Tf *yaf* xJt) *xat To* TOtSrov wto/xaot, *xat (itxets tti avru* oXXaf *tffnyot) nxtr TTftxr- ttrotttro.* aSs *tfH m Tihz Toiocitw cifi tavTu* yfafnv *rrpoo-i!itl; aro, xanrtf tut X. oli ct Tutu asfiiwuat.* 1. *$7. OOJ.* E. 8. A.

Most eminently exemplary, great, just, and humane.

Pater. culus. – O rem diftu non eminentem, fed folida veraque yirtute atque utilitate maximam, experientia fuaviffimam, humanitate fingularem ! Per omne belli Germanici Pannonicique tempus, nemo e tjobis, gradumve noftrum aut praecedentibus aut fequentibus, imbecillus . fuit; cujus falus ac valetudo non ita fuftentaretur Caefaris cura, tam- quam diftraftiffimus ille tantorum onernm mole huic- uni negotiovacaret animus. Erat defiderantibas paratum junftum vehkulum; Icftica ejus publicata, cujus beneficium com alii, turn ego fenii. Jam media, jam apparatus cibi, jam in hoc folum importatum inftrumen- tnm balinei nullius non fuccurrit valetudird, domus tatttm ac domestic i dearant; caeterum nihil, quod ab illis aut prxftari aut defiderari poflet . Adjiciam illud, quod, quifquis illis temporibus interfuit, at alia, quae retuii, agnofcet protinus. ii. 114.

Sepultaeque ac fitu obfita e juftitia, aequitas, induftria

civitati redditx; acceffit magiftratibus auctorhas, fenatoi ma-eras, judiciis gravitas; ii. 126.

t Cumque fit imperio maximum, exemplo major eft. 126.

V. Maxim vs. – Cujus caelefti providentia virtutes de quibus diftu- rns fum, benigniiTune foventur: *Prtl. ad Ttb.*

Lib. v. cap. t, De humanltate.

Lib. vi. cap. 5, De juftitia.

Princeps parenfque nofter ...... auftor ac tutela i

eolumitatis noftrae. ix. ii.

Seneca. – Quid aliorum tibi fuaera Cxfarurn referam? quos ia hoc mihi interim videtur violare fortuna, ut fie quoque generi humano profint, oftendentes, ne eog quidem, qui diis geniti deofque genituri dlcantur, fie fuam fortunam in poteftate habere, quemad- modum alienam. *Divus Auguftm,* atniffis liberis, nepotibus, exhaufla Caelanun turba, adopdone defertam domum fulfit. Tulit tamen for- titer: tanquam ejus jam res ageretur cujus cum max! me intererat, de diis neminem queri. *Tib, Cafar* et quem gennerat, et quern adopta- verat, amifit : Ipfe tamen pro roftris laudavit filium, fteritque in con fpeftu pofito corpore, interjefto tantummodo velamento, quod pontificis oculos a fonere arceret, et flente populo romano non fiexit vultcm : experiendum fe dedit Sejano ad btus ftanti, quam patienterpoflet fuos perdere. Videfne quanta copia *virorum tnanimarum* fit, quos non excepit hie omnia profternens cafns, in quos *tat animi bana,* tot ornamenta publicc privatimque congefta erant ?

Confel. adMaretam c. 15.

– – – Nomen Attici perire Ciceronis epiftola e non finunt. – Nihil illi profuiflet gener Agrippa, Tiberius progener, et Drufus nepos *inter tarn magna nomina* taceretur, nifi Cicero ilium applicuiflet.

Efift. 2r.

Suetonius- – Atque haec eo notabiliora erant, quod ipfe in appel- landis venerandifque fingulis, et univerfis prope exccilcrat humani- tatis rnodum. iii. 29.

Neque tam parvum quidquam, neque tarn magnum publici priva-
tique negotii fuit, de quo non ad P. C. referretur Nunquam
curiam nifi folus intravit: leftica quondam introlatus aeger, comites a fe removit. –
. 30.
Qasedam adverfus fententiam fuum decerni ne queftus
quidem eft Cum Senatusconfultum per difceffionem forte
fieret, tranfeuntem eum in alteram partem in qua pauciores erant, fecutus eft nemo. Caetera quoque non nifi per Magiftratus et jure ordinado agebantur: tanta Cofs. auftoritatc ut Legati ex Africa adierint eos, querentes trahi fe a Caefare, ad quern miffi forent. Nee mirum, cum palam eflet ipfum quoque eifdem aflurgere et decedere via. – .31.
Quorundam illuftrium exfequias ufque ad rogum frequen-
tavit. Parem moderationem minoribus quoque et perfonis et rebus exhibuit: &c. , iii. 32.
– – – - Paullatim Principem exercuit, praeftititque ; etfi varium diu, commodiorem tamen faepius, et ad utilitates publicas proniorem-. Ac primo eatenus intetveniebat ne quid perperam fieret. Itaque etconftitutiones quafdam feoatus refcidit: et Magiitratibns pro tribanali cognofcentibus plemmque fc oSerebat connliariont, affidebatqne miflim vel ex adrerfo in parte primori: ct fi quem reorum elabi gratia rumor eflet, fabitus adetat, jadicefqne ant e piano, *sat c* qiuefitoris tribunal!, legurn et religionis, et noxx de qua cognolcereat, admo- nebat: atque etiam fi qua in publicis moribos defidia aut mala con- foetudine labarent, corrigenda fufcepit. iii. 33.
Statimque revocante affidua obteftatione populo, prop- ter cladem, q-ua apud Fi-
denas, fupra xx. hominum miilia gladiatorio munere amphitheatri ruina perierant, tranfiit in continentem, potes- tatemque omnibus adeundi fui fecit; tanto magis quod ab urbe egredi ens, ne quis fe interpellaret, edixerat, ac toto itinere adeuntes fub- moverat. iii. 40.
– – – Nee abftinuit confuetudinc, quin *tmnc* quoque inflans in medio triclinio, adftante liclore, fingulos valere dicentes appellaret.
– .72.
Tacitus. – Tiberiumque ipfum viftoriarum fuarum, quaeque in toga per tot annos egregie feciflet, admonuiL *Ann* L t2.
– – – Egregium vita famaque quoad privatus vel in imperils fub Augufto fuit. vi. 51.
Congruens crediderim recenfere citeras quoque reipub-
licae panes, quibus modis ad earn diem habita e fint: quando Tiberio mutati in detenus principatos initium *tlls* annus attulit. Jam primom publica negotia, et privatorum maxima, apud patres traftabantur:
dabaturque primoribus diflerere: fua confulibus, fua prxtoribus
fpecies. minorum quoque magiftratuum exercita poteftas; legefque,
fi majeftatis qux-ftio eximeretur, bono in ufu Res fuas Caefar
fpe&aliffimo cuique, quibusdam ignotis ex fama mandabaL iv. 6
– – – Nondum ea clades (at Fidenae) exoleverat, cum ignis violentia urbem ultra folitum adfecit, deufto monte *Cxlio.* feralcm- que annum ferebant et ominibus adverfis fufceptum principi confi- Jium abfentiae, &c. ni Caefar obviam iflet, tribuendo

pecunias ex modo detrimenti. Aftaequc ei grates apud fenatum, ab inluflribus : famaque apud populum, quia fine ambitione, aut proximorum precibus, ignotos etiam et ultro accitos munificentia juverat. iv. 64.

- Magifque fama quam vi, flare res fuas. vi. 30.

DlON C. – tXaj$tr yaf *ts* atm'v Savawv, *tretr ts* To xooov

I'. sv us tttittv ra Sv/xo(Tt tfya, *rot* /fv *atotmoolf.-Z'v, fa ot etnxoo'itMt.* woXXa St *xat nouTt xxt uSturats ttrafxut, Tuv re* /3vXvtTwv *avytns lumens, xat f.* nxsn /t)Ss Ttt' tfleXovTar, twXtTTfV. a csvroi *xat axftrws auro ttntn,* aXXa x/ TBf iucv vtro *aunyuas, res $e vuu tnto trructast amt* /xnofva *avrns .0yta-//. ou* owroSSt/ tSwvro. wav Tt a tSafecro Tio-iv, tuflw xat *rots*

ttntSv yaf m Tt Ayya. vs /xtyatXa Fx raI Toibtwv oi SorSftr *avrut o, snus tfyvatmro fun xau elf tavra ran ytvso-Q&t. xat ravrat lumt TTayrat ex rut* vfto//,/o-jU, fvaiv wfoaoowv tSrrasv. Stf yap aTTfXTfivt sm *utnav nms rare yt* A/mwtfv, XX eS v§ *tmtfstas n , tu* yvv Pnxtci; *yjptma. rat wore vru* wXeiw wafa To TfTy/svot tx Tw AyutrTS

Kxt futrot xat ttvfoaoos xau twffocrwyofos ury)us m, ins yat r.0(ous ao-trafyffQxt avrot fXfXfufftt, tva tu urivTat. To, Tt *avpTTav, tTftemt'av tto-xst, ut ttteiSn mn 0i PoStut* afotTfS f7ri5"ftAavTet *n aura,* H rs nnroXti Tkto Sv To *toliufyftsvsv, tt%as avru tromium*

offaSi *us xat* xaxot Ti *(au; av,* tXflotTa? Se Stv Sfivov *ttfyaurotro, M? waoyfaatrs* To fvcot atntn/(/f. T&; *re atet afxftras us et y. oxfan tnIiuz, xau rots vrrotms xat vtr&vtratro, ovsore re auras $eustt(flt, raro* /uv, *ecmmzs a$Ks wpos rots Ovfats* tltffro, Tuto Sf, xai *atlannr&s* rofofEJf/AWfv. ct Tt mm csrt Tu *o,* a5s 01 w anoAsflfttv, owwv /3a? tEUT))Vj AA e5 Iwwf Twv

tat, a n tat. s cs-rr/zftr., u n Tt

tftssjn, t 5v av ty *trrt*

aTa ya; *vet tas* 9txvagJi/7a, Tw Tt T.-iit T MStn. rr-v *ns* re c. n9t tt. vrfu2, T Tt w–fTiis. t crf7i JcttTt. s 7.; r

TMxTM fAf, KTf JvXn TX, t &U 9VTBOA T. K,

to-os tuu tftont v, Hot fXro Twa Tv Jtfta fftAf-4jfau on t *Cfc, nfot cwBxntffx., Cfu T-. i ltrtKT-n* airs

re *troufea, us* §*10 a unmx, f. nt-* ' *ff* 0, xJU flts? t *o-vntffTX;. K-erras n mu tfy at ft rat frif Ttfjmnun* nv *fstrafat ttmt uvt.*

p. 608. 609.

t *not annfut* (Drufum-fcil.) xoj tS. xat *otyuxr' "mtXms.* K Cote *ftau amafvt* oWftv *vxfnTut ttwn* en, " Zwtk fu ;, tn

-; if : . v of ri x

Ti xaTa Tmv

auras CTt. fv5t, n xun *Ttft-Ttftft artKat.* ttt fuI ya sn rw foC *euayyns xat lUTftowrou Ta eamn, wft xt laJRn trtyft(Jtffat. t* S' a o

T– rrr p-. o-tWJ IXviX565, /AJlJsv OEVT8 *fttlfUtrfll. tUU ft: - -.1.:*

tcctx, not t(jnfJ. tunt . Ltre 01 tv waniyvffl Thi *rftKliutm, $x. xv fi. xi2vrnv ttfntv.* Kxx'

rare Bxjt' eottr urwr *aUwat tafafut fftoav na. fi. T, t.* Ta:9' ara vatra, *usu o Ttffi. attxos tfyt, tvorft. f/. tra vxf ram m-x vrut tureGaAn, nr'* t *STus ccao trfwrnv, us* vftfov *otf$tt%f,* XftTotftsv0t ot tf 03Dv txl/v0f *sGtu, tTftt-tratf ttSfttmrrx Oivtw Tv vytfutntx utfot.* nn *not n$mf ftn* mJ fl oxXiu S' *vn Th arratyuttrB* tsfnflt). p. 6lO.

- - Tohj tv r5 Ao-i trons'i Tajr Ito Tb *ffcurfJ. a xxaQtmts* ...... n/x, aT tx Twv 9c/iwv)tt9n, B-cXXa Sf xai 97fa Tb *TtGtftu* tScfln. Tjiv y *orfiut nrvfus, ptxfi ye xtai rm aMw apimt iwtTwiivo-ir, anrixottos , f-t, rr ras xAyptoiMxs, as This avru evyyutis iorrts xar&iirov, irfoditfios,* 7r/t7roAX. *tis re ras irofais xai rus iSiuras anitna.* xai art Tiwiv, *en iiratvot udtta itf Avrois irfotnitro,* p. 614. D.

,- *Tot n itpayfAx ro xxrut la $tHayfMera iptrpiayv, xai* S1o-Xiar *xzi iteirot S&s ra Syfuyiv eduxtr, tict r avras vn aifut fiaivrut armn rZit rfia em etu$avtio-Qytai*. p. 634. E.

- - llrs St S *noiirma fura Ktntrs* nXwT *virarivyat1 'ot* o, *n TiGifts iroMa Tr. s mfavs iirtxf. vyn,* oift wXE-jo-feasi, xai *irvpi itdhi irteiu irtft* ri ro *iiruwSp0ar* xati *-ffipi* ro AnTrot *ttyQapy. are rot TiGtfim Sio-jiias xai itwromoyias ftvpittSas mis tyiptu&tia-i ri ? r' aura $uai.* . p. 68. A.

An eater of human flesh and a drinker of human Hood.

a *rori rys xaroerarius sow,* xai i *fins taita* To *f-ii a xai* Tot *yapxsat civra ijStus eixytit.* p. 6 2 1 E

Suetonius. – Faftidit vinum, quia jam bibit ifte cruorem :
Tam bibit hunc avide quam bibit ifte merum.

The universal dispenser of the blessings of Peace.

Paterculus. – Quando pax laetior? Diffufa in orientis occiden tifque traftus, et quicquid meridiano aut feptentrione finitur, pax Augufta per omnes terrarijm orbis angulos nos a latrociniorum metu fervat immunes. ii. 126

Philo. – *ris yap* jSwv Taiot *p-tro . rm ra TiGifia Kaia-afos nsvni ira $ora nit vyenat itairris ytis xai Qaara-ys xsixo-iasot xai* cuvo/xot *xai irao-i rois fif syin vpp, o!rp. s/iv as* ro Tr/poo. *Leg. ad. C.* p. 7"9. '

- - *rvt ri tip iint xai ra ms tipwny ayaQa irafafjfiitim api Tvs ru /3*j *BtpButv xai 'xeiriu X, i'f Kat yxlAl' Ib.* p. 7 "3' "

Suetonius. – Imprimis tuendae pacis a graflaturis ac latroeinh-s fcditionumque licentia curam habuit. Stationes, militum folito fre- quentiores difpofuit. Romae caftra conftituit, quibus Praetorianze cohortes, vagae ante id tempus, et per hofpitia difperfae, conrinerenter. Popularcs tumultus exortos -graviffime coercuit; et ne orirentur fedulo cavit. Caede, &c. – Cum Pollentina plebs, &c. Hi. 37.

Tacitus. – Nobis in arto, et inglorius labor immota quippe aut tnodice laceffita pax maeftae urbis res, et princeps proferendi irr- curiofus erat. *Ann,* iv. 32.

-. t-...- ' -

Permitted the worst of all civil -wars to rage at Home.

Seneca. –Noftri faeculi exempla non praeteribo. Sub Tiberio Caefare fuit accufandi frequens et paene publica rabies, quaa *cmni civi/i bello gravius* togatgm civitatem confecit.. Excipiebatur ebriorum fermo, fimplicitas joeantium nihil erat tutum: omnis faeviendi place- bat occafio. Nee jam reorum exfpeftabatur eventus, quum eflet unus. Coenabal Paullus praetorius in convivio quodam, imaginem Tiberii Caefaris habens, eftypam, et eminente gemma. Rem ineptif- fimam fece/o, fi nunc verba quaefiero, quemadmodum dicam ilium matellam fumpfifle. Quod faftum, fimul et Maro, ex notis illius temporis veftigatoribus, notavit. At fervus ejus cui neftabantur in- iidiae, ei ebrio anulum extraxit. et cum Maro convivas teftaretur, ad- triotam efle imaginem obfcaenis, et jam fubfcriptionem componerat : oftendit in manu fua fervus anulum. 1. iii. c. 26. *de ben.*

Tacitus. – Non alias magisanxia et pavens civitas, egens *(agens?)* adverfum proxiulos, congreflus, colloquia, notae ignotaeque aures *(aural?)* vkari: etiam muta atque inanima teftum et parietes circum- fpeftabantur. v iv. 69.

Neque fenatus in eo cura an imperil extrema dehoriefta- rcntur: pavor internus occupaverat animos, &c. iv. 74., "" Inritatufque fuppliciis, cunftos qui carcere attinebantur

accufati focictatis cum Sejano, necari jubet. Jacuit immenfa flrages: omnis fexus, omnis aetas: inluftres, ignobiles, difperfi aut aggregati. neque propinquts, aut amicis adfiftere, inlachymarc, nc vifere quidem diutius dabatur ; fed circumjefti cuftodes, et in maerorem cujufque intend, corpora putrefafta adfeftabantur, dum in Tiberim traheren- tur: ubi fluitantia, aut ripis adpulfa, non cremare quifquam, non contingere. interciderat fortis humanae commercium vi metus : quan- tumque faevitia glifceret, miferatio arcebatur. vi. 19.

DION C. – *vxnts yctf 0i Tivoi rotavrm xtnat* Xatffotnf, *u% otrus mtHts, atx xat* $tXniT/, aS' *ovtas attyts,* XX *xat yvtaxts, ts To iStfft, urvftor lTvvtaQStrn. xxt* xTat4/t)Uo-6tvTff, *ot fAtt txtt txoa(pnftt at* St *xat aTro ra Kaanruta tnto rut xzt Tut vTfaTut xare(niMtfyitr0 : xat K Tt Tm tfyofat Ta O'upxtx*

M *SfflTTTlTO,* Xal I/. ITIZ TTO IS T0v 7TOT/X. Ov t? XXtTO. p. 6jO. E.

e *yaf* /u, otot *0i xaTVycf txrmnt Tttut txfttotro, .* Xa xat *0i ,* v9nAti7XGv ro. *UTus x9 o TtGtftos Tmwv ftyttuSTo,* aXXa *x&t froifftv av, Tots trexfrno,* ar' aXXot ftfaiov pov aSsta *"Xf' '* lv T lO-"

t ro *avay. afnrov,* To, Tt *uTtotr t-suot n xat To adcts, vfos rm Tut " attaxf tatl, lytyten, ,* p. 6jl. C.

' ' TOaSrov *yaf* Xi)8or Twv Ti aAXstv xgt r$v *iHafavTut atwktro, uft Tus tm*

p. 636. B.

Query – If Tiberius was the caufe of all this civil ftrife why does Paterculus, in the x6tia year of his reign, fpeak fo highly of him ? Why does V. Maximus fay of him, after the death of Sejanus – Princeps parenfque nofter ..... auftor ac tutela incolumitatis noftrae ? Why does Seneca fay of him – that he was fuperlarively great – that he had fo many good qualities, and – that he, at his death, went tothe abode of the Gods? And why does Dion fay, in two places, that the people thought that Tiberius knew nothing of the matter, and expefted that things would, after the death of Sejanus, be better ?

At page 629, A. B., he lays – oXiyov Tt *va; v To Qafo-av m, xrt* tl iu *-n ntrsvt* xa9ti$i)xtJ, *xat rut TtGfftot tnnwnfot ytnfftfQat fpxn&oxa. ra re y:ff avt$tGnxonx atau ts rot* avoXwXor *(annf tro ifttet yt-ycaQat') trfnrav, xat txtttot* n *x&ms* v v *tntareo. ra yaf vfatyta, rot fttt wytMnutat, ra* St *xai axatra*

, *tr.:-/-, i.* – And at p. 635. C. – SoxSvTef *yaf at atQfxmt tnn* T *watnt ra xar- avrus vforffot ytmfuta xat tvtaums mtQvivuT&xt rore x. r.* X.

Overcome by the pressure of family afflictions.

Paterculus. – Quid, ut juvenes amitteret filios? Quid, ut ne- potem ex Drufo fuo? Dolenda adhuc retulimus: veniendum ad erubefcenda eft. Quantis hoc triennium, M. Vinici, doloribus lace- ravit aniutum ejus ? *Quamdiu* abftrufo, quod miferrimum eft, peftus
N.
ejus flagravit incendio ? Quod ex nuru, quod ex nepote *Jo/ere,* indig- nari, erube- fcere coaftus eft? Cujus temporis aegritudinem auxit mater eminentiffima, &p. ii. 130.

Tacitus. – Profeftio arto comitatu fuit caeteri liberalibus
ftudiis praediti, ferme Graeci, *quorum fermonibus levaretur.*
Ann. iv. 58.

At Caefar dedicatis per Campaniam templis, quanquam edifto monuiflet, ne quis *quietem* ejus inrumperet, concurfufque oppi- danorum difpofito milite prohiberentur; perofus tamen municipia, et colonias, omniaque in continent! ftta, Capreas fe in infulam abdidit.
Ann. iv. 67.

Suetonius. – Sed orbatus utroque filio &c. – feceflum Campaniae peliit: conftanti et opinione et fermone pene omnium, quafi neque rediturus unquam, et cito mortem etiam obiturus: iii. 39. Peragrata Campania Capreas fe contulit;

Statimque revocante affidua obteftatione populo, propter cladem, qua apud Fidenas, ... tranfiit in continentem, poteftatemque omni

bus adeundi fui fecit ; tanto magis quod ab urbe egrediens, ne quis fe interpellaret, cdixerat, ac toto itinere adeuntcs fubmoverat. iii. 40.

DION C. – -ap' a Jv *xat etfvxsvat Tuts aunt rut (ffntut VtttfBTtwaa. a ftnrot v. au vtrus* irafzffKKH rx rsra *Stfitiuito. tat yaf* XXa *xat vattv travra Hewrac*
IttlMl. X. T. X. 1. 57. p. 618. E.

Negligent of Hte Gods but attentive to some one God.
Suetonius. – Vicina vero urbi oracula etiatn dejicere conatus eft. iii. 63.

- Circa Deos et religioncs negligentior : quippe addiftus Mathematicae : per- fuafionifque plenus cunfta fato agi. – . 69.

- Supremo natali die fuo Appollinem Temenitem et am- plitudinis et artis eximiae adveftum Syracufis, ut in bibliotheca novi templi poneretur, viderat per quietem affirmantem fibi – Non pofle fe ab 'ipfo dedicari. – . 74.

Josephus. – Jofephus fays, in the beginning of A. xviii. 7. *Q.,* that Tiberius, the day before he died, prayed to the Gods of his country to be direfted in the choice of a fucceflbr, and, in the fequel of that feftion, he alfo fays, three times, that fome *one God* direfted him according to his requeft, and that he obeyed the direftion of that *one God,* though contrary to his own wifh. – /§iv Se So$ur *n tun vrn tsfatftm. us* Tb psy"D3ib To *tts avrots*

N. B. – t. – How contradidory the evidence of ancient writers on this point feems to be.

Paterculus. – Sacravit parentem fuum Caefar, non imperio fed religione: non appellavit cum, fed fecit Deum. ii. 126.

Quam pia munificentia, fuperque humanam evefta fidem, templutn patri molitur ? ii. 130.

V. Maximus. – Deos enim reliquos accepitnus, Caefares dedimus. Et quoniam initium a cultu Deorum petere in animo eft, de con- ditione ejus fummatim difleram. *Prol. ad Ttb.*

Seneca. – Appiae viae curator eft: qua fcis et divum Auguftum et Tiberium Caefarem, ad Deos ifle. *Afiocolacynt. Cl. Ctss.*

Suetonius. – Peragrata Campania, cum Capuae Capitolium, Nolae Templum Augufti, quam caufiam profeftionis prsetenderat, dedi- caflet, Capreas fe contulit; iii. 40.

Tacitus. – Sanftos acceptofque numinihusClaudios: etaugendam caerimoniam loco, in quo tantum in Principem honorem Dii often- derint. A. iv. 64.

At Caefar dedicatis per Campaniam templis. – . 67.

JoSEPHUS. – *Mitral rots trarftots Qtots irtfi. tat n trf tft ra.* T)iv *tffnunuH* StaSt| a/tut8. A. Xvlii. 7. *Q.*

3"his Jofephns fays of Tibertus the day before he died. And, that . it was fignified to him, by an omen, that he fhould appoint that fon, for his fucceflbr, who mould come firft to him in the morning.

N. B. – 2. – How contradiftory the evidence of Jofephus and Tacitus, concerning the time when Tiberius appointed a fucceflbr, from that of Suetonius? Suetonius fays, iii. 76. – Teftamentum duplex *ante blennium* fecerat : alterum fua, alterum liberti manu, fed eodem exemplo: obfignaveratque etiam humillimorum fignis. Eo teftamento haeredes aequis partibus reliquit Caium ex Germanico, et Tiberium ex Drufo, nepotes; fubftituitque inviccm.

4

SECTION 4

A friend of Jews and the maintaincr of Jewish Rites.

JoSEYHUS. – *Hfvfas* St *o nrfafxps,* nrj *pay Vt " rw TtGtfttt Qtktas*
A. xviii. 2. y.

t *Ttdftot St aSct trotao-as, r n* XX *avru yfaftt*

rt fuy, svos. tn St *puftn ttoaninfntat ttn ru o-ut nratnxtn ttn rat Katrftas. tvtt* at *xtytxtttrav,* f)Sfr *etyAut ru tv rots yfappaffnt trfo6vlAa, ntmaXf to nau ttf-, tCf.* – . 7. S.

N. B. Jofephus alfo fays that Tiberius reprimanded Pilate for attempting to infringe the cuftoms of the Jews. – And, that he permitted them *agatn* to keep the facred veftments. ' A. xviii. 5. y.

Tacitus. – Sub Tibeiio quies. *Hlft,* v. 9.

John. – Ye have a cuftom that I ihould leleafe unto you one at the Paflbver. XviiL 39.

Whofoever maketh himfelf a king fpeaketh againft Caefar – that is, Tiberius. xix. 12.

t We have no king but Czsfar. – . 15.

Luke. – I perfecuted even unto ftrange cities. *Alls.* xxvi. 11.

N. B. According to Jofephus, B. i. 24. &. Auguftns feems to have conferred this favor on Herod. – And who, but Auguftus, could have granted them the privilege of demanding yearly one at the Paflbver ? Tiberius, however, mud have continued both thofc cuftoms.

A hearer of the Law and a partial doer of it.

Suetonius. – Diogenes Grammaticus difputare *Sabbath* Rhodi folitus, vcnientem, ut fe extra ordinem audiret, non admiferat; ac per fervulum fuum *infe/uimum* diem diftulerat . Hi. 32.

Quinctilian. – Theodorus Gadareus, qui fe dici maluit Rhodium : qucm ftudiofe audifle, cum in earn infulam feceffiflet Tiberius.

1. iii. c. t.

N. B. Quin&ilian, 1. v. c. 13, reprefents this celebrated teacher of Gadara as the leader of a feft. – And fo does Strabo, L xiii. xvi. – M. Seneca Controv. ix. p. 103. introduces Syriacus as fpeaking thus to Niger – Pritnum non apud eundem praeceptorem ftuduimus. Tu Appollodorum habuifti, cui femper narrare placet : ego Theodorutn cui non femper.

Agr. ippa. – In his letter to Caius, he reminded him, that Augustus had, at his own expence, ordered a bull and two lambs to be offered daily to the moft high God. – This facrifice, fays he, has been continued to the prefent time – i xi *fufi* v"v *mtrAturou.* – Tiberius muft, of courfe, alfo have continued this cuftom.

Epijl. ad Catum. p. 801. F.

– – n $t 8 *tnfos as vawms TtGtftes Katraf ; ut ravr tyamrou*
n yaf rfto-tt xat nxaan tnffH ots ourroxf&ruf lyttero rm Katru, -n ufot
Xjlvtut vatfaiotopcm fluxetav *rrKftHTer.* p. 799. F.

Philo. – Of Auguftus he fays – he had fo great a reverence for our holy worfhip, *that all his dome/lies,* after his example, made prefents to our temple. – He mentions the daily facrifices, which, he fays, are Hill continued – *Imiwia&* Tjiowv *iurus avroxfanftvtwt.* – *A. nd* after having thus extolled the piety of Auguftus, he fubjoins – *t Itu TtGtfta* v *avrot rpotaor. Leg.* p. 785.

Remarkably inquisitive about Futurity.

Tacitus. – Jaftis tamcu vocibus per quas intelligeretur providus futurorum. *Jm.* vl 46.

JoSEPHUS. – *vatfat yaf* I *avra* Xtwtr tnXay. svw *nfavrav uroptwv,* S/atp9t'f (9-9t Tw *tfpotytuxuf* -nix Iito/ahw *vjvyym rut iftrantt nfavreit.*

A, xviii. 7- .

By the evidence of Tacitus it appears, that Tiberius, though, as he fays, a fatalifl. was, at his laft hour, concerned about futurity. – And, by that of Jofephus, it appears, that Tiberius, though he had, a day or two before his death, prayed to be direfted which of his two grandfons he fhould appoint for his fucceflbr, was very much concerned at the dicifion, but did as he was direfted. – 'How differently do thofe five hiflorians – Philo, Jofephus, Suetonius, Tacitus, and Dion C., fpeak of the conduft of Tiberius on, this occafion – of the time when he thought of appointing a fucceflbr – and – of the manner in which he difpofed of the young Tiberius? – Tacitus feems to fay that he did not think of appointing a fuccefTor till a few days before he died, and, that he then, being unable to come to a determination on the point, left the decificm of it to fate. Jofephus fays, that he, a day or two before he died, prayed to-his God, to be direfted whether he fhould leave Caius or Tiberius his fucceflbr, and that he was fo dtrefted, that though the decifiort was contrary to his wifh, yet he complied with it, and only appointed Caius. – The other three, on the contrary, fay that he appointed both Caius and Tiberius. Dion fays, p. 636. A., that it was well known, nearly four years before his death, that he very readily – *xrptw*—intended to leave Caius his fucceflbr, and, in conjunftion with Tiberius. Suetonius fays, iii. 76., – Teftamentum duplex ante biennium fecerat; alterum fua, alterum liberti manu, fed eodem exemplo: obfignaveratque etiam humillimorum fignis. Eo teftamento haeredes aequis partibus reliquit, Caium ex Germanico, et Tiberium ex Drufo, nepotes: fubftituitque invicem. This will Dion fays, 1. 59. ink., Caius fent to the Senate, by Macro, and took care to have it invalidated. – And, that he, by difregarding the confideration of futurity, might have died in peace. – Jofephus alfo tells us, that Tiberius forewarned Caius that the Gods would avenge the murder of his grand- fon Tiberius. E

A believer in the divinity of Jesus Christ.

V. Maximus. – Quod caetera divinitas opinione colligitur: tua *prafenti fide* paterno avitoque fiderl par videtur. Pro/, *ad.* 7 *it*

Query – Would any author have prefumed to fpeak to any Autocrat, who had publicly notified his abhorrence of his being thought a God, of his inherent divinity ? If V. M. does mean to do this, what can he have meant by – praefenti fide ?

Paterculus, – Si aut natura patitur, aut mediocritas recipit hominum, apud aures Deorum de his queri; quid hie meruit?

ii. 130.

In the fentence immediately preceding, it mould be obferved, Paterculus fpeaks of a levy which Tiberius was then making – and – without caufing any uneafinefs – Quanta cum quiete hominum, rem perpetui praecipuique timoris, fupplementum, fine trepidatione de- leftus providet ? – Now when did he make this levy, if not in the Cxteenth year df his reign? For Paterculus, we fee, ufes, not the paft tenfe of the verb, but the prefent – */irovidet.* – That he had no occafion to make it, before the eleventh year of his reign, we find, by Tacitus, A. iv. 32, – Nobis in arto, et inglorius labor. Immota quippe aut modice laceffita pax, &c. – That he muft have made it, after the fourteenth, we alfo find, by the fame author, iv. 74, – Clarum inde inter Germanos Frifium nomen: diffimulante Tiberio damna, ne cui bellum permitteret. – That he made it more than a year after he redded at Capreae, we may prefume, becaufe Paterculus had, immediately before, fpoken of his beneficence to the fufferers by the fire that happened on Mount Ccelius. – And – that he made it, not before the fixteenth year of his reign, why mould we not conclude for the reafon above affigned ? – But for what reafon did ke make it? Suetonius, we find, fays, iii. 37, that he, for fomereafon, (lationed the military, at lefs intervals than ufual, throughout Italy, but of any levy he fays not a word – on the contrary, he feems to fay that he rendered fuch a ftep unneceflary – that he was very intent on preferving the peace from being difturbed by banditti and depredators, and the lawlefs – that he punimed rioters moft feverely – that he put a flop to foreign commotions by difcreet negotiations, ; and that he never after undertook any foreign expedition. – Was it to put a flop to that internal alarm which caufed fo much anxiety at Rome? – If fo, he could never, as fome have fuppofed, have encouraged it. – Was it to oppofe Sejanus? Dion fays, 1. 58. p. 623. A., that Sejanus was then every thing with the Senate, the people, and the guards, and that Tiberius was next to nothing. – Befides – Suetonius fays, iii. 65, that he fupprefled Sejanus. rather by craft and fubtilty than by any princely means. Why then mould we not fuppofe that he muft have made it after the introduction of Chriftianity, when the unbelievers were fo exafperated againft believers – and – that this new levy confifted of Chriflian foldiers ? Does not Dion feem to acknowledge fomething like this, 1. 58. p. 628. E., where he fays that the military, exafperated at finding that nofturnal guards, more in the faith of the Emperor, were employed – oi wxroptAaxsf o-pv *ts rm rv*

– became incendiaries and depredators ?

But the chief thing to be confidered is whether this levy is any way connefted with this complaint to the . Gods of fome Gods? By the expreffion, in this fentence – de *his* queri ; it mould feem that thofe fentences are connefted. What then is the meaning of this ? In vain have the learned endeavoured to explain this paflage, they have not been able, even with the help of various readings, which they quote abundantly, and among the reft, the following – De Deo cum Deis queri – Apud aures Deorum Deis queri – Auribus Deorum de dis queri – Audeo cum deis queri. – Now if the firfl of thofe various readings mould happen to be the right one, what God couldhe have meant? Had the God of the Jews ever given the Romans caufe to complain ? Why then fhould we not fufpeft that he may have meant the myfterious Trinity of Chriftians ? Or, if any of the other three fhould happen to be the right one, why fhould we not fufpeft that he improperly fpeaks of him as a plurality of Gods?

Seneca. – His inftirlftus, abflinere animalibus coepi: et anno perafto non tantum facilis erat mihi confuetudo, fed dulcis. Agilio- rem mihi animum efle credebam: nep tibi hodie affirmaverim, an ftterit Quaris, quornodo defierim ? In Tiberii Caefaris principatum juventae tempus inciderat: *alienigenarum facra movebantur;* fed inter *argumentafufterjlitionis* ponebantur, *quarumdam animaltvm* abftinentia. Patre itaque meo rogante, qui non calumniam timebat, fed philo- fophiam oderat, ad priftinam confuetudinem redii: nee difficulter lnihi, ut inciperem melius coenare, perfuaftt, *Ep.* cviii. p. 635.

Now why were the facred rites of other nations difcufled by the Senate, and in what year of Tiberius ? Was it not the cuftom of the Romans to adopt the Gods of other nations? And did they not know that the religion of the Jews, who chiefly ufed to abftain from fome forts of meats, was fecured by compaft at the depofition of Archelaus? Did they not know that Julius Caefar, Auguftus, Agrippa, and Tiberius had always encouraged them in the exercife of it, even at Rome ? That they had favored them with the moft extraordinary privileges ? Did they not know that Auguftus had contributed yearly a large fum towards defraying the expence of their facrifices? That moft of his houfehold had followed his example ? Did they not know that Tiberius continued the fame yearly contribution ? That he, before the death of our Lord, reprimanded Pilate for attempting to profane the faniSity of the temple ? Was not Livia acquainted with Salome ? – Antonia with Berenice ? And Drufus with Agrippa ? Why then we fuppofe that the facred, rites of the Jews were, at any time, taken under confideration ? Tacitus, we however find, tells us that they were, and in the fifth of Tiberius. And Lipfius, takes it for . granted, that this was the year meant by Seneca. But why this report of Tacitus mould be taken in preference to that of Philo, and Jofephus, and of Suetonius too, who, fpeaking of the fame event, fay that it took place, after the death of our Lord, or, about the time that Tiberius abolifhed all the afyla, we cannot fee. By the report of Jofephus indeed, it appears,' that Agrippa muft have been then refident at Rome, and in high favor with Drufus. But is it not rather more probable, that by this, Seneca alludes to what happened in the eighth or ninth year, when fays Tacitus, iii. 60., the Senate in- fpefted the religions of the very Gods – r-introfpexit ipforum numinum religiones? The only objeftion which can be made to this fuppofition, is, that the abufe of afyla was the caufe of this enquiry; and, that it does not appear that any religion was then calumniated, and efpecially for abftaining from certain forts of meats; whereas, in this cafe, it feems, the reafon was becaufe fome fuperftitioufly abftained from meats, and feemingly through a fpirit of philofophy to which fome calumny was attached. A philofophy which the father of Seneca, who feerns by his own account, 1. ii. Controv., and by his fon's account, Confol. ad Helviam. c. 16., to have had no prejudice againft philofophy, hated, and, for that reafon perhaps difluaded his fon from abftaining from meats. – Neither of thofe events, then, mentioned by Tacitus, feems to anfwer the defcription of this here mentioned by Seneca.

Let us now then proceed to confider whether this event does not appear to be the fame as that mentioned by Suetonius, Philo, and Jofephus, when external ceremonies in general, and the rites of . ifcgytians and Jews, and firailar Seftaries, were fuppreffed at Rome, that is, a year or two after the death of our Lord.

Now that the Jews, the only people that abftained from meats, Ihould have been expelled from Rome, in the reign of Tiberius, for exercifing their religion, is very improbable, not only becaufe he was much attached to them, but alfo becaufe they enjoyed the right by compact with Auguftus, and Tiberius held all his afts inviolable: befides – the fuppofition refts only on the report of Suetonius, for neither Philo nor Jofephus fay it – indeed, they affign a ery different reafon for their expulfion. Philo does not fay that they were then expelled for their fuperftition, but for their ftrong attachment to Tiberius. – And Jofephus fays, that they were expelled for the mifconduft of a pretended Rabbi, and two or three other vagabonds who had been driven from their own country. That this, however, could not have been the time here alluded to by Seneca, may be inferred from his faying that he perfevered in the obfervanqe of this fuperflitious ceremony a year after the enquiry was made. This event then does not feem to correfpond with that mentioned by Seneca, any more than thofe two mentioned by Tacitus. Befides – that Seneca was not at Rome in the t7th year of Tiberius appears from the laft chap, of hisConfol. ad. Helviam, where he fays, that his aunt loft her hufband (Vetrafius Pollio) as he was returning from the praefefture of Egypt, where he had been fixteen years, that is, from the return of Emilius Reftus, who as Dion fays, 1. 57. 608. D., was recalled the firft 1 Tiberius, u. c. 767. – And, that he was then, with them, *a witnefs* of it.

What then if we fhould fuppofe that thofe facra alienigenarum were agitated, at the fame time as Tiberius firft introduced chriftianity at Rome, or, when, as Tertullian, Eufebius, and Jerom fay, he recommended Chrift to the Senate, as a God, that is, as it feems, in the fourteenth year of his reign, for then, the internus pavor happened, –

then the Senate went to the coaft of Campania to defire to be favored with an interview with him, but were not – and, then, he, for the firft time, feems not to have been willing to venture among them. Aboutthree years after this, the graviffimum exitium, or, execrabilis fuper- ftitio, which crept in under the proteftion of Tiberius, was again re- prefled, that is, when the Jews and fimilar Seftaries or Chriftians were expelled from Rome. That all this is not far from the truth, why mould we not infer from that expreffion – anno perafto – in the paf- fage above quoted from Seneca ? – And, from that other – fed inter argumenta fuperflitionis ponebatur, quorumdam animalium abftinen- tia? For we know that fome evil difpofed perfons commanded Chriftians to abftain from meats, i. Tim. iv. i., that their religion was faid to be a deftruftive fuperftition.

Seneca. – Cum interim ufque eo *feeleratijfimis gent is* confuetudo convaluit, ut per omnes *jam* terras recepta fit: *vifli viflorlbus* leges dederunt. *Contra. Superftltiones.*

This quotation is fuppofed to be from a work of Seneca the younger, and, to be fpoken of Jews, but this does not feem to be at all likely, becaafe he could not but have known that Auguftus, Tiberius, Caius, and Claudius patronized them: and becaufe he fays of them, not only, when, *in the mean time,* their praftice fo prevailed – and – that they were, even then, fpread over all countries – but, that they had been, before the death of Nero, conquered, and had conquered their conquerors. Befides, Auguftin, who, vi. II, quotes this paflage, fays, we find, in two places ot that chap., that the author, in the context, fpeaks of *their facraments.* – Hie inter alias civilis theologiae fuperftitiones re- prehendit *etiamfacramenta* judaeorum, et maxime fabbata: &c. – And, then again, immediately after he has adduced the above quotation, he fubjoins the following remark – Mirabatur haec dicens, et quid divinitus ageretur, ignorans. Subjecit plane fententiam qua fignifi- caret, quid illorum facramentorum ratione fentiret. Ait enim: – Why then mould we not fuppofe, for thofe reafons, that it is rather likely that he means Chriftians ? Of this, fays Lipfius, there can be nodoubt. But would Seneca, the younger, who, in his youth, for a year, abftaincJ, in compliance with a certain fuperftition, from eating certain forts of meats, and who is faid, by fo many eccleﬁaftical writers, to have been a Chriftian, have faid, at any time, and ef- pecially in the latter part of his life, of Chriftians – that they were the moft wicked of all people ? – Again. If Seneca, the younger, was the author of this work, and here fpeaks of Chriftians, when had they, before he died, been conquered? Was it before, or after, they had been received every where? Was it not before, and at Rome only ? When we confider what Tacitus fays of the fuppreffion of the execrabilis fuperftititio, and, of its having, afterwards burft forth, not only in Judea, but at Rome; and, alfo what he fays of the fuppreffion of the graviffimum exitium, and of its having, afterwards, blazed out, and overcome every thing, who can doubt, that Seneca, or whoever was the author of this work, alludes to this by – fceleratiffimas gentis confuetudo – and, by vifti viftoribus leges dedere ? Now if he does, can we fuppofe, that Seneca would have fpoken of it forty years after it happened, as having happened *jam,* and, be fore they had been conquered, and had conquered their conquerors ? Or, that he was but a little more than twenty when he faid it ? Is it not then very likely that Seneca jun. did not write it ? And, on the other hand, when we confider that Seneca fen. endeavoured to difluade his fon from conforming with the fuperftition of abftaining from meats, and, becaufe he hated the philofophy, is it not very likely that he was the author of it? Now if Seneca fen. was the author of this work, we have ftill ftronger evidence that he' could not have meant Jews, and that he could not but have meant Chriftians. – Would he have fpoken thus of the religion of the Jews, knowing how it had been patronized both by Auguftus and by Tiberius? Could he have faid, before the death of Tiberius, (for he died before Tiberius) that the *Jews* had been conquered, and, that they had given laws totheir conquerors ? Was it any news to the Romans that they had been every where received ? Who then can doubt but that he Was the author of this work, and that he meant Chriftians ? Now if he did mean Chriftians, we find that the Chriftian religion, was, before his death, that is, before the death of Tiberius, received in every country, – that Chriftians had been conquered, and were even then conquerors, and gave laws to their conquerors.

Seneca Sen. – Hie eft Corvus, quiquum tentaret fcholam, Rom, *fummo till, qui Judteos fubegerat,* declamavit controverfiam, de ea, quse apud matronas diflerebat, liberos non efle tollendos, et ob hoc accu- fatur Reip. laefae. In hac controverfia, fententia ejus haec ridebatur. Inter pyxides et redolentis animffi medicamina conftitit mytrata concio. *Suas.* ii. p. 24.

In all the foregoing part of this ii. Suas. Seneca introduces feveral learned men celebrating the greatnefs of the refiftance made by the Spartans, at Thermopylae, under Leonidas, to Xerxes, who, it feems, defied the Gods. At the end of it, he adverts, and feemingly abruptly, to the attempt of Corvus to raife a fchool to that eminent commander, who fubdued the Jews. How this is connefted with the main fub- jeft of this Suaforia – viz. the oppofition which the Spartans alone made to Xerxes, at Thermopylae, it is not eafy to difcover: but fo, it feems, it is fuppofed to be. Let us try to difcover, if this account of Corvus be really fo abruptly introduced as it appears to be.

Corvus attempted to fet up a fchool, at Rome, and, to that mod eminent perfon who had fubdued the Jews. What fort of a fchool was this ? And, who was this mofl eminent perfon ? – Pompey, fays the annotator. But was he the only conqueror of the Jews? Was not Anthony after him? Was Pompey entitled – ille fummus – the moft eminent ? Was he more eminent than either Auguftus or Anthony?

And admitting that Pompey was the moft emment fubduer of the Jews, why fhould a fchool have been eftablimed to him, and, feem- Jngly, on that account ? What fort of a fchool can we fuppofe this to have been ? Does not all this feem to point out the neceffity of looking out for a very different, and ftill more eminent conqueror ? one who could, with a much lefs number of followers than thofe who fell with Leonidas, effeft a much more extenfive conqueft ? – – What then if we. turn our eyes to the greateft of all great captains, Jefus Chrifl, who, with an inconfiderable party of unarmed followers, obtained a much greater viftory over the world ? That it is not altogether improbable that Seneca may have meant to allude to this moft eminent conqueror, rather than to Pompey, why fhould we not conclude from what Seneca had before fuppofed Leonidas to have faid of the vain attempt of Xerxes – viz. ponat fane contra coelum aftra – commilitones Deos habqo.

But though Seneca may not be allowed to have here thought of contrafting thofe two celebrated viftories, obtained by fo few combatants, in a good caufe, over an immenfe holt of aflailants – yet, if it be allowed that he meant, by what he fays in this quotation, to allude to this then recent viftpry obained by this moft eminent conqueror, we begin to perceive why Corvus Ihould have thought of eftablifhing a fchool to him, and why he was accufed of Reip. laefar, for having contended, in that fchool, before an audience of motherly women, that their children ought not to be brought up – that is, as we fuppofe, as ufual.

" Sabinus Clodius, in quem uno die et Graece et Latine dcclamantem multa urbane difta funt. Dixit Haterius quibufdam querentibus, pufillas mercedes eum accepifle, cum duas res doceret,

Rectius *tiabel/o* – et *castra,* ex conjcctura et veteribus libris tribus. – Vulgati eniin *astro.* Alludit ui fallor ad *fiytHrofMtn* Cyelopmn, qui cum Ciis fcella gerentea, &c.

nunquam magnas mercedes accepifle eos qui vfinntiftr docerent.

L. iv. *Controv.* 26. p. 183.

L. ix. *C* . p. 66.

What were thofe teachers of wuiwvpsra, or, interpretations ? Where elfe, in the works of the Roman or Greek writers do we read of them, but in one or two of the writings of Paul ? If they taught extraordinary things, ought they not to have been extraordinarily rewarded ? And yet we find they were not rewarded as well as others.

Thofe teachers of *tfuwvif.psy"D4,* it may not be amifs to obfcrre, appear to have followed their profeffion before the death of Seneca, that is, before the death of Tiberius, and even before the death of Sejanus, for Sabinus, we are told, was, about that time, imprifoned.

Tacitus. – Haud pigebit referre in Falanio et Rubric praetentata c. rimina: ut quibus initiis, quanta arte Tiberii, graviilimum ex ilium irrepferit, dein repreflum fit, poftremo arferit, cunftaque corripuerit, nofcatur. *Ann.* i. 73.

Here we are told of fome crimes, committed by two Roman knights, which were hard to be found, by detefting which he pro- mifes *to let tts know how a certain moJJ grievous prji, by the no little artifice of Ttberius, at firft, crept in:* how it was then reprefled, and then again blazed forth, and overcame every thing.

Now what were thofe groped for crimes ? And how fo intimately connefted with this moft grievous peft, that the bare mention of thofe, would, of courfe, lead to a knowledge of this? What moft grievous peft did Tiberius, with no Kttle contrivance, at firft, introduce ? And ia what part of his reign ?. Is it not rather ftrange that neither V. Maxi- mus, nor Paterculus, not either of the Senecas, nor Suetonius, nor either of the Jewifh writers, nor Dion C., mentions his having done jt fNor, any fuch peft having been introduced? In order to get foma infight into the nature of this undefcribed moft frightful phenomenon, let us hear what Tacitus here fays of thofe crimes of darkness which he tells us will lead us to a knowledge of it – for no where elfe does he fpeak of them.

In this chap., we find, he fpeaks of a certain crime or two of each of thofe knights, but then there was not the leaft occafion to grope for any of them, for they were, by his own account, manifeft to every body. To Falanius, he fays, that it was objefted, that he had admitted, among the worfhippers of Auguftus, who, he fays, aflembled ' *in every houfe,* as a fort of collegiate body, one Caffius, a mimic, and of a difgufting perfon. – And alfo that he had difpofed of, together with a garden, a ftatue of Auguftus. – Thefe were the two charges againft Falanius. To Rubrius – that he had taken a falfe oath by Auguftus. But were either of thofe a crime of darknefs? Or, will they lead us to a knowledge of this moft grievous peft, which Tiberius, fo artfully, introduced? Does Tacitus, in the fequel, give us any encouragement to think fo ? As foon, continues he, as Tiberius knew it, *he wrote* to the confuls an apology for each of them. In

which, after having obferved that heaven was not decreed to Auguftus for the deftruftion of any one, he vindicated Falanius, by faying that Caffius, the aftor, ufed, as others of the fame way of life, to be prefent at the fports, which his mother *had* cpnfecrated to the memory of Auguftus: And, that it was not contrary to religion, to difpofe of his effigies, with gardens or houfes, any more than to difpofe of thofe of any other Deities. And Rubri&s, by faying that he had committed no greater offence than if he had committed it againft Jupiter, Offences againft the Gods were only to be punjfhed by the Gods.

If now thofe crimes were fo very notorious, and Tiberius did not think that they were c. rimes, at leaft cognizable by man, why wouldTacitus have it thought that they were works of darknefs, and that the bare fpecification of them would tend to elucidate this moft grievous peft, and as furreptitioufly introduced by the no little artifice of Tiberius ? Surely, if Tacitus meant no more than what he here fays, ho appears to have rendered his own teftimony queftionable. And, inftead of rendering it credible that Tiberius introduced this moft grievous peft, to have faid what makes not a little againft the fup- pofition.

But did Tacitus here mean to fay all that he had to fay of this matter? And that thofe crimes were committed in the fecond year of Tiberius ? If he did mean to fay this, may we not fuppofe that Tiberius introduced this graviffimum exitium, foon after? But how can we fuppofe this when we recolleft what Tacitus fays in two or three places of his iv. book ? In the firft chap, he fays that every thing was well managed by Tiberius till the ninth year of his reign, and, that he then began to be cruel himfelf, or to permit others to be fo. But however cruel he may then be fuppofed to have begun to be, it is pretty plain, from what Tacitus again fays, c. 32., that he could not have introduced this graviffimum exitium before the thirteenth year of his reign was pretty well ended, for he there complains, that he had till that time only a contrafted and inglorious talk, that the peace of the empire was fixed, or, at moft, but little difturbed, that the affairs of Rome were (not furely mournful, unlefs on account of the fall of the Amphitheatre, at Fidenae, and the burning of a con- fiderable part of the city,) but dull, or uninterefting,–And after having faid this, he propofes to tell us of what advantage it may be to contemplate this *even* furface of things. – " Yet it will not be ufe- lefs to infpeft clofely that even furface from which the grcateft commotions often arife." – Non taincn fine ufu fuerit introfpicere ilia prime afpeftu levia, ex queis magnarum fepe rerum motus oriuntur. Now after having faid all this in the 32 chapter who would haveexpefted to find him faying in the next, what appears to be of a very different tendency ? In that chap, he proceeds to obferve how much more interefting the works of former writers muft be fuppofed to be than his who had nothing more to record than – cruel mandates, continued accufations, fallacious friendfhips, *the dejlruflion of innocent perfons,* and fuch like tranfaftions. Of all this, it mould be obferved, he complains, but a little before Tiberius retired from Rome, which ftep, he would have us to believe, he was compelled to take in order to avoid being a witnefs of the domineering pretenfions of his mother, who was then near ninety, and, as the learned, he alfo obferves, thought never to return, though by what he fays, chap. 66, the Senate was of a very different opinion. Indeed, if it was generally thought that he would never return, why mould the people, as Suetonius fays, iii, 40, attempt to recall him, *from Caprea,* by a conT tinued importunity, when the Amphitheatre, at Fidena:, fell?

Again – that Tiberius was, by no means likely to have encouraged any of thofe evils, before the end of the thirteenth year of his reign, is evident from what Tacitus fays, iv. 62, of his humane conduft to the fufferers at Fidenae; – and alfo, 64, to the fufferers at Rome, when, a little after, a great part of the city was burnt; – and, from the reception which he met with from the people, on the former occafion, and from the Senate, on the latter; – and from the honor, which, he fays, the Gods then mewed him. And that Tiberius had not, at that time, begun to encourage accufers, in particular, is evident, from what he fays, in chap. 66, of the accufation of his kinfman Varus Quinftilius, and of the Senate's having deferred to pafs fentence on him till the arrival of Tiberius, who, as he acknowledges, was then the only fuffugium in fuch hard cafes. Indeed if he was then overcome by the preflure of family affliftions, how can he be fuppofed to have encouraged any of thofe evil praftices, and much lefs can he during the three following years, for Paterculus, we find, aft, sYinicius, II. 130. – Quantis, hoc triennium, M. Vinici, doloribus, laceravit animum ejus ? Quamdiu abftrufo, quod miferrimum eft, pcftus ejus flagravit incendio ?

The graviffimum exitium then does not appear to have been any way connefted with thofe crimes of Falanius and Rubrius, that is – if thofe crimes were committed in the fecond year of Tiberius. But is it not likely that thofe crimes -were committed after the death of Livia? May we not conclude from his faying that Tiberius *wrote* to the Confuls on this occafion, that he was then not at Rome ? – Or, rather that he was then at Capreae? Was it his ufual praftice to write, to the Senate before he retired ? Does not Tacitus fay, iv. 55, that he ufed to attend the Senate *frequently* ? And does he not fay, c. 66, that the Senate, in the cafe of Varus Quinftilius, waited his return ? And becaufe he was, in fuch cafes, the only fuffugium ? and may we not alfo conclude from his having faid that his mother *had* confecrated thofe fports to the memory of Auguftus, that thofe crimes were committed after her dc:eafe ? Would he have faid, in her life time, of any thing appointed by her to be continued during her life, that ihe *had* appointed it ? Would it not be more proper for him to have faid that Ihe hath appointed it ?

- Quos per flagitia invifos vulgus Chriftianos appellabal.

Auftor nominis ejus Chriftus, Tiberio imperitante, per Procuratorem Pentium Pilatum fupplicio affeftus eft. *Rept ejjaque in prfens exitla- Hlis fuperftitlo rurfus crumprbat,* non modo per Judaeam originem ejus malj, fed *per qrtem* etiam. A. xv. 44.

Whoever will be at the pains to compare the laft claufe of this paflage with that paflage immediately preceding, quoted from Ann. i. 73, will no longer doubt of the meaning of that. Exitiabilis fuperftitio, correfponds to graviffimum exitium – dein repreflum fit, to, repreflaque in prsfcns – rurfus erumpcbat, to, poftrerao arferlt – and, non modo per Judaeam fed per urbem etiam, to, cunftaque corri- puerit. – And whofoever will be at the pains to compare both of thofe paflages with the laft of thofe adduced by Auguftin, vi. c. i r, from Seneca, will be inclined to think that they all mean the fame thing. Indeed, if Auguftin quoted that from Seneca, the father, who can (as he is faid to have died before Tiberius) help thinking that thofe three paflages evidently do fo ?

If now Tiberius, by no fmall artifice, introduced this moft grievous peft and deftruftive fuperftition, who can doubt of his having been a believer in Jefus Chrift, that is – in his divinity ? For what occafion was there for any artifice to introduce a preacher of morality at Rome ? Would the Romans have thought of engaging in the worft of civil wars on that "account ?

Manebat quippe fufpicionum etcredendi temeritas. iv. 67.

Non alias magis anxia et pavens civitas, egens *(agens ?)* adyerfum proximos, congreflus, colloquia, nota e ignotaeque aures *(aural?)* vitari : etiam muta atque inanima, teftum et parietes circumfpefta- bantur. – . 69.

, Neque fenatus in eo cura, an imperii extrema dchoneftarentur: pavor internus occupaverat animos cui, &c. – Et revenere in urbem trepidi, quos non fermone non vifu dignatus eft : quidam male alacres, quibus infauftae amicitiae *gravis exitus* imminebar. – . 74.

Ne *(ni?)* caeleftis religio decerneretur. fie ipfam maluifle,

V. 2.

Novas condones, nova patrum confulta. – 4-

DlON C. – *xai 0i SfariZroti, ayaaanratns on avm n ts rni ra*

*tvioiau vnaittivtyyaaa, Kxi 0i wxrofvaxcs 7$ut ss fifi ra avroxpanfos iriTH irfotnpy Quam, ip. itfna-tis ri xat xpsixyxs imoiuvro, xairoi fHHrut rut a rats apx?'* vrai To rv v$t tx, rTts ra Tifepi erToi *tyvurronw* p. 628. E.

Query – If the foldiers, that is, the praetorian (Softpo/o, as Dion fays, p. 623, B.) were fufpefted of favoring Sejanus, why does Suetonius tell us, chap. 48, that they were rewarded by Tiberius for not having favored him ? And, if they were fo diflatisfied, becaufe night-watches more in *the faith of the Emperor* – *ts rr* T *avroxfanfos* wifiv-r-were thought more truft-worthy, as to become incendiaries and depredators, even though the magiftrates were ordered by Tiberius to keep the peace, why fhould they be fuppofed to have been rewarded by him at all? – Efpecially fo very handfomely? Do not both Suetonius, chap. 37, and Tacitus, ii, fay that he was for nothing fo anxious as to keep every thing quiet? Populares tumultus exortos graviffime coercuit; et ne orirentur fedulo cavit. – Nihil enim ipfum tam anxium habuit, quam ne compofital turbarentur — How differently does V: Maximus fpeak of this affair, 1. ix. n. – Arae pulvinaria, templa praefenti numine vallata funt : *Nihilque* quod pro capite Augufti, ac patria excubare *debuit* torpere fibi permifit. – Would Maximus have faid fo, a year or two after, if the praetorian bands had been attached to Sejanus, and if they had been incendiaries and depredators?

Tertullian. – Tiberius ergo cujus tempore nomen Chriftianum in feculum introivit. Annunciata fibi ex Syria Palaeftina quae illic veritatem illius divinitatis revelaverunt, detulit ad fenatum cum praerogativa fuffragii fui. Senatus, qui non ipfe probaverat, refpuit : Caefar in fententia manftt, comminatus periculum accufatoribus chriftianorum. *Apol.* c. 5.

EUSEBIUS. – Tattra TtfrtAXtavot *rat Pxlaxicm topus etuftiwxuv,* at-tf, ra re ; *Mr, s, XXI* Twv ftaXtf JCTJ *Pufixts* Xa/xWf-tv, *tt rn azrsvytx. x. T. X. $ft. h-1l.* ii. 2.

Tttfnu rot Xutx vat Survfa xvxya/av xat ra vf *txtm&ct ttt tfwra* tr/ftwf. *TtGtftot Ti vfos rr.* v *iTu/xnmv txo*

Tlffl TtiC fIS %ftfov *VttJS. . . C/tl'OH,* Jehom. – Pilato de chriftianorum dogmate referente, Tiberius re- tulit ad fcnatum, Ut *inttr aeterafacra recijuretur.*

Query – Did this latent monfter of luft and cruelty, who was, as Tacitus fayst afhamed to be feen, who, as Jofephus fays, was indifferent about moft things, and who as both Suetonius and Tacitus fay, was notoriously a fatalift, not only permit a fupcrftition fo deftruftive to creep into Rome, in fpite of the Senate, but by his inconceivable artifice procure an entrance for it ? – If he did how did the Senate aft ?

Tlte abolisher of all Sanctuary Protections.

Tacitus. – Sed Tiberius vim principatus fibi firmans imaginem antiquitatis fenatui praebebat, poilulata provinciarmn addifquifitionem patrum mittendo. Crebrefcebat enim Graecas per urbes licentia et im- punitas afyla ftatuendi: complebantur templa peffimis fervitiorum: eodem fubfidio obaerati adverfum creditores, fufpefttque capi- talium , ctiminum receptabantur. Nee ulhim fatis validum imperium erat coer- cendis feditionibus populi, flagitia hominum nt caeremonias Deum pro- tegentis. Igitur plac- itum ut mitterent civitates jura, atque legates..... Magnaque ejus diei fpecies fuit, quo fenatus majorum bcncficia, fociorum pafta, regum etiam, qui ante vim Romanam valuerant. decreta, ipforumque numinum religiones introfpexit, Jibero, ut quondam, quid firmaret, mutaretve. . A. iii. 60.

Suetonius. – Abolevit et jus moremque afylorum qua e ufquam erant. iii. 37.

The first Prohibilor of immediate Executions.

Suetonius. – Nam cum Senatus confulto cautum eflet ut pxna damnatorum in dccimum femper diem differretur. iii. 75.

Tacitus. – *Igitur* faftum S. C. ne decreta patrum ante diem deci- mum ad acrarium deferretur. A. iii 15.

DtON C. – iiririfti) Ti *avms xii l* Soy/xa Ti *nttv tins* Stx *npipxi* To xaT4")po&vT uw' uriI, &C.

1. 57. p. 617. A. *Tlie nursing Father of the Infant Catholic Church.*

Clemens Of R. – Cumque nullum yideremus exitum rei, fuper- venit Cornelius Centurio, miflus a Caefare ad praefidem Caefareae, publici ncgotii causa : hunc accerfimus ad nos folum, caufamque ei qua maefti eflemus exponimus; ac *fi* quid poflet, ut juvaret, hortamur.

VJr/

Turn ille promptifllme repromittit fe cum protinus fugaturum, li tx. ncn condlio ejus etiam nos adniteremur: cumque nos polliceremur impigre cunAa gefluros, ail ; C? efar in urbe Roma, ct per provincial malcficos inquiri juflt ac perimi ; ex quibus multi jam perempti funt. *Recogn.* 1. x. c. 55. 55' c. 56. 58. 59. – and *Ajnjl. Conft.* vi 8.

"' o Si *tuLUv axtaras nri$yfiuia-sn mas ex rns irforxyvs* Bo-iXixr *ti vm, mil tyamtrois* xad' *an Katirap* woXAar *fui-/is anuv, lira Hai ra xara* Zifii'ix Koflopo *tti nrifyirv? iv aura* ire/xtitv, *oirus xai avm aottit x&aru.*

E/iit. de ge/iis S. Pctri – Cxxxiv.

N. B. In each of thefe extrafts Clemens fpeaks of Simon – and, in the former, he fays, that Cornelius, the Centurion, had then been converted to the faith – that he was fent, on fome public bufinefs, by Tiberius, to the Prefident of Caefarea – that is, furcly to Pilate ; that Cxfar had, both at Rome, and through the provinces, caufed inquifition to be made for the maleficent – and, in the latter, for Simon in particular – and, in both he fays, that he had, *before that time,* but how long we know not, caufed many of thofe maleficent – or – magi, to be put to death. How long then, before this miffion of Cornelius to the Prefident of Caefarea, had Caefar caufed the maleficent to be fought out and put to death – and, in particular, at Rome ?

In his Homily, i. 6. 7., Clemens alfo fays that, in the courfe of the year in which our Lordfuffered – that is, in the fourteenth of Tiberius, there were frequent meetings all over Rome to enquire what this new naeflenger from God had done and faid; – that before the autumn of that year Barnabas, ftanding in the moft frequented place in that city, preached eternal life in the name of the f6n of God – that tumults enfued, and that Barnabas was obliged to take fhelter in the houfe of Clemens.

Tacitus, we have feen, fays, that the execrable fuperftition, was for the *prefent* – in praefens – reprefled, and – that the *moft grievous peflt* which was introduced by the no little artifice of Tiberius, was alfo reprefled – and, that unaccountable uaeafinefs prevailed all over Rome in the fourteenth year of Tiberius. ' '

Early in the year following the Sanhedrin, on the accufation of certain libertines – that is, furely, Jews made free of Rome, ftoned Stephen, as a blafphemer, and continued tjhe praftice of ftoning Jewifh believers, as blafphemers, (even thofe of ftrange cities) a year or two from that time. – Confequently, why fhould we not conclude from this, that thofe libertines were, on their return to Rome, very forward to feize Jewifh believers, as blafphemers, for the purpofe of getting them ftoned by the Sanhedrin ? And that great difturbances were, by that means only, if the Senate had not then refufed to acknowledge the divinity of Chrift, occafioned as Tacitus feems to fay, A. iv. 70., at Rome? – That the Senate encouraged the perfecutors – and Tiberius, protefted believers ? Of this, we however, are aflured by both Jofephus and Suetonius that, after the refurreftion, Tiberius fent 4,000 libertines to Sardinia – and by Philo, that it happened before the fall of Sejanus. All thofe hiftorians agree that the Jews alfo were then expelled: and not the Jews only but the Egyptians – and, as Suetonius fays, the funilia feftantes. Confequently – whyfhould we not fuppofc, that the execrable fuperftition of the fimilia feftantes was, as Tacitus fays, reprefled, about the fame time that thofe libertines were fent to Sardinia ?

Tertullian. – Comminatus periculum accufatoribus chriftian- orum. *jf/wL c.* 5.

Elf SEE I US. *Tys lr py* ireiflo/xm)r, *aM, x p, tifi*
OLvfa, *o aunis* Qatarot i, y$io-xTv Kara rut $iuktv rvv
js-opi. *Chron,*

Jerom: – Verum quum ex conlulto patrum Chriftianos eliminari urbe placuiflet, Tiberius per ediftum accufatoribus Chriftianorum comminatus eft mortem. *Chron.*

32   THE HISTORY OF THAT INIMITABLE MONARCH TIBERIUS

N. B. It feems to have been, on this account, that Tiberius, who in the ninth year of his reign, acquired no little praife for difcouraging informers, is accufed, by Tacitus, Suetonius, and Dion C. of having encouraged them.

The Protector of Jewish Christians as not Blasphemers.

Talmud Of J. – A tradition: forty years before the Temple was deftroyed, judgement, in capital cafes, was taken away from Ifrael. – *Lightfoot Hebrew and talmudical exercitations on Matth.* xxvi. 3. – *John* xviii. 31. p. 248.

Luke. – And he (Saul) fpake boldly (at Jerufalem) in the name of the Lord Jefus, &c. – *Then* had the churches reft, throughout all Judea, and Galilee, and Samaria. *Ails* ix. 29. 30. 31.

What? – Did the Sanhedrin, who had commiffioned him to feize, not only in Judea, but in ftrange cities, Jewifh believers, and to im- pvifon them for the purpofe of trying them as blafphemers, and ftoning them, fuffer their own officer to fpeak boldly, even at Jerufalem, in the name of the Lord Jefus, and without attempting even to molefthim ? How is this unexpefted forbearance on the part of the San- hedrin to be accounted for ? Why did they, who had been fo zealous and aftive in endeavouring to fupprefs this new feft, and as Tacitus fays, had aftually fucceeded, fo tamely fuffer their own fervant to preach Chrift, as it were in defiance of them ? Had they relinqnimed the praftice of ftoning Chriftians as blafphemers ? If fo – why did they relinquifh it – and when? Could Tiberius have interpofed his authority between the Sanhedrin and believers? Tertullian, we find, fays that he threatened periculum to the accufers of Chriftians. – Eufebius and Jerom fay that he threatened death to them. And their report feems to be fupported by that of Clemens of R. But may not Tertullian have, by periculum, meant the punifhment which Tiberius threatened before the ftoning of believers as blafphemers ? Would Tiberius have threatened death to fuch as mould accufe Chriftians of worfhipping a God not authorifed by the Senate ? Was death the punifhment for introducing an unauthorifed Diety ? If fo, was not Tiberius himfelf liable to that punifhment? Jerom, we find, fays that the Senate ordered Chriftians only to leave Rome. May not Tiberius then, have firft threatened periculum, and afterwards death?

Of all Kings or Autocrats the most venerable.
vni Xiaij *ttiti iroios*
780 F.

As some affirmed, prefigured by that of a Phoenix.

Tacitus. – P. F. et L. V. Cofs poft longum feculorum ambitum, avis Phcenix in . fligyptum venit; praebuitque materiem do&iffimis indigenarum, et Graecorum multa fuper eo miraculo diflerendi.

A. vi. 28.

DlON. – E Si T *xxi rot Aiywirria irfos ras Pvpatur wfooiixti,* o $awj *txtitt i ru trii v$Q, ttiu* tSol e *ret* flxTo *ru Tiftfiu irfocn(aintt.* 1. 58. p. 638. B.

Solemnized with due pomp and at the public Expence.

Suetonius. – Tiberio cum plurimis lacrymis pro condone laudato, funeratoque arnpliflime: iv. 15.

DlON C. – *Kai $viMitnats ndfns trv%v, Kcu tmntht vno ra Thus.*
Sub. fine. 1. 56.

Foliowed Augustus to the residence of the Gods.
Seneca. – Appiae vix curator eft: qua fcis et divum Auguftum, el Tiberium Cxfarcm ad Deos ifle. *dpocolocynt. Cl. Cat.*

A SYNOPSIS of CHRONOLOGY
DURING THE LIFE
TIBERIUS.

7U. – Tiberius born, Nov. 16.

714. – Herod made king by Ant. and Oct. in the 184 Oly. (I) – Oct. takes Livia Nor.

Tib. then *Irimut.* (2)

?17 – Drusus born, Feb. – Jer. taken in the harvest *after* a sabbatical year. (3)

722. – The first lustrum, which ended with a Census by Caesar, begun.

723. – The battle of Actium fought on the 2d Sept. (4)

725. – The temple of Janus shut. – The Actian, &c. triumphs, Tib. *pubescens.* (5) Ctesar entitled *Anlomttoor* in a new sense.

726. – The first Census by Caesar ended. – Made Prin. Sen. – The first Actian games. (6) 727. – Augustus made governor of the provinces for ten years. (7) 729. – Tiberius made sedile in Spain. – The temple of Janus shut. 730. – Tib. made quaestor, and permitted 10 take offices five years before others.

(1) *Jot. A.* xiv. – (2) *Paterc.* ii. 94. (3) *Jos. A. xiv.* . (4) *Dion* 1. 50.
(5) *Suet,* iii. 6. – (6) *Dion* 1. 53. – (7) *Ibid.* 53. p. 496. C. D.

A SYNOPSIS of CHRONOLOGY
DURING THE LIFE
TIBERIUS.

731. – Augustus dangerously ill. – Marcellus dies.

732. – Augustus goes to Sicily.

733. – Agr. marries Jul. – Augustus goes to Greece, and winters at Samoc.

Tib. marches through Macedonia – and is sent against Armenia. (1) 734. – Aug., in the spring, goes to Asia – thence to Syria – Caius born. – Aug. gives to
Herod the tetrarchy of Zen. – Sends for Tib. to expel Anabar, and to restore
Tigr. – Tib. begins to expect the Monarchy. – Aug. returns to Saruos, and there again winters.

735. – Augustus returns to Rome.

737. – Lucius born.

742. – Agrippa died. – Tiberius marries Julia.

747. – Aug. begins his second Census. – Christ born.

748. – Tib. invested with tribunitial powe-r for five years – retires to Rhodes.

749. – Caius puts olt the Toga virilis.

750. – Herod dies after having reigned about 36J years.

(1) *Slrabo.* 1. xvii.

A SYNOPSIS of CHRONOLOGY
DURING THE LIFE
TIBERIUS.

751. – Caius, /? *hts travels,* and, *before he took the command in the east,* beard the

validity of Herods wtll discussed. (I) 752. – The second Census by Aug. ended. – Censore me et Caninio Coss. (2)

Lucius puts on Toga virilis.

755. – Lucius died. – *I* iberius recallecl. – Drusus puts on the Tog. vir.
757. – Caius died. – Tiberius adopted.
759. – Archelaus deposed. – Christ went up to Jer. – 12 years old.
760. – Agrippa banished, and bis effects put into the military chest.
762. – Tiberius made Princeps Senatus, and coll. with Aug. in the Censorship."
7)'7. – The third Census by Augustus ended.

(I) *Jos. A,* xvii. 9. *s.* – (2) *Ancyr, mar, – Falerculus* ii. 100.

A SYNOPSIS of CHRONOLOGY
DURING THE LIF5
or
TIBERIUS.

777. – Pilate made Proe. of Jutltcs. – Our Lord baptised, when near 30.
778. – The Temple 46 years building. – Begun 732, in the 15tb of Herod. (1)
779. – Tiberius makes the tour of Campania. – The last Jubilee begins.
781. – Tiberius retires to Capren. – Our Lord when about 32, crucified, 42 years before

the fall of the Temple. – Great disorders at Rome.

782. – Livia dies, and leaves orders to refuse all honors ne *(ni?)* coelestis, &c.
783. – The power of stoning Jewish believers as blasphemers taken from the Jews 20 years before the fall of the temple. (2)

784. – The Christians expelled by the Senate from Bome, and protected by Tiberius.
788. – Pilate sent to Rome and dies on his passage. – Cornelius converted by Peter wba

was blamed for eating with him by the other Apostles.

(I) *Jtsephvs B.* i. 21, . – (2) *Talmud of Jer.*
THE HISTORY
TIBEBIUS,
THE
First Defender of the true Faith.
THE HISTORY

TIBEM1US,
mil
First Defender of the true Faith.
CHAPTER I.
Tiberius born u. c. 711.

SUETONIUS fays, iii. 5, that Tiberius was born, either in the firft confulfhip of Auguftus, or in that of Plancus and Lepidus, or in that of L. Antonius and P. S. Ifauricus, that is, either u. c. 711, 712, or 713. The fame writer adds – that it appeared by the public records, that he was born 712, and that moft chronologifts, and, among them the better informed, were convinced that he was born in that year. The opinion of thofe better informed, Suetonius himfelf feems, by what he fays, c. 73, of the age of Tiberius, at his death, to have followed: He there fays that Tiberius died 17 kal. April—!, e. the 16th March in the year of Rome 790, and that he was then in his 78th year. – Confequently if h had lived till the i6th of November he would have been full 78. – Whether Suetonius was always of the fame perfuafion we may, as we extend our enquiries, be able to difcover.

Tiberius born Nov. u. c. 711.

Tacitus alfo feems to have followed the opinion of thofe better informed, for he fays, Ann. vi. 50, that Tiberius, at his death (which, he fays, happened in March 790,) was in the 78th year of his age. In which cafe he muft Iiave been born in November 712. Now if he was born in November 712, he muft, in November 741, when he was the firft time conful, have been 29 only – and, in November 747, when he was a fecond time conful, have been 35, and, in the year following, 748, (when, as Dion fays, 1. 55, p. 554, D., and, as Pater- culus, ii. 99, and Suetonius, iii. 9, appear to fay, he was firft invefted with the tribunitial power,) have been in his 36 year. – And, therefore, Drufus his fon, muft, when he was firft made colleague with his father in the tribunitial power – that is – in the year of Rome 775, have, according to Tacitus, been in his 36 year – for, fays Tacitus, iii. 56, Tiberius himfelf then remarked to the Senate, when he applied for the tribunitial power for his fon, that he was of the fame age as himfelf when he was firft made a tribune. And confequently Drufus muft have been born 739. – But does he really appear to have been born in that year ? – Let us endeavour to fatisfy ourfelves.

Drufus, fays Suetonius, iii. 7, was his only fon by Vipfania Agrip- pina, the daughter of M. Agrippa, and the grand-daughter of the famous Caecilius Atticus. When Tiberius married her, it does not appear. But fays Suetonius, in the fame chapter, he, when he put her away, had Drufus by her, and Ihe was with child again – fublatoque ex ea filio Drufo, quamquam bene convenientem, rurfumque gravi- dam dimittere, ac, &c. – Dion fays, 1. 54, p. 543, C., when fhe had brought him one child and *vasfuckling it,* and was going with another

– *xat nxnt to* fttt *nti TftQuo-cH, To* St sv *yarft tyfaaa* – he was Compelled

to put her away, and marry Julia. This, according to Dion, happened in the confulfhip of M. V. Barbatus, and P. S. Quirinus, u. c. 742.

Tiberius born Nov. u. c. 711.

And, according to the joint reports of Paterculus and Dion, early in that year, becaufe, fay they, he was immediately obliged to take the command in Pannonia, which Agrippa had, in the preceding winter, been, through ill health, obliged to refign. Drufus then appears to have been, in the fpving of the year 742, about one or two years old. And confequently to have been born in 741, if not in 740. Dion fays, 1. 56, p. 586, A., that Drufus was quaeftor in the year 764.

That Drufus is likely to have been born in 740, Suetonius has rendered credible by what he fays, iii. 15, – viz – that Tiberius, on his return from Rhodes (which according to Paterculus, ii. 103, and Dion, 1. 55, p. 556, A., happened in the year 755 – and to Cardinal Noris about July in that year) introduced his fon into the forum, and that he, having done this, immediately quitted Pompey's houfe, in the Carinae, (which furely feems to imply that he had been refiding there fome time at leaft) and removed to that of Maecenas, in the Efqui- liqi. His own words are – Romam reverfus, dedufto in forum filio Drufo, ftatim e Carinis ac Pompetana domo, Efquilias in hortos Maecenatianos tranfmigravit: – of courfe, if Tiberius foon after his return from Rhodes in the year 755, introduced Drufus to the company of men, and – at the ufual age – viz – foon after he was 15, (for at that age Suetonius fays, ii. 8, Auguftus took the Toga,) he muft have been, at lateft, born before July 740, or, in the courfe of the year before Tiberius was conful the firft time. – And confequently, muft, in the year 775, when he was made his father's colleague in the tribunefhip, have been 35 years old. Tiberius therefore muft have been born the year before Tacitus fuppofes, and, by his own report, have been firft made colleague with Auguftus in the tribunitial power, not as Dion fays in the year 748 but in the year 746 – the year before he was the fecond time conful.

Tfbertus born Nov. u. c. lll.

If then Tiberius and Drufus, wete, when they were invefted witli the tribunitial power, of the fame age, (as Tacitus informs us, . Tiberius Himlelf obferved,) and Drufus was then 35, Tiberius muft alfo have been 35, – and, if Tiberius was, as Dion fays, invefted with that power 748, he muft have been born, not as Tacitus and Suetonius fay in 712, but 713. Tacitus then feetns, by this report, to have rendered his other report queftionable, and, of courfe that of Suetonius too.

Let us now then hear what Dion fays of this matter. – He feems to have been of a different opinion from thofe two' writers, and, of courfe, from all the better informed, for he feems to think that he was born not in 712 but either in 711 or 713. – L. 57,, p. 603, A., he fays that Tiberius was u. c. 767, when Auguftus died, 56 years old- ill *yvf xat tranxotra m* tytyotu – meaning, perhaps, not that he was then 56, but in the 56th. Confequently, he feems by this to have thought that he-was born 16th November 711 – or about two months after Auguftus was firft conful. And that he was, at his death, u. c. 790, in his 79th. But was Dion always of this perfuafion ? – Let us fee. – He fays, 1. 58, p. 639, B., that Tiberius was, when he died, not in his 79th year, but in his 77th, which implies that he muft have thought that he was born 713, and this he inconfiderately affirms, notwithftanding he there fays that he reigned 2 2 years 7 months and 7 days.

As then no fatisfaftton on this point can be obtained from thofe three writers, let us confult one or two of his cotemporaries.

Paterculus fays, ii. 75, that Tiberius was, when his parents fled from Italy to Sicily, on the defeat of their party by Oftavius, and the confequent diftribution $f their lands among his veterans, *minus biHum.* – When then did this infurre&ion happen, and, how long did itlaft?

Tiberius lorn JVoz?. u. c. 711.

Livy Epit. of B. 125, fays that L. the brother of M. Antomus, while conful, made, at the mftigation of Fulvia, war on Caefar – and that he was joined by thofe who had been difpoflefled of their lands by Oftavius. – L. Ant. onius conful, M. Antonii fratcr, eadem Fulvia conciliante, bellum Qvfari iatulit: receptis in partes fuas populis, quorum agri veteranis affignati eflent. – Florus, B. iv. 5,. fays nearly the fame thing. – Confeq. uently this infurre&ion of the land-holders muft have happened u. c. 713. And as to the continuance of it, w$ may fafely conclude from what Patercuhts fays, ii. 75, that it could not hare been long, for he there fays of it – id quoque adventu Caefaris fepultum atque difcuffitm eft. – Tiberius Claudius Nero, who, Paterculus fays had been the inftigator of this infurreftion, finding hia party difperfed, fled with Livia, and her infant fpn, then not two years old, to Sicily. Confequently Tiberius feems, by the report of Paterculus, to have been, in the year 713, lefs than two years old. – And. therefore he muft, as Dion affirms, 1. 57, and Suetonius admits to have been poffible, have been born u. c. 711.

Again – When Tiberius was three years old – *qw trlmo* fays Pater- culusr K. 94, a reconciliation of all parties took place. Qa- whicfr oceafion Tiberius Claudius Nero who bad then returned from Achata, whither he had removed from Siciry, refigned his wife, who-was then- fix months advanced in pregnancy for her fecond fon- Drufus, *to-* Oftavius. – Now when did this general reconciliation of the hoftile leaders take place ? – Or rather in what year did Tiberius transfer his wife Livia to Oftavius ?

Livy we have feen, tells us that Oftavius befieged L. Antonius while conful, in Perufia. – And Suetontus tells us, iii. 4, that the- fiege was begun toward *the end* of the year – *exitw anni – aad,* again 51. 15, that it was cmted- before, the ides- of Marchv – When *us* Livy-

, *Tiberius torn* JVbu. *u. c.* 711.

further fays, in the next chap. 126, Oftavius forgave both Anthony and all his troops, and by fecuring all the forces of the adverfe party, put an end to the war, without any further bloodfhed – bellum citra ullum fanguinem confecit. – With Livy, Paterculus, ii. 74, 76, alfo agrees. Suetonius fays further, iii. 4, that Nero *foon after* the fiege was ended – *brevi* – returned from Achaia, with Mark Anthony, to Italy, when, as Jofephus fays, A. xiv. 14, *i,* before the end of the 184 Olympiad – that is – before Midfummer 714, a reconciliation of all parties took place. And before the end of the year Oftavius married Livia. – Confequently, if as Paterculus fays, Tiberius was then three years old, he muft, as Dion fays, 1. 57, have been born 711.

Let us next confult Suetonius again and endeavour to difcover if he appears to have been always perfuaded that Tiberius was born 712.

He fays, iii. 6, that Tiberius was, at the Aftian triumph (which it appears by Dion, 1. 51, p. 459, B., took place in the month of Auguft u. c. 725, Oft. Caes. V. et S. A. Cofs.) old enough to ride one of the horfes which drew the car of Oftavius; – and, that he was, at that time, *pubefcens* – that is, furely, not 12 years and nearly 9 months old, but 13 years and 9 months. Confequently it feems by this that he muft have been born in the year 711.

, x

Again – Suetonius, Hi. 9, mentions another office, to whichTiberius was promoted, and, the junfture when it took place – a due attention, to each of which circumftances may enable us to fettle the year of hi? birth. – He there fays that Tiberius firft ferved in the Cantabrican war – and, as a tribune. – Stipendia prima expeditione Cantabrica Tribu- nus militum fecit. – At which time he muft have been, at leaft, 17 years of age. – Now when did that war begin-and, when did it end ?*Tiberius lorn* JVbil. *u.* & 7 11.

Dion fays, 1. 53, p. 513, D. E., that it began 728, and feemingly late in that year, and, p. 515, that it ended in 729, and feemingly early in that year. He alfo fays that the temple of Janus, Was, in the laft mentioned year, fhut. Dion moreover fays, p. 514, D., that Tiberius was not only in Spain in the year 739, but that he together with

Marcellus, in that year, performed the office of aediles at the fports which Auguftus gave, in the field, for the amufement of thofe that Were then of a military age – Jtou Si Sa rfTEa-j/o Xjai It *iHa-i, Sias nix:, Six. n ra* MafxcXXa *xai* Ta *TtGifiu tis nai ayopanfiLarfuv, n*

tiv-rois rois ffaroirtSoit twwtwt. – As then Tiberius was a tribune in 728, and an aedile in 729, he muft, of courfe, have been born in 711.

To this evidence of Dion, it may not be amifs to fubjoin that of Livy, Epit. of chap. 134, 135. – In the former title he mentions the Gallic cenfus – and in the latter, the Thracian war, which was con- dufted by Craffiis – and the Spanifh, which was condufted by Caefar. – Bellum a Marco Craflb adverfus Thracas. et a Caefare adverfus Hifpanos geftum refertur. – Now the Thracians were fubdued by Craflus, fays the Chron. Syn. in the third year of the 1 88 Olympiad, or 728, 729' – -OA – PI1H – F. *K. patra-os rii*

Again Paterculus fays, ii. 94, that Tiberius was, when in his year, made a quaeftor – quaeflor undeviceffimum annum agens capef- fere ccepit Rempublicam. – That he was then, with Auguftus, at Rome, and very aftive in fupplying the city with corn in the time of the greateft fcarciry. – - Now in what year did this happen ?

Dion, 1. 53, p. 516, B., fays that Auguftus in his tenth confulate, u. c. 730, was at Rome – that Marcellus was then made aedile, and Tiberius quaeftor. – Jofephus alfo fays, A. xv. 9, . that in the

Tiberius born Nov. u. c. 711.

of Herod – u. c. 730. – x. con. of Auguftus a very great fcarcity prevailed all over Judea and Syria. – As therefore Tiberius was in the year 730 in his t9th year, he muft have been born u. c. 711.

Not long after this – that is – not long after he was quaeftor, he, fays Paterculus, ii. 94, was fent to the eafl, by Auguftus, with an army, to fee the Provinces and to fettle the affairs of thofe that wanted it. – Nee multo port miiTits ab eodem vitrico cum exercitu ad vifendas, ordinandafque, quae fub Oriente funt, provincias. – In all thofe regions, he, continues Paterculus, gave *the mojl Jlriking proofs of all virtues.* – Having, with his legions, entered Armenia, and reduced it under the control of the R. P. he gave the command of it to Arta- vafdes, for which, he afterwards remarks, c. 122, that he deferved a triumph. – And concludes Paterculus, he fo terrified the king of Parthia by *the greatnefs of his name* that he fent his fons as hoftages to Caefar. – Of thofe exploits Horace takes notice in his ep. to Iccius.,

1. I. 12,

Cantaber Agrippae, Claudi virtute Neronis
Armenius cecidit: jus imperiumque Phraates
Caefaris accepit genibus minor.

Suetonius in two places of his gth chap, fays nearly the fame as Paterculus. – In the beginning of that chapter, after informing us that he made his firft campaign in Cantabria, as a tribune, he immediately proceeds to tell us that his next military ftep was to lead an army to the eaft, &c. – *Deinde* dufto ad orientem exercitu, regnum Armenia? Tigrani reflituit, ac pro tribunal! diadema impofuit. Rccepit et figna quae M. Craflb ademerant Parthi – This he fays in the beginning of this chap. – In the conclufion of the fame, after having faid, in general, that he difcharged all offices fooner than others, and pafied from one to another almoft without intermiffion – Magiftratus et

Ttberius lorn Nov. v. c. 711.

maturius inchoavit, et pene junftim percurrit – he adds – Quaefturam, Praturam, Confulatum: interpofitoque tempore, Cos. iterum, etiam Tribunitiam poteftatem in quinquennium accepit. – May we then conclude from this that he was made praetor when he, as Suetonius fays, in. 14, led the army, through Macedonia, to the eaft ? If fo, he feems to have been made praetor u. c. 732, for in that year, Strabo fays, Auguftus fent him from Samos into Armenia – and in the next year Eufebius Chron. Can. and the authorf of Chr. Syngr. fay that he was in Armenia and recovered the ftandards which were taken by the Partisans from M. Craflus.

Dion, we know, fays, 1. 52, p. 447, C., that the age recommended to Auguftus by Maecenas for prators was 30. And, 1. 53, p. 515, B., that Tiberius was permitted to enter on all offices 5 years before the ufual ftanding, but he alfo fays, 1. 54, p. 527, D., that Auguftus, the very next day, after his return from Syria, u. c. 735, when Tiberius was in his 24th, gave him praetorian honors, and at the fame time permitted Drufus alfo to ftand for all honors 5 years before the ufual time. – And, 1. 54, p. 534, B., that the Senate, u. c. 738, paffed a decree that Drufus, who was then in his 25th year, fhould be praetor, for the remainder of the time, inftead of Tiberius, who was then going to attend Auguftus into Gaul. Where he commanded, fays Suetonius, iii. 9, a year.

Another office which we fhall notice in order to difcover the age of Tiberius, is that of conful. – Now Tiberius difchargcd this office in the year of Rome 741, that is, as Dion fays, 5 years after he had re-

AOAAIOS *iuxt* AEntAOZ – *TtGefto* f PnO- – I. – KIo-f *rots lfifJ. utts as Kfao-o-os* nro

Tiberius born JVbv. u. c, 711.

eeived praetorian honors – or 5 years after 735 – as did alfo Drufus in the year 745, and as Paterculus fays, ii. 97, at the age of 30, which was fomewha$ more than 5 years after Drufus was praetor. – Now as Prnrus was made conful at 30, why fhould we not conplude that Tiberius alfo was made conful at that age ?

CHAPTER II.

Tiberius -went to Rhodes early in 749, *and returned in*
July 755.

little before Tiberius was made conful ii. he had, fays Pater- culus, ii. 94, conquered all Germany. – It was on this account that he, as Dion fays, 1. 55, p. 553, C., obtained, early in that year, afecond triumph. – In the mean time, continues Paterculus in the next chap. 98, Pifo fubdued Thrace, and procured fecurity for Afia and Macedonia. – By thofe two chapters, it appears that all nations were, in the beginning of the year 747, when Tiberius was ii. conful, at peace.

Soon after the aforefaid events had taken place, Tiberius was, fays Paterculus, ii. 99, invefted with the tribunitial power, and, in that refpeft, made equal to Auguftus. This mark of diftinftion, Dion feems to fay, 1. 55, p. 554, D., was conferred on him, u. c. 748, not as a reward for his fcrvices, but to check the afpiring pretenfions of the youths Caius and Lucius. But obferves he, inftead of anfwer- ing the end intended, it only ferved to render both parties more diflatisfied. Wherefore to avoid giving them offence, or, for fome, as Paterculus hints, more fubftantial reafon, this, as he fays of him, ii. 99, moft eminent of all citizens, but Auguftus, and fubordinate to *Tiberius at Rhodes from* 749 *to July* 755.

him only by choice – this greateft of generals – this moft renowned as to charafter and fuccefs – and, to fpeak out the truth, this other luminary and head of the republic, when C. Caefar had juft put on the toga virilis – cum C. Caefar fumpfiflet jam togam virilem – u. c. 749, petitioned for leave to retire – and affigned as a reafon – " left the fplendor of his exploits Ihould difcourage the enterprifing fpirits of the youths," – to this his father-in-law and mother, fays Suetonius, iii. 10, ftrenuoufly objefted – this made him, fays he, abftain from food four days, in the courfe of which time Auguftus feems to have complained in the fenate that he was deferted, (which furely implies that Tiberius was not banifhed, if not that Auguftus did not procure for him the tribunitial power, merely becaufe of the petulance of his grandfons.) – And not only Auguftus and his mother were moft deeply affe&ed at the thought of lofing him, but alfo all his fellow citizens. To recite, fays Paterculus, ii. 99, what was the condition of the flate at the time – what the feelings of every individual – what tears were ihed at the thought of parting from fo great a perfon – how his country could fcarcely refrain from ufing force to detain him, would too much interrupt the prefent hiftory, and therefore would be better referved for a feparate narrattve. – At laft he obtained his requeft. – r But before he left Rome, he, fays Dion, 1. 55, p. 554, E., opened his will before Auguftus and Livia, and read it. – Another proof that he was not bammed. – All things being fettled, he, leaving his wife and fon behind him, went, with very few attendants, to Oftia. And then inftead of going immediately to Rhodes, he, fays Suetonius, iii. 11, travelled from place to place in Campania, for, as we fhall come to fee prefently, nearly a year, and early in the fpring 749 proceeded to Rhodes, not without office, but as praefeft of Armenia, which had, in the mean time, revolted, for no fooner had the rival ftates intelligence of his intention, than they entered into a confederacy – Senfit

Tiberius at Rhodes from 749 *to July* 755.

terrarum orbis digreflum a cuftodia Neronem urbis, nam et Parthus, defcifcens a focietate romana, adjecit Armeniae manum; et Germania, averfis domitoris fui oculis, rebellavit. ii. 100. – At Rhodes he refided almoft as a private man, and on the moft cordial terms with the inhabitants more than fix years.

Heic modicis contentus aedibus, nee multo laxiore fuburbano genus vitae civile admodum inftituit: fine liftore aut viatore gymnafia interdum obambulans: mutuaque cum Graeculis officia ufurpans, prope ex aequo. – Here too, fays Suetonius, iii. u, he gave the firft proof of his moft extraordinary philanthropy – for having one day early, intimated his intention of vifiting the fick, his attendants, mif- taking his meaning, ordered all of them to be carried to a public portico, and to be placed according to their diforders. Struck at the inconvenience which the miftake had caufed, and, at a lofs for fome time how to. aft, he, at laft, went to every one of them, and made an apology to each for what was done, even to the pooreft and moft obfcure. – His conftant employment, while he refided here, ufed to be to attend the public fchools, and to liften to the leftures of the profeflbrs, ftudying, as Tacitus fays, vi. 20, the chaldaean art – viz – aftrology or aftronomy, or, perhaps, mathematical truths, as, we find, by Suetonius, iii. 69, he was addifted to mathematics, with the

Whoever attends to what Paterculus says, ii. 99, of the time when Tiberius applied for leave to retire – viz – cum C. Caesar sumpsisset jam virilem togatn, Lucius item matnrus esset viris – u. c. 749 – may stand a chance of understanding what Suetonius meant by – tantum non adversis tempestatibus, iit. 11; – and whoever attends to what Paterculus says of the ttme when Tiberius returned to Rome – viz – ante utrinsque horum obitum – that is – before the 20th August u. c. 755; – or, as Cardinal Noris says – July 755, will be inclined to think that he could not have been resident at Rhodes more than 6 years and 4 or 5 months. – And as he resided at Rhodes no longer, and us Suetonius says, iii. – , that he returned the Sth year after his secession, may re not suppose, that he spent, at least, one year in Campania ?

Tiberius at Rhodes from 749 *to July* 755.

famous mathematician Thrafyllus, who, it feems, abode with him – quern et fapientiae profeflbrem contubernio admoverat, S. iii. 14 – or, religious doftrines, under Jewifh Rabbi's – viz – Theodoras of Ga- dara, (S. iii. 57,) and Diogenes the grammarian, who ufed to difpute at Rhodes, on the fabbaths, iii. 32, by whom he probably was brought acquainted with the ftate of affairs in Judea, among the reft, with the difientions in Herod's family, and with his uneafinefs in confequence of the arrival of the eaftern magi by the guidance of a new ftar, and the convocation of a fynod on that account, and the confequent maflacre of the infants at Bethlehem. – All the while he was in this ifland, the greateft honors were, fays Paterculus, ii. 99, and Suetonius, iii. 12, paid to him by the eaftern praefefts, (a third proof that he was not fent to Rhodes in difgrace) and, in particular by Caius, both on his viftt to the provinces, and on his expedition to Syria. – On his vifit to the provinces he, fays Suetonius, iii. 12, and Dion,]. 55, p. 555, D., faw him either at Samos or Chius, and on his return he again faw him at one of the fame iflands. Paterculus, who ii. 101, fays that he was prefent at the interview between Caius and the Parthian potentate, fays alfo, in the fame chapter, that Caius, in his way to Parthia, waited on Tiberius and mewed him, as his fuperior, every mark of refpeft.

In the year 755, fays he, ii. 103, P. V. Cos., while Caius and Lucius were ftill alive, a fhip was, without the knowledge of Tiberius, about Midfummer, fent for him. – A fourth proof that he was ftill in favor. Thus, fays Paterculus, did fortune reftore to the republic her wonted fupport, to the incredible joy of all ranks. When he arrived at Rome, Auguftus, not at all doubting whom he mould choofe, but knowing that the eminent was the only perfon, wifhed to adopt him

Query – May not Diogenes have been the aine as Theogenes mentioned ii. 94.

x *f*

-Tiberius -was at Rhodes from 749 *to July* 755.

immediately before the death of Caius, but Tiberius refolutely declined ttte honor. After the death of Caius, about July u. c. 757, Auguftus, at laft, prevailed. – The joy of that day, the meetings of the people, the devotions of thofe who almoft thruft their thankful hands into heaven, and the hope that they entertained that the fecu- rity of the Roman empire was eternally eftablifhed, I, fays Paterculus, cannot here recount. – Let me only fay how very dear he was to all. Then fhone forth again a certain hope of children to parents – of marriage to men – of patrimony to mafters – of fafety, quiet, peace, tranquility to every one – fo that nothing could be wifhed for more, nor more happily anfwer their expeftations. The fame joy was manifefted all through Italy, and the provinces of Gaul. Every one feemed to rejoice more on his own account, than on his. The foldiers fhed tears of joy, and prefled to touch his hand – exclaiming – Do we then fee you general again, and in fafety ? – I have fought under you in Armenia – I in Rhaetia – I was rewarded by you in Vindelicia – I in Pannonia – I in Germany.

5

SECTION 5

CHAPTER III.
Augustus and Tiberius colleagues five years.

the preceding chronological fynopfis of the years of Tibe rius, it appears, that the 36 year of Herod ended in the 750 of Rome, and, as Jofephus 'fays, A. xiv. 14, E., before Midfummer in 'that year – confequently if Herod died in that year and before the 2[th of December, our Lord muft, if he was, as both Matthew and Luke fay, born before the death of Herod, have been, at lateft, born in 749, and, as is thought on the 25th of December – and confequently, muft have attained his 3Oth year, not in the year of RomeSa, as we fupppfe, but in the year 779, or, the lath of the monarchy of Tiberius. But was a cenfus begun in the year 749 ? – And was there *then* an univerfal peace ? Auguftus himfelf tells us that he finifhed the fecond cenfus, not in the year 746 when Cenforinus and Afinius Gallus were confuls, but in the year 752 when he hirnfelf, *the cenfor,* and Gallus Caninius were confuls – Cenfore me et Caninio Cofs. – and if he ended it in the year 752 he muft have begun it, in the year

Ancyr. mar.
Augustus, and Tiberius colleagues five years.

747, when Tiberius was conful, in which year there was, as Pater- culus fays, ii. 98, an univcrfal peace, which, fubjoins he, did not laft long after Tiberius had determined to retire – that is – after 748. And if he had not told us fo, we might, as we know that Tiberius, who was, by all accounts, the conftant defence of the republic, was then conful, and at Rome, and prefently after retired, havo readily believed it. – That a cenfus was about that year made, Jofephus him- felf feems to have attefled, A. xvii. 2, ., where he refers to a certain fine which had been laid on 7,000 Pharifees, who, when an oath to Caefar was required of all the Jews, refufed to take it. When this oath was required he does not direftly intimate, but it is not very difficult to guefs pretty nearly at the time by almoft indubitable criteria. For in the end of A. xiv, Jofephus fays, that Jerufalem was taken in the year of Rome 717 – and before Midfummer, and the xv and xvi books contain, he fays, the tranfaftions of 30 years, and therefore end before Midfummer 747, when Herod had reigned 33 years. And confequently as this event is referred to in the fecond chap, of the xvii book, and as haying taken place fome time before, we may fairly fuppofe that it is probable that it happened about 747 or early in 748. Was then our Loid born in the year 747 ? If fo, he muft have attained his 3oth year u. c. 777, and in the beginning of the loth of Tiberius. – That our Lord was born before December 749 cannot be eafily made to appear from what Matthew and Luke fay – but from what Matthew and Jofephus fay, it might be made to appear that he was born December 747. For Matthew, we know, by faying that Jofeph, was, while in Egypt, informed that *they* were dead, intimates that one or two others, befide Herod, fought to kill the young child. – Now who were thofe other corifpirators ? – Jofephus

Augustus and Tiberius colleagues five years.

informs us, A. xvii. t. .. 2. s., B. i. 29. ., that Herod, about 3 years before his death, refigned the management of public bufinefs to Anti- pater and Pheroras, who had been the caufe of the deaths of Alexander and Ariftobalus. Soon after, 3. 8, thofe two had obtained the direftion of affairs, they, unaccountably, both became very un- eafy, and contrived to withdraw from Judea. Antipater firft obtained leave to go to Rome – and Pheroras, A. xvii. 3. y. B. i. 29. $., went foon after to his tetrarchy, under a vow never to return more. When Antipater went to Rome, it is not faid, but may be inferred from the fequel – Syllatus, A. xvii. 3. /3. – B. i. 29. "v-f went to Rome *at the fame time,* and Saturninus was then governor of Syria. – Now Saturninus, we know, was fucceeded by Varus, u. c. 748, as appears by a fmall coin which the latter ftruck, of which Pagi. Appar. ad Baron, n. 1 36 on the authority of Cardinal Noris, fays, that there are ftill extant feveral which were ftruck by him while prefident of Syria – the earlieft of which has on the reverfe a woman fitting with her foot on the figure of the Orontes, with a palm in her right hand, with the following infcription – Em Otapon ANTtoxEnN – and in the middle the letters – KE – that is – xxv. – By which it appears that Varus muft have been in Syria before September 2d, u. c. 748 – For the aera which the Antiochians ufed, at that time, was that of the viftory of Aftium, which was obtained September the 2d, u. c. 743. – Con- fequently the xxv. of this aera muft have ended September the 2d,

Probably for having accused them of being in the interest of the Parthians.
oe Koci ZuXXoKof o Af4/ *etn Puffwf, r. tntas* /xsv *rut Kato-atfot*
Vfos AmvaTfot. B.
Augustus and Tiberius colleagues Jive years.

v. c. 748. If then Varus fuccceded Saturninus before the ad September in that year, it is clear that Antipatcr muft have gone to Rome, nobody knows how long before. – That Antipater muft have been a long while at Rome we may infer from the various particulars which, Jofephus fays, happened during his abfence – for, after he left Jeru- falem, which it fcems, he did, not long after he was made every thing – that is – not long after the 33d year of Herod was ended, Herod quarrelled fo mach with Pheroras, on account of the proteftion which his wife afforded the 7,000 Pharifees, that he forbad him his prefence, and Pheroras fwore that he. would never fee him more. – A little after this Herod was taken ill, and fent for Pheroras, who, as he had fworn, rcfufed to fee him. – Pheroras was then taken ill and Herod went to fee him. Soon after Pheroras died. After his death, it was fufpefted that he died of poifon, and on an enquiry it was found that he did, and that Syllceus, the Arabian, was privy to it. – This enquiry led to a difcovery that Antipater had been plotting againft the life of his father. – His guilt was proved feven months before he knew it at Rome. From Rome he went to Tarentum, where he was informed of the death of Pheroras, from thence he failed to Cilicia, and, at Celendris, received a letter from Herod, in which his mother was blamed, which made him fufpeft all was not right, however he proceeded on to Sebafte. and fo to Jerufalem, where he was imprifoned, and put to death five days before Herod died.

It is pretty clear then that Antipater went to Rome before Varus went to Syria – that is – before the 2d September, 748. And therefore as our Lord was more than a month old when the children were mafTacred at Bethlehem, that he may have, with Pheroras, been coa- ceined in that maflacre.

Augustus and Tiberius colleagues Jive years.

Befides – Tf, as the Talmud of Jerufalem fays, the power of puniftt- ing capitally was taken from Ifrael 40 years before the deftruftion of that city – that is – 40 years before 823 – or – in 783 – and in the 16th of Tiberius, the perfecution of Saul muft have then ceafed. – And, if that perfecution did not begin till the year following the crucifixion, and lafted about two years, our Lord muft have been, at lateft, crucified u. c. 781, or – the t4th of Tiberius.

By the help of the fame evidence of the above-mentioned document, we may perceive that Jofephus too feems to have intimated the fame thing, A. xviii. 4. *t.,* where he, after having mentioned the crucifixion of our Lord, fays that a vagabond Jew, who had fled from lus own country to avoid the punifhment due to his tranfgreffions of the laws, and had found an afylum at Rome, was the caufe of the expulfion of ail his countrymen from that city – for, if that Jewifh vagabond left Judea to avoid the penalty of the law, he muft have left it before the power of punifhing capitally had been taken from Ifrael – that is – before 783. And, ofcourfe, our Lord, who appears to have beea crucified before this wretch left Judea, muft have been crucified, nobody knows how long, before that year. But why, it may be afked, if he left Judea before the power of inffifting capital punifhment had been taken from the Jews, did they not avail themfelves of their boafted privilege and endeavour to feize him at Rome, as Saul did other delinquents in other ftrange cities ? If he was not a

Hv *amf ludatos, fytuyas* itv Tijj *avra, xarnyofta re trafaGato-tus* v-'/'.-'v *xat octt Ttfftns Tns tv"* avrotf, vomfos St *sts* Tiz *vanat, xt* St) ron tv Tt) Pxi/xJ) *otatrut, etos,* trfoi7S7roifiro /afv *cj-yvturQat aotyton* Ki/aoit *tut Muvo-sus, vfoo-'TKMaaty. tws re rfus atiofas us rat, jrattx oiMmfoTtus, ts-rots tvfyowtaacmv* 8X? taVf Txiv *ct yvtatxut xat mfiufMts wfoo-ttovQt/xt rots* IbSaKOJf, *tntQvvt TTOftyvfat aat t us To tv*

Augustus and Tiberius colleagues Jive years.

worfhipper of Chrift they furely had ftill the power of feizing him any where. May we not therefore furmife that this notorious tranf- greilbr of the laws was no other than a worfhipper of Chrift ? And that he was therefore, in the eftimation of Jofephus and his unbelieving brethren, fo very execrable? This fuppofition, however novel it may appear, we find ourfelves obliged to adopt, not only by noticing the negleft of the Jews to profecute him, but by obferving that he, bad as he was, could obtain accefs to Fulvia a profelyted lady of diftinftion, and that Tiberius, on his account, permitted the expulllon of all the Jews from Rome, and the banifhment of the Jewiih libertines to Sardinia. And though it does not tend direftiy to eftablifh. our original point – viz – the year in which our Lord was put to death – yet, as it implies that the gofpel was, *without molcjlation,* permitted to be preached at Rome before the expulfion of the Jews from Rome and the tranfportation of the libertines to Sardinia – that is – before the 18th year of Tiberius, it will be found to imply pretty fatisfaftorily that our Lord was crucified, nobody knows how long before the I5th of Tiberius, and confequently that he, as he is faid by John to have celebrated three, if not four paflbvers, in the courfe of his miniftry, poffibly attained his 30th year in the loth of Tiberius.

But what ? Does our Lord really appear to have been born 747 ? And to have entered on his 30th year u. c. 777 – that is the loth of Tiberius ? Why then has Luke told us that he entered on it, on the T5th of Tiberius, u. c. 782 ? Did he by the I5th mean only the loth? Of this we may be affured that if he really means the ijth of his

This accounts for Josephus' appearing, A. xviii. 3, 4, lo have omitted the events of 8 or 10 years in the short period of 32; – in the end of chapter 3, he mentions the death of Germanicus, who died u. *c.* 772; – and in the begin- Brag of chapter 4, he mentions the offence of Pilate by introducing the Roman standards at Jerusalem after *v.* c. 180.

Augustus and Tiberius colleagues five years.

monarchy he pofitively aflerts that he was born u. c. 752 – that is after the death of Herod – and confequently contradifts not only the evidence of Matthew, but alfo his own in the two preceding chapters, if not in the Afts iv. 27 – for in the beginning of the firft he fays – " There was in the days of Herod, the king of Judea," – and, in that of the fecond – " And it came to pafs in tiiofe days, &c." – And he not only appears to contradift his own teftimony, and that of Matthew too, but likewife that of John, who fays that our Lord, at the firft paflbver which he celebrated after he begun his miniftry – that is – in the 15th of Tiberius u. c. 782, obferved to the Jews, at Jerufalem, that the temple had been building 40 and 6 years, and confequently it muft, if Luke has been underftood rightly, have been begun 736. – But what fays Jofephus of the time when it was begun? – He fays, B. i. 21. ., that Herod, in the I5th year of his reign u. c. 732, at a vaft expence, began both to decorate the temple, and to enclofe a fpace around it as large again as the

former – *atvrot re* vov *tvnnuvxrt Kjxi Tth vtft aunt xvsTettfaro yu(aw ns atms Snrteunmt* – as a proof of the immenfe expence it muft have coft, he inftances the *jlatdy porticos* around the temple, (among which, no doubt, was that called Solomon's,) and the fortrefs on the north, where the pontifical habits ufed to be kept. Now if he began to do all this in the I5th year of his reign, why may he not be faid to have then begun the building of the temple ? And if fo it muft have been 40 years a building, not in the year 782, but in 778 – the loth year of the monarchy of Tiberius, and the 30th of our Lord's age. – He alfo fays indeed, A. xv. n. *a.,* that it was begun in the 18th year of Herod, u. c. 735 – after the arrival of Caefar in Syria. – But then he feems to refer to the fame event – 5z – to the beautifying of the temple – and the enlarging of the feptum – Totf yav *oxTwxatxara Ttts* HfwSa @*atnuas* ysyowros *tvtavra, peroc ras Vfottftpas trfatets, t[yw a r*

Augustus and Tiberius colleagues five years.

nreGatro, ro Mw Tb 0i5 Si' aura *mxTxa-xivairxTQai, ptia re fit*

o, *xai irfot* ii4oi *aZioirfivirxm lyeifw. x. r. x.* – Confequently, why fhould we not fuppofe that, by thofe two dates, Jofephus meant to refer to the two commencements of Herod's reign – viz – by the former, to the capture of Jerufalem – and by the latter, to his firft being made king ? And, that he therefore in both works means the fame thing? If he does not, but by the i8th of Herod he alfo means from the conqueft of Jerufalem – and therefore u. c. 735, then our Lord muft have faid this 781, for 735x46=781 – which was not the I5th but the I3th year of Tiberius, and the 3oth year of our Lord- in which cafe our Lord muft have been born after the death of Herod, and, could not, as a fabbatical year did not, in that cafe, happen in the courfe of his minifny, have celebrated a jubilee. – That it is, at leaft, not certain that he meant to fay that Herod began the temple 18 years after the capture of Jerufalem – or – u. c. 735, is clear, becaufe this book contains only the events of 18 years from that time, and yet in the conclufion of it, we find, he fpeaks of the finifhing of the temple, that is, at leaft, of the ferviceable part of it, which he fays, was completed in a year and fix months, and, that it was opened on the anniverfary of Herod's reign – that is – exaftly at the expiration of 18 years from the taking of Antigonus and Jerufalem – or – u. c. 735. Now if the priefts finifhed the more facred part in a year and fix months, can we fuppofe, that the materials, for that part, were collefted in lefs time ? If not, we find, that Herod muft have begun to build it 3 years before the end of the iSth year of his reign – that is–at the end of the

He says it in the title – and, wo find it contains the transactions from the capture of Jerusalem, u. c. 717, till the anniversary of Herod's reign, after the arrival of Cswar in Syria, v. c. 735.

Augustus and Tiberius colleagues Jive years.

Luke then, notwithftanding his profeffion, at the outfet of giving us a more corrett account of the life of Chrift than others, notwithftanding his precifion in this very cafe, appears to have made a nroft glaring anachronifm; – and, in contradiftion, not only of his own previous teftimony, but alfo of that of two companions of that moft extraordinary perfon.. – But this furely we cannot fuppofe that any biographer would have done in the fhort life of any one, efpecially of one fo eminent and a cotemporary, much lefs a biographer, who wrote to correft the inaccuracies of others, and on whofe produftion the eyes of the unbelieving world were fixed.

Now if, even by the account of Luke, as well as by that of Matthew, John, and Jofephus, our Lord appears to have been born before the death of Herod, and to have entered on his joth year, not as Luke fays, in the I5th of Tiberius, but in the icth, may not Luke have called the loth of his monarchy the I5th of his reign. – Let us not fpare any pains to fatisfy ourfelves.

It is generally admitted by hiftorians that Auguftus, a few years before he died, made Tiberius his colleague in the government of the Roman affairs. – But in what year this event happened none of thofe hiftorians have attempted to fhew. Some think it took place in the year of Rome 764, when M. *J$m.* Lepidus and T. S. Taurus were confuls – and, about three years before the death of Auguftus. – Clemens of Alexandria, fays, Strom. p. 339, that fome maintained that the reign of Tiberius lafted 26 years 6 months and 19 days. – If this account be true, Tiberius muft have begun to reign in the year of Rome 763 – but, according to Luke, he muft have begun a year earlier. – Let us enquire which of thofe three opinions appears to be neareft the truth. – And firft let us confultthe evidence of Paterculus on this point.

Augustus and Tiberius colleagues five years.

Paterculus, fpeaking of what happened after the conqucft of Bato and Pinetcs, u. c. 761, F. C. and S. N. Cofs. ii. 114, fays, in the end of that chapter – Autumno viftor in hyberna reducitur exercitus, eujus omnibus copiis a *Cafare* (a Caefaribus?) M. Lepidus praefeftus eft, vir nominis ac fortunae *eorum* proximus. – In the courfe of that winter, or, rather perhaps, in the end of it, o. c. 762, after Tiberius had, as Diou fays, I. 56, init., triumphed, either Tiberius alone, or, Tiberius in conjunftiou with Auguftus, placed M. Lepidus over all the forces.

In the next chapter – viz – H5th, he fays of the fame Lepidus – Initio aeftatis – fcil. 762, Lepidus, edufto hibernis exercitu, per gentes integras immunefque adhuc clade belli, ct eo ferociores ac truces, tendens ad Tiberium imperatorem, &c. pervenit ad Caefarem; et ob ea, quae fi propriis geffiflet aufpiciis, triumphare debuerat, ornamentis triumphalibus, confentients cum judicio *prlnctjtum.* voluntate fenatus, donatus eft. – By thfs extraft it appears that Lepidus was, in the year 762, by the joint approbation of *Hoe princes,* rewarded with triumphal honors.

In the t2pth chapter, he faya – His auditis revolat ad patrefn Caefar; perpetuus patronus romani imperii *adfuetam* fibi caufam fufcipit. – Paterculus is here fpeaking of the defeat of Varus, who, as Dion fays, ! 56, p. 582, C., was defeated in the winter of 763 By this it appears that Tiberius, o'n hearing of that defeat, haftened immediately to Rome, to give direftions, as ufual, for the fecurity of the Roman empire.

Omnino " a Cxsaribus" Lips.

Augustus and Tiberius colleagues five years.

In the next chapter, the t2tft, he fays – Eademet virtus ct fortuna *fubfcquenti* tempore ingrefla . animam impcratoris Tiberii fuit, qu$

initio fucrat; qui cum molliflet, et fenatus populufque

fomanus (poftulante patre ejus ut aequum ei jus in omnibus provinces exercitibufque eflet, quam erat ipfi) decreto complcxus efiet, (elenim

abfurdum erat) *in urbem reverfus,* jampridem debitum, fed

continuatione bellorum dilatum, ex Pannonicis Dalmatifque egit triumphum. – By this we learn that Tiberius, after he had been inverted with authority equal to that of

Auguftus, returned u. c. 765, to Rome, and triumphed not only over the Pannonians but alfo over the Dalmatians.

In the t23. d chapter, he fays – -Commendans illi *faa atque i/tfas opera.-Bj* this we are informed that Auguftus, on his death bed, recommended to Tiberius their joint works.

Laftly, in the 1291!!, he fays – Sed propofita quafi univerfa principals Tiberii forma, fingula recenfeamus Quibus praeceptis in-

ftruftum Germanicum fuum, imbutumque rudimentis militiae fecum aftae, domitorem recepit Germaniae? – Quibus *juventam* ejus exagge- ravit *honoribus,* refpondente cultu triumphal! rerum quas geflerat Ktagnitudini, &c. ? – By this we are informed, that one of the moft jnemorable deeds of Tiberius, while *prince,* was, the heaping of honors on Germanicus while a *youth,* that is furely, as Dion fays, 1- 5v P- 582. B., at lateft, in the year 763, for he was then decorated with triumphal infignia, and admitted to praetorian honors, and allowed to ftand for the confulfhip before the time appointed. But whether he could then be properly called *a youth* will perhaps be queftioned, for he was then 24. – Befides – it feems that this was not the firft time that he had been fent to announce a viftory,- for Dion fays – x

Augustus and Tiberius colleagues five years.

He may have been fent to announce the viftory for which Tiberius triumphed u. c. 762, for we find by Dion, 1. 55, p. 569, C., that he was in 760, foon after the breaking out of the Pannonian war, fent, when qucdlor and only 19, with the new levies to Tiberius.

The fum of the teftimonics of Paterculus on. this point, amounts to this – In the year 762 cither Tiberius alone, or Tiberius in con- jun&ion with Auguflus, placed M. Lepidus over all the forces. – Tiberius and Auguflus rewarded Lepidus with triumphal honors. – Tiberius, in the year 763, on hearing of the defeat of Varus badened to Rome immediately, to give direftions, *as ufual,* for the fecurity of the Roman empire. – Tiberius, after he had been invefted with authority equal to that of Auguflus, triumphed over the Pannonians and Dalmatians. – Auguflus, on his death bed, recommended to Tiberius their joint works. – Tiberius, while prince, heaped honors on Germanicus when a youtL

This being the fum of what Paterculus fays – why fhould we not conclude from it that Tiberius was, u. c. 762, made equal to Auguflus in every thing?

Let us now attend to what Suetonius fays of the length of this important period.

He fays, iii. 15, that from the banifhment Of Agrippa in the year 760, nothing was omitted that might ferve to increafe the *majc/Jy* of Tiberius. – Nihil ex eo tempore praetermifTum eft *ad maje/iatem* ejus augendam, ac multo magis poftquam, Agrippa abdkato ac fepofito, certum erat, uni fpem fucceffionis incumbere.

Dien seems to intimate also that Augustus sent him because he suspected that Tiberius was dilatory. – Had Dion seen the letter from Augustus to Tiberius, at that very time, commending his caution and prudence, (wltich letter nay be still seen Suetonius iii. 21,) he would hardly have said so.

Augustus and Tiberius colleagues five years.

In the next chapter – viz – t6th, he fays – that Tiberius, being again invefted with the tribunitial power *for foe years,* was fent into Germany to fettle the affairs of that country – and – that while he was there, ambafladors from Parthia arrived at Rome, who, having . delivered their credentials to Auguftus, were ordered to attend Tibe- rius in Germany. – Data *rurfus* poteftas tribunitia in *quinquennium:* delegatus pacandae Germaniae flatus: Parthorum legati, mandatis Augufto Romae redditis, eum quoque adire in Provinciam juffi. – 'Now that thofe Parthian ambafladors mould, after having delivered their credentials to Auguftus, at Rome, have been ordered to attend Tiberius in Germany, muft be allowed to be not a little remarkable. – But when did thofe Parthian ambafladors arrive at Rome ? – Scil. – When Tiberius was in Germany fettling the affairs of that country. But when did he fettle the affairs of Germany ? – Was it before or after the Pannonian war ? Clearly before – as appears by the fequel. For he proceeds thus – Sed nuntiata Illyrici defeftione, tranfiit ad curam novi belli: – which, continues he, next to the Punic, was the moft grievous, and lafted *three years.* But, at the expiration of that time, he was viftorious, having fubdued all the country between the Adriatic and the Danube.

Thofe Parthians then, it feems, arrived at Rome about the year

759, and juft after Auguftus, as Dion fays, 1. 55, p. 567, B., ordered three confulars to hear moft foreign embaffies.

In the next chapter – viz – I7th, he fays that, for the exploits which he performed in the courfe of thofe three years – that is – 759,

760, and 761, a triumph and many and great honors were decreed him, and among the reft, that he mould be entitled Pannonicus. – This triumph, fays he, was deferred, on account of the "defeat of

Augustus and Tiberius colleagues Jive years.

Varus, which, fays he, happened at the fame time. Neverthelefs, fays he, he entered Rome wearing a praetexta, and crowned with laurel, and, the Senate flanding, he afcended a tribunal placed in the fepta, and there, with Auguftus, fat between the two confuls.

In the aoth chapter, he fays that Tiberius ordered Bato, the chief of the Pannonians, whom he had rewarded with coftly prefents, to refide at Ravenna. – A *Germania* in urbem *poft biennium* regreffus, triumphum, quern diftulerat, egit: .... Batonem Pannonicum ducem, ingentibus donatum pramiis Ravennam tranftulit. Prandium dein populo et congiarium dedit. Dedicavit et Concordiae aedem: item, &c. f

In the 2ift chapter he fays – Ac non multo poft (Lege per Cons, lata, ut provincias cum Augufto communiter adminiftraret, *Jimulque* cenfum ageret, *condho lujlro)* in Illyricum profeftus eft. – By this it appears that this law was paffed, before the laft cenfus or luftrum wa? begun, becaufe, at the fame time that it gave to Tiberius the fame power as Auguftus had over the provinces, (and, indeed, if we may believe Paterculus, chapter 121, over the armies,) it alfo gave him a power over the civil organization of the Romans equal to that of Auguftus. And as that cenfus or luftrum was ended before the death of Auguftus, and lafted, as every cenfus or luftrum did, five years, why mould we not fuppofe that it began five years before his death – that is – in the year of Rome 762, when Q. S. Camerinus and C. P. Sabinus were confuls? – And again, in the courfe of the fame chapter,

"*Augustus and Tiberius colleagues Jive years.*

Dion, who will not allow that Varus was, at this time defeated, say, 1. 56, init, that this was a perfect triumph, attended, as usual, wilh sports – and – beside those several circumstances mentioned by Suetonius, adds some others, one of which we shall presently have occasion to notice.

f Dion sayi, 1. 56, p. 586, B., that the dedication of this temple t Concord happened v. c. 764.

Suetonius fays, that Auguftus, in feveral of his letters, addrefled Tiberius, as a moft experienced general, and as being the only fafe- guard of the Roman people – unicum praefidium populi romani – a copy of one of thofe which he wrote to him in Pannonia, before the concrueft. of Bato, he fubjoins – in which, he fays, every one fpoke with admiration of his prudence and circumfpeftion, and laments that he can no longer confult him as ufual. – *Vale jucundijfime Tiberi et remgerc j'dicker, i/x xai rait Mea-ais r/iTnyv. – JucundiJJime, et ita jim felix, vir fortijflme, et dux, mitiiMra-et. – Vale, et ordinem teftivorum tuemm – – – . Ego vero, mi Tiberi, et mter tit rerum difficultatest xai na-avrm paQvfuxi rfanvofuiai non potuijje quenquam prudenlius gerere fe, quam tu gefferis, ex'iftimo. Hi quoque, qui tecum fucrunt omnes, confitentur verfum ilium in te pojje dici,*

Unus homo nobis vigilando reftituit rem.

S'fUe (inquit) *quid incidit, de quo fit cogitandum diligentius, jive quid jiomachor valde, medius fidius Tibet ium mcum dejidcro: fuccurritque verfui ilk Homericus.* –

Tra JT *itntapnoio, xai tx irvfor aiQofumiio*

Ap-fa vsyaatpw, nrti iripi oi$i vmrai.

Altenuatwn te effe continuatione laborum cum audio et lego, Dii me per- dant, niji cohorrefcit corpus meum: teque rogo ut pcrcas tibi: ne ji te languere audierimus, et ego et mater tua expiremus; et de fumma imferii fui P'opulus Romanus /icriclitttur. Nihil interejl valeam i/ife nee ne, fi tit non valebis. Deos obfecro ut te nobis conferment, et valere nunc et femper /tatiantur, Ji non Populum Romanum pero/i funt.

Now if this letter of Auguftus to Tiberius was written during the Fannonian. war – that is – before the year 762, Tiberius muft, even then, and by the teftimony- of Auguftus himfelf, have been generally; eonfidered, as the *only* fupport of the Roman greatnefs, and, con-

Augustus and Tiberius colleagues Jive years.

fequently, muft have been thought worthy of being made equal to Auguftus – and – as Anguftus declared himfelf even then fo very defirous of his advice on great occafions, and fent the Parthian am- bafladors to him when in Germany, and afterwards permitted him to appoint Lepidus commander in chief, and Sabinus conful, and made him his colleague in the cenforfhip, can we wonder, if he alfo made him his colleague in other things, efpecially if Auguftus was then fo very infirm as not to be able to tranfaft bufinefs without the affiftance of others ?

Again – chapter 42, he fays – Poftea *Princess* in ipfa publicorum morum correp- tione cum Pomponio Flacco et L. Pifone noftem con- tinuumque biduum epulando potandoque confumpfit: quorum alteri Syriam provinciam, alteri praefefturam urbis *confeftim* detulit. – By this we learn that he, in the time of a cenfus, which always lafted five years, made Pomp. Flaccus the governor of Syria, and L. Pifo praefeft of the city. – But in what year did Tiberius difpofe of two fuch important offices? By the report of Tacitus he did it in the year 765 – for he fays, vi. 10, n, that Pifo had then been 20 years prefeft of the city. – Confequently he muft have have been made praefeft, by Tiberius, in the year 765.

The laft paflage which we fhall notice in this writer occurs in the 4th chapter of the fifth book, in which he gives a tranfcript of another letter of Auguftus, not indeed to Tiberius, but to Livia – Collocntus fum, cum Tiberio, ut mandafti mea Livia quid nepoti tuo Tiberio faciendum eflet ludis Murtialibus. Confentit nutcm uterque noftrum,

femel efle nobis ftatuendum quod confilium in illo fequamur

Nam femper aeftuabimus, fi de fingulis articulis temporum deliberabi-

Augustus and Tiberius colleagues five years. mus, *Im, trfevmxtttuvs* nfttv pofleeum gerere honores arbltremtir hec ne

Cur enim non *pnsjicitur urbi,* fi poteft fratrem fuum fequi in tnontem. By this letter of Auguftus to Livia, as well as "by that befote tncited to Tiberius, it feems that Auguftas confuted Tiberius oft itfiportant cccafions. It has been thought that the occafion which produced this letter was the appointed proceffion of Germanicus, the brother of Claudius, as conful, to the Alban Mount. – If that was the occafion on which it was written, it muft have been written in the year 765 – the very year in which Tiberius, we have juft feen, made L. Pifo the prefeft of Rome, in preference to Claudius.

By thofe feveral extrafts from Suetonius, it appears that Tiberius exercifed feveral afts of fovereignty before the year 765 – or rather – five years before the death of Auguftus – viz – from the year 762 – and – that in that year the law was paffed to enable him to affift in making a cerifus.

Let us now attend to what Tacitus fays of the imperial fun&ions of Tiberius before he fucceeded Auguftus.

In the firft book of his annals we meet with feveral references to his having been, feveral years before the death of Auguftus, invefted with them – and, in other parts of that fame work with as many more.

B. i. c. 3. – -He fays – Drufoque pridem exftinfto, Nero folus e privignis erat: illic cunfla vergere: filius, *collega tmperii,* confers tribu- nitiae poteftatis adfumitur, omnifque per exercitus oftentatur: non, &c.

– . – . c. 6. – He fays – Primum facinus *novi* principatus fuit, Poft- humi Agrippsp cades.

He alfo fays in the fame chapter – Salluftius Crifpus monuit ne . . . . neve Tiberius *vim principalm* refolveret, cunfta ad fenaturn yocando.*Augustus and Tiberius colleagues five years.*

– . – . c. 8. – He fays – Addebat Mcflulu Valerius, *renovandum* per annos facramentum in nomcn Tiberii.

– . – . c. 10. – He fays – Etenim Auguftus, *Jiauch ante annis,* cum Tiberio tribunitiam a patribus *rtirfum* poftularet, quanquam honora oratione, quaedam de habitu cultuque et inftitutis ejus jecerat, quae velut excufando exprobraret.

– . – . c. ii. – He fays – Verfae inde ad Tiberium preces. Et illc varie diflerebat, de magnitudine imperii, fua modeftia: folum Divi Augufti mentem tantae molis capacem: fe *in partem cur arum ab ills vttatum,* experiendo didicifle, quam arduum, quam fubjeftum for- tunne, regendi cunfta onus.

– . – . c. 26. – He fays – Tiberium olim nomine Augufti dcfideria Icgionum fruftrari falitum.

– . – . c. 46. – He fays – that the Roman populace, difiktisfied with his having fent two ftriplings to quell the mutiny of the legions – viz – Germanicus and Drufus, obferved – ire ipfum, et opponsre majeftatem imperatoriam debuifle cefluris, ubi *principiem langa expcrientia,* eun- demque feveritatis et munifieentiae fummum, vidiflent.

Thofe feven teftimonies on this point, we find in the firft book only – in the next book – viz – ii. c. 42, we find an ambiguous expreflion which appears to tend to the eftablimment of the fame conclufion – viz – Ut verfa Caefarum fobole, imperium adeptus eft. – Now as he had before faid that Tiberius was by Auguftus made his colleague in the empire – and alfo in the tribuuitial power a few years before the death of Auguftus, what can he have meant by this, but that he obtained fovereign power foon after the exile of Agrippa? – That is – 760.

Augustus and Tiberius colleagues Jive years.

Again – iii. 30, – he fays of Crifpus SallufHus – Igitur incolumi Maecenate proximus; mox pnecipuus cui, fecreta *imperatorum* inni- terentur, et interficiendi Pofthumi Agrippae confcius, aetate provefta fpeciem magis in amicitia principis quam vim tenuit, idque et Maece- nati acciderat, &c.

In the vi. book we meet with three references more to this joint power of Auguftus and Tiberius, the firft of which occurs c. 10, ir. It fays, as we have already obferved, that L. Pifo governed Syria 20 years. – The fecond is of a piece with it. – It occurs chapter 39. – Fine

anni – -u. c. 788 – T. 22 – Poppaeus Sabinus conceffit vita *prin-cijmm* amicitia, *confulatum* ac triumphale decus adeptus: maximifqUe provinces per *quatuor et viginti annos* impofitus. – Now P. Sabinus was, we know, conful u. c. 762, feveral years after the deaths of Caius and Lucius, and the fecond after the banifhment of Agrippa. – Confequently, by – principum amicitia – can only be underftood that of Auguftus and Tiberius. – Now if, in that year, P. Sabinus was made conful by the favor of the */trinces,* why fhould we not conclude that Tiberius was, in that year colleague with Auguftus ? – And if P. Sabinus, had, in the year u. c. 788, prefided over the largeft provinces 24 years, he muft have been made prafeft of Madia, by the fame princes, 764. – This, at leaft, we learn from Tacitus himfelf, i. 80 – that Tiberius in the firft or fecond year of his reign to the praefefture of Maefia added that of *Achala* and *Macedonia,*

The laft paflage relevant to our purpofe in this book, occurs in the laft chapter – viz- – 51 – egregium vita famaque quoad privatus, vel in *Imperils* fub Augufto fuit. – On this we have no remark to make pertinent to our prefent purpofe. – But though we have nothing more to fay as to the power of Tiberius under Auguftus, yet we think it not amifs

Augustus and Tiberius colleagues five years.

to point out to the admirers of Tacitus the different manners in which he fpeaks of the charafter of Tiberius in this place and in a pafTage of the i. book already quoted.

– He here, we find, fays that Tiberius, as long as he lived under Auguftus, was fo very exemplary that every body noticed it – Now if his charafter was, during all that time, egregioufly fair – why would Tacitus have us to believe that Auguftus, when, a few years before his death, he again demanded the tribunitial power for him of the Senate, think of making excufes for his defects, and in fuch a manner too as tended only to expofe them? Quae velut excufando exprobraret. – Did Auguftus, who as Suetonius, we have feen, fays, wrote that moft affe&ionate and laudatory letter to Tiberius, then, by the account of Paterculus, in Pannonia, (for what Paterculus fays, ji. tn – viz – quantis prudentia ducis op- portunitatibus, furentes eorum vires univerfas evafimus partibus? – correfponds exaftly with the purport of Auguftus' letter tranfcribed. by Suetonius,) fpeak thus of him,- a year or two after, to the Senate – and, when he, as Tacitus fajs, *demanded* a renewal of the tribunitial power for him? – Impoffiblc ! – And it is not only impoffible that Auguftus fhould, within five years of his death, have mentioned Tiberius with any kind of obliquity – it is by the evidence of Dion, as we fhall come to fee prefently, almoft as incredible that Auguftus, was at that time, capable of going to the Senate.

The fum of w, hat Tacitus fays on this point, feems to be. this – that Tiberius was colleague with Auguftus in fovereign power, and confort in the tribunitial – that Auguftus demanded a renewal of the tribunitial power for him, not as Dion fays, 1. 56, p. 588, B., the year before he died – but a few years before he died. – And that Tiberius was, as prince, partly the caufe of the promotion of Sabinus to the confuHhip u. c. 762.

Augustus and Tiberius colleagues Jive years. Let us now then attend to what Dion fays on this point:

Dion fays, 1. 55, p. 567, B., that Auguftus was, a little after the banifhment of Archelaus, and a little before the Pannonian war, u. c. 759, rendered by age and by bodily infirmities, incapable of deciding on every point fubmitted to him, and that he, with the affiftance of co-afleflbrs, tranfacted at home, as much bufinefs as he could. – And as for embaffies, as well thofe from the provinces as *from kings,* he deputed three confulars to hear them, and to return anfwers – excepting in fuch cafes, as it was neceflary for him and the Senate to join in the decifibn. – x *mtitiat* x r *yefa aafitnix.* tiix/vEV, *ari* ; Stwao-fla *Ttxiti rois iioHois n Ocvtb* XX *avros fiarx rm avntifut siai* W4'*aro x* tSixai.'W, *sv ru iro&omu tirt itpoliaQynos fas* Si *irftirGmas,* Txs Te *irafa rut* Su/xwv, xa *ras irtxfa* /3o-iXEoiv aiitvHfteasr, *rfiyi t vat vlrxnvxorivv eirirfs4isv* T' *auras oifis* Y. *ou viaxuctt* Tivsjv, *xai lXiFoxpirir avrois imoai,* /./ r. vv *irx av&yiim yt*

Tv Ti /3aX, xi txeitot *mi$ienfimi.* – If now this report of Dion be true, and what Suetonius fays, iii. 16, be alfo true – that the Pannonian war lafted three years, Auguftus muft have been, nearly three years before the end of the Pannonian war, fo infirm as not to have been able to do bufinefs in public. – Paterculus, ii. no, feems to have pointed out one of the principal caufes of his malady – he there fays – quin tantus etiam hujus belli (viz – the Pannonian) metus fuit, ut ftabilem ilium, et fhmatum tantorum bellorum experientja, Caefaris Augufti animum quateret atque terreret. – And no wonder if it alarmed him fo very much, as it was by the account of Suetomus, iii. 16, a fecond Punic – quod graviffimum omnium externorum bellorum poft Punica, per xv. legiones, paremque auxiliorum copiam, triennio geffit. – Another caufe which tended to render him ftill weaker, happened in the courfe of the next year, 760, jnft before the coa*Augustus and Tiberius colleagues five years.*

clufion of the Pannonian war, when fays Dion, 1. 55, p. 569, 570, he found it abfolutely neceflary to difinherit and confine his only remaining grandfon Agrippa for his contumacity, not only to Livia, but to himfelf.

Again – Dion fays, 1. 55, init., that Tiberius, u. c. 762, when Camerinus and Sabinus were confuls, after the winter was pafled, and therefore nearly a half a year after the Pannonians were fubdued, went to Rome – that he was met by Auguftus, in the fuburbs, by him condufted to the Septa, and, as Suetonius fays, iii. 17, made to fit by his ftde, between the two confuls – that he congratulated the people, performed the ufual ceremonies, and, by the 1 confuls, gave *public /ports,* (a pretty fure proof that no public difafter had then taken place.) And that, at thofe *very ffiorts,* the knights demanded a repeal of the law relating to batchelors and to thofe married folks who had no children. On which occafion, Auguftus, as fome un- derftand Dion, notwithftanding he had, twice before, permitted the Senate to take cognizance of almoft every thing, notwithftanding he had declared his incapacity to attend them, notwithftanding he was, as Dion himfelf fays, oppvefled with grief, on account of the un- dutiful behavior of Agrippa – and, notwithftanding he was, as Suetonius fays, ii. 84, unable to fpeak in public – notwithftanding all this,

he is fuppofed to have delivered thofe two long, animated, and very

eloquent harangues, which we read in Dion, to the married and unmarried knights, aflembled in *the forum.*

But is it not juft as likely that Tiberius himfelf, who, as Suetonius obferves, iii. 21, was then made cenfor, and, as he alfo obferves, iii.-70, was thought to have fpoken better extempore than by premeditation, thus addrefled the knights on this occafion? If as Pater- culus, we have feen, fays M. Lepidus was, by him, juft before,

Augustus and Tiberius colleagues five years.

placed over all the forces – if as Suetonius, we have feen, fays, the Parthian ambaflkdors were, before the Pannonian war, commanded to attend him in Germany, when Germany was not yet tranquillized – if, as he alfo fays, he was now made cenfor. – If as Tacitus, we have feen, fays, Sabinus was by him and Auguftus made conful, it feems

not a lit. tle likely, as fome have furmifed, that he did harangue the

t knights on this occafion. – And if he did, the confequence of this

triumph feems to have been as honorable to him, as the triumph itfelf.

Again – Dion fays, 1. 56, p. 582, A., that a triumph was again decreed to Tiberius in 763, and feemingly for his exploits in Pan- nonia and Dalmatia – but, fays he, C., this triumph was deferred on account of the defeat of Varus, which, adds he, happened at the fame time – viz – in the winter. – On the receipt of this news, fays Dion, p. 585, B., Auguftus was overcome by grief – and at F., that he would not, on that account, permit, as before, *any Jfiorte*

Again – Dion fays, 1. 56, p. 587, B. C., u. c. 765, that Auguftus, when old, wrote a letter to the Senate recommending Germanicus to the fathers and them to Tiberius – this letter, fubjoins Dion, Auguftus did not read himfelf, for he was not able to do it, but Germanicus, *as ufual*. – And then he enjoined them, on account of the *Celtic war,* which, by his own report, began 763, and ended about this time, not to attend him, at the palace, with any more falutations, and not to be offended if he did not give them any more entertainments –

fHI *St nft yvftas uo, rot n* Ttf/xavixot *n* /3sXt, *xatt* raurnv *ra TtGtftu trafatxarsQfro. amyta Ss ro* (3iCxiov *ax avros (u yaf otos r* 'tv *ytyutnTxtn) atM.'* o *Ttfpunxos, ftuQn xatt y. tra Tnro tmo-aro ttat(avrwt ttn Tv ru* KsXnx8 tro 0ix0i *avroo aintat(fo-Qt, fwr ayxtxxrm tt fJ. nxen*

Augustus and Tiberius colleagues Jive years.

The next teftimony of Dion, which feems to be relevant to this point, occurs in the next page – viz – 588, C. D., where he fays – " and on account of his great age (which would not permit him, but " very feldom, to attend the Senate) he demanded 20 annual counfel- ." lors – and a decree was paffed- – that whatever he, and *Tiberius,* and " thofe counfellors, and the confuls for the time being, and the con- " fuls eleft, and his fons – that is – his *adopted fans,* and whoever they " fhould call in to their affiftance, fhould enaft, fhould be valid, as if " decreed by the whole Senate." – K *avpSuxs, mo* Tb *yyfus* (up' *amp* Se iiSii, *irm yiraiiurarx yvntyoira) tixoyit rnritis vneavo. Kai itaiff oyx xt aura itrx rc rs TiGifiu, xai ftir' txcituv, rut ri aiti wiranvotriM, xai rut ts raro* iroSsSEi7/xEvwv, *rut n eyywut avra, rut itwrat noion, rut re aw turns at txxrore irpoimrafaxGy (2uKivop, etut* Sofy, *xvpia, us xai irxrn ry yypmrix apia-xtra titan.* – The mention of Tiberius, in this decree of the Senate, and of him only by name, has appeared to ibme rather remarkable.

The laft paflage in this hiftorian, which we confider as a proof that Tiberius had, before the death of Auguftus, imperial authority, and that it had been confirmed to him by a decree of the 'Senate, occurs in the next book – viz – 1. 57, p. 602, D.

Dion, in the beginning of that book, fays – Tiberius, immediately on the death of Auguftus, wrote, as Autocratoor, from Nola to the armies and to all the allies, not faying exprefly that he was Autocratoor, for this title he would not receive, though voted to him, with others, by the Senate. – Tixaro B Ss *ns ai tis ri ra* r/iroiri&a *xai*

ct ra aflni Trarira, *us Auroxparup tvQv: Xiro rys Nuyr onreriifa. fJ. y tyxt AvroKforiiip* E;. *ytyia-QtY yap avru xai rvro ptrx- rut xXxv otopar:vvt ax*

s? El *aro*. – By this Dion fecms to acknowledge that Tiberius had,

Augustus and Tiberius colleagues five years.

before the death of Auguftus, been, by *a decree of the Senate,* made emperor – and – that he, immediately after the death of Auguftus – ta6vr – itfued, as if he was emperor, notices to the armies, and to all the allied powers, from Nola. – Now when did the Senate confer on him this title ? – Or when did Tiberias refufe it ?- – That the Senate had, fereraHimes before, voted him this title, and, that Tiberins did not refufe it, but on the contrary, feemed pleafed with it, we learn from feveral writers. Paterculus fays, ii. 104, that the fbkliers, fall of joy to fee him again after his retirement at Rhodes, exclaimed – Videmus te, Imperator, &c ? – Ego tecum, Imperator, in Armenia, &c. And, ii. 115, he himfelf fpeaks of him as being, in the beginning of his monarchy, an old imperator – Sed haec omnia veteris imperatoris maturitas, &c. Dion too fays himfelf, 1. 55, p. 552, B., that he was honored with this titlt the year before he was

ii. coufot that is – u. c. 746. – And, 1. 56, p. 582, A., that it was, wkh feveral other marks of honor, given to Auguftus and Tiberius on the conqueft of the Dalmatians u. c. 763, and adds, that Auguftus did not, infirm as he was, refufe it. Eufebius fays, that he was, for his conqueft of Germany, entitled *Autocratoor.* – *T$ifns Kaifat - woXi/twaj Ttfuaw; avroxfaruf* Trfoouyofivfln. – An. p. 6a. – And adds, immediately after, that he twice triumphed over the Panndnians. – Why then fhould Tiberius be faid to have refufed this honor though decreed to him by the Senate ? – After he had fo often accepted it from them? May we not fvtfpeflt then that Dion muft have ufed this word in a different fenfe here from what he had before ? – And in that fenfe which, he acknowledges, 1. 52, p. 493, E., was fometimes affixed to it ? – If he has, why did not Dion tell us fo, and when it happened?

Two triumphal arches in Paononia.

Augustus and Tiberius colleagues Jive years.

The fum of thofe feveral teftimonies of Dion fccms to be this – that Auguftus, in the year 759, began to be fo very infirm, as not to be able to attend to public bufinefs – that his infirmity ever after gradually increafed – that he, infirm as he was, u. c. 761, con- defcended to meet Tiberius, when he triumphed over the Pannonians, in the fuburbs, and thence attended him to the Septa – that he, in the year 763, made Tiberius princeps fenatus – and, that he, at fome time, not mentioned, caufed Tiberius to be, by the Senate, inverted with power equal to that which he himfelf had.

Having now difcovered that the evidence of Paterculus, Suetonius, Tacitus, and Dion tends to prove the fame thing – viz – that Tiberius was, in the year 762 made equal with Auguftus in every thing, it feems to be unneceflary to adduce that of any other writer – and yet that of a later writer, may, after all that has been faid, be ad- duced with propriety.-? rlt is an extraft from a Panegyric cap. tt, of which Pagius. Critic, A. *Q.* tj, n. Hi, fpeaks highly – it is as follows Quoufque hoc Maximiniane, patiar, me quati, te quiefcere, mihi libertatem adimi, te ufurparc, tibi illicitatn ntiffioncm ? An quod Divo Augufto, poft feptuaginta aetatis, quinquaginta imperil, non licuit anttos, tarn cito licuit tibi ?

By the accounts then of thofe five hiftorians, Tiberius appears to have reigned five years with Auguftus. And this, for the feveral reafons affigned at the outfet, is no inconfiderable point to be afcer- tained. For if ILue be underftood to have reckoned, the tth of his reign from the time when he had imperial power given him by the Senate over the . provinces as well as the armies, he mull have meant , that our Lord was baptized, by John, in the loth of his monarchy –

Augustus and Tiberius colleagues Jive years.

in which year, we perceive, by the chronological fynopfis prefixed to this work, our Lord entered on his 30th year. Confequently this report of Luke agrees with thofe of Matthew, John, and the Talmud of Jerufalem, and with that concerning the expeftation of the Jews that the Meffiah Ihould appear at the laft jubilee.

As we have thought it neceflary to be very particular in our enquiry concerning the length of this period in the reign of Tiberius, in order to juftify the accuracy of the report of Luke in his gofpel, it may not be amifs to add a word or two more concerning the impropriety of fuppofing that he would have made a wrong report concerning the year when Tiberius began to reign.

Before Luke wrote his hiftory of the life of Chrift, many others, he fays, had done it. But as none of their hiftories were fo complete as they mould have been – he, who, though of Antioch, had a perfect under/landing of all things from the beginning, undertook to write a more particular account of the birth and miniflry of our Lord. And this, it fhould be obferved, he did for the more ample inftruftion of Theophilus, a man of rank of Antioch.

Now as Luke prefaces his gofpel with this account, who would expecl to meet with any mis-ftatement in his work ? – Efpecially with refpeft. to the name of the governor of Syria when our Lord was born ? – Or – with refpeft to the year when Tiberius began to reign over Syria?

He begins his gofpel, as Matthew alfo does, with faying that in the days of Herod the king of Judea, the annunciation took place.- – He not only fays this, he alfo fays what the other three Evangelifls have omitted to fay – viz – that Cyrenius was, when our Lord was born, the governor of Syria. – He moreover fays that a taxation, or *Augustus and Tiberius colleagues five years.*

rather enrollment, which he feems to fay was called the firft, then took place every where. – Afterwards, he fays, that our Lord was baptifed by John, in the I5th year of Tiberius – and – that Pilate was, at that time, praefeft of Judea. Befides the name of the praefeft of Judea, he alfo mentions thofe of the rulers of the feveral diftrifts contiguous to it, and that of the Jewifh high-prieft, – He fays ex- preflly that an interval of 29 years took place between the birth and baptifm – or – between the firft taxation under Cyrenius (which, we have obferved, he fays happened in the reign of Herod the king of Judea,) – and – the Jjth of Tiberius. – Now Herod, it appears, died in the year It. c. 750. – Confequently, reckoning, not from the birth of our Lord, . which clearly preceded the death of Herod, but from the death of that prince – and – admitting that our Lord was full 30, when he was baptifed, he muft have have been baptifed u. c. 780 – or – the 13111 of the monarchy of Tiberius. But if our Lord was born two years before the death of Herod, and, was, when he entered on his miniftry, only 29 years complete, lie muft have been baptifed the loth of Tiberius.

Now can it be fuppofed that Luke, who aflures us that he was per- fecHy acquainted with all things from the beginning, and wrote for the purpofe of giving a fuller account of the birth and miniftry of our Lord than others had done, who was of Antioch, the capital of Syria, and publiftied the gofpel in that city, mould have committed1 fo great an error with regard to the name of the governor of Syria, at our Lord's birth, and the tax which then took place, and the duratton of the reign of Tiberius over Syria ? Cit cumftances with which myriads in that province then alive were as well acquainted as himfelf. "

Augustus and Tiberius colleagues five years,

But if, by the t$th year of Tiberius, Luke meant the the I5th yar of his government psy"D2f Syria, and the loth of his monarchy, and fays that Pontius Pilate was in that year the governor of Judea. – rHow is it that Jofepbtts in three places of his A., – viz – xviii. 2, 5, 7, feems to deny it ?

C. 2, *P.,* he fays, that Annius Rufus governed Judea when AuguftllS died. – A/dffTan Se *xat rant* Amor *Pufos,* tp' *a* 017 *xau ntevrZ f. auo- of.-rAnd* that Tiberius fent Valerius Gratus to fucceed him, who governed Judea 11 years – evStx *m* – which alone is enough to fatisfy US that Pilate could not have governed Judea in the roth. – Again – C. 5, §. (3., he fay$ that Pilate governed Judea 10 years – Je *tnin*- and he has alfo been underftood to affirm, in the fame fentence, that Tiberius died, as Pilate was returning to Rome. Now, if that be his meaning, it proves that Pilate could not have been the governor till the middle of the t3thyear – for 22f – *10=12%*. – Laftly, c. 7, §. e., he fays that Tiberius, in the courfe of his reign, fent only two governors of Judea – viz – Gratus and Pilate.

This is the account which Jofephus gives of the commencement and duration of the government of Pilate. – An account which has been always thought unobjeftionable.

But if Jofephus fhould be underftood as having faid that Pilate" governed Judea till the death of Tiberius, how is it that he alfo fays, c. 5, §. &., that ViteUius, (who, Suetonius fays, was from the conful- Iblp – that is – in the 2Qjth year of Tiberius, made praefeft of Syria,) on his arrival ift that couijtryor – rather, before he weflt up to Jerufalem, which he feems to have done at the enfuing pa. ffoyer, and before he did any thing elfe in the eaft, fent – *txttsas* – Marcellus to fupply the place of Pilate, whom he ordered to go to Rome, not to.

Augustus and Tiberius colleagues Jive yeafs.

anfwer the charge of the Samaritans, but – *trpos a vjtrwyofotet* tsSatw SiSaivT *To,* avrolTrof. x. – If thfiri Pilate was fent to Rome, befort the paflbver in the tft of Tiberius, and foon after the arrival of Vitcllius in Syria, he may have been fent in the end of the aoth year, and if he had then governed Judea 10 years, he may, by the evidence of Jofephus,- have been appointed in the 10th of Tiberius. Does it not then appear by this evidence of Jofephus that Pilate was fent to Rome before the paflbver in the 2tft year of Tiberius ? That this rrmft have been his meaning will appear by confidering what he fays, in the next fe&Jon, where he fpcaks of VitelliuS as being at Jerufalem at the paiTover – he there fays, that Viteltius conferred fevetal favors dn the Jews – that he permitted them, once more, to keep flte facrei ftole–arid' that he then depofed Calaphas, and fubfthuted in his room Jonathart, whom he fays, C. 6, 7., Vitellins alfd depofed, when he went np again to Jerufalertt to attend the paflbver after Tiberius died. – Pilate then was undoubtedly fent to Rome, and Marcellus appointed by Vitellius to fucceed him, before Caiaphas was depofed : and Tiberius died juft before Jonathan was depofed. – Again – Tiberius, we know, died l7th kal. April, (t 6th of March) – that is – ' before arty of the days on which the paflbver could fall. But Jofephus fays, A. xv. it, S., that Tiberius was /till alive at the paflbveT next after the difrhiflal of Pilate – (which paflbver we are told by Mann, Bacon, Scaliger, and Fergufon happened t6th April,) – for he there fays that Vitellius *"wrote* to Tiberius to know if he would grant per- miflidh to the Jews to keep their facred ftole again, and that Ttberius lent an acknowledgement of his approbation – *tyfat* St *tnft rurut ttftftu* Kato-aff, xaxnvot twrftj/t. – Jofephus adds, in the fame paflage, that the ftole was kept by the Romans – *xt'* psy"D4v Tt&fia *yfmut.* – If then it was given up to the Jews at the paflbver after Pikte left

Augustus and Tiberius colleagues five years.

Judea, and in the days of Tiberius, Tiberius rnuft have been alive at the next paflbver, and therefore could not have died the 16th of March.

Thofe three considerations are enough to prove that Jofephus could not have meant to fay that Tiberius died as Pilate was on his paflage to Rome. But thofe are not the only confederations – for Jofephus has, in the fequel of the xviii, mentioned feveral other things which Vitellius did afterwards in feveral places of the eaft before the death of Tiberius.

He fays, in the next §. – viz – S – that Tiberius again wrote to Vitellius, after his return to Antioch, ordering him to enter into an alliance with Artabanus – and, again, §. t., that Artabanus was by Vitellius perfuaded to fend his fon Darius, an hoftage to Tiberius – that Herod, the Tetrarch, who attended at the interview, immediately reported the whole tranfaftion to Tiberius – and – that Vitellius was fo offended at it that he never forgave Herod. – And all this he feems to fay, §. *s.,* happened, not in the 2oth year of Tiberius, according to our reading,, but in the 22d year, according to the reading of Epi- phanius. – But befides all this, which Jofephus relates in the fifth chapter – he fays, in the next, 6. , that at the fame time there was a difagreement between Herod, the Tetrarch, and Aretas – Ev *Tutu ro-ta&w,* &c. that Herod, by the treachery of fome foldiers, who had ferved under Philip, was defeated – that he complained of it to Tiberius – that Tiberius inftantly ordered Vitellius to affift Herod – that Vitellius, notwithftanding his inveterate hatred of Herod, not only marched to his affiftance, but even went up to Jerufalem with him and his friends to worfhip, where, on the fourth day after their arrival, they heard that Tiberius was dead. – The day before, Vitellius had depofed Jonathan from the high-prieft-hood, and promoted his brother Theophilus to it.

Augustus and Tiberius colleagues five years.

To all this may be added, that Jofephus fays, that Vitclluis, when he ordered Pilate to go to Rome, appointed Marcellus to fucceed him, who feeins to have governed Judea the remaining year or two of Tiberius – for he alfo faysf i, that almoft the firft thing Caius did was to fend Marullus. – And Clemens of Rome, in his Recogn. x. 55, appears to confirm this – for he there fays that Cornelius, the Centurion was, by Catfar – that is – by Tiberius, fent to the praefeft of Caefarea – miflus a Caefare ad praefidem Caefareae. – But if Marcellus was prsefeft of Judea a year or two under Tiberius, why does Jofephus fay afterwards in this fame book, 7. ., that Tiberius fent only Gratus and Pilate ? – Of this prefently.

t

Now as Vitellius is faid to have been fent to Syria – ex confulatu – and as he is faid by Jofephus to have ordered Pilate to go to Rome before the following paflbver, and of courfe long before he did any thing elfe in the eaft,' why fhould we not conclude that Jofephus cannot have meant to fay that Tiberius died while Pilate was on his paflage ? – Let us attend to his own words.

He fays – Wfo 5t *n* m *Pupn vto-ytn atr ot,* fdatft *TtGtftos ff. trXfats.* –

Now about the meaning of the firft part of this fentence there feems to be very little doubt – and if *psra-as* here means dying, the latter part of it mould clearly be rendered thus – Tiberius anticipated by dying – without faying who or what Tiberius anticipated – and the whole fentence will run thus – before *he* got to Rome, Tiberius anticipated by dying, and, it may be faid – by dying voluntarily – for fttrarai – means a voluntary tranfition from one flation or fyftem of opinions to another – neither of which could then be faid with truth of Tiberius – and if either of them could – is it not a very unufual mode of fpeaking to fay of an emperor, expefting vthe arrival of his*Augustus and Tiberius colleagues five years.*

accufed praefeft, that he foreftalled him by dying ? – What then if we fuppofe that a fmall error has crept into the text of Jofcphus, and, that the whole pailage is defcriptive of the proceedings of Pilate ? – Before he arrived at Rome he anticipated Tiberius by killing himfelf, which we are told by Eufebius, E. H. ii. 7, he did. – Has not Jofe- phus himfelf, by omitting to acquaint us with the refult of the accu- fation, apparently confirmed this reading ? – If he lived to reach Rome, and was acquitted, would he not have been permitted to return to his government ? And if he was found guilty, would he, as Tiberius was then alive, and had before, as Agrippa faid in his letter to Caius, L. ad C. p. 800, C. IX, reprimanded him moft feverely, have been permitted to efcape with impunity ? – And if he was found guilty would not Jofephus, who feems to fay that he was partly accufed by the Jews, have taken care to tell us fo ? – Or – would not Agrippa have adverted to this recent inftance of the juftice of Tiberius and of the delinquency of Pilate, in his remonftrance to Caius?

CHAPTER IV.

Agrippa Ppsthumus not murdered by Tiberius.

has been aflerted by Tacitus, Suetonius and Dion that Tiberius, foon after the death of Auguftus, caufed Agrippa Pofthumus to be affiiffinated. – Let us enquire what reafon there to is think that he may have done it,

Paterculus, iL 112, defcribes the exploits of the army nder Tiberius in Pannonia, the year the war commenced u. c. 759 – that part of the army which was under the command of Meflalinus, he fays, was viftoripus, but that under A. Caecina and S. Plautius was nearly vanquifhed by the improvidence of the generals. – Having faid this, he, quite unexpeftedly, proceeds in the end of the fame chapter to give an Account of the difgrace and death of Agrippa, the fon of Julia, and the adopted fon of Auguftus. – Hoc fere tempore, fays he, Agrippa qui eodem die, quo Tiberius, adoptatus ab avo fuo naturali erat, ct jam ante biennium qualis eflet, apparere coeperat, mira pravitate animi atque ingenii in praecipitia converfus, patris atque ejufdem avi

Agrippa Posthumus not murdered by Tiberius.

fui animum alienavit fibi. – Having thus informed Vinicius, that Agrippa had, the year the Pannonian war began, given proofs of his depravity, and that he was now become fo ungovernable as to alienate the affeftions of his grandfather, he fubjoins – Moxque crefcentibus in dies vitiis, dignum furore fuo habuit exitum.

Now if Agrippa did not ferve in Pannonia the year the war commenced – or-ru. c. 759, and by fome rafh aft, while ferving in that country, forfeit the regard of his grandfather, why fhould Paterculus have inferted an account of his flagrant mifconduft in this place ? – Efpecially, as he had immediately before, mentioned the fevere lofs which that part of the army, under A. Coecina and S. Plautius, had fuffered by the temerity of thofe commanders – for to their temerity he imputes it – qui, multum a more imperatoris. fui difcrepantes, ante in hoftem inciderunt, quam per exploratores, ubi hoftis eflet cog- nofcerent. – This however we know that Dion fays, 1. 55, p. 569, E., that Germanicus was, u. c. 760, fent into Pannonia, inftead of Agrippa, who had, by his vile conduft, fp offended his grandfather that he difinherited him, and banimed him to Planafia, and caufed his effefts to be placed in the military cheft. – That Agrippa was always very ferocious we are allured by the evidence of other hiftorians.

Suetonius, ii. 65, having obferved that he was adopted with Tiberius, immediately fubjoins – E quibus Agrippam *brevlt* ob ingenium fordidum ac ferox, abdicavit (that is, as Quinftilian explains it, in Declamat, difinherited him) fepofuitque Surrentum. – This feverity of Auguftus was fo far from making him better, that it only ferved to make him worfe. – He was, fays Suetonius, in that chapter, fo far from being more traftable, that he was daily more outrageous. – Agrippam nihilo traftabiliorem, immo in dies amentiorem. – This jncorrigiblcnefs made Auguftus think it neceflary to tranfport him –

Agrippa Posthumus not murdered by Tiberius.

In infulam tranfportavit – and there to keep him confined under a guard – fepfitque infuper . cuftodia militum, – –And moreover, adds Suetonius, Auguftus, not fatisfied with all this coercion, prevailed on the Senate to make a decree to render his confinement there perpetual – Cavit etiam fenatus confulto, ut eodem loci in perpetuum contineretur – which by the accounts of all other hiftorians was done, for they fay, that he was, after the death of Auguftus, in the cuflody of a tribune. – Why then fhould Auguftus have fhewn fo much dif- pleafure to the only fon of his only daughter, whom he had but a few years before, adopted, if that fon was not, as all hiftorians fay, very depraved, vicious, and ungovernable ?

Both Suetonius and Tacitus, who acknowledge that fuch were his faults, fay that he was not made better even by this fevere punifh- ment. – Of whom the former fays, that Auguftus, at every mention of him and Julia, ufed to exclaim, in the bitternefs of his mind –

Atfl' osXov ayaftof T' C///x. fvzi *ayoms* T' aTToXfo-fti – and that he llfcd to Call Julia and her two children, his – treis vomicas – and, his – tria car- cinomata. – Tacitus fays, that by far the greater part of the Roman people had the fame opinion of him, and, that they confidered him as more enraged by his ignominious confinement – pars multo maxima imminentes domjnos variis rurnoribus differebant – trucem Agrippam,- et ignominia accenfum, non setate neque rerum experientia tantae moli parem.

But though Tacitus fays, that by far the greateft part of the Roman people were, after the death of Auguftus, perfuaded that Agrippa was not in the leaft tarned by his long confinement, yet in the next chapter, i. 5, he thinks it not amifs to relate a rumour which, he fays, *had* prevailed before the death of Auguftus – Quippe rumor inceflerat – viz – that he, attended only by Fabius Maxitnus, a *few* months

Posthumus not murdered ly Tiberius.

before he died, failed to Planafia, where Agrippa was confined, to fee him – that they were both much affefted – that Maximus, on his return, difcovered the whole affair to his wife Martia, fhe to Livia, and fhe again, inftead of concealing the difcovery from Auguftus, could not forbear from letting him know that fhe had been brought acquainted with the whole proceeding. – Soon after, fays Tacitus, Maximus died, but whether naturally, or by fome contrivance he could Hot fay – this, however, he fays – that his widow, was, at his funeral, overheard to lament that fhe had been the caufe of his death. – Seemingly intimating by this that Auguftus was fo much under th control of Livia, that he, infirm as he was, contrived to take this trip to Planafia (which is faid to have been near the ifland of Corfica) by ftealth – and that fhe, after all his contrivance to conceal it from her, got intelligence of it, and contrived to make the quietus, not only of his trufty confidant for having been at the interview, but of her own hufband too – at leaft, fome, fays Tacitus, fufpefted it – et quidam fcelus uxoris fufpeftabant.

Such is the ridiculous ntmour which Tacitus has thought proper to infert in his annals. – A ftory the credibility of which, he himfelf, we have juft feen, has, in the very chapter immediately preceding, completely deftroyed. – For, if by far the greater part of the Roman people, as he had, c. 4, faid, were perfuaded, but juft before the death of Auguftus, that Agrippa was ftill as fierce s ever and enraged by his ignominious confinement, how can it be fuppofed that Auguftus, who, not long before, could not, as Suetonius fays, bear to hear his name mentioned, was entirely ignorant of it ? – And if he knew that he was not at all foftened by his confinement, why fhould we believe that Auguftus was fo fond of feeing him as to undertake a clandeftine voyage acrofs the Tyrrhene fea for that purpofe ? – And at

Agrippa Posthumus not murdered by Tiberius.

a time too, when, as Dion, we have feen, lays, he was unable to receive the fenators, as ufual, at his own houfe ? Does not Paterculus, who lived at the time, fay enough, ii. 112, to lead us to fuppofe that he died not long after his banifhment – and – by his own ferocity ? – What elfe can he have meant by – *maxque* dignum furore fuo habuit exitum? – And does he not fecm to mean the fame thing, ii. 123, by leaving us to fuppofe that Auguftus, in his latt moments, took not the leaft notice of him ? – He there fays – et ingravefcente in dies valetudine, cum fciret, quis volenti omnia poft fe falva remanere, accerfendus foret, feftinanter revocavit filiutn. – And what fon, if Agrippa was then alive, could he have meant ? – Or rather – which of them attended his fummons ? – fcil. – Not Agrippa, but Tiberius – ille ad patrem patrias expeftato revolavit maturius.

Agrippa then, if alive in the laft illnefs of Auguftus, was even then, by the evidence of Tacitus himfelf, thought by moft people to be very unfit to govern. – He moreover was, by the evidence too of Tacitus himfelf, in a fmall ifland under the cuftody of a *tribune.* – He moreover, had been, and by the evidence too of Tacitus himfelf, ex-filiated, by a decree of the Senate at the requeft of Auguftus – why- then fhould Tacitus have faid that the firft aft of the *new* princely power of Tiberius was to order Pofthumus Agrippa to be affaffinated. -rFrimum facinus *novl* principatus fuit Pofthumi Agrippae caedes.-r What had Tiberius, who was fq incomparable a general and fo egregious a charafter, to fear from him, whom he fays, almoft every body knew to be a raw, unexperienced, ferocious youth, and was then under a military guard in a remote ifland? – But defpicable as Agrippa was generally known to be, he tells us further, ii. 39, that one of his Haves- found intereft enough to procure a fhip of burden, and refolu- tion enough to-attempt to refcue him from the place of confinement, and that he failed in his attempt only by the'heavinefs of his fhip. "*Agrippa Posthumus not murdered by Tiberius.*

Suetonius agrees with Tacitus in faying that Agrippa was aflaffina- tedi – He fays, that he was atfafiinated by the contrivance of T. iviu, and, before the death of Auguftus was known. – He alfo fays, that Clemens, the zealous flave of Agrippa, contrived to aflemble a no defpicable body of men to revenge the death of his mafter before Tiberius had refolved on accepting the government – and – that this was one of the caufes of his hefitation.

So abfurd are the attempts of thofe two hiftorians to make it appear that Tiberius ordered Agrippa to be ailkffiuatecL – But after all that they have faid on this point, it will not be difficult to prove, even by their own evidence, that it was the well-founded opinion of many that Agrippa died, as Paterculus feems to have faid, before Auguftus. Dion fays, 1. 57, p. 604, A., that it was the perfuafion of fome that Auguftus himfelf, *before his death,* ordered him to be aflaffinated – *an o Avyafos avrot wo* Tuv TtXsvrJiv

Tacitus, we find, even in the chapter in which he confidently ac- cufes Tiberius of having been the caufe of the death of Agrippa, admits that fome thought that Auguftus himfelf was the caufe of it. – His words are – ceterum in nullius unquam fuorum necem duravit; nequa mortem nepoti pro fecuritate privigni illatam, credibile erat. – Now why fhould he have faid this, unlefs there had been a report that Auguftus himfelf was the caufe of his death? – Indeed that Agrippa was dead before the death of Auguftus, Tacitus, we find, admits, iv. 57, where he fays, that Auguftus had thoughts of making Germanicus a monarch, but that he being entreated by Livia not to do fo, made Tiberius the head and placed Germanicus under him.

The evidence of Suetonius on this point will be found to comport jiretty much with that of Tacitus and Paterculus.

Postbumus not murdered by Tiberius.

He, Hi. 23, gives an account of . the preamble of the will of Auguftus, which, he fays, begun thus – Quoniam finiftra fortuna Caium et Lucium filios mini eripuit, Tiberius, Sec. – He here feems to regret the lofs of Caius and Lucius, but of Agrippa he fays not a word. – And, in the body of it he direfts, that neither Julia nor *her daughter* fhould be buried wjth him, but of Agrippa he here alfo fays not a word. – This furely is fomething like a proof that Agrippa was then dead. – Now when does Suetonius fay Auguftus made his will? – viz – ii. 101, a year and four months before his own death, at which time he depofited it, under feal, with two codicils, written partly by him- felf, and partly by his freedmen, Polybius and Hilarion, with the veftal virgins.

Let us now hear what Dion fays of this matter. .

He fays, 1. 56, p. 59l, C., that Auguftus left fourTxroks containing accounts of the refources of the ftate, with direftions for his fucceflbr, &c. – He there enumerates the contents of thofe books, and in the fourth, he fays, that he gave to Tiberius and the community – *ta* uA-certain commands and direftions, one of which was this – that they Ihould not make many free. – Dion fays, moreover, that to all the reft he fubjoined this advice – viz – that they fhould commit the republic to the care of more than one, and, to men of *jkill and expertence,* and by no means to let it depend on the caprice of any individual, left he (hould be fond of tyranny. – By which furely it appears that Auguftus was, at that time, perfeftly uncontroled by Livia. – The name of Agrippr, Dion d)es not fay was mentioned in any of thofe volumes.

t

By the evidence of thofe hiftorians then, as well as by that of Paterculus, it appears that Agrippa was, when Auguftus made his
- i Q .

Agrippa Posthumus not murdered by Tiberius.

will, dead – that is – as Suetonius fays, ii. 101, before the third of April u. c. 766. – Teftamentum, L. Planco, C. Silio, Cofs. iii. – Nonas Aprilis ante annum et quatuor menfes quam decederet, fai$lum ab eo, &c. – a year and four months before Auguftus died. – Nay it appears by what Dion fays, 1. 56, p. 587, B. C., that Agrippa was dead before the year u. c. 766 – or rather, before the fecond of September u. c. 765 – for in that page he fays, that Auguftus, when old, and before he accepted the management of the republic the laft time commended Germanicus to the Senate, and the Senate to Tiberius.

We have in the preceding chapter proved that Auguftus was unable to undertake the voyage to Planafia – and, we have in this proved, that he appears not to have had any inclination to fee Agrippa, but it will not be amifs here to fay a few words of the danger of croffing the Tyrrhene fea, and likewife to fhew that he was otherwife engaged during the few months fpecified-by Tacitus.

Horace, in an ode, 1. iv. 15, addrefled to Auguftus himfelf, defcribes a voyage acrofs the Tyrrhene fea as remarkably hazardous. – Ne parva Tyrrhenum per aequor vela darem. – How then can we fuppofe that Auguftus infirm, as he is reprefented by Dion to have been, and overcome by fear, as he is reprefented, both by him and Paterculus, to have been, would, a few months before he died, have ventured his aged frame acrofs that fea merely to condole with Agrippa ? – And if he was able and inclined to fee his exiled grandfon, and to go in. a fmall bark acrofs the Tyrrhene fea for that purpofe, yet if he did it only a *few months* before he died, and *byjlfaltb,* how will it appear to agree with what Suetonius and Dion fay ?

Suetonius fays, that the ceremony of concluding the luftrum re quired his attendance at Rome, but a few months only before he died – that he then ordered Tiberius to conclude the folemnity – and

Agrippa Posthumus not murdered by Tiberius.

t after that ordered him to Illyricum, and accompanied him fo far as

Beneventum – and after that again removed from place to place on the coaft of Campania, and in the iflands nearefl it, till he was fo ill that he could go no further. – Paterculus and Dion too agree with Suetonius in faying that Auguftus fpent the laft three or four months of his life in going from place to place in Campania. – Now if Auguftus was thus employed duriug the laft three or four months of his life, how can he be fuppofed to have had an opportunity of going, incog, to Planafia?

Suetonius moreover appears to have flatly contradifted the prevalence of fuch a rujnour, for he fays, iii. 22, that it was, in his days, ftill an unfettled point whether Auguftus himfelf had not left orders for the execution of Agrippa. – Quos codicillos, dubium fuit, Auguftus ne moriens reliquiffet quo materiem tumultus poft fe fubduceret: An nomine Auguftj Livia, et ea confcio Tiberio an ignaro diftaflet. – Now if it was, from the days of Auguftus to thofe of Suetonius, a matter of doubt whether Auguftus had, in his laſt moments, himſelf given the order for the execution of Agrippa, of courſe the report of his trip to Planaſia muſt have been then, if known, quite diſcredited.

Suetonius then has, beſides the having given us an account of the rooted antipathy of Auguſtus tp Julia and her children, and, of the total omiſſion of the name of Agrippa in his will, ſaid enough to convince us that it was generally undcrſtood that his reſentment againſt his adopted grandſon continued to the very laſt.

Dion too ſeems not only not to have been aware that ſuch a report was ever current, but to have almoſt as flatly contradiſted the poſſibi- lity that it could ever have been received as Suetonius – for, beſides taking no notice of it, he not only ſays, 1. 56, p. 588, C., that

Agrippa Postiiumus not murdered by Tiberius.

Auguſtus was, in the conſulſhip of Munatius and Silius – and therefore the year before he died, ſo infirm as to be feldom able to attend the Senate – and – with Suetonius, that he ſpent the laſt three or four months of his life in making the tour of Campania, – He even ſays, 1. 56, p. 589, D., that is was fufpecled by ſome, but, ſays Xiph. p. 97, E,, by himfelf never, (and perhaps for the reaſon affigned 96 E.) that Livia was the cauſe of the death of her huſband – and, (as they ſay) for fear leſt he fhould recall – *xaryayv* Agrippa from his infular confinement to make him a *monarch*. But how could this be, if Tiberius was, by a decree of the Senate, made colleague with Auguſtus in every thing five years before his death ?

But does not the belief of this report by ſome – viz – that Livia haſtened the death of Auguſtus, becauſe ſhe was afraid that he would recall Agrippa to make him a monarch, ſeem to imply that ſome thought that Auguſtus would not be direfted by Livia, in any matter, to the very laſt. – Why then mould we believe that he would have concealed his voyage from her ? Are we not told, by Suetonius, that he would not permit Tiberius to return from Rhodes, even though importuned by Livia, without the confent of Caius, and then indeed, only on condition, that he ſhould not interfere in ſtate matters ? – And are we not told, by the fame writer, that he ordered Tiberius to conclude the laſt luſtrum that he made – that he then ordered him to Illyricum – and, that when he found his ſtrength decaying, he recalled him to take his laſt farewell of him. And are we not told by Dion, 1. 58, p. 622, A., that Livia was, to the laſt, remarkably fub-

miffive to Auguftus – *-rotuvrn yxt v tavuc eyttsro.*

This ftory then of Auguftus having failed to Planafia, by ftealth, which is recorded by Tacitus, (and by him only) in the beginning of his annals, appears to be a defpicable fiftion, and a fiftion invented,

Agrippa Posthumus not murdered by Tiberius.

not improbably, by himfelf, to calumniate Livia, and to imprefs his reader, at the outfet, with a moft horrible idea of the manner in which Tiberius began his new princely career.

As to his infinuation that Livia poifoned Auguftus, what ftronger proof can be given of her innocence of that crime, than what Suetonius and Dion ſay, of the tranquil manner in which he died ? – Suetonius ſays, ii 99, that Auguſlus was, at the time of his death (which, by the bye, he ſays, happened not at Rome but at Nola) furrounded by his friends – that he afked them – if they thought that he had afted his part on the theatre of life well – and that he then

faid – Aott *xforot, xatt trmns vptts y. tra X, afas* wwti. – SlietOIliuS allb

adds – fortitus exitum facilem, et qualem fcmper optaverat. Dion fays, p. 589, 590, nearly the fame.

On reconfidering the whole of what has been faid – the acknow ledged fiercenefs of Agrippa, his inexperience as a general, and the means which Auguftus took to reclaim him, and the precaution which Auguftus afterwards took to difinherit him, by ordering the Senate to pafs a decree for that purpofe, on the one hand – and, on the other, the moft excellent charafter of Tiberius at that time, (which is acknowledged even by Tacitus himfelf, and in two places – viz – A. i. 12, and vi. 51,) and his tranfcendent abilities as a general, (which were acknowledged by Auguftus himfelf,) – when we confider all this, we fhall not have the leaft reafon to fuppofe (if Agrippa was then alive) that Auguftus would have appointed him a colleague with Tiberius in the fucceffion, much lefs, as Dion would perfuade us, a monarch – or – that Tiberius would have been fo jealous of his influence as to think of cutting him off.

6

SECTION 6

CHAPTER V.
Germanicus died naturally.
JHLAVING now difcovered that there is, at leaft, fome reafon to think that Agrippa did not furvive Auguftus, as Paterculus feems to fay, and confequently that the reports of Suetonius, Tacitus, and Dion, as to the time and caufe of his death, appear to be wrong – and – that their reports, as to the caufe of it, appear to be rather in- confiftent – let us now proceed to inquire whether the reports of the fame three hiftorians, concerning the caufe of the death of Germanicus, appear to be lefs objeftionable.

Suetonius fays, iv. t, that Germanicus died, at Antioch, of a lingering diforder, not *without a fufjticion* that it was occafioned by poifon – diutino morbo Antiochiae obiit, *not fine veneni fuf/ticione-*. – He then proceeds to mention the fafts on which the fufpicion was grounded – of which the principal Ohq ferves to deftroy the credibility of the other two. – In the beginning of chapter 2, he fays, that Germanicus, *as was thought,* died by the contrivance of Tiberius, and by the means of Cn. Pifo, whofe obloquy and offenfive behaviour was too much for his *weak* ftate. – Obiit autem, ut *-opinio* fuit, fraudc
Germanicus died naturally.

THE HISTORY OF THAT INIMITABLE MONARCH TIBERIUS. John Rendle   **69**

Tiberii, minifterio et opera C. Pifonis: qui fub idem tempus Syria prapofitus, nee diffimulans offendendum flbi aut patrem aut fllium, quafi plane ita necefle eflet, etiam *tegrum* Germanicum graviffimis verborum ac rerum acerbitatibus, nullo adhibito modo, affecit. – The fame thing he fays, iii. 52 – Germanico ufque adeo obtreftavit, ut et praeclara fafta ejus pro fupervacuis elevaret; et gloriofiffimas viftorias, feu damnofas Reipublicae increparet. Quod vero Alexandriam propter immenfam et repentinam famem inconfulto fe adiiflet, queftus eft in Senatu. Etiam caufla mortis fuifle ei per Cn. Pifonem legatum Syriae creditur: – And again, vii. 2, V., he fays, that Pifo was the caufe of of his death, and that he was condemned for it, on the accufation of P. Vitellius.

Tacitus fays, A. ii. 69, that Germanicus himfelf fufpefted Pifo, who had retired from Syria to Coos, of having, before he left Syria, either *poifoned* or *bewttched* him – that there however appeared ftronger marks of witchcraft than of poifon – fuch as human relics found about the houfe, charms, devotions, the name of Germanicus infcribed on plates of lead, half burnt afhes, and other devices ufed by witches. – And again, 73, he fays, that the body of Germanicus was expofed in the forum, at Antioch, for the purpofe of difcovering whether there was any reafon to think that he died, not of poifon, but of witchcraft. – He fays nothing of the livid fpots, nor of the ftill more remarkable circumftance that his heart remained unconfumed by the fire that confumed his body, fafts mentioned by Suetonius.

Jofephus fays, A. xviii. 2, *c.,* that Germanicus was poifoned by Pifo.

f F

Dion fays, 1. 57, p. 615, D., that he died by the contrivance of Pifo and Plancina – and by witchcraft – the tokens of which were . found in bis own houfe.

Germanicus died naturally.

Thofe reports that the death of Germanicus had been accomplifhed either by witchcraft or by paifon appear to be not at all fatisfaftory. – And as to Tiberius having been privy to his death, both Suetonius and Tacitus have faid enough to prove the futility of the infinuatiqn – Suetonius, in one place, iii. 56, and Tacitus, in feveral, A. iii. 5$, and iv. 52, 53, 54. – Tacitus, iii. 56, fays, that Tiberius, three or four years after the death of Germanicus demanded the tribunitial authority for Drufus, and pbferved to the Senate, that he, as long as Germanicus lived, had defifted from making the demand out of re- fpeft to him. – Now why fhould Tiberius, if he had been . confcious sto himfelf that the people fufpe&ed him of having been the caufe , pf the death of Germanicus, have thought it at all neceflary -to mentipn him on this occafion? – This alone feems to be almoft enough to prove that he knew nothing of the matter.' The remark, however, which, Tacitus fays, he fubjoined, proves more clearly that he "was innocent of the charge. – For he fays, that he alfo obferved that his fon Drufus then had a wife and *three children* – wiry then fhould Tiberius, who, by the account of Paterculus and Dion, feems to have been much interefted in the welfare of Germanicus, be fufpefted of having been the caufe of his death? – And of having fent 'him to Syria to be murdered, and fhortly after Cn. Pifo to kill him in that country ? – Again – iv. 52, 53, 54, he fays enough to convince us that Agrippina muft, if fhe was fuch a termagant, as he reprefonts her to have been, and if fhe was perfuaded that Tiberius had been the caufe of the death of her brother and hufband, have a&ed

very inconftftentliy, for he fays, c. 52, that fhe, in a rage, intruded on Tiberius, while facrificing to his father, and told him that it was of no ufe to do fo while he perfecuted his pofterity, alluding to the cafe of her coufin Claudia Pulchra. – And, in the next chapter, 53, 4te fays, that when Tiberius once, in her illnefs, paid her a vifit, (he, in a ftt

Germanicus died naturally.

of refentment, refufed to fpeak for fome time, and at laft, aftef havfng llied tears profafely, fhe complained to him – not of his having been the murderer of her firft hufband and brother, but that fhe wanted another hufband. – And what reply does Tacitus fay Tiberius made to her ? – Not the leaft. – For *fear* of giving any *offence* he immediately left her. – This private aneedote of the family, fubjoins Tacitus, I found in the commentaries of her daughter. – Laftly, in the 54th chapter, Tacitus tells us a ftill more unexpefted ftory – viz – that Agrippina, notwithftanding the butcheries of her brother and hufband – notwithftanding her ferocity and hauteur, was in the habit of frequenting the banquets of Tiberius, and that me once attended even though fhe had been informed, by the agents of Sejanus, that Tiberius intended to poifon her – but with, it feems, a predetermination, not to look at Tiberius, not to fpeak to him, not to touch any thing at table. – Tiberius obferving her total referve, but whether he had been apprifed of the caufe of it, or not, Tacitus could not fay – to make himfelf fure, offered her, with his own hand, fome choice apples. – This ferved to convince her of the truth of what fhe had heard, and fhc therefore, ordered the fervants to take them all away. – Tiberius, fays Tacitus, faid not a word to her, but, turning to his mother, obferved that no one could wonder if he never invited her more, as fhe fufpefted him of a defign to poifon her. – Suetonius fays, iii. 53, that he never invited her afterwards.

Now though thofe two hiftorians appear to have faid enough to ' render their own in/inuation that Tiberius was the caufe of the death of Germanicus queftionable, yet let us not fpare any pains to examine

whether there be any thing like a foundation for it.

Germanicus, the younger, was the only fon of Drufus, firft fur- named Germanicus, and of Antonia, minor, who was the daughter of

Germanicus died naturally,

M.- Anthony and Oflavia. – He was alfo the adopted fon of his uncle Tiberius, the only brother of Drufus. The attachment of Tiberius and Drufus to each other is fpoken of by hiftorisns (a) as very remarkable. And that of Tiberius and Antonia (who is re- prefented by all hiftorians (b) to have been a moft excellent woman) is fpoken of, by many writers,. as having been no lefs remarkable. – It was Ihe who contrived, by the means of her freedman Pallas (c) nd her maid Caenis, .(d) to apprife Tiberius, then refiding at Capreae, of the treachery of Sejanus. It was fhe too who difTuaded her grand- fon Caius, by Germanicus, on his fucceeding Tiberius, (for Tiberius, it feems, after having murdered his father and unde, appointed him his fucceflbr) from. liberating his and her friend Agrippa, whom Tiberius had, about fix months before his death, imprifoned for treacherous expreffions, as Jofephus would, A. xviii. 7, i r, have us to believe, in favor of Caius.

Germanicus had a' fifter, named, as Tacitus fays, Livia, but as Suetonius and Dion fay, Livilla, who was married to her coufin Drufus, the fon of Tiberius, by Vipfania, the daughter of Vipfanius Agrippa, whom Tiberius was compelled to divorce in order to marry Julia u. c. 742. – The mutual fondnefs of Germanicus and Drufus' was, as Tacitus obferves, A. ii. 43, as remarkable as that of Tiberius and Drufus – fed fratres egregie Concordes, et proximorum certami- nibus inconcuffi.

Thus was Germanicus – the nephew and the adopted fon of Tiberius – and the brother by adoption, and the brother-in-law of his only fon Drufus. – By fo many ties was Germanicus connefted with the family of Tiberius.

(a) – . Liry. Epit. HO. (b) – V. Max. iv. 3. (c) – Joi. A. xiiii. 7.. (d) – Dionl. 66. p. 75[. B.

Germanicus died naturally. Let us now proceed to enquire a little about his vrife Agrippina.

She was the daughter of Agrippa and Julia, and me became the'

daughter-in-law of Tiberius, by his marriage with her mother. – She

was alfo the fifter of that Agrippa, the caufe of whofe death we have been juft confidering, and the half-fifter of Vipfania Agrippina the firft wife of Tiberius. – The haughtinefs of her fpirit is acknowledged by every writer, and by no one more than by Tacitus, who, in feveral places of his annals – viz – i. 33, ii. 72, 75, 78, iv. 52, 53, vi. 25, defcribes her as a fort of female fury – even after the death of her hufband – and, in the lafl mentioned place, as being greedy of dominion – dominandi avida. – Dion, fays of her, 1. 57, p. 105 – tv *yaf xaxcm qiflmtparu&ts yt/vn.* – Her hufband, Germanicus, was, fays Tacitus, fo well aware of her unbounded ambition, that he, while dying, gave her the following advice – Turn ad uxorem verfus, per memoriam fui, per communes liberos oravit, *exueretferaciam,* faevienti fortunae fubmitteret animum; neu regreflain urbem aemulatione poten- tias validiores irritaret. – This advice, obferves Tacitus, Germanicus gave his wife before all their friends. – -And, fubjoins Tacitus, he gave other fecretly, by which, fays he, he was thought to have cautioned her againft offending Tiberius – et alia fecreto, per quae credebatur oftendere metum ex Tiberio.

This is the account which Tacitus gives of the laft words of Germanicus to his wife, by which it feems, fhe could not have been much better than her brother Agrippa, whofe fiercenefs we have feen haftened his death. – But why does he fay, that Germanicus, in the prefence of his friends, advifed his wife, on her return to the city, not to emulate the power of the more powerful – and then again, in

Xiph.

Germanicus died naturally.

fecrct, to have cautioned her againft offending Tiberius? – Did he fuppofe her to be fo high-minded as to think of vying with Tiberius for monarchy ? – If not, what reafon had he to be apprehenfive that fhe might have any thing to fear from him ? Had he not, but juft before, depofited with his friends his dying requefl – viz – to report to his father and brother, that is, to Tiberius and Drufus, how miferably he had ended his life – referatis patri ac fratri, quibus acerbitatibus dilaceratus, quibus infidiis circumventus, miferrimam vitam peffima morte finierim ? – And does not this feem to imply that Germanicus had, to the laft, the greater! expeftations from the known regard of his father and brother ? If not that he thought it more advifable to requeft his friends than his wife to report to Tiberius and Drufus in what a miferable ftate he died ?

Agrippina, we may well fuppofe, took care to follow the laft advice of her dying hufband – at leaft – as to any competition for power. Hiftorians, we find, agree in faying that me did not. Even Tacitus, we have feen, reprefents her as having been not afraid to intrude on Tiberius at any time, and any where, and to interrupt any buiinefs, however folemn, with indecent clamours. And both he and Suetonius even reprefent her as fo daring in her complaints as to have provoked the following folitary expodulation from Tiberius – are you therefore hurt, my child, becaufe you cannot govern? – And that fuch was her predominant paffion, to the very laft, Tacitus affirms, A. iv. 25. Paterculus fays, of her, ji. 130, and her eldeft fon Nero – Quod ex nuru, quod ex nepote, dolere, indignari, erubefcere coaftus eft ? – And all this Paterculus feems to fay of her before the death of Livia, for he immediately fubjoins – Cujus tempoiis aegritudinem auxit amifla mater eminentiffima, &c. Tacitus himfelf appears to have confirmed what Paterculus fays of her – for he fays, A. v. 3, miflaeque in Agrip- pinam ac Neronem litterae, quas pridem adlatas et cohibitas at

. *Germanicus died naturally.*

Augufta crcdidit vulgu – baud enim multum poft mortem ejus recitatae funt. – And what does he fay was the fubftance of this epiftle of Tiberius to the Senate? – Scil. – verba inerant quaefita afperitate: fed non arma, non rerum novarum ftudium – amores juvenum et impudi- citiam nepoti objeftabat – in nurum ne id quidem confingere aufus, *adroganttam oris* et contumaccm animum incufavit. – But was this really the fubftance of the charge? – Would Tiberius, who was not overfond of troubling himfelf about trifles, who was then, as Dion fays, 1. 58, 623, not the autocrat of the Roman empire, but of Capreae, who was then, as Juvenal fays, in a ftate of fecurity, have thought of bringing fo unimportant a charge againft the widow and the eldeft fon of Germanicus, and in the Senate, at a time when, as Tacitus himfelf fays, in the chapter before, one of the confuls ufed to divert the fathers with farcaftic jokes on him ? – What fays Suetonius of this matter ? – He, iv. 30, fays, that Caius himfelf ufed to inveigh againft all the fenators for having been the accufers of his mother and brothers, and to fay that the feverity of Tiberius was really excufable, confidering who were the accufers. – All the fenators then, and not Tiberius, were, by the confeffion of her own fon, the accufers of Agrippina. – Pretty nearly the fame thing we find atteftcd by Philo, in his work againft Flaccus, p. 748, F., where he fays, that Flaccus, the governor of Egypt, adminiftered the affairs of his province five years under Tiberius, better than any former praefeft – that he, foon after the death of Tiberius, was fo worn out with continued grief on that account, that he was, at laft, when he heard of the murder of his grandr fon, a few months after, incapable of attending to the duties of his ftation – and, perhaps, adds Philo, he was confcious of having been one of thofe who, by their accufations, were the caufe of the death of

the mother of CaiUS. – *stn run mmttQc. tvut n* ria *fiwnft* xafl' *xt fOvot ttt ras Germanicus died naturally.*

By this it appears that it was generally thought that many were her accufers – and – that there was more than one article of accufation. – And if Flaccus did not accufe her' of endeavouring to prevail with him to fecond her treafonable defigns againft

Tiberius, does not Philo feem to be a little inaccurate in faying that Flaccus was one of thofe who were, the caufe of her death? – For how could Flaccus be faid to have been any way inftrumental in her death, if he, in the 17l!1 year of Tiberius, was fent to Egypt? Agrippina, fays Tacitus, vi. 25, died in the igth year. And, if we may believe Suetonius, iv. 10, was banifhed to Pandataria before the death of Livii – et ea relegata in Liviae Auguftae proaviae fuae contubernio manlit. – Confequently Flaccus muft have been fent to Egypt two years before her death, and, at leaft, three years after her banifhment.

Have we not then reafon to fufpeft that fome other muft have been the offence of Agrippina befides that affigned by Tacitus. – If me was . accufed of arrogance only, why were the fenatbrs faid by Cains to have accufed her to Tiberius? – Why was Flaccus faid to have joined others in her accufations ? – Why does Tacitus himfelf fay, v. 4, that the populace befet the fenate-houfe with her banners ? – Simul populus effigies Agrippinae ac Neronis gerens, circumfiftit Curiarn, &c. – That Sejanus complained in the Senate' that the grief of Tiberius was defpifed – that the people were difaffefted – that new difcourfes – conciones – were now heard and read – new decrees – confulta – of the fathers – that nothing remained but to take arms, and to place themfelves under thofe leaders whofe banners they bore. If her offence was no greater, why has Paterculus told us that Tiberius *was forced* to grieve, to be indignant, to be afharned ? If it really was no greater, had he not feveral other incomparably greater caufes to grieve ? – And efpecially for the recent lofs of his mother?

t
Germanicus died naturally.

Tacitus then appears to differ, in three points, from every other hiftorian, who has fpokcn of the offence of Agrippina – viz – with regard to her accufers, the alleged offence, and the time when fhe was banifhed. – Indeed what he fays of the two former feems to he almoft contradiftory of the latter. – For if Tiberius had fo long borne the termagant rants of Agrippina, with fo' much compofure, and had then retired from the management of ftate affairs indifguft, and, after the death of his mother, permitted Sejanus to tranfaft all public bufinefs, and if he, as Tacitus himfelf fays, fpent his time in amaenity – or, as Juvenal fays, in fecurity, would he have given himfelf the trouble to accufe her of arrogance only ? As to the third particular – viz' – the time when fhe was accufed – Tacitus difagr'ees with Pater- cuhas and Suetonius not a little. – Paterculus, we have feen, mentions the grief which Tiberius fuffered on account of the mifdemeanor of Agrippina and her fon immediately before that of the diflrefs which he fuffered for the lofs of his mother. Suetonrus, we have juft feen, fays, that fhe was banifhed *before the death of Livta* – and – that Caius, her youngeft fon, was, on the banifhment of his mother, placed under the care of Livia. Tacitus fays, that fhe was tried *after the death ef Livia,* who, he alfo fays, v. 3, was, by the populace of Rome, fuppofed to have prevailed on her fon to fupprefs this charge againft Agrippina and her fon Nero.

But is it poffible that Tacitus could have erred concerning the order in which two fo remarkable events happened ? If he has, can what he fays of the pcrfuafion of the populace – viz – that the fame charge had long before been bro'ught and given up on account of Livia, be true? – And alfo, what he fays, of the interference of Livia in ftate matters be alfo true? – If Agrippina was banifhed before the death of Livia, and Livia had before interfered in her behalf why did fhe not now ?*Germanicus died naturally.*

Let us now endeavour to bring ourfclves acquainted with the laft year or two of the life of her hulband, in order to enable purfelves to judge of the caufe of his death.

He was, fays Jofephus, A. xviii. 3, i., fent, by *the Senate,* into the eaft, after the death of Antiocims, king of Comagene, to fettle a difpute between the higher and lower ranks of people in that country, of whom, the one party were for continuing the government, and the other for putting themfelves under the proteftion of the Romans – and there, fays Jofephus, he Was murdered by the contrivance of Pifo, and his wife Plancina. This report of Jofephus is, we find, nearly attefted by Tacitus, A. ii. 42, who there fays, that Tiberius, in the year of Rome 770, after he had, in the name of Germanicus, dif- tributed among the populace of Rome 300 fefterces, and had defigned him for his colleague in the confulfhip the year following, (which acls of benevolence, fays Tacitus, the people did not think proceeded from any real regard to him,) either contrived, or took the advantage of contingencies, to fend him away from Rome, under a pretence of conferring honor on him. – Ceterum Tiberius, nomine Germanici, trecenos plebi feftertios viritim dedit, feque collegam confulatui ejus dcftinavit, nee ideo fincerae caritatis fidem adfecutus, amoliri juvenem *f/iecie honoris* ftatuit, ftruxitque caufas aut forte oblatas arripuit. – By this then it appears that Tiberius, and not the Senate, fent Germanicus from Rome to fettle the aflairs at Comagene. But, befides this, Tacitus, in the fequel of the fame chapter, mentions another caufe, not noticed by Jofephus – viz – that Syria and Judea, unable to pay their tributes any longer, prayed to have them leflened. – This he fays in the 42d chapter, but in the 43d, he feems to affirm, that all the eaft was in a ftate of confufion. – Igitur haec, et de Armenia quae fupra (chapter 5) memoravi apud patres difTeruit; nee pofle motum

Germanicus died naturally.

Orientem nlfi Germanici fapientia componi, nam fuam aetatem ver- gere, Drafi nondum fatis, adolevifle. – After having faid this, he fub- joins what has a little too much the appearance of a contradiftion to what he had before faid – viz – that Tiberius fent him, and, that he lent him with no good view. – Then, by a decree of the Senate, the tranfmarine provinces were affigned to Germanicus, with much larger powers, every where, than either thofe poflefs who are appointed by lot or *fent by the emperor.* – By this it appears that *the Senate,* as Jofephus fays, fent Germanicus to the eaft. – Suetonius, iv. i, fays, that Germanicus was, when he was fent to compofe the differences in the eaft, *expelled,* and therefore, we prefume, he was expelled, not by the Senate, but by Tiberius. – Conful deinde iterum creatus, ac priufquam honorem iniret, ad componendum orientis ftatum *expulfus,* &c. &c. – But if all the eaft was then in a perturbed ftate – and he had larger powers, every where, how could he be faid to have been expelled ? Tacitus fays, chapter 5, that Tiberius was glad of the difturbances in the eaft, becaufe, on that pretence, he could withdraw Germanicus, from his favorite legions, and expofe him to new deceit and dangers in new provinces. But, if it was only a contrivance of Tiberius to remove Germanicus from the command of the German legions, did not the Senate know it? Why then did they fo pompoufly fecond it? And at a time when, if we may believe Suetonius, iii. 30, 31, Tiberius had not attempted to control their deliberations? – But what fays Paterculus of this matter? – He, before the death of Agrip- pina, obferves, to a conful, with how great honor Tiberius fent his Germanicus into the tranfmarine provinces. – Qnanto cum honofc Germanicum fuum in tranfmarinas mifit provincias? – ii. 129. Now how can Paterculus be fuppofed to have recorded this of Tiberius, in

S, ,

i . - :. ' -'

Germanicus died naturally.

the face of all the Senate, if they had fent him to the eaft ? – And with greater power than. any imperial prafeft ? That this report of Pater- culus is more credible than any of the foregoing appears likely from this confideration – that not only Syria, but the eaft in general, was under the care of the emperor, as Tacitus himfelf has admitted, A. ii. 43. – For he there fays, notwithftanding he had immediately before aflerted, that the Senate had given to Germanicus greater power than any imperial prfeft, that Tiberius removed Creticus Silanus from the government of Syria, becaufe his daughter was engaged to Nero, the eldeft fon of Germanicus, and appointed Cn. Pifo, becaufe he was hoftile to his interefts. And if the primary objeft of his mif- Jion was, as Tacitus fays, to fettle the affairs of Armenia, and to prevent the interference of the Parthians in the political arrangement of that country, we may well fuppofe that Tiberius, who, as Dion fays, 1. 55, p. 554, D., was, when he went to Rhodes, made praefeft of Armenia, by Auguftus, would not permit the Senate to appoint a governor of that country.

But why fhould Tiberius have fent Germanicus rather than his fon Drufus to fettle the affairs of the eaft? – Tacitus informs us, A. ii 43, that Tiberius confided more in the wifdom of Germanicus than he could in that of his own fon Drufus. And what reafon does he affign for this fuperior confidence ? – Becaufe, as he would have us to believe, Germanicus had more wifdom, and was the older of the two. Igitur baee, et de Armenia quae fupra memoravi, apud patres difleruit: nee pofle motum Orientem nifi Germanici *fapientia* componi, nam fuam . aetatem vergere, Drufi nondum fatls adolevifle. But would Tiberius, who was, by all accounts, of all men the moft fagacious, and who knew as well as Tacitus, how very familiar his two fons were at the very time – fed fratres egregie Concordes, et proimorum certamini*Germanicus died naturally.*

bus inconcuffi – A. ii. 43, have made, thus publicly, this invidious companion between them, at any time of his monarchy, efpecially in the year 770? – What reafon had he for faying that Germanicus was much older than Drufus – or – much wifer ? – Drufus was, in the year 770, as Tacitus himfelf allows, A. iii. 56, 31 years of age: and Germanicus was, in the fame year, 32. – Befides, long before Germanicus arrived in Syria, he was fent to oppofe Maroboduus, and as Tacitus himfelf fays, A. ii. 62, while Germanicus was making the circuit of the provinces, he contrived to fubdue Maroboduus. – Dum ea aeftas Germanico plures per provincias tranfigitur, *haud leve decus* Drufus quafivit inliciens Germanos ad difcordias, utque frafto jam Maroboduo ufque in exitium infifteretur. – And for this exploit, he was, fays Tacitus, A. iii. 11, honored for it by the Senate the very year in which Germanicus died, with an ovation. Atque interim Drufus rediens Illyrico, quanquam patres cenfuiflent, ob recep- tum Maroboduum, et res priore aeftate geftas, ut, ovans inirct, prolato honore urbem intravit. – Confequently the reafons faid by Tacitus to have been affigned by Tiberius for fending Germanicus to the eaft appear to be without the leaft foundation. And therefore we may well doubt whether Tiberius really affigned fuch. Indeed if he fpoke fo difparagingly of the experience and age of his own fon in the year 770 – how can it be fuppofed that he forgot himfelf fo very much in the year 775, as to recommend him to the fame Senate, as duly prepared, for eight years paft – that is – from the year 767, by his experience and military achievements, to be colleague in the tribuni- tial authority ? Neque enim propere, fed per ofto annos capto ex- perimento, compreffis feditionibus, compofitis bellis, triumphalem et bis confulem, noti laboris participem fumi. – A. iii. 56. The fame

Germanicus died naturally.

enormous contradiftion Tacitus has reprefented Tiberius as having made, on thofe two occafions, with regard to the age of his own fon. For in the year 770, Tacitus fays, he obferved to the Senate – Drufi aetatem nondum fatis adolevifle – and – in the year 775, he fays, Tiberius obferved to them – efle illi conjugem et tres liberos, eamque a? tatem qua ipfe quondam a divo Augufto ad capeflendum hoc munu$ vocatus fit, A. iii. 56. – Now Tiberius was, when he was firft honored with the tribunitial authority, as we have feen, 36. – If then Drufus was, in the year 775, in his 36th year, he muft have been in his 3ift in the year 770. – How then can it be fuppofed that Tiberius then obferved of his age – nondum fatis adolevifle ?

Thofe contradictions Tacitus has reprefented Tiberius himfelf to have made publicly with regard to the age and military experience of Drufus, within a period of four or five years. – And a no lefs glaring contradiftion, it fhould be obferved, he appears to have reprefented Tiberius as having made to the general opinion of the populace of Rome, with regard to the qualifications of Germanicus as a general. In the year 767 he reprefents, A. j. 46, the populace of Rome as dif- fatisfied, becaufe Tiberius did not go himfelf to quell the mutinous legions in Germany and Illyricum – - and becaufe he fent two ftriplings to fupply his place – neque duorum adolefcentium nondum adulta auftoritate comprimi queat. – If then the populace of Rome thought that neither Germanicus nor Drufus was fit, in the year 767, to be fent to the mutinous legions, who can fuppofe that Germanicus could, in the year 770, have been fo much more fit to be fent to the eaft than any other perfon, and efpecially than Drufus, who was but a year younger?

Germanicus then, we prefume, on the evidence of Tacitus, was, in the year 770, fent by the Senate, with powers exceeding thofe of

Germanicus died naturally.

imperial prefers, to fettle the affairs of the eaft, and efpecially of Armenia, then in diforder. – And Tiberius, he fays, in the next fen- tence, ii. 43, was fo jealous of his plenipotentiary fenatorial com- miffion, that he thought it prudent to remove Creticus Silanus from his command of Syria, becaufe his daughter was likely to become the wife of the eldeft fon of Germanicus, and to fend Cn. Pifo to fucceed him, becaufe he was always hoftile to Germanicus. – But can it have been true that Tiberius removed Creticus Silanus from the government of Syria merely becaufe it was likely that he would be induced to fide with Germanicus? – What fays Dion of this fame Creticus Silanus? – He fays, 1. 59, p. 646, A., that Tiberius honored him much (and for his virtues, as Philo alfo fays, no doubt) that he took care never to oppofe him, and gave up to him in every thing – o . tv *yxp TiGifms arvs*

Etijawev *ufi /aiti txxX)Tot iron air' avra oixayiai iQe%. vxrai, aJ? txttvti vQn rx ntxvrx f/ti'fla-ai.* – Is it at all likely then that Tiberius would have recalled fuch a praefeft from Syria, merely becaufe it was thought there would be, at fome remote time, a match between his daughter and Nero, the fon of Germanicus, then, perhaps, not more than ten or twelve years old ? If, indeed, Tiberius recalled Silanus for this reafon only (and, admitting the truth of what he had faid before, A. ii. 5 – viz – Tiberius was glad to hear of commotions in the eaft, becaufe by that means he had a pretence for detaching Germanicus from his favorite legions – it is not altogether unlikely) how are we to underftand what he fays in the next chapter, 44 ? – There he fays, that Tiberius thought himfelf more fecure by trufting the legions to each of 'his fons – feque tutiorem rebatur, utroque filiorum legiones obtinente. – If then Tiberius thought himfelf more fecure becaufe his fons commanded the armies, did he not fee that his fecurity j was likely to be increafed by retaining his friend Silanus in his government?

Germanicus died naturally.

But if the affairs of the eaft were in general in fuch a ftate of anarchy in the year 769 – for fo Tacitus himfelf fays, A. ii. 5 – and – if Tib.&- rius was glad of the opportunity to fend Germanicus far away – and – if the Senate were fo ready to fecond his wifhes, may we not expeft that he, in that year, went to Armenia ? – Let us make it our bufmefs

to inquire.

In the year 770, fays Tacitus, A. ii. 51, he was ftill at Rome, eleftioneering with Drufus, and did not leave Rome till after Drufus had arrived in Dalmatia. – Germanicus then began his journey. – Firft he went to Illyricum, and from thence to Dalmatia to fee Drufus, and from thence again along the coaft of the Adriatic to Nicopolis, in *Epirus*, where he entered on his fecond confulfhip. From Nicopolis he removed to Athens, where he was received with, every mark of adulation. Thence he went to Euboea, and fo on, not to Afia, but to Byzantium. Then he entered the Euxine fea, the coafts of which he explored, and then returned along the coaft of Afia to Rhodes, where he met Cn. Pifo, haftening to Syria. Thus it feems that Pifo was fent, not before Germanicus, but *after* him, and, it may be added, a long while after him, notwithdanding the affairs of the eaft had been in a confufed ftate, as Tacitus fays, A. ii. 5, two years before. As then Germanicus delayed fo long to execute the primary objeft of his miffion, why fhould we not fufpeft that Tiberius found it necef- fary, to fend, in the mean time, Pifo into Syria' – Thither, however, he fent him, and there Pifo arrived before Germanicus, notwithftand- ing Germanicus had been fent, by the Senate, with more ample powers than any imperial praefeft, to fettle the affairs of the eaft, which had now been in confuiion about two years.

And how did Germanicus behave when he anived in Syria?

Germanicus died naturally.

He firft placed a royal diadem on the head of Zeno, as king of Armenia – then he reduced Cappadocia into the form of a province, and appointed a praefeft for the firft time over Comagene. – Thus every thing being fettled, he ordered Pifo, or his fon, to march, with a part of the legions, into Armenia. – This Pifo refufed to do. – This difobedience of orders caufed a mifunderftanding between them, which, by the interpofition of friends, feems to have been accommodated. – After this Germanicus vifited the king of the Nabathaeans, and permitted him to fet a heavy crown of gold on his own head and on that of Agrippina. – This offended Pifo and drew fome offenfive animad- verfions from him.

The year following Germanicus, in the time of immenfe and un- expefted fcarcity, under a pretence of procuring a fupply of provifions for the people of Syria, without the permiffion of Tiberius, entered Egypt. – Of this ftep, fays Suetonius, iii. 52, and Tacitus, ii. 59, Tiberius complaine'd very much. – For, fays Tacitus, Auguftus ordered that no fenator nor knight fhould enter Egypt without leave from the prince. – In the mean time Pifo reverfed whatever orders he had left for the legions or for the cities. – This ftep revived their mutual criminations, in which their wives bore a very confpicuous part. – Soon after this Germanicus, on his return to Antioch, fell fick, and, in his laft moments, furrounded by his friends, he, as we have feen, gave his wife fome prudent advice, which feems to imply that much of the oppofition which he had experienced, had been occafioned by her hauteur – and – moreover, faid fomething to her afterwards in private. – Having fmifhed his exhortation to his wife, and requefted his friends to report to his *father* and brother, what he had faid, he expired.

Germanicus died naturally.

Pifo was foon after accufed of having poifoned him – and condemned for it by the Senate, contrary to the inclination of Tiberius, who was therefore fuppofed to ha e given private orders to Pifo to cut him *off.*

Let us inquire how far Tiberius is likely to have given this order.

That Tiberius was confidered by Agrippina as any way privy to the death of her hufband is rendered not a little improbable by what we have already feen Suetonius and Tacitus fay of her fubfequent behavior to him at Rome – her intrufions – her repeated attendance at his entertainments – and her complaint to him of her want of another hufband. – But this is not the only proof of the innocence of Tiberius in this matter. – The' conduft of Antonia, the mother of Germanicus, if examined, will afford a proof equally ftrong that ihe alfo confidered Tiberius as perfeftly innocent of the death of her fon.

Antonia, we have feen, was the widow of Drufus, the mother of Germanicus, and the firft coufin of Julia, the mother of Agrippina. – Confequently ihe muft be fuppofed to have known all the circum- ftances of her fon's death. – How then do hiftorians fay Ihe behaved after the lofs of her only fon ? – Tacitus fays, iii. 3, that (he did not attend his funeral, and why ihe did not, he fays, he could never dif- cover, by any written document whatever – poffibly, fays he, Ihe may have been unwell – or, the excefs of grief may have prevented her – to thofe two conjeftures he adds a third – which, he takes care to let us know, he thinks more likely to have been the real caufe of her abfence – viz – that Ihe was kept from attending the proceffion by Livia and Tiberius. – Arid does not this look like an infinuation that Livia too was a party concerned in the death of her grand-fon ? – But if Antonia was thus deterred from attending the funeral proceffion of

Germanicus died naturally.

her grand-fon by the contrivance of Tiberius and his mother – how is it that fhe, a few years after, as Jofephus fays, A. xviii. 7, ., apprifed Tiberius, by her freed-man Pallas and her maid Caenis, that Sejanus was ploting to overthrow the government ? – And how does Tacitus fay Sejanus contrived to do it – fcil. – by promifing to marry Livia, the widow of his friend Drufus, the fon of Tiberius, and the daughter of the fame Antonia. – And would Antonia have voluntarily done all this for Tiberius, if me had fufpefted that he had been the murderer of her only fon ? – And how is it that me, as Jofephus alfo fays, A. xviii. 7, i., defired Caius, who was going to liberate Agrippa the day after Tiberius died, not to do it fo foon, becaufe it would appear difrefpeftful ?

Another thing that looks like a plain refutation of the infinuation, Is mentioned by Tacitus himfelf, and, among the events of the fame year. A. ii. 88, he relates how Adgandeftrius, the prince oftheCatti, offered to poifon Arminius, and what Tiberius faid in the Senate on that occafion. He fays, that Tiberius rejefted the offer with ditdain, or rather with indignation – and – that he acquired the fame of an ancient Roman for his abhorrence of the deed. – Qua gloria aequabat fe imperatoribus prifcis. This noble refufal of the offer of Adgandeftrius, it fhould be remembered, happened in the courfe of the year in which Germanicus died, and probably but a very few months after that event – and is faid, by Tacitus, to have been recorded by the writers and fenators who lived at the time. Would then Tiberius have acquired fo much credit for expreffing himfelf fo indignantly oa this occafion before the expiration of that year, if he had been thought to have been the caufe of the death of his adopted fon and nephew, and the hufband of his daughter-in-law Agrippina ? – This teftimony of Tacitus is not a little remarkable, if not alone fufficient to prove that Tiberius was confidered by every body as innocent of the death

of Germanicus.

Germanicus died naturally.

But Seneca, in three of his works – viz – Confol. ad Marc., Confol. ad Polyb., and Nat. quaeft., has afforded us ftill ftronger proof that Germanicus died a natural death – for – in the firft mentioned work, he himfelf fays, c. 16 – that Tiberius Caefar et quern genuerat, et quem adoptaverat amifit: – in the fecond, he, c. 35, introduces Claudius as faying – Amifi Germanicum fratrem: quem quomodo amaverim, in- telliget profefto, quifquis cogitat quomodo fuas fratres pii fratres amant. – And in the lair, he, 1. i. c. t, fays – Vidimus circa divi Augufti excefTum fimile prodigium: vidimus cum de Sejano aftum eft: nee *Germanici mors* fine denunciatione tali fait. – Now if Germanicus had been poifoned, would both Claudius and Seneca have fpoken thus of him ? – And, if Tiberius had caufed him to be poifoned, would Seneca, have propofed to Marcia, under extreme grief for the lofs of her fon, the example which Tiberius exhibited of fortitude for the lofs of Germanicus and Drufus?

7

SECTION 7

CHAPTER VI.
' *When Tiberius began to be a bad Prince.*

JL HE charafter of Tiberius is, we know, reprefented, by all hiftorians, as having been very excellent till he was 56 years old – that is – till the death of Auguftus. Even Tacitus admits, and, in two places, i. 12, vi. 51, that it was during fo many years, fo very excellent. He alfo fays, i. 54, that his manners were more dignified than even thofe of Auguftus, who, in compliment to Maecenas, then fond of Bathyllus, a pofture mafter, and to pleafe the vulgar, ufed to be prefent at the loweft diverfions – Indulferat ei ludicro Auguftus, dum Maecenati obtemperat effufo in amorem Bathylli: neque ipfe abhorrebat talibus ftudiis, et civile rebatur mifceri voluptatibus vulgi.

Tacitus, who here seems to condemn Augustus for being present at such low sports, and to commend Tiberius for not following his example, says, i. 76, of Tiberius, on a similar occasion – cur abstinuerit spectacnlo ipse, varie trahebant: alii tzdio coetus, quidam trislilia ingenii, et metu coinpara- iionis, quta Augustus comifer interim!.

Suetonius, iii. 72, Castrensibus Imlis non interfuit solum, sed, &c.
47, Et iis, quse ab aliquo cderentur, *rartsstme* interfuit.
Dion, p. 609, 1!., ovvfffr *yaf ffn vats Qts*
When Tiberius legan to be a bad Prince.

But, continues he, the manners of Tiberius were different – alia Tiberio morum via. Tacitus not only fays this, but he adds, that Tiberius had it in contemplation to check that diflblutenefs of manners, to which the generality of the people were, in confequence of the long connivance of Auguftus, fo much habituated – but that fuch was the diflblute ftate of them, that he dared not, *as yet,* attempt to do it – fed populum per tot annos molliter habitum, *nondum* audebat ad duriora vertere – which, furely, feems to imply that he did, afterwards, attempt to do it. Indeed, we find, that both Tacitus himfelff and Suetonius tooj fay exprefsly thai; he, more than once, attempted to correcl the manners of the people – though as Suetonius fays, iii. 59, not always without many inveftives for his good intentions from mife- rable verfifyers, who dared to reproach him for his having been an exile at Rhodes – for his abftinence from wine – for his morofenefs towards his mother – and, ftrange to fay – for his cruelty and blood- thirftinefs. And how does Suetonius fay this blood-thirfty tyrant behaved on thofe occafions ? – fcil. – he calmly faid, let the bad hate me, provided the good like me – Oderint dum probent.§ '

In the 74th chapter of this same book Tacitus says – inevitabile crimen, cum ex moribus l'rincipis foedlssima quaeque deligeret accusator, objectarel- que reo.

t A. ii. 34, 48, 85. – iv. 14, 62.

tii. 33, 35, 59.

Suetonius, iii. 28, Sed adrersus convitia malosque rumores et famosa de se ac suis cannina firmus ac patiens subinde jactabat. – In civitate libera lin- guam mentemque liberas esse debere.

Tac. A. ii. 50 – In se jacta nolle ad cognitionem vocari.

A. iii. 10 – ? pentendis rumoribus validum. – "Dion, p. 637, C.

vi. 38 – Contemptor suae infnntitf.

When Tiberius began to be a bad Prince.

But notwithftanding Tacitus has, in feveral places above noticed, fpoken fo highly of the conduft of Tiberius till the death of Auguftus, yet he fays, A. 72, 73, 74, that he was a very bad prince, and, feem- ingly, fo early as the beginning of the fecond year of his reign, though be had then been, as he fays, in the beginning of the firft mentioned chapter, requefted by the people to accept the title of *father of his country,* feveral times. In the end of that fame chapter he fays, that he was, as Suetonius, we have feen, alfo fays, fo notorioufly *cruel,* proud, and quarrelfome with his mother, that certain unknown faty- rifts attacked him for thofe bad qualities moft feverely, and, as Tacitus fays, exafperated him. – Hunc quoque afperavere carmina, in- certis auftoribus vulgata, *mf/evitiam* fuperbiamque ejus, etdifcordem cum matre animum. – C. 73, he proceeds to let us know how furrep- titioufly he contrived to introduce a moft grievous but namelefs pell into Rome, how this namelefs peft, was, by fome unknown means then expelled, and how it then again, after fome time, found means tore-enter, and, at lafc, blazed forth, and before the end of his reign, infefled every thing. – Haud pigebit referre in Falanio et Rubrio, modicis equitibus romanis pretentata crimina: ut quibus initiis, quanta arte Tiberii, graviffimum exitium irreplerit, dein repreflum fit, poftremo arferit, cunftaque corripuerit nofcatur. – C. 74, he informs us how Romanus Hifpo, a poor, unknown, reftlefs wretch, began, ioon after the affair of Falanius and Rubrius – nee multo poft – to follow a courfe of life whidi the mileries of the times, and the audacity of men, afterwards rendered fa. nous, and, that this wretch began it by finding means to become an agent to the *cruelty* of the prince – fsevitiae principis adrepit – that is – by obtaining his permiflion to fend him private accounts, not of any one, but of any one of

Does not this appear, lo have been contradicted by Tacitus himself, by what he sajs in the three places referred to ia the last note?

When Tiberius began to be a bad Prince.

eminence, to the great danger of all that clafs. Thereby rendering himfelf odious to all, in order to pleafe one, and fetting an example to the reft of his fort, how to enrich themfelves by feeking the deftruftion of the great. This bafe wretch, fubjoins Tacitus, and all his fort, at kit, met the fame fate.

This is the account which Tacitus gives of Tiberius in thofe three chapters abovementioned. An account which clearly feems to imply that his cruelty, &c. muft have been, even in the very beginning of the fecond year of his reign, notorious, fince thofe fatyrifts then attacked him for it, and Hifpo, low as he was, thought of ingratiating himfelf with him, by becoming the agent of his cruelty.

But can Tacitus here have really meant that Tiberius was, even in the fecond year of his reign, fo notoriously cruel, and at variance with his mother, and was then the introducer of this moft grievous peft, and the encourager of this poor wretch to the deftru&ion of the moft eminent? – Or – mould he be only underftood to fpeak by way of anticipation ? – Whether he can really have meant to fay that all this happened in the beginning of the fecond year of his reign, or, cannot – we hope, as we go on, to be able to qualify ourfelves to judge.

Dion, in feveral places of his, 1. 57, bears pretty nearly the fame teftimony to the charafter of Tiberius, as Tacitus, we have feen, does, not only till the beginning of the fecond year of his reign, but till the death of Germanicus – that is – till the fixth year of his reign, and the 6ift of his age, he fays nothing, during that period, of the cruelty of Tiberius – of his introducing this moft grievous peft – or –

This worthless fellow, not long after, that is, as we suppose, not long after Tiberius had surreptitiously introduced the most grievous evil, accused Granius Marcsilus, the praetor of Bythynia, of having spoken disrespectfully of hjs prince. An inevitable crime! adds Tacitus, especially when, according to the manners of the prince, he objected to him, Ihe most filthy things.

When Tiberius began to be a bad Prince.

of the accufations of Hifpo – on the contrary, he, in feveral places, fpeaks moft highly of his conduft, and therefore, it feems likely that Tacitus only mentions thofe events by way of anticipation. – p. 603, D., he fays, that he was, by the Senate, chofen emperor, for his greater excellence in virtue than even any of their own body – ir *xarot aftrw o-Qut* wfotDtwv. – p. 6to, C., he fays, that he, for fome time, lived very rationally – *aotyun-arx* – and that he would not permit others to Jive diflblutely, but punifhed many for living fo. – p. 614, D., he fays, that he, as long as he praftifed other virtues, was remarkably careful to proteft the property of others, f and that he would not accept a legacy from any one who had relatives. J – p. 715, D., he fays, that he was not, till after the death of Germa- nicus, at all changed – that is – till after the 151!! year of his reign and the 6til of his age – or – u. c. 773, when he was, of a fudden,

totally changed – Tifeftor S, tt *n tfytoftvtn mar'* v'Xvi f 'av T0 Ttvavtiov *rut TTfooQtt ttfyxirocfJ. tn aura,* oXXam *atnn xatl* xaXwv wtfnpt – where, it IS obfervaWe, he intimates that Germanieus was his competitor, and attributes this fudden and total change to the want of one. – Laftly, in the next, p. 616, D., he fays, that this total and fudden change excited (as it well might in any one, and efpecially in a man of the

Tacitus, A: ii. 48 – Ceterum ut honestam inuoceatium paupertatem leva- rit; ita prodigos & ob flagitia egeutea Vribidium Varonem, Marium Nepolem, Appium Applaaum, Cornelium Sullam, ft. Vitellium movit geaato, aut sponte cedere pass us cst.

+ A most remarkable instance Dion mentions, 1. 57, p. 609. C., being once at a publtc exhibition, when the people would have an excellent daucer made free, he would not consent till his master had consented to part with him and to receive the full value of him. – Tacitus, A. iii. 18, satts firmus, ut saepe memoravi, adversum pecuniam.

Tacttus, A. tt. 48 – Neque hereditatem cujusquam adiil, nisi cum amicitia tnernisset: ignotos et uliis iofeusoj, eoquc paacipem nuucupaatcs, procid ucebat.

When Tiberius began to be a bad Prince. moft virtuous habits, and more than threefcore years old,) univerfal

aftoniffllient – To fv av *mf.-xr ara t–. tx, m Ttfff. xttxn Qxtarot ff. sn8xM. tfo, ufe* avrot, *fiuyxus* xa trforefov tTTatvatstov, woAXw Sx Totj //. atXXot flv//. a; sT!Xt.

Of this total change in the conduft of Tiberius Dion, p. 618, C., mentions an inftance or two which he thinks worfe than all the reft. He was, fays he, fo hardened in wickednefs, juft after the death of Drufus, who, he fays, died, in the cons, of Sulp. and Hater, u. c. 775, that he would publifh whatever , any one might fay of him in privatef – and – that he would puuifh others for impiety! a crime of

which he himfelf was guilty – *X. xkx ram avtfGamv avru, vnvrat re Sxsdx,* tp' *ots ras* aXXaf *us* xt *amGatras* eicoXa$tt, *xvros ts cattrot* wXt)/x/!Xeo, *xat vftxnn xat* Xswatr/xot *oip. to-xouett* – for which reafon, fotne, fays he, thought he was befide himfelf, though many, on the contrary, did not think fo, and, becaufe he did almoft 'all things well – *rat yaf* xx xi *trxw tsxtra. Itnrus -hum* – of which difpofition to adminifter moft things fairly he mentions two very ftriking inftances, and then fubjoins this remark of his own – fo great inequality was there in the aftions of Tiberius F – roo-Sror [/. *ft* Su To SiaXTrov tt *rats "TtGtfta vfatan* jjv. – And in the end of

the next book – viz – 1. 58, p. 639, B., he denies, moft expreffly, that fuch a total change fo fuddenly took place in his virtuous habits – for he there fays that, to the very laft, he had very many, if not, moft virtues.

How different is this from what Suetonius says, iii. 26 – Verum liherattu metu, civilem adinodum inter initia ac paulo minus quam privatum egit.

+ See p. 637, C. – Tacitus, A. vi. 38 – contemptor sux infamix.

$ Can Dion be correct in this ? – Does not Tacitus say, iii.'57, that the Senate decreed temples, &c. to him ? – And, iv. 52, that he worshipped Augustus .' – And,

c. 64, that the Gods were, on his account, favorable to the Romans ? – And, does not Suetonius say, iii. 36, that he expelled from Rome profaue rites ?

When Tiberius began to be a bad Prince.

But what reafon have we to think that Tiberius confidered Germa- nicus as a competitor ? – What competitor could he have had, who, as Tacitus fays, A. iil. $6, had been, by Auguftus, invefted with tribunitial authority, as being the perfon who was to fucceed him – who, as both Paterculns, ii. 104, and Suetonius, iii. 21, fay, had, at his adoption, received that public teftimony from Auguftus – " *this I do for the fake of the republic"* – who, as we have proved, chapter iii, had, five years before Auguftus died, been, as Paterculus fays, ii. 121, at his exprefs command, made equal to himfelf in every thing – who, as Suetonius contends, iii. 21, 23, was, by that moft prudent and raoft circumfpeft prince Auguftus, who did nothing rafhly, efpecially a thing of fuch importance, appointed his fuccefTor in confideration of his paft fervices and his excellent charafter – who, as Tacitus, Suetonius, and Dion fay, had demanded a colleague or colleagues and had been refufed – who, as Tacitus, A. i. 11, and Suetonius, iii 24, fay, would not confent to be a monarch, till the Senate, on their knees, entreated him to refufe no longer ? – Who, as Suetonius fays, iii. 67, was, immediately on being made emperor, faluted with the appellation of – " *father of his country"* – and, who, as Tacitus fays, A. i. 46, was reflefted on, by the terrified populace of Rome, as foon as they heard of the revolt of the army of Germany, for having heil- tated fo long to accept the fovereignty, as to have caufed that mutiny. – What competitor, it may well be a/ked, could fuch a monarch be fuppofed to have had ? – Was Germanicus, at his death, of age fuffi- cient to be cgnfidered by him, or any one elfe, as a competitor? – If he was only, as Tacitus fays in the laft mentioned chapter the

Taritus, A. i. 11, !. – Suetonius, iii. 25. – Dion, 1. 57, p. 603, A.

f U
! '

When Tiberius began to be a bad Prince.

Roman people complained, an adult, was he at all likely, but five years after, to be confidered by them as the competitor of his father? – Had nof Tiberius a fon, at the very time, nearly of the fame age as Germanicus ? – Does not Tacitus fay, i. 34, that Germanicus, high as he was, only devoted himfelf to the fervice of Tiberius ? – And, ii. 57, 58, that he, in his laft moments, difclaimed, before his friends, any pretenfion to competition, and exhorted his wife to take care of offending him ? – If Tiberius had confidered him as a competitor, would he not, inftead of complaining to the Senate of hi$ going into Egypt, have ordered him to be punifhed for fo doing ? – And as to the fudden and total change which, as Dion pretends, took place in his good habits, immediately after the death of Germanicus, to the aftoniflunent of every body, is it noticed by any other writer?

The evidence of Tacitus and Dion then, as to the excellence of the charafter of Tiberius, in the beginning of his reign, is precifely the fame. But how long that excellence continued they feem to difagree not a little. -Tacitus, we have feen, fays, that he was, in the beginning of his reign, fo notorioufly cruel, &c. that fatyrifts had then taken the liberty of writing againft him. Dion, we find, fays, that he remained the fame till the fixth year of his reign. Confequently, if Tacitus really meant to fay that Tiberius was fo foon changed, Dion evidently contradifts him. But as he appears to contradift Tacitus, fo Tacitus, we fhall find, in return, flatly contradifts him, and, fays enough to convince any one that he did not mean to fay that Tiberius was fo cruel in the fecond year of his reign.

Tacitus takes not the leaft notice of this moft furprifing change it the habits of Tiberius, immediately after the death of Germanicus – on the direct contrary, he has, in the end of chap, ii, recorded feveral celebrated afts which he did in the fhori refidua of that fame year –

When Tiberius began to be a bad Prince.

two of which, it may not be amifs to adduce – chapter 87, he fays, that he again refufed to accept the title of " father of his country" – which was now voted him for his beneficence to the commonalty, in the time of fcarcity; – and, in the next chapter, he fays, that he acquired the fame of an ancient Roman for rejefting the propofal of Arminius to poifon Adgandeftrius. – Tacitus not only fays this of Tiberius after the death of Germanicus – but he alfo fays, iv. t, that it was not till the beginning of the 9th year, when this fudden change took place. – C. As – C. An. Cofs, nonus Tiberio annus erat com- pofitae reipublicae, florentis domus: (nam Germanic! mortem inter profpera ducebat) cum *repente* turbare fortuna caepit; faevire ipfe aut faevientibus vires praebere. – And again – chapter 6 – Congruens Crediderim recenfere caeteras quoque reipublicse partes, quibus modis *td earn diem* habitae fint: quando Tiberio mutati *in detenus* principatus initium ille annus attulit. – Where, it mould be obferved, he does not fay, as Dion does, that either his government, or all his moral habits were, of a fudden, totally changed from the beft to the worft, nor, that he was fo loft to all Ihame that he publifhed an account of all his vices (indeed he, iv. 57, fays – that it was his opinion, that he left Rome for the purpofe of concealing his cruelty and luft – fsevitiam ac libidinem – -and, in the end of the vi, that he pretended to be virtuous during the life of Drufus – that he had as many good as bad qualities during that of his mother – that he concealed his lufts, during that of Sejanus – and that he, when 74, and we prefume, a chriftian,

How is this to be reconciled with what he had before said, i. 72 – viz – hltnc quoque asperavere carmina, incettis auctoribus vulgata in *savtttam* et superbiam ejns et discordem cum matre animum ? – If he was notoriously cruel in the second year of his reign, how can he be-said to hare *begun* to be cruel in the eighth ?

When Tiberius began to be a bad Prince.

purfued all manner of wicked ways openly and in defiance of decency,) but only, that he began to be cruel himfelf, or, to permit others to be fo – alluding, no doubt, to his having made Sejanus his prime minifter. – But where, in all this iv. book, do we find any inftance of the cruelty of Tiberius? – Indeed, if his cruelty was, as Tacitus fays, vi. 51, inteftable – inteftabilis faevitia – what reafon have we to expeft any inftance of it recorded ? – Let us, however, not think it too much to infpeft the particulars recorded in it with clofe attention.

Chapter 6, he prefents us with an admirable pifture of his admi- niftration of public affairs – a pifture fcarcely inferior to that of Pater- culus, which has been thought adulatory – in the end of which chapter he mentions an inftance of his beneficence to the diftrefled people of Rome, and of his conftant endeavors to prevent his provincial praefefts from extorting by cruelty. – Res fuas Caefar *Jfuflatijfimo cuiquc,* quibufdam ignotis ex fama mandabat; femelque adfumpti *tenebaritur,* prorfus fine modo, cum plerique iifdem negotiis *infenef- cerent.* Plebes acri q. uidem artnona fatigabantur: fed nulla in eo culpa ex principe: quin infecunditati terrarum, aut afperis maris ob- viam iit, quantum impendio diligentiaque poterat. Et ne provtnciae novis oneribus turbarentur, atque vetera fine avaritia et crudelitate magiftratuum tolerarent, providebat. *Corfwrum ttcrbera,* ademptiones bonorum, aberant. – So beneficent and humane does Tacitus fay Tiberius was, long after the death of Germanicus, and as he fays, chap. 7, Till a little after the death of Drufus. – Quae cunfta, non quideiH comi via, fed horridus ac plerumque formidatus retinebat tamen, *donee morte Dtujt "vertereniur: nam dum fuperfuit, manfcre.* – In this fame year, it fhould be obferved, Drufus died. – And, fays Tacitus, chapter 8, Tiberius entered the Senate and complained that his mother's age was now extreme – that is – above 80, and his own verging – or, 65. – After the burial of his fon, fays Tacitus, chap. 13,

When Tiberius began to be a bad Prince.

Tiberius attended to the concerns of the public with unremitting attention, his folace, fays he, was bufmefs – he frequented the courts of juftice, he heard the petitions of the allies. – At Tiberius nihil in- termifTa rerum cura, negotia pro folatiis accipiens, jus civium, preces fociorum traftabat. – Chapter 14, he fays, that Tiberius, after the praetors had, in vain, made many complaints againft the indecency of aftors, at laft referred it to the Senate to deliberate about taking fome fteps to prevent their immodeft behavior – and particularly about the low buffoonery of one Ofcan, who did much mifchief. – It was, fays he, agreed to expel all players from Italy. And Suetonius, who feems to fay, chapter 37, that they caufed riots, fays alfo, that Tiberius would never after permit them to return. – Chapter 15, he fays, that L. Capita, procurator of Afia, was, by the people of his province, (which, it fhould be obferved was imperial,) accufed of having op- prefled them, and was, by the permiiTion of Tiberius, tried by the Senate, (who had even then, as both Tacitus, in this fame chapter, and Suetonius, iii. 33, fay, the cognizance of all things,) and was, after a fair hearing, by them condemned to be banifhed – for which aft of juftice, continues he, and for a fimilar one, the year before, on C. Silanus, for embezzling money while procurator of Afia, the ftates of that country defired permiffion to ereft a temple to Tiberius, to his mother, and to the Senate. – A flrong proof how very few, even of his cotemporarics, as Dion remarks, confidered him as infane – and – as ftrong a proof that as few of them confidered him as irreligious – though Dion did, and the prefent race of fcavans, flill do.

Thefe are the inftances of the jnft government of Tiberius, which he has recorded as having taken place, in the end of the Qth year – or – the beginning of the loth. – Confequently why fhould we not think that he feems to have eontradifted himfelf, very little lefs than Dion-

When Tiberius began to be a bad Prince.

Let us now proceed to enquire whether he has recorded any fuclt IJke inftances among the tranfaftions of the loth year.

Chap. 29, 30, he fays, that Vibius Serenius, an exile at Amorgos, (one of the Cyclades) who had, eight years before, on the death of Libo, (who had endeavored to excite a rebellion, and who, to evade a public punifhment, had ftarved himfelf,) been banifhed, was, in the loth year of Tiberius, accufed, and by his own fon, of a plot againft: the government and life of Caefar – and – moreover that Carnutus, a praetor, was alfo accufed of having engaged to fupply Serenus with money for the above purpofe. And what was the fentence of thofe two confpirators? fcil. – Carnutus, before fentence was paffed, deftroyed himfelf, which, furely, feems to imply guilt. And what was the fentence of Serenus – fcil. – he was fent back to Amorgos. – Chapter 31, he mentions three inftances more of the upright conduct of Tiberius, as a monarch. He fays, firft, that C. Cominius, a knight, was accufed of having written an opprobrious poem on Tiberius – that he was tried for it, by the Senate, and convicted. And what punifhment was inflicted on him? – Tiberius, he fays, forgave him, and, at the interceffion of his brother who was a fenator. – He fays, fecondly, in the fame chapter, that P. Suilius, a quaeftor, was, in the fame year, convicted of having received a bribe, as judge, and banifhed. Laftly – Catus Firmius, a fenator, was, fays he, convicted of having brought a falfe accufation of treafon againft his own fifter – and, by the permiffion of Caefar, was expelled the Senate. – Chapter 32, he complains that he was aware how uninterefting his hiftory muft appear to moft of his readers

Under Tiberius, says Philo in Flac. p. 158, some proefects, who had been oppressive to their subjects, were, on their return to Rome, punished for it, and especially when complaints were made against them by the injured persons. – This subjoiqs he, p. 759, made them very careful to adminster justice to all.

When Tiberius began to be a bad Prince.

– that he had no external events to record, and as to internal, they were by no means fo remarkable, as thofe of former times – that every thing (notwithftanding Tiberius was fo cruel, and had introduced the moft grievous peft, and had encouraged Hifpo,) moved fmoothly. – Ofcourfe, if things moved fo fmoothly, in the beginning of the loth year, how can we be expected to believe that either he or his deputies began to be cruel in the beginning of the fecond or in that of the 9th? In the next chapter, 33, he complains again that fo far were internal things from moving fmoothly, that he had nothing to do but to make a chain of cruel mandates, continued accufations, falfe friendfhips, the deftruction of innocent perfons, and fuch like events – of courfe, why mould we not fuppofe that this change took place, not in the 9th, but in the beginning of the loth ? – And, why mould we not expect to find, that the fequel contains nothing elfe befides' a continuation of fuch like occurrences – at leaft for the following year – for after that, it feems, he was forced from his feat of government either by his mother, or the cunning of Sejanus. – And yet if he, as Tacitus fays, - had, from the death of his fon, to that of his mother, as many good qualities as bad – and retired from Rome in order to conceal his bad qualities – that is – as he fays, 'chapter 57, his cruelty (meaning, furely, if he was obliged to give way to his mother, not his political cruelty,) and luft, we cannot fuppofe that Tacitus knew enough of his vices, which he took fo much care to conceal, to be able to retail the particulars. Indeed, he, on the contrary, avoids giving us a continued account of thofe cruel mandates, &c. and takes care to furnim us with many aneedotes of his good deeds, and even two or three moft remarkable ones, and, it maybe remarked, even after he went to Cap- reae. Chapter 37, 38, he tells us how nobly he behaved when deputies from further Spain applied fo the Senate, for leave to build a temple to him and to his mother, (which, of courfe, feems to imply that*When Tiberius began to be a bad Prince.*

the people of Spain, as well as thofe of Afia, did not confider him as an inhuman monfter, for furely the people of Spain did not worfhip the devil, but rather as being one of the beft of men,) he, fays Tacitus, went to the Senate and deprecated the projeft moft earneftly, and ended his fpeech with thofe moft remarkable words – Proinde focios, cives, et Deos ipfos precor: (which, furely, is no proof of his impiety,) *has,* ut mihi ad finem ufque vitae, quietam et mtelligen- tem humani divinique juris mentem duint; *Hlos,* ut quandocunque conceflero, cum laude et bonis recordationibus, fafta atque famam nominis mei profequantur – which refufal fome, fays Tacitus, attributed to *modefty,* many to *diffidence,* and a few to *degeneracy* – to the opmion of which laft fet, Tacitus himfelf feems to fubfcribe, by an obfervation or two of his own, which he fubjoins – Optumos quippe mortalium altiffima cupere – and – nam contemptu famae contemni virtutes – *the former* of which feems to imply that Tacitus thought him ftill the beft of men – and the *latter* that he fufpefted that he then began to defpife fame, and, ofcourfe, the fincerity of what he then faid in the Senate. – But if he had before encouraged the hTuing of thofe cruel mandates, &c. why mould any one have thought him the beft of men? – Or – why fhould any one have thought of requefting permiffion of the Senate to ereft a temple to him ? – -. Chapter 57, he fays, that (notwithftanding what moft had faid) he was inclined to fufpeft that the real caufe of his retirement from Rome was to conceal his cruelty and luft, which he could not do at Rome. – But what occafion was there for endeavouring to conceal his cruelty, if he had ifiued cruel mandates, &c. ?

This alone is fufficient to prove that Tacitus, like Dion, has contradifted himfelf with regard to the time when this fuppofed change in Tiberius took place. – But there are ftill other chapters in

When Tiberius began to be a bad Prince.

this book, to which we think it proper to refer on this point, which relate to tranfaftions which, Suetonius fays, iii. 40, took place after he went to Capreae – they are 64 and 66. – In the &4th chapter, he mentions the fire on Mount Coelius, which, he fays, the populace imputed to his abfence – feralemque annum ferebant, et ominibus ad- verfis fufceptum principi confilium abfentias Now, if Tiberius had been fo very cruel, would the populace have thus regretted his departure? Or, would he have flown to their affiftance? So, he fays, he did – and received the thanks of all ranks for his beneficence – and for his being fo great a favorite with the Gods as to be the means of flopping it? But would the Gods have fhewn fo particular a favor to fo inhuman, fo lewd a wretch ? What an inconfiderate fool then muft this prince of hiftorians have been ? – The laft chapter, to which it feems not amifs to refer, on this matter, is the 66th – in which, after having again adverted to the beneficence of Tiberius, on the before mentioned occafion, he complains that the power of accufers grew ftronger and more dangerous, without oppofition, every day – that Varus Quinftilius, a relative of Caefar, was, among others, attacked by Domitius Afer and Publius Dolabella his kinfman – that the Senate agreed to defer the matter till the emperor mould return

– becaufe he was, for the time, the only fuffuge from urging evils – quod unum, urgentium maJorum fuffugium in tempus erat.

From all that Tacitus has faid in thofe. feveral chapters, why fhould we not conclude that Tiberius, muft have been, not cruel, but moft humane, till after the fall of the Amphitheatre of Fidenae – that is – as Suetonius fays, till after his retirement ? And why fhould we not alfo conclude from what he fays, iv. 57, and v. 3, that he had it not in his. power to do much harm before the death of his mother ? –

When Tiberius began to be a, bad Prince.

For, in the firft mentioned chapter, he fays, that tradition affirmed that he had been extruded from Rome by her impotency – and, i in the laft mentioned, he fays, that while fhe was alive, neither he nor Sejdnus could prefume to counteraft, her will – but that after her death, their tyranny was exceffiye. – Caeterum ex eo (namely the death, of his mother) praeruptam et urgens dominatio: nam incolumi Augufta, erat adhuc perfugium, *quia* Tiberio inyete- ratum erga matrem obfequium: neque Sejanus audebat auftoritati parentis anteire, *tune* velut franis exfoluti proruperunt.

Tacitus then, we find, not only contradifts the report of Dion concerning the time when this great change in the conduft of Tiberius took place, but alfo his own. Let us now then try to fatifiy ourfelves which of their reports Suetonius follows – and, in order to do this the more effeftually, let us hear what he fays of his conduft, from the fifth or fixth year of his monarchy, till that in which he retired to Capreae.

Chapter 26, he begins with faying, that when Tiberius was, on the death of Libo, and not as Dion fays, on that of Germanieus, releafed from the fear of competitors, he, at firft, behaved, not like a hypocrite who had been releafed from reftraint, but with the greateft civility and almoft like a private perfon. – Verum liberatus metu, civilem admodum inter initia ac paullo minus quam privatum egit. And when many of the greateft honors were ioted him, he, would accept but few, and thofe of the leaft value. – Ex plurimis maximifque honor ribus, prarter paucos et modicos non recepit. – Suetonius then pro-? ceeds to mention leveral inftances of the honors which he refufed. *In the zjth chapter,* Suetonius mentions feveral inftances of his antipathy to adulation. *In the z8tA,* he gives us two or three moft ftriking inftances of his regard for civil liberty – or rather of his tole*When Tiberius began to be a bad Prince.*

fation of the abufe of it. *In the 291/1,* he fays, that the manner in which he accofted perfons, of every defcription, almoft exceeded humanity – and, of this too he gives an inftance or two. *In the yth,* be fays, that he referred all cafes to the Senate, however triffing or important, whether relating to public or to his own private matters, to the army, or to foreign affairs: and he concludes it with this remarkable inftance of his confidence in the members of it – " he never " but once entered the Senate with any attendant – and that was when " lie was fo unwell as to be unable to go without aflvitance – and, then " no fooner had he entered, than he difmifled the very few that were " with him." – Nunquam curiam intravit nifi folus : leftica quondam introlatus aeger, comites a fe removit. *In the* 317?, he gives feveral inftances of motions that were carried againft him in the Senate. At which, fays Suetonius, he mewed no fort pf difpleafure. On one of thofe occafions, he obferves, that when a divifion took place, he went over to the minority and not a single fenator followed. – This chapter too he concludes with an account of the very condefcending manner in which he received foreign ambafTadors, fome of whom, it feems, the confuls took the liberty of fending for and opening their credentials. *In the %ld chapteri* he mentions feveral inftances more of his condefcenfion both with regard to the Senate and to private individuals of every clafs – that with regard to the Senate is of fo remarkable a nature that it muft not be overlooked, and becaufe it feems to be a pretty complete refutation of thofe who entertain doubts of the afta Pilati. It is this – Corripuit confulares exercitibus prapofitos, quod non de rebus geftis Senatui fcriberent – this he fays in the beginning of . this chapter – and he concludes it with as remarkable an inftance of the proteftion which he (as Tacitus, we have feen, alfo notices)i. I

When Tiberius began to be a bad Prince.

afforded the provinces – viz – when the prafefts of provinces advifed him to augment his tributes – his reply was – a good fhepherd would not think of flaying his fheep – Boni paftoris efle tondere pecus, non deglubere. Of this reply, it may not be amifs to obferve, both Jofephus and Dion take notice. Laftly – *In the* 33 *chapter,* he begins with telling us, not as Tacitus does, iv. i, that his adminiftration was, in the ninth year of his reign, all at once deteriorated – cum repente turbare fortuna ccepit: faevire ipfe aut faevientibus vires prae- bere – but, on the contrary, that he afted the prince very gradually, and for a long time varioufly, and he might, it feems, have added, till his. feceffion, for in all that interval he does not produce a fingle inftance of tyranny. – But let us attend to the whole of this chapter, as it appears to afford fome curious information.

Paulatim Principem exercuit, praftititque – by which it appears that, for a long time, he did not aflume the prince – and, that when he began to put on the real prince, he only did it by degrees – and,' fo it appears, by what follows – viz – etfi *varium dm* commodiorem tamen faepius, et ad publicas utilitates proniorem. By which it appears that when he did begin to aft the prince, he was, *for a long time,* rather a good than a bad one. – So he feems to fay, by what he again fub- joins – viz – Ac primo eatenus interveniebat ne quid perperam fieret. And what did he do better than this before he began to be a bad prince ? Itaque et conftitutiones quafdam Senatus refcidit. What ? Did he *therefore* refcind certain degrees of the Senate, becaufe they were con- feffedly wrong ? – And is this any inftance of his variety ? Is it not rather of that of the Senate ? – Et, continues he, Magiftratibus, pro tribunaK cognofcentibus plerumque fe offerebat confiliarjum, affi- debatque miftim, vel ex adverfo in parte primori: – a pretty ftrong proof that he was not, as Tacitus fays, iv. 57, afhamed to be feen – and that he was ftill only anxious that ftrift juftice fhould be*When Tiberius began to be a bad Prince.*

adminiftered – as appears more clearly by what he fays in the feqnel - - viz – et, fi quem reorum gratia elabi rumor eflet, fubitus aderat, judi- cefque aut e piano, aut e quaefitoris tribunal!, legum et religionis, et noxae de qua cognofcerent admonebat. And then he concludes the chapter with an inftance of his conce-rn for public morals – viz – atque etiam fi quae publicis moribus defidia aut mala confuetudine labarent, corrigenda fufcepit – which, Tacitus obferves, i. 54, he did not dare to attempt to correft in the beginning of his reign. – *In the* 34/$ *chaft.* he mentions fome inftances of his attention to public manners and public expences – and in the conclufion of it records an inftance of the great refpeft which the people were inclined to mew him. –

In the 35 *chapter,* he mentions feveral inftances of his attention to the private morals of individuals of every rank, both male and female. *In the* 36.' *chapter,* he mentions two or three inftances of his concern for the tranquillity of Rome by expelling feveral religious fefts who were fuppofed to entertain opinions hoftile to thofe of the Romans. – Laftly, *tn the yjth chap.',* he tells us how careful he was to preferve the peace of the public – by ftationing the military all over Italy in more numerous parties than ufual – and by collecting the praetorian guards at Rome – which, we are told by Dion, 1. 57, p. 619, D., he did in the tcth or nth year of his reign – how he punifhed fome popular tumults moft grievoufly – and took care to prevent them for the future – how he baniftied fome for making a riot in the theatre – and im- pvifoned others for life for having made a difturbance at Pollentia. – In the fame chapter, he alfo tells us how he abolimed all the afyla in the empire – and how he fupprefled, by his legates, fome *hoftilc commottons* – and that he never after undertook any expedition.

This is the account which Suetonius gives, us in thofe 12 chapters of the monarchical charafter of Tiberius, till very near the time of his feceffion. Suetonius then, we find, does hot give us the leaft *When Tiberius began to be a bad Prince.* encouragement to think that this fuppofed change, in the moral habits of Tiberius, happened in the 5th year of his reign, after the death of Germanicus, though it, as Dion fays, caufed fo great an aftonifh- mcnt, nor, in the 9th, when he firft employed Sejanus as his prime minifter, on the contrary, he, we have feen, gives us a moft excellent account of the former part of his reign, till, at leaft, the time when he collefted all the praetorian troops at Rome, if rot till after he loft his fon, and went into Campania. He expreffly fays, chapter 42, that he became totally vicious, not before he went to Capreae, nor before the difafter at Fidenae – but after that event – and not after the death of Sejanus, as Tacitus intimates, but before that event, when he was about 70 years of age. – Cseterum fecreti licentiam naftus, et quafi civitatis oculis remotus, *cunfla jlmul* vitia male *dlu* diffimula"ra *tandem* profudit. Suetonius moreover fays, chapter 61, that, *after* Ttberius became fo totally vicious he alfo became cruel. – Mox in omne genus crudelitatis erupit, nunquam deficiente materia: but againft whom principally did he exercife his vengeance ? – fcil – cutn primo matris, deinde nepotum et nurus, poftremo Sejani familiares atque etiam notos perfequeretur. Poft cujus interitum vel *favijfimus* exftitit. '

On reconfidering all that thofe writers fay of this furprifing change in the habits of Tiberius, what do we find but felf-contradiftions and contradiftions of each other ? And, fo many that we feem to have reafon enough to doubt whether any fuch change took place in him at all.

Tacitus fays, vi. 30, that accufers were, when opportunity offered, . punifhed. – And that Tiberius would not attempt to moleft Lentulus Gaetulicus, though a relative of Sejanus, becaufe he was aware that . his government flood by *fame rather than by force* – magifque fama

When Tiberius began to be a bad Prince.

quam vi, ftare res fuas. And again, 45, that when a great part of Rome was deftroyed, in the laft year of his reign, he, once more, obtained, from all ranks of people, the greateft honors for his beneficence to the fufferers.

Dion, besides saying, as we have seen, that Tiberius had very many if not most virtues to the last, says also, I. 58, p. 633, A., that he did not attempt to molest Sejanus the prsetor, though he had, the year after the death of his brother, dared to insult him publicly. And in the end of the next page, he says, that Tiberius, in the following year, commanded all the most aftive of the accufers to be put to death in one day. Now if Tiberius had been fo cruel a tyrant would L. Sejanus have dared to infult him publicly, and, but the year after the death of his brother.

Josephus, A. xvii, gives the fulleft account of any, of the manner in which he spent three or four of his last years at Capreae. And though he says that he was fond of detaining accused persons a long while in prison, yet he says nothing of his extreme vicioufnefs.

Juvenal describes his residence at Capreae as remarkable only for his inaftivity, and his inattention to bufinefs, and his being furrounded by a party of Chaldaeans – he likewife says nothing of his extreme vicioufnefs.

Paterculus, who ferved under him nine fucceffive years, and wrote the-hiftory of the firft fixteen years of his reign, and addrefled it to one of the then confuls, says, ii. 126, that he was the moft excellent,' in every refpeft, of all princes. So admirable, indeed, is the defcrip- tion which he gives of his reign during that period, that it has been confidered by the conduftors of one of our principal feminaries of cJaflRc learning as merely adulatory, though both Tacitus and Sueto*When Tiberius began to be a bad Prince.*

nius fay nearly the fame of him – the former, iv. 6, in the ninth year of his reign, and the latter in the 12 chapters above referred to, no one knows how much later/

Valerius Maximus, who wrote after the death of Sejanus, and dedicated his work, which is all through of a religious and moral tendency, to Tiberius, addrefles him, in the preface, as the patron of virtue and the enemy of vice – cujus cselefti providentia, virtutes de quibus difturus fum benignimme foventur: vitia feveriffime vindicantur. – And, ix. u, he says, both the Gods and men were, as foon as they knew of the treachery of Sejanus, ready to crufh him. Itaque, fays he, flat pax, valent leges, fincerus privati ac publici officii tenor fefvatur – which, furely, feems to imply that fuch had been the ftate of things before.

Seneca, the elder, finds not the leaft fault with the conduft of Tiberius in any part of his works. On the contrary, he, in one or two places, fpeaks of him as a pattern of filial piety, of patiently enduring the greateft affliftions, and, as being one of the greateft of men, on whom nature had beftowed more good qualities than he could eafily enumerate. In his Confol. ad Marc, (for moft certainly that Confol. was written by him, and not, as Lipfius fays, by his fon, nor, as he alfo fays, after the death of Tiberius, but juft before that of Livia, when his fon was not arrived at manhood,) he propofes the example of the moft eminent men to her, and laft of all, that of *Tiberius,* not as delighting in human mifery, (for, it feems, by what he fays, chapter xix, that at that time Marcia had not witnefled any public calamity,) but of patient fortitude under the lofs of relatives. – Tiberius Caefar, et quern genuerat, et quern adoptaverat, amifit: tpfe tamen pro roftris laudavit filium, ftetitque in confpeftu pofito corpore, interjefto tantummodo velamento, quod pontificis oculos a

When Tiberius began to be a bad Prince.

funere arceret, et, flente poputo romano, non flexit vultum: expe- riendum fe dedit Sejano, ad latus ftanti, quam patienter poffet fuos perdere. Videfne quanta copia virorum maximorum fit, quos non excepit hie omnia profternens cafus ? In quos tot animi bona, tot ornamenta publice privatimque congefta erant ? Thus Seneca, the elder, fpeaks of Tiberius, even to Marcia – of Sejanus, he, in the fame work, fpeaks of his having caufed Cordus, her father, to be perfecuted, not for extolling, as Tacitus fays, Brutus and Caffius as the laft of Romans, but for fpeaking difrefpeftfully of himfelf, and as having fed his dogs with *human blood:* but though he fpeaks thus of him, yet he does not fay that Tiberius was the caufe of it – or, that he was the caufe of that vaft power of Sejanus, he fays, that Sejanus had ufurp- ed it – Sejanum in cervices noftros nee imponi quidem fed afcendere.

SENECA, the younger, too, though he, De Benef, 1. iii, 26, fpeaks of the infamous praftice of accufing – yet he does not fay that Tiberius encouraged it. He too, on the contrary, fays, that Sejanus, was the enfetter – and, Ep. xxi, that Tiberius was great while he lived – and, Apocol., that he followed Auguftus to the manfion of the Gods.

PHILO, ad C. p. 783, demands of the Egyptians, who had been the worfhippers of Caius, why they had not worfhipped Tiberius, the predeceflbr of Caius, who, during the whole courfe of his monarchy, had enjoyed fuch a peace as had never before been known, (the feveral bleffings and extent of which he enumerates p. 769.) Was it, iays hes becaufe l'iberius was inferior in erudition ? Who, replies he, among all the celebrated geniufes of his time – *rut* Xt' *avm awto-ntrv* – was more prudent or more rational – . *oytxunfos.* – Was it, fays he, becaufe Tiber:as was, in years, inferior to Caius? – What king or emperor prev? old more honorably ? – Even in his youth, he was, fays

When Tiberius began to be a bad Prince.

he, for his difcernmcnt called *the fage* – and yet, fubjoins Philo, this fo great and fo excellent a prince has been neglefted by you. And, afterwards, in the fame work, p. 799, Philo, reprefents Agrippa, who refided at Capreae with Tiberius during the laft three years of his life, and who was imprifoned by Tiberius, as fpeaking of the conduft of Tiberius towards the Jews, even to Caius, as having been but a continuation of that of Auguftui.

CLEMENS, of Rome, too, who, in feveral of his works, fays, that he was related to Tiberius, fays alfo, Kecog. x. 55, and again, in his account of the proceedings of Peter, 13$, that he, after the Gofpel had been preached to Gentiles, made, both at Rome and in the provinces, inquifition for the maleficent, for the purpofe of punifhing them, even with death – and that he ordered Simon, the adverfary of the Apoftles, to be apprehended. And, de G. P. 143, he even fays, that this fame unfeeling tyrant, fhed tears abundantly – *Qifpus sxam* – at feeing again Fauftus and Mathilda.

The charafter of Tiberius then was, by the account of even Tacitus, Suetonius, and Dion, moft excellent till he was 56 years old, and his government was, by the evidence of the fame writers, alfo, moft excellent for many years of his monarchy, and though they fay, that it was intolerably bad afterwards, yet they cannot agree about the time when it began to be fo very bad. Suetonius fays, that it was not extremely bad for a long time – that is – till he went to Capreae. And Tacitus fays, vi, that it was a mixture of good and bad while his mother lived – that it ftood almoft to the laft by fame rather than by force. And Dion fays, 1. 58, that it always had a great mixture of good. But by the account of thofe who lived under it, not only Romans, and the beft of Romans, but Jews, and Chriftians, it was always moft excellent.

When Tiberius began to be a bad Prince.

Now as fo many and fo very refpeftable cotemporary writers, of different religions, declare, with one confent, that the whole reign of Tiberius, was fo very excellent – and even Tacitus fays, that his government, in the 2tft year of his reign, flood more by fame than by force ; – and – that he was, but about fix months before he died, thanked, by all ranks of people, for his beneficence to the fufferers by fire at Rome; – and, as Suetonius too, fays, that he was buried moft magnificently, at the public expence, and praifed by Caius with many tears – how can any one expeft to be believed who dares /to aflert that the confuls, in any fuccedding reign, confidered him as unworthy of a place in the line of Roman emperors ? And yet Dion, we find, 1. 59, p. 646, C., dared to aflert it – and moreover, 1. 60, p. 667, D., that he continued to be confidered fo from the firft of Caius, u. c. 791, till his own time. The evidence of the Senecas alone would, one would think, have kept him from aflerting it – or – that of Suetonius concerning Caius and Claudius – for of the former, he fays, 30, that he vindicated the cruelty of Tiberius to the Senate, on the fcore that they were the caufe of it – and of the latter, he fays, v. u, that he erefted the marble arch near Pompey's Theatre, which the Senate had, on fome great occafion, voted to him.

8

SECTION 8

CHAPTER VII.
Why Tiberius left Rome, and why he went to Capreee.

J IBERIUS, we are told by Tacitus, iv. 57, went, in the conful- ftiip of Cn. Lentulus and C. Calvifius, and in the 12th year of his reign, and the 68th year of his age, (which, Tacitus obferves, iii 59, was acknowledged, four years before, to have been lefs qualifted for bufinefs than it had been,) from Rome into Campania, for, as both he ' and Suetonius fay, the pretended purpofe of dedicating two temples, the one at Capua, and the other at Nola, but as Tacitus alone fays, with a long formed defign of livfng at a diftance from Rome. – Inter quae *dm* meditato, prolatoque faepius confilio, tandem, &c.; fed certus procul ab urbe degere. – /This, it may not be amifs to obferve, Tacitus fays, was the fecond time he went from Rome into Campania, and, with the fame defign. – He, fays Tacitus, A. iii. 31, went thither about five years before – viz – in the beginning of u. c. 774, when he and his fon Drufus were confuls – by degrees meditating a long and continued abfence – longam et continuam abfentiam paulatim medi- tans. – At that time, he remained there till the following year, when Ms mother was taken fuddenly ill, and, he was obliged to return in

Why Tiberius left Rome, and why he went to Caprea.

THE HISTORY OF THAT INIMITABLE MONARCH TIBERIUS. John Rendle hafte. – The reafon of his going into Campania this firft time, was, fays Tacitus, not to leave Rome for ever, (though, he fays, he then had it in contemplation,) but either to re-eftablifh his health, or, to leave the management of affairs to Drufus. But can either of thofe reafons have been the right one ? – Had Tiberius then been ill ?- – Suetonius fays, iii. 68, that he was always moft remarkably well – Valetudine profperrima ufus eft – and efpecially after he became emperor – tempore quidem principatus, pene toto, prope illaefa. – -And, as to the other reafon, does not Tacitus himfelf fay, that Drufus was, in that year, extremely ill ? – And, that Tiberius, though worn out with age, was obliged to give, as ufual, direftions about every thing – efpecially about the revolt in Africa, under-Tacfarinas, and that in Gaul, under Sacrovir, and that in Belguim, under Julius Florus. – And does he not fay, c. 44, that Tiberius was blamed, by difcontented perfons, for permitting accufers to occupy all his attention, when affairs of fuch moment demanded it moft imperioufly ? – Incre- pabantque Tiberium, quod in tanto rerum motu, libellis accufatorum infumeret operam. – And does he not again fay, c. 52, 56, that Tiberius was, in the following year, when every thing was quiet, and a law was propofed to reftrain luxurious living – and by the means of informers, confulted on that occafion – and – that he then obtained univerfal applaufe for having objefted to the means ofenforcing. it – Tiberius faivia moderationis parta, quod ingruentes accufatores repref- ferat. – Why then, all this confidered, fhould we fuppofe that Tiberius left Rome, either for the fake of his health, or, to leave the management of public affairs to Drufus ?

How is it that Tacitus has given so different an account of the conduct of Tiberius towards accusers in so short a time? – Is it at all likely that any prince would, in the course of a year, be censured for encouraging informers, and applauded for discouraging them.

Why Tiberius left Some, and why lie went to Capreee.

Tiberius however, as Tacitus, we have feen, fays, went into Campania both in the year 774 and 779 with the fame fixed defign – viz – to live continually at a diftance from Rome – but if fuch was his intention, in the laft mentioned year, where was the propriety of telling us that the aftrologers foretold that he would never return? And if he had fo long made up his mind on that point, where was the neceffity of pretending that he was only going to dedicate temples ? – And if he gave out that he was only going to Capua and Nola to dedicate temples, where was the neceffity of publifhing, as Tacitus fays, iv. 67, an edift forbidding any one to come near him, and to place fentinels, here and there, on the road to keep off the people ? – Had not the people of Campania feen enough of him, when he fpent more than a year with them about four or five years before ?

Tacitus, befides telling us, iii. 31, that fuch had been his fixed' defign feveral years before, and even the year before his mother was fo alarmingly ill – and, iv. 58, that he was, eleven years, voluntarily abfent from Rome, and, iii. 59, that his age was, four years before, worn out with labour. – -Befides telling us all this, Tacitus who, it feems, was neither fatisfied with the reafon affigned by *mojl writers* for his leaving Rome and continuing to remove from place to place in Campania, for about two years, and then retiring to Capreae, and refiding in folitude nine years more – nor with that affigned by *general tradition* – nor with that affigned by *the few* – (for they all feem to have thought that the fame motive which determined him to take the firft ftep, alfo determined him to take the other,) – fets himfelf, A. iv. 57, to affign the real motive which, he flatters himfelf, may have been this – viz – to conceal his cruelty and luft – fevitiam ac libidinem. – But though this may have been the reafon of his feceffion to Capreae, is it likely, to have been that for his traverfing Campania

Why Tiberius left Rome, and why he went to Caprea.

fo long ? – And in company with fo many men of learning ? – Could he, during his peregrination in Campania, have concealed either of thofe vices? – What occafion had he, who, ten years before, had introduced the graviffimum exitium into Rome, who had then been publicly fatyrized for his cruelty, and who had, two years before, ilfued cruel mandates – feva jufla – to conceal his cruelty ? – And by what luft could a man, who had been twice married and had grandchildren, be fuppofed to have been aftuated ? – Does not the former part of this double infinuation feem to militate againft the latter ? – If he was fo cruel a tyrant, would he, at the age of 70, have been afhamed of his vices? – Was he not, as Tacitus himfelf fays, iii. 10, valid in defpifing rumors – Contra Tiberium fpernandis rumoribus validum. – And was he not, as he again fays, vi. 38, a defpifer of his own infamy – Contemptor *fuae* infamiae ? Not only Tacitus fays fo, but Suetonius and Dion too. Suetonius, in two places – viz – iii. 28, 66. – In the firft mentioned chapter, he fays – Sed adverfus convitia malofque rumores et famofa de fe ac fuis carmina firmus ac patiens fubinde jaftahat – In civitate libera linguam mentemque Hbe- ras efle debere. – In the other, he fays – nonnunquam eadem Contem- neret, et proferret ultro atque vulgaret. – Dion, 1. 57, p. 618, fays the fame as Suetonius does in the chapter laft quoted – and, 1. 58, p. 633, B., he fays, that Sejanus, the praetor, had the audacity, after the death of his brother, to expofe the baldnefs of Tiberius, and that he took no notice of it. – If he was fo vicious why did the Romans perfift in worfhiping him, in fpite of his edift to the contrary? – Suetonius, we have feen, in the laft chap., fays, c. 42, that he was not noto- rioufly vicious before he went to Capreae, but, after the fall of the Amphitheatre at Fidenae – that is – after he became a Chriftian. – And cotemporary writers, Jews, Romans, and Chriftians, we have alfo feen, in the fame chapter, fay that he never was vicious.

Why Tiberius left Rome, and why he went to Capreoe.

But as the reafon affigned by Tacitus as being, in his opinion, preferable to either of the others, is not at all likely to have been the true reafon. – Let us proceed to examine the other three which he rejefts, for the purpofe of fatisfying ourfelves whether any of them be fo probable as to render all enquiry on this fubjeft ufelefs.

Firft, he fays, that *lnofl authors* had left it on record, that Tiberius had been prevailed on to leave Rome by the artifice of Sejanus, and, in order that he might be able to get the management of the government into his own hands – the credibility of which report he himfelf combats, and with the greateft fuccefs, by obferving that Tiberius continued a voluntary exile fix years after he had caufed Sejanus to be put to death. – This fingle objeftion he thought quite fufficient to fet afide the report of moft of his biographical predeceflprs. – But this objeftion is not the only one which he makes to their report, nor the leaft forcible. – He, both before and after this chapter, has, without intending it, furnimed us with feveral others equally good. – A. iii. 31, he, we have feen, fays, that Tiberius had, while his -fon Drufus was alive, and two or three years before he thought of employing Sejanus, by degrees meditated a long and continued abfence. – In the firft chap, of this fame book, he fays, that Sejanus was no match for Tiberius in craft, or, rather he fhould have faid, in wifdom, or, the right application of knowledge – non tam folertia (quippe iifdem artibus viftus erat.) – In the 39th and 40th he relates a remarkable inflance of it – he there fays, that Tiberius, but the year before he left Rome, on being folicited by Sejanus to grant him permiffion to marry Livilla, the widow of his deccafed fon, contrived, in the moft exquifite and delicate manner, to evade his requeft, and to convince him of the vanity and abfurdity of his pretenfions. – In the 58th chapter, he fays, that Tiberius, when he left Rome, took Sejanus with him as one of

Why Tiberius left Rome, and why he went to Caprea.

his chofen companions, and detained him all the while he was in Campania – and that he alfo took him to Capreae, where he alfo detained him fo long, that the Senate, at laft, found themfelves obliged, notwithflanding the mother of Tiberius was then alive, to petition, both of them, repeatedly, to return – and, finding all their petitions difregarded, they thought it neceflary for them to go, in a body, to the very coaft of Campania, to intreat them to return, if not, merely to get a fight of them. – Which, furely, feems to imply not only that Sejanus, though, by fuppofition, the direftor of every thing, would not go near them, but that Tiberius, as well as Sejanus, was confidered, by the Senate, as not lefs the direftor of every thing – and – that he alfo would not go to Rome. – Which, furely, feems to imply further that fomething of no common import muft have then happened at Rome – and, fomething, as Tacitus fays, iv. 74, like a moft extraordinary commotion. – And what, but the preaching of Chrift, could have then happened to caufe fuch diftraftion ?

Other writers confirm what Tacitus here fays of this matter.

Philo fays, that Tiberius, a little before the death of Sejanus, at his inftigation, or – as Jofephus fays, at the complaint of Satuniinus, againft the pretended doftors, expelled the Jews from Rome.

Suetonius fays, of Tiberius, iii. 66, that he, kept Sejanus at Caprea e till juft-ibefore he was conful, and that he at laft effecled his fubver- $on (who, he had before faid chapter 55, was one of his privy coun- fellors,) by artifice and cunning – aftu et dolo fubvertit – and that feveral others of his privy counfellors were then furviving.

Dion fays, 1. 58, p. 621, D. that Tiberius was praifed, in the i5th year of his reign, for not neglefting public bufinefs

Why Tiberius left Rome, and why he went to Caprea.

ttrxtteo-xoTts on rut rut X. iiiui ioihiktixs St *ron amurytro,* – And, again, in the next page, C., that many deputies were, in the next year, fent, by the Senate, to him, and, among the reft, Gallus. – And, again, 1. 59, p. 643, C., that he would never fuffer others to govern' him in the fame manner as Caius did.- – *TtGtftot t/. tv yaf avms n vff tuu (nrnftreta*

rotf XXoi$ *trfos yt To avra jii-nft. x tftTO.*

Paterculus fajs, ii. 127, 128, that Sejanus was, till the xvi year of Tiberius, nothing more than an affiftant. – C. 127, he fays – fingu- larem principalium onerum adjutorem in omnia habuit atque habet. C. t48, he fays – ad juvanda vero onera principis, Sejanum protulit. Paterculus alfo defcribes him as being, at that time, very faithful and unatfuming – ipfum vero laboris ac fidei capaciffimum – nihil fibi vindicantem.

Jofephus fays, A. xviii. 4, 3, that Tiberius, in that year, gave orders for every tiling.

V. Maximus fays, ix. n, that Sejanus attempted to take the reins of government from Tiberius by force – Tu videlicet efferatae barbariae immanitate truculentior habenas romani imperii, quas princeps, parenfque nofter falutari dextera continet, capere potuifti?

Seneca, Confol. ad Marciam xxii, feems to intimate the fame thing – Sejanum in cervices noflros nee imponi quidem fed afcende.

Now as cotemporary and latter writers, friends and foes, with one confent, tell us that Tiberius did not omit to tranfaft public bufinefs while at Capreae, why does Tacitus, fo confidently tell us that moft writers had left it on record that Tiberius had been prevailed on by Sejanus to leave Rome and the management of every thing to him.

Another reafon which, Tacitus fays, *feme perfens* affigncd for hts retirement was, a *conftitufnejs* of his perfonal defedts – Erant qui ere-

Why Tiberius left Rome, and -why he went to Capreee.

derent in feneftute quoque corporis habitum pudori fuifle – quippe, fays he, (and it particularly deferves to be noticed, becaufe it feems to intimate that he admitted that it might, after all, be the true reafon) – praegrandis illi et incurva proceritas, nudus capillo vertex, ulcerofa facies et plerumquc medicaminibus interftinfta. – And, as a fort of proof, he adds – et Rhodi fecreto, vitare coetus, recondere voluptates infuerat. – But how is this at all reconcileable with what Paterculus and Suetonius fay of him ? – Paterculus fays, ii. 94 – -Tiberius Claudius Nero juvenis genere, forma, celfitudine corporis inftruftiffimus. – Again, chapter 97, he fays – Nam pulchritudo corporis (Drufi. fcil.) proxima fraternae. – Suetonius, we find, agrees with Paterculus on this point, and, chap. 68, defcribes his perfon, fo particularly, that any one may fancy his figure to have been very majeftic – Corpore fuit amplo atque robufto: ftatura quae juftam excederet. – Latus ab humen's et peftore: caeteris quoque membris ufque ad imos pedes aequalis ej: congruens, &c. – And is this a form for any man of 70, who had never experienced any ill health, to be afhamed of? – Suetonius fays this of his perfon – he next proceeds to defcribe his countenance and his features – Colore erat candido, capillo pone pccipitium fummif- fiore, ut cervicem etiam obtegeret: quod gentile in illo videbatur. – Facie honefta, in qua tamen crebri et fubtiles tumores cum praegran dibus oculis, &c. – Laftly, he fpeaks of his mien and manner of con- verfation – Incedebat cervice rigida et obftipa et addu6to fere vultu, plerumque tacitus.

Such is the account which Paterculus and Suetonius give of the perfon of this moft excellent monarch. – How different from that of Tacitus.

Why Tiberius left Rome, and why he went to Capreoe.

But had his perfonal defefts been as remarkable, as Tacitus would have it thought, yet why fhould we be expefted to believe that any veteran defpot, and efpecially one who was fo cruel as Tacitus re- prefents this to have been, would have been fo fond of concealing them from the eye of the world as to leave the feat of his government for that purpofe ? – Does not his public appearance in Campania, at leaft, at the dedication of the temples, in two of the rnoft populous towns in that diftrift, fhew the futility of that fuppofition ? – Had the people of Rome the leaft fufpicion that fuch was his motive, would they, either when the Amphitheatre, at Fidenae, fell, or when a great part of Rome was burnt, have importuned him to return, and, as Suetonius fays, from Capreae ? – And would he, if that had been the cafe, have fo readily returned to affift the fufferers, and have made himfelf fo very acceffible to people of all ranks? – Or would the Senate, &c. have prefumed to requeft him to return to Rome – and, to go to 'the coaft of Campania, for the purpofe of importuning him to favor them with an interview ? – This however Tacitus himfelf fays, iv. 74, they did. – Dion alfo fays, that A. Callus, the year after, defired to be one of the delegates whom the Senate fent to him. Juvenal fpeaks of his being furrounded by a company of Chaldoeans. – Jofephus fays, that Agrippa fpent two or three years with him at Capreae, and that he went to Tufculanum. – And laftly, Suetonius fays, chapter 72, that he was, juft before his death, prefent at the military fports at Circeii, and, in the fame chapter, that he ufed to fee much company.

The *loft* reafon which Tacitus fays was affigned for his leaving Rome, is this – that he could not bear the thought of his mother's ufurping a paramount authority in the direftion of public affairs, and, that he could not make her defift – nee depellere potc-

Why Tiberius left Rome, and why he went to Caprets.

rat. – This, Tacitus obferves, he had by *tradition* – that is – by common report. – But how is it that common report appears to have con- tradifted that of moft writers ? – *Mojl records,* Tacitus, we have feen, informs us, faid that the caufe of his retirement was the artifice of Seja- nus. – And now he fays, that *tradition* faid that the caufe of it was the intolerable arrogance of his mother, whofe age was, as he himfelf obr ferved of it, iv. 8, three or four years before, extreme – that is – as Dion fays, 1. 58, p. 621, C., at the time when her fon retired, 83. – If this laft be the true caufe,. the firft cannot have been the true caufe, for this reafon as well as for that before affigned by him – viz – that Tiberius remained at Capreae (ik years after the death of Sejanus – unlefs he would have us to think that Sejanus could do no more under Livia, than he could under Tiberius, which, furely, would feem to imply that there was no great occafion for contriving to get Tiberius out of the way – that he, however, could do no more under Livia than under Tiberius – he, we find, v. 4, denies – for he there fays – Neque Sejanus audebat auftoritati parentis anteire. – And this refpeftful diftance, he, we find, fays, Sejanus obferved till the death of Livia, or two

years after Tiberius feceded.

But let us examine this laft reafon which Tacitus fays tradition affigned for the feceffion of Tiberius, independently of the channel through which he derived it.

Dion who, I. 57, p. 610, B., admit! that tradition, said that Tiberius retired *to Caprea:,* on account of some disagreement with his mother, then, at least, 84, is so far from saying that she directed every thing, that he, immediately before, says, that Tiberius would not suffer her to do any one thing–

Y. xi riM rat pn Sn/xoo-iiiv *itixironrayH avtni aina%ii.* – And, I. 58, p. 621, D., he says – KXiTTip ro TiGipiot ivainwins, on This rut Kvhu ihoixsyEwr a? E Tots

Why Tiberius left Rome, and why he went to Capreas.

Did not Tacitus fee that the only argument which he produced againft the fuppofition that Sejanus contrived to get Tiberius out of the way, is, when applied to the prefent cafe, a little more forcible ? If his continuance at Capreae more than five years after the death of Sejanus be any thing like a proof that Sejanus was not the caufe of his-retiring, why mould not his continuance there more than nine years after the death of his mother be confidered as fomething like aftronger proof that he did not remove from Rome on her account? – This con- fideration Tacitus has unaccountably contrived to overlook. – That Tacitus himfelf could not have believed this pretended tradition is very clear from what he fays of the occurrences which happened during the two or three years between his feceffion and the death of his mother. – For, firft he fays, that the people of Rome complained in their diftrefs of his having left them – feralemque annum ferebant, et ominibus adverfis fufceptum principi confilium abfentiae – which, furely, feems to imply that the feceffion of Tiberius was voluntary – as Tacitus himfelf aflerts, iv. 58 – libens patria careret – though, by the remark which he fubjoins, he himfelf feems to have thought that it was merely accidental. – He alfo fays, that both the Senate and people thanked him for his beneficence on that occafion. – Again, he tells us, that the Senate, in the cafe of Varus, did not think ofcon- fulting Livia how to proceed, but agreed to wait the return of Tibe - rius – and, becaufe he was, the *only* fuffuge, for the time, from the impending evils. – Again, he complains of his not having paid the leaft attention to the revolt of the Frifii, which, furely, implies that he confidered him as ftill the direftor of military proceedings. – Laftly, he fays, that the Senate petitioned him, again and again, to return, before they went, in a body, to wait on him, on the coaft of Campania, for the purpofe of requefting an interview.

Why Tiberius left Rome, and why he went to Capreee.

i In fhort – from what Tacitus fays of this matter, it appears almoft incredible that there could have been fuch a tradition.

Let us now proceed to enquire what Suetonius fays was the caufe of his retiring from Rome.

He, chapter 39, fays, pofitively, that the caufe of his going into Campania was the lofs of his fons – Sed orbatus utroque filio feceflum Campaniae petiit. – The laft of whom – viz – Drufus, it fhould be ob- ferved, died three years before, and therefore fome may be inclined to think it ftrange that his grief for the lofs of him mould have continued fo long: but to thofe who know what Jofephus fays, of his grief for the lofs of his fon, it cannot appear fo. – Again, he fays, 51, not as Tacitus does, that it was generally thought that his difagree- ment with his fuperannuated mother was the chief caufe of it, but, *ikiztfome* might think fo – ut quidam putent inter cauflas feceflus hanc ei vel pracipuam fuuTe – but, if he grieved fo much and fo long for the lofs of his only fon, can it be likely that he would difagree with his fuperannuated mother? – But does he agree with Tacitus as to the caufe of their difagreement ? – By no means. So far is he from faying that Livia ever obtained fuch an afcendancy over her fon, as to take from him the management of public concerns, that he, on the contrary, fays, c. 50, that Tiberius permitted her to do fcarcely any thing at all – and that he ufed to tell her often to mind her own concerns, and to leave ftate matters alone. – How then can Livia be fuppofed to have forced him, by her interference, to retire ? – Would not any one be inclined to fuppofe from this that he managed every thing moft arbitrarily, and that me had the greateft reafon to retire ? – Suetonius proceeds, in the next chapter, to point out the very inftance, which, it was pretended – ut ferunt – caufed the breach between them – Dehinc ad fimultatem nfque proceffit, hac, ut ferunt, de cauffa – *Why Tiberius left Rome, and why he went to Caprete.*

fcil. – Ihe wifhed to have a certain libertine made a judge, and, therefore, *often entreated* her fon – inftabat faepius – to grant her requeft – at lafl, he, on condition that a memorandum fhould be entered in the roll, oppofite the perfon's name, purporting that his mother had forced him to confent, granted her requeft. – Whether it was accordingly done, Suetonius does not fay – but this he fays, that me was *to* much offended at this reply, that fhe inftantly went to her clofet and produced certain papers of Auguftus, which fhe had always kept concealed, complaining of his morofenefs and intolerance. – This, fays Suetonius, he took fo much amifs, that, as fome *may* think – ut quidam putent – it was the chief caufe, not of Livia's retiring from court, but of his retiring from Rome.

So contradiftory is the evidence of Tacitus and Suetonius concerning the interference of Livia in political matters. – Let us proceed to enquire with whom Paterculus feems to agree.

Paterculus, H. 127, fays, of the government of Tiberius till the 16th year of his reign, that Sejanus was and is the flngular affiftant of all his princely burdens – fingularem principalium onerum adjutorem in omnia habuit atque habet. – And of Livia he fays, chapter 130 – Cujus temporis aegritudinem auxit amifla mater eminentiffima, et per omnia Deis quam hominibus, fimilior femina; *cujus potentlam nemo fenfit,* nifi aut levatione periculi aut acceffione dignitatis.

In fhort – to reprefent the greateft general that ever commanded an army, who militated in almoft every part of the empire, and who never fuffered a defeat, who, when he fucceeded Auguftus, took care, as Tacitus fays, i. 7, to have it undei flood that he was not indebted either to him or to his mother for his advancement, but only to the . free choice of the Roman people, who, at the very beginningvof his

Why Tiberius left Rome, and why he went to Caprete.

reign, refufed her, as Tacitus fays, i. 14, the honor of a fingle liftor, and afterwards the titles which the Senate voted her, who, during twelve years, would not fuffer her to interfere in any political matter, and when Ihe only requefted him t'o make a certain perfon a judge, would not, for a long time, confent, and then only on condition that" – *exterted by Livia* – was entered in the margin of the roll oppofite his name – to reprefent fuch an one as driven from the feat of his government, when he was near 70 years of age, by his mother, who was' then not lefs than 84, is fuch a piece of abfurdity, as could not be expefted from any hiftorian – not even from one who wrote for the fole purpofe of calumniating the beft of charafters.

We have now paid due attention to each of thofe four reafons affigned by this, as he has been, by fuppofed fcavans, flyled, prince of hiftorians, for the feceffion of this prince of princes, and we have found every one of them to be fuch as no honeft hiftorian would have thought of affigning. – Thejfr/?, which, he himfelf fays, *mojl writers* confidered as the true one, he himfelf rejefts, and, for a very good reafon. – And the laft which he mentions as traditional he therefore ought a fortiori to rejeft. – The *fccond* evidently confifts of two con- tradiftory parts. – And the *third* is flatly contradifted not only by Paterculus and Suetonius but even by Tacitus himfelf.

Let us then endeavour to difcover a reafon that has, at leaft, the appearance of a probability.

If aH this was true, why do we read of the following legend and inscription : –

Tristanus T. 1, p. 123, JVLIA. AVGUSTA. GENETRtX. ORBtS.

Crater, p. tcxxxiv. 2, JULI. E. AVG. DIVI. F. MATRI. TI. CLARIS. AUG. PRINCIPIS. ET. CONSERVATORIS.

Why Tiberius left Rome, and why he went to Capreee.

Suetonius, we have obferved, fays, iii. 39, that after Tiberius had loft his two fons, Germanicus and Drufus, (and, he, it feems, might have faid, as Tacitus has faid, iv. 15, after he had alfo loft one of the twin fons of Drufus – and moreover, his old friends Lucilius Longus, Qnirinus, and Cn. Lentulus – the former of whom died u. c. 776, Tib. 10, and the latter 778, Tib. 12,) he fought retirement in Campania. – Before he left Rome, he, as both of thofe hiftorians fay, publifhed an *edifl*, forbidding any one, as Tacitus fays, to difturb his *quiet* – or, as Suetonius fays, to *falute him*. – And he not only pub- limed an edift for the above mentioned purpofe, but he, as they both fay too, ftationed guards to prevent the people of the feveral towns through which he intended to pafs from coming near him, which (by the bye) feems pretty clearly to intimate that he expected from them no little attention, notwithftanding the edift – if not that he was unwell, either in body or mind. – In body, Suetonius tells us, iii. 68, he never was unwell. – Was then his mind difordered? – If it was, what but grief for the lofs of relatives and friends could have made him take this *peregrination,* for fo Suetonius calls it. – And that it was fo appears from what Tacitus fays, iv. 58, of his attendants – viz – that they were few, and, that they were men of learning and felefted for the fake of their converfation – quorum fermonibus levaretur – among: whom, he fays, was Cocceius Nerva, who; he alfo fays, vi. 26, was the conftant companion of the prince, and, well /killed in all law, human and *divine* – continuus Principis, omnis divini humanique juris fciens. – With this felelt learned party he ufed fometimes to amufe himfelf in grottos – neglefting to dedicate the temples till nearly the end of the following year – viz – 780, or the beginning of his I4th

If the people thought he was so very vicious and tyrannical, and, that he would die soon, what necessity could there have been either for the edict or for the guards to keep people from paying thajr respects (o him?

Why Tiberius left Rome, and why he went to Capreoe.

year. – In the courfe of which year of Rome three remarkable events, as Tacitus fays, happened – viz – the fall of the Amphitheatre at Fidenae – the fire on MounfCcelius – and, the profecution of V. Quinc- tilius, a relative of Caefar. – But did thofe three events really happen before Tiberius went to Capreae ? – Does not Suetonius tell us ex- preffly that the firft of thofe events happened after he went thither? – And muft not the other two of courfe? – However by what this writer fays of his extremely kind behavior towards the diftrefTed fufferers at Fidenae – and, by what the other fays, of the Senate having agreed to defer paffing fentence on V. Quinftilius till he fhould return, his malady, whatever it was, feems, for the prefent, to have left him: but, fays Tacitus, v. 4, and Paterculus, in the end of his hiftory, a relapfe foon followed, and his diforder was much worfe than before.

Grief then for the lofs of his only fon and of two or three very old friends feems to have been the only caufe of his retiring from Rome and remaining fo long in Campania – that is – from the year 779 to nearly the end of 780, if not till 781, in which laft mentioned year, he was 70, and Chrift was, rather early in that year, firft preached at Rome. – If then grief was his complaint, and it was, when the difafter at Fidenae happened, fo far abated that the Senate began to expeft his return when V. Quinftilius, his kinfman, was accufed, and in hopes that he would counteraft the then enormoufly increafing prevalence

of accufers, why did he, inftead of returning, withdraw to Caprene, and though requefted, by the Senate, again and again, to return, in order to counteraft the caufe of the internal alarm, refufe to comply with their requefts, and even to confens to an interview with them on the coaft of Campania ? – In that year, we have feen, Chrift fuffered, and, as Clemens, of Rome, fays, in the fpring of that year his faith

Why Tiberius left Rome, and why he went to Caprettt.

began to be preached at Rome, and, as both Tacitus and Tertullian fay, under the patronage of Tiberius, and, as the fame two writers fay, great oppofition was made to it, and, of courfe to Tiberias, both by a majority of the Senate and of the people – how, then as all this happened in the courfe of the year 781, are we to be fure that Tiberius may not have retired for perfonal fafety ? – Of this, at leaft, we feem to be pretty well allured, and even by Tacitus, that Tiberius, who ufed, without any attendant, to enter the Senate, then, for the firft time, complained to the fathers, by letter, that his life was in danger – that he fufpefted the plots of his enemies, and would not go, as ufual, to the Senate, not even with a guard, nor be feen by them on the oppofite coaft, and, that fome of them, from that time, took the liberty to fpeak difrefpeftfully of him, even in the Senate, and others, among whom were even condemned perfons, ufed to write any thing, however fcurrilous, againft him, and to publifh it in the moft frequented places, and not only of all this do we feem to be affined, but of this alfo, that the praftice of accufing perfons, for what we know not, unlefs it were for not worfhipping Tiberius, began then to be in fafhion, and that Tiberius refufed the honors voted, by the Senate, to his mother – ni coeleftis religio decerneretur.

How much more credible the preceding mode of accounting for his feceffion from Rome is, than either of thofe mentioned by Tacitus, muft appear to every one. – And how much more credible this other mode of accounting for his retiring to Capreae is, than that of Suetonius, may be made to appear from what Tacitus fays of fome of the events of the two following years – viz – 781, 782 – A. iv. 68, he tells u how a fcheme was laid, by four candidates for $he confulmip, and therefore, we prefume, fqnatorials, to enfnare Titius Sabinus, a knight, who was notorious for his attachment to the family of Ger- manicus, and for his difaffeftion to Tiberius, and who had, three*Why Tiberius left Rome, and why he 'Went to Caprete.*

years before, been profecuted by Sejanus, for the fame offence, when his trial was, for fome unknown reafon, put off. – Chap. 69, he fays, how one of them pretended to pity the family of Germanieus, and, by that means, got him to fpeak difrefpeftfully of Tiberius and Sejanus, while the others overheard every word that he faid. – Of this they immediately fent off an account to Tiberius, who, it fhould b obferved, is faid, by all, to have difregarded fuch reports, and had, but the year before, been confidered, by the Senate, as the only fuffuge in fuch hard cafes, and was then at Capreae, driven from th Management of public affairs by Sejanus or his mother. – And, flrange to relate, he alfo tells us, that, though Sabinus was then almoft the Only ftauneh friend of the family of Germanieus, inconceivable horror feized all ranks of people at Rome, as if the cafe of Sabinus, a knight, might be every man's own cafe: – " The city, fays Tacitus, was never feized with greater dread; one neighbour accufed another, fo that reports, known and unknown, began to be avoided, nay even dumb and inanimate things, roofs and walls, occafioned dread and circum- fpeftion." – Non alias magis anxia et pavens civitas, egens *(agens?)* adverfum proximos, congreflus, colloquia, notae ignotaeque aures *(aurai?)* vitari; etiam muta atque inanima, teftum et parietes cir- cumfpeftabantur. – But if fuch were the accufers and fuch was their motive, and fuch the crime which they alledged againft Sabinus – what reafon had the commonalty of Rome to be alarmed left a fimilar accufation might be brought againft any of them ? – Why fhould they have accufed one another ?–But did the Senate, on this evidence alone, proceed to pafs fentence on Sabinus ? – In the next chapter, 70, Tacitus proceeds to fay, that Tiberius himfelf, magnanimous and benevolent, as he is faid to have been, let loofe fome of the moft corrupt of the libertines againft Sabinus, then in prifoa – that Sabinus was tried

Why Tiberius left Rome, and why he went to Caprete.

before the Senate, condemned, and, contrary to the edift of Tiberius, immediately executed – and, as he was on the way to the place of execution, every body, through fear, fled from the fight – the flreets and public places were deferted – and, that fome of thofe who had fled, returned to their occupations again, afraid of being punifhed for having fhewn figns of fear – quo iutendiflet oculos, quo verba acci- derent, fuga, vaftitas: deferi itincra, fora: et quidam regrediebantur, oftentabantque fe rurfum, id ipfum paventes, quod timuiflent. – And, laflly, Tacitus fays, that Tiberius returned thanks to the Senate for ' having put to death a perfon *hoftile to thejlate.* – Tiberius, though, as- Tacitus himfelf fays, v. 2, *habitually placid,* though, as Juvenal fays, X. 75, *fecure in his old age,* though, as Suetonius fays, iii. 59, *haftfty in himfelf,* at the fame time, fays Tacitus, added – that his life was in danger – trepidam fibi vitam – and that he fufpefted the plots of his enemies – fufpeftas inimicorum infidias – no doubt, fays he, meaning Agrippina and Nero. – And in this conjefture, he feems to be fupported by Paterculus, ii. 130, who fays – Quod ex nuru, quod ex nepote, dolere, indignari, erubefcere coafltus eft ? – And immediately fubjoins – Cujus temporis aegritudinem auxit amifla mater, &c.

This then is the ftrange account which Tacitus has given us, in thofe three chapters, of the accufation, trial, condemnation, and immediate execution of Titius Sabinus. – An account which is liable to various and great objeftions. Let us proceed to confider fonte of the chief.

Titius Sabinus had, three years before, fays Tacitus, iv. 18, been attacked by Sejanus, for having been concerned with C. Suilius, in endeavouring to raife a diftur- bance in favor of the family of Germa- nicus. – But though attacked, he was not, for fome unaccountable reafon, then tried – if he was then imprifoned, he appears to have beer!*Why Tiberius left Rome, and why he went to Caprece.*

fet at liberty again, and probably without fecurity for his future good behaviour. Suilius, however, was tried, and fearing the iflue, put an end to himfelf. – Sabinus, regardlefs of thelenity which he had, fo lately experienced, permitted himfelf to be decoyed into a repetition of his offence, and, not only fo, but an aggravation of it, by fpeaking againft Tiberius, and, what is ftill more furprifing, by one whom he could not but have known to be a creature of Sejanus – and, at a time too, when Tiberius was either driven from the feat of his government – or, obliged to retire by grief, and when he had, but the year befoie, or, it may have been but the fame year, endeared himfelf to all ranks of people by his benevolence and beneficence on two moft extraordinary occafions. – And who, does Tacitus fay, were his accufers ? – fcil. – four candidates for the enfuing confulate, who, to obtain their objeft, took this ftep to ingratiate themfelves, not with either Livia or Tibe- . rius, but with Sejanus. – How four competitors, for an office that was difcharged only by two, Ihould have entered into fuch a confpiracy againft Sabinus, Tacitus has forgot to tell us. – Certain it is, however, that not one of the four obtained the expefted reward for his raoft difgraceful fervice. – On their information, Sabinus was, to the inconceivable confternation of the whole city, dragged away to prifon – and an account of the whole proceeding was fent away to Tiberius, then at Capreae. – Tiberius, then, as if the evidence of thofe fenators might be fufpefted, contrived, after he was in prifon, to fet fome of the freedmen againft him, in order, it mould feem, to do the work,, which the others had begun under Sejanus, the more completely, and to crown the report, Tiberius, fays Tacitus, demanded vengeance – ultionemque haud obfcure pofcebat – and, by fo doing, prejudged the whole matter himfelf. – The Senate, in obedience to the demand of Tiberius, immediately proceeded to pafs fentence on him, and, in

Why Tiberius left Rome, and why he went to Capreoe. .

defiance of his former edift, (made ia a fimilar cafe fix or feven years before, commanding them to allow the condemned perfons ten days' refpite,) immediately *executed* him – to the ftill greater confirmation of all Rome. – Tiberius, continues he, returned thanks to the Senate, by letter, for having punifhed a man *hojiile to the Jlate* – but of the principals, Agrippa and Nero, he, fays Tacitus, took no notice, at leaft, by name, though he fufpecled them of a defign upon his life.

In this inftance, then, we find that fenators themfelves fometimes became accufers, and even of the friends of the family of Germanicus, and, that the Senate, even in fuch a cafe, feconded their views, and were entirely fubfervient to the will of Tiberius and received his thanks for it – and, we alfo find, that the citizens were imprefled with vmfpeakable abhorrence at the atrocity of the deed, fuppofing that the cafe of this knight might be that of every one amongft them. – But how could they have 'been fearful of this, unlefs they were confcious to themfelves that they were all equally attached to the family of Germanicus, and Agrippina and Nero had then encouraged them to revolt – which furely would imply that they had too foon forgotten their late difafters at Fidenae and at Rome. But how long did the Senate continue fo fubfervient to the will of Tiberius – and – fo oppo- fite to the views of Agrippina? – And, why, as they were fo very obfequious to his will, even in oppofition to the hopes of Agrippina and Nero, fhould he have faid that his life was in danger ? – And that he was afraid of the plots of his enemies ? – What plots or what enemies could he have meant? – How long had his enemies been plotting againft him – and – how long did they continue to do fo ?

In the next chapter – viz – 71, Tacitus proceeds to fay, that Afinius Gallus, a brother-in-law of Agrippina, pretended to be fo very ignorant of the perfons meant by Tiberius, (though, as Tacitus fays,

Why Tiberius left Rome, and -why he "went to Caprea.

every body elfe had no doubt that they were Agrippina and Nero,) that he propofed, in the Senate, to petition the prince to difclofe the Caufe of his fear, and, in order to have it removed. – But if it was, as Tacitus fays, generally underftood that Tiberius meant; Agrippina and Nero – and – as he fays too, that Tiberius could not bear the thought of having his thoughts known, was there not great danger in preffing him to difclofe them ? – Was then Afinius Gallus the moft likely of all men to'have madeihe propofal to the Senate? – But, fays Tacitus, his propofal was overruled by Sejanus, on the fcore that the prince did not lik$ to reveal his thoughts – And why then, it may furely be afted, did he, while refiding at Capreae, complain that his life was in danger ? – That he feared the plots of his enemies ? – What enemies could he, whp had but juft before fo endeared himfelf to every body, have had? – Or what plots could be formed againft his life, while he was refiding at Capreae ? – Or againft his government, who, by his own account, had then no government ? – Or rather, had fo much intereft with the Senate as to prevail on them to execute one of the moft (launch and zealous friends of the family of Germanicus, merely for his attachment to them. – Does not Tacitus then appear to have made a very incomprehenfible report of this whole affair ?

Let us next proceed to attend to one occurrence more, which, Tacitus fays, began to take place foon after the execution of Sabinus, and before the year was expired – -and which occurrence was, he alfo fays, incomparably more terrific than the revolt of a warlike people, and, ofcourfe, than the execution of Sabinus.

His account of this internal confirmation, for that is the name he gives this political phenomenon, he introduces with faying that the Senate, at a time when a warlike people were incroaching on the

Why Tiberius left Rome, and why he went to Cnprea.

torders of the empire, regardlefs of that difgrace, were totally occupied about devifing a method to obviate it – and, that the only thing they could think of, as likely to accomplifh their purpofe, was adula- tion-rCui remedium adulatione quaerebatur. – A ftrange application for fo great apolitical diforder! – But to whom, does he fay, this adulation was to be paid ? – by whom – and – how ? – fcil. – to Tiberius and Sejanus – by the Senate – and – by erefting altars to clemency and amity around the ftatues of Tiberius and Sejanus – ita quan- quam diverfis fuper rebus confularentur, aram dementiae, aram Amicitiae, effigiefque circum Caefaris et Sejani cenfuere. – But how could they think that adulation of any kind, efpecially of a religious nature, was likely to be the means of conciliating Tiberius to cq- operate in remedying this evil ? – Did they not know that he hated adulation of every kind, and efpecially fuch as was of a religious nature ? – That he had forbidden that by edicT: ? – Does not this mode then of adulating him imply fomething of a very unaccountable nature ? – However, whether they did, by this fort of adulation, intend to pleafe him, or, whether they did not, does it not feem to imply that they confidered Tiberius as the caufe of this fudden alarm, if not, that he was able to remove it and would not? – But what political evil could he, who had been driven from Rome by his mother, and was then redding at Capreae, and afraid that his enemies had a defign on his life, have introduced at Rome? – Would he, who, as Suetonius fays, iii. 37, had moft grievoufly fupprefled fome popular tumults, not only at Rome but throughout Italy, and taken great care that they fhould never happen again – Populares tumultus exortos graviffime coercuit; et ne orirentur fedulo cavit. – And, as he feems to have intimated immediately before, by ftationing the prxtorian guards at Rome. – And who, as Tacitus fays, A. iv. 64, but the year before had recejved the thanks of the Senate and *of* all ranks of -the*Why Tiberius left Rome, and ixihy lie went to Caprea.*

people of Rome for his beneficence to them, have thought of difturb- ing them fo inconceivably by the introduftion of any evil ? – That he did, at fome time of his reign, by great artifice, introduce what Tacitus is pleafed to call a moft grievous evil – exitium – he, and he alone, we find, allures us, A. i. 73, and, as we hate already feen, p. 40, after the i3th year of his reign. – Was then the introduftion of this moft grievous evil the caufe of this amazing internal coufterna- tion ? – If it was, we have feen that we have no little reafon to think the introduftion of the execrable fuperftition – alias – df the Chriftian religion, was the caufe of all of it. And, confequently, that it may alfo have been the caufe of his retiring to Capreae, as, it feems, his life tnuft have been in danger from the enemies of the Chriftian religion – if not of its being faid that the people were fo terrified at the execution of Sabinus – and – of its being alfo faid that he turned the moft worth- lefs of the freedmen againft him. – That this was really the faft why Ihould we not infer, even from what, we have already feen, Tacitus fays of this internal dread, and ftill more from what he fays in the fequel ? – Tacitus proceeds to fay that the Senate repeatedly importuned them to fhew themfelves – crebrifque precibus efflagitabant vifendi fui copiam facerent – with this repeated requeft they would not comply – Non illi tamen in urbem aut propinqua urbi digreffi funt. – How differently did he behave only a few months before, towards the fufferers at Fidena e and towards thofe on Mount Ccelius! On the former occafion, he, as Suetonius fays, went, at the requeft of the people, from Capreae *inftantly,* and made himfelf acceffible to all. – But now he would not comply with the repeated prayers of the Senate, who, inftead of begingthat he would order out the pnetorian troops,

Orig. Quot.

t /

Why Tiberius left Rome, and why he "went to Caprece.

went, with the knights and great part of the commonalty, while Rome was in the greateft confufion, to the coaft of Campania, and, merely, as Tacitus pretends, to get a fight of them. – This, however, Tiberius himfelf took care not to indulge them with, and, no doubt, for fear of any attempt on his life. – This, fays Tacitus, made them return in trepidation. – Some, fubjoins he, a little cheered at their better reception, on thetr return foon met with a grievous exit.

9

SECTION 9

CHAPTER VIII.
Why Tiberius did not see His dying mother.
AND
Whether she refused honors ne – or – nit $c.

A ACITUS, v. t, fays, that Livia died u. c. 782 – or – in the 7 tft year of Tiberius. – Now if fhe died in that year, and her foh was jhen in his 7 tft, Ihc muft have been, at her death, not as Pliny fays, xiv. 6, 82 years old, but, as Dion fays, 1. Iviii, p. 621, C, at leaft 86 – -v! ' oySixovTa rm *to-xo-x*. – Tacitus had, it fhould be obferved, before faid, A. iv. 8, where he is fpeaking of the events of u. c. 776, that her age was, in that year, extreme.

During her illnefs, Tiberius, fays Tacitus, Suetonius, and Dion, . never favy her, and, when fhe was dead, did not attend her funeral, neither, fay they, would he permit her body to be confecrated. – All this, they fuppofe, proceeded from dilrefpeft. – Tacitus fays, that he, though juft before afraid that his life was in danger, made no change, all the time fhe was ill, in his ufual amenity – and – that he, at her death, though inattentive to the revolt of the Frifii, told the Senate

Why Tiberius did not see his dying mother.

that the preflure of public bufinefs was fo great that he could not attend. – Let us proceed to enquire why he was fo inattentive to her in her laft moments and after her death.

If he was, as Tacitus, we have feen, in the laft chapter, feems to fay, 1. 72, fo very early on fuch notorioufly bad terms with her as to have excited the obloquy of fatyrifts, it furely cannot be a matter of furprize that he paid no attention to her in her laft illncfs. – But Tacitus, we have difcovered, could not have meant to fay fo. – Indeed, if he had meant to fay fo, he would be found, by what he fays afterwards, in the following books, to appear to contradift himfelf. – For, ii. 34, he fays, that Tiberius, *to pleafe his mother,* went to the Senate, to plead the caufe of her favorite Urgulania, who had refufed to attend the fummons of Pifo, the praefeft of the city, and had been pro- tefted, by Livia, in her contumacy – Tiberius indulgere matri civile ratus, &c. – And again, in three or four places of the third book, he fays enough to induce us to fuppofe that Tiberius could not have difagreed with his mother fo early as to have their difagreement pub- licly known in the courfe of the year after he was made emperor, if not enough to convince us that their concord muft have been fincere till a year or two after the death of Germanicus. – In the 3d chapter, he fays, that both Tiberius and his mother did not attend the funeral of Germanicus, and poffibly, as he hints, that their pretenfions to grief might not be difcovered. – In the 16th chapter, he reports the dying words of Pifo – who, after complaining that he had been falfely accufed, and that the evidence in his favor had not been attended to, faid, in a codicil to Caefar, which he left – " I call the immortal Gods

Dion says, 1. 58, p. 621, D., *xattnf na TtGtftot vsxunymrnt n m rut* mtvwv *lottnenus* a$t ron *xtttxytro*. – Suetonius says, iii. 41, that be cared nothing for the republic – and – 51, tbat he encouraged them to hope that be would attend.

Why Tiberius did not see his dying mother.

to witnefs that I have lived faithfully towards you, and pioufly towards your mother; and I befeech you both to think of my children." – Confpiratione inimicorum, et invidia falfi criminis oppreflus, quatenus veritati et innocentiae mea e nufquam locus eft; deos immortales teftor vixifle me, Caefar, cum fide adverfum te, neque alia in matrem tuam pietate: vofque oro liberis meis confulatis. – In the next chapter, r 7, he fays, that Tiberius, *at the earmjl Intreaty of his mother,* fhamefully and fcandaloufly, defended, in the Senate, Plancina, the murderer of her grand-fon, who, he fajs, chapter 14, was not poifoned, and, who, we have feen, CHAP. V, was not murdered. – Pro Plancina cum pud ore et flagitio difleruir, matris preces obteridens. – And, in the 64th chapter, he fays, that Tiberius, who, in the beginning of the year 774, went into Campania, and, with a defign never to return – - longarn et continuam abfentiam paulatim meditans – and, who, feem- ingly, n purfuance of his intention at the outfet, remained there till the following year, on hearing of the fudden illnefs of his mother, thought it 'neceflary to return inftantly, – Sub idem tempus Julise Auguftae valetudo atrox *necejfitudinem* Principi fecit *ftftinati* in urbem reditus; – Now as Tacitus has declared that the illnefs of Livia made Tiberius think it *neceffary* to return to the city *in kafle,* notwithftand- ing he had, before his outfet, formed a defign never to return, who would fuppofe that he meant to have it underftood that he was offended at her – And yet he, we find, fubjoins this very fapient and unexpefted alternative – their concord was hitherto fincere – or –

their refentments were concealed – fincera adhuc inter matrem filiumque concordia, five, occultis odiis – that is – as we prefume, juft as if he had faid – they ftill either agreed, or, difagreed. – But after what he had faid, i. 72, who would have cxpefted to hear him admit that their Concord might ftill have been *jlncere?* – And, who, after what he had faid, ii. 34, and iii. 3, 17, and what he fays here, would have ex-

Why Tiberius did not see his dying mother.

peftcd him to infinuate that their enmity might have been concealed? If Tiberius, notwithftanding his defign of living continually at a great diftance from Rome, thought it neceflary to return quickly, as foon as he heard of his mother's illnefs, does not this feem to prove that their concord was ftill fincere? – Why then fhould Tacitus, after having produced an urjqueftionable proof that their concord was ftill fincere, have thought it at all to his credit to intimate that it may ftpt have been fo, and only becaufe, it was *fuppofed,* that Tiberius had, a little before – paulo ante – been offended at her? – And why, does he fay, fome fuppofed that he was offended at her? – fcil. – Li via had, not long before, i. e. – not long before 775, canted her flame to be infcribcd on a ftatue of Auguftus before that of Tiberius, and this, *as was fuftfiofed,* offended him – idque ille credebatur, ut inferius majcftate Principis, gravi et diflimulata offenfiorie abdidifle. – Put whatever he might have been, he, it feems, was not fo offended now as to negjeft to fee her – or – to refufe any of the honors voted to her, on this occafion, by the Senate. – Tacitus then, here' afierts that Tiberius had a due regard for his mother in the year 775. – Jn the year following, he fays, iv. 8, that he bewailed, in the Senate, the extremity of her age – rMiferatufque Auguftae extremam feneftam. Laftly he, v. 3, once more aflerts pofitively that his obfequioufnefe towards her, was, to the laft, inveterate – quia Tibcrio, invetcratum erga matrem obfequium.

This is the evidence on this point which we colleft from what Tacitus fays of the conduit of Tiberius towards his mother before fhe died. – Let us now attend to what he fays of the conduit of Tiberius towards her memory after fhe was dead,

He, fays Tacitus, would receive but very few of thofe many honors bountifully decreed her by the Senate – honorefque memoriae ejus ab

Why Tiberius did not see his dying mother.

Senatu large decretos, quafi per modeftiam imminuit, paucis admd- dum receptis. – What honors thofe were which were liberally decreed her by the Senate, after her death, he does not fay – nor what thofe many were, which he refufed – neither does he fay what thofe very few were which he accepted. – To this he fubjoins the reafon why he refufed thofe many – ne cceleftis religio decerneretur – and afterwards informs us, that Tiberius obferved, it was her own option – fie ipfam maluifle. – But what? – Did me order moft of thofe honors to be refufed – ne cceleftis religio decerneretur? – What celeftial religion could fhe have meant? – Had not Tacitus, A. i. n, informed us, that celeftial religions in general had been already decreed to Auguftus? Had not the Senate before, *v.* c. 776, ordered her to be worfhipped? And:did fhe not then cohfent to it? – Why then fhould fhe be thought to have had any concern about celeftial religion? – Efpecially about the decreeing of it? – Or – how coul'd fhe have thought that the ac ceptanee of any of the honors which fhe ordered to be refufed would tend to accelerate the decreeing of any religion,? – Would the decreeing of any religion neceflarily follow her acceptance of thofe honors? And what if it did? – Why would fhe wifh to hinder celeftial religion from being once more decreed ? – But of this more hereafter ?

In the vi. 5. Tacitus mentions a faft which feems to Jinply that Tiberius muft have had the greateft veneration for her memory in the year 785 – that is – nearly three years after fhe was dead – if not that what he had before faid of his refufal of almoft all the honors decreed to her by the Senate is not a little likely to be falfe. – He there fays, that Cotta Meflalinus, who, he admits in the fequel of that chapter, was one of the moft intimate friends of Tiberius, was accufed, in th Senate, of having faid the following thing of an entertainnje, nt, given,

Tiberius did not see his dying mother.

either on *t/a-* birth-day of Augufta to certain, priefts, or, on *a* birth-day . to the priefts of Augufta, of which he hinii elf partook – " that it was a funeral, or, expiatory luppcr – et cum die natali Augufta." inter facerdoles cpularctur, uovendialcm cam ca-nam dixifle." Cotta, being pt cllcd hard on the fubjeft, appealed to Tiberius, who, inftead of ftnding fault with him for having been prefent at fuch a feaft, inftantly wrote a letter tp the Senate, in which, after reverting to the commencement of their intimacy, and enumerating his many ferviccs, he enjoined them to take up notice of exprelftons ufcd ia the hour of conviviality, which, at Inch times, were liable to. be mifunderftood. By this then we find that either the birth-day of Augufta was kept three years after her death – or, that priefts were continued to officiate to her, (as they did to her in her life-time) in coojun&ipn with, Tiberius and the Senate – that a friend of Tiberius attended their convivial meeting – and that Tiberius was, not offended at it – though he would npt be worfhipped himfelf. – Was fhe, as Tiberius himfclf, we fhall find, ajfo was, worfhipped in fpite ? – Why, then, fhould Tacitus hay faid that Tiberius refufed almoft all the honors decreed to, her by the Senate. – And. what can he have meant by faying – et addito nc coeleftis r, eligio decerneretur – and – . fie ipiam maluiife ?-,-Ijf fltc had any objeftion to make to her own deification why did me not make it before her death?

Having now considered all that Tacitus has advanced on this fub- – Jet us. proceed, to conitder what other writers have faid on it.

Seneca, in his Confol. to Marcia for the lofs of her fon, chapter 4, quotes the example of Livia, who, it feems, by two or three places in this work, was then alive, and intimately acquainted with Marcia. Livia, fays he, was inconfolable for the lofs of her fon Drufus, but Ihe attended to the confolation of Ajeus, whofe perfuafions were of

Why Tiberius did not see his dying Mather

More avail than even the filial piety of Tiberius – plufqbam Tiberhim filium, *fujtts /tietat* efficfebat, ut in illo aeerbo et defleto gentflwfe fiinert, hihil fib! ttifi humerum deefle feritiret. – This teoatblation, it mould be obferved, Stneca Wrote after the death of Cordus, the father ef Marciav who, a.; TdcitiS ftys, iv, 35 Milted Mmfetf ti-.-6. *jf$4tid* therefore two years after h pretended that ftlfee thoUglrt that lhe pitty of Tiberius towards his mother Jtt *v. c.* 5, was not iktcere, Ad ten years aftef he Was, as Tacitus fty A. i.)i, laih pooned by the anonymous fatyrifts for his (impiety towards liter.

Paterculus, who wrote the ydar after thfe death of Ltvia u. c. 783, and addrefled his work to Vinicius, the then cohful, fpeaks of Tiberius as having, for the three years paft, been overcome with grief oft fevral accounts – and, as having been, nobody knows how iowg, inwardly devoured by a eertairt kteht fire – and, moreover, as having had his grief iWt a little increafed by lhfe idfam0us proceedings of Agrippina and fett-AArK having deplored all this to Vinicius Paterculus concludes his hiiiory With this remark – the grief of this ptfiod has been ittteaffed by the leTs of his rhoft eminent mdtlter – & woman, in very thirtg tnftfe like the Gods than men; whofc power nobody felt unlefs by the risrrtoval of danger, or, the aeceffiort of dignity.

Suetonius, iii. 51, gives a quite different account of the con- duft of Tiberias towards his mother juft before and after her death.-He fays that Tiberius never faw her but once in the courft of the laft three years-that he would not attend her funeral – that he would not execute her Will – that he perfecuted all her friends' and acquaintances – efpecially thofe to whom fhe had left the care of her.

Ccfc

Why Tiberius did not see his dying mother.

funeral – that he forbad her body to be confecrated – -and that he pretended fhe had left orders that it mould not. – But though Suetonius fays all this, iii. 51, yet he has faid enough in the next book, c. I, 15, to convince us that he did not refufe any other honor befides confe- cration, if not to convince us that all the reft cannot have been true- chapter t, he fays, that Tiberius permitted Caius to fpeak her funeral oration – and, chapter 15, he fays, that Caius heaped, by one decree of the Senate,- all the honors on his grand-mother Antonia, which had been ever conferred oh Livia.

Dion fays, 1. lviii, p. 621, C. D., that Tiberius would not accept of any other honor befides a public funeral and images, &c. and that he ftrenuoufly deprecated her. irnrnortalization-ix9vrio-flDvai *vnxfvs* aMwvofsus-H. – Dion further fays, that the Senate not only decreed her *what Tiberius ordered – svtnAt* – but that they' alfp decreed her a mourning of matrons, for a year, and (what was never before granted to a woman) an Arch, and,, for this reafon – becaufe fhe had faved many fenators, and had provided for their, children.-rTras Arch, he fubjoins, Tiberius undertook to ereft-at his own expence, but 'never did it. Dion alfo feems to fay, 1. lix, p. 648, B., that a profufion of honors were voted her, and, among the reft, immortality – i

ra n a/Cf. x, aaat rn n Atatat fStSoro, zvj/t)p'o-flt, *xat tvat aQxtxno-Q xxt ttt , !. . - t ;.. ..- .. .. t -*

Seneca and Paterculus1then, we find, contradict. Taeitus concerning the piety of Tiberius towards his mother. – -And Syetoniqs tand. Dion, we alfo find, contradift him with -regard to the honors accepted and re- fufed by him – they fay that the Setvate voted her, befides thofe which

Suetonius sajs, v. 11, that an Arch was decreed to Tiberius by the Senate, but never built.

Why Tiberius did not see his dying mother.

Tiberius ordered, many other – and, that Tiberius did not refufe any other befides her confecation. – Now if cohfecration or immortalization was the only honor refufed by him why did not Tacitus tell us fo? Was he afraid that his report of what Tiberius added – viz – ne coeleftis religio decerneretur – would, in that cafe, become queftiorioable.

?-r- How could the decreeing of her immortalization or confecration be confidered as any thing elfe but the decreeing of celeftial religion ?, – What elfe could it have been ? – Do not Seneca, Suetonius, and Dion fecm to intimate that it was really fo ? – Seneca, we know, fays of Claudius. Apoc – *Divam* Auguftam aviam fuatn quam ipfe Deam efle juffit. – Suetonius fays of him, v. n – A viae Liviae divinos honores decernendos curavit. – And Dion fays of him, 1. Ix, p. 667, that, ho gave her immortality – xx i amftzrxriopsy"D4. – All which furely imply that to deify her and to give her divine honors were the fame as to decree her immortality. – Would Tiberius then have added fuch a ridiculous reafon? – Or, would he, who had feveral years before pub- limed an edift prohibiting his own worfhip – and was then notorioufly a worfhipper of Chrift, have permitted, on any condition, the wor- fh-tp of his mother? – Or, would me, who, as Jofephus fays, had always been intimately acquainted with Herod and his family, and honored by them as their patronefs, and who, as Philo fays, had contributed to the fupport of the wormip of the temples, have been, to the laft, concerned about the religion of the Romans? – It is true-that fhc had, but four years before, confented to be worfhipped in conjunftion with the Senate and her fon, and that a coin, with this inscription – *fsia Kxto-xfos* ZsCac-a *(Suas letas* Zf$, z? tjis – if not another with this – Divae Julia – had, before that again, been ftruck, yet as fhe had been prSvioufly acquainted with the religion of the Jews, and Chriftianity*Why Tiberius did not &ee his dying mother.*

Tristanus T. I. p. 1$27.

had then beten publifhed, how are we to be fare that (he was not in clined to favor diat. And as Tiberius Irimfelf was worihipped, in op- pofttion to his own edift, how flvaJl we be fure that the Senate may not bave decreed her divine honors in oppofition both to h6r owtt inclina- tion and to hfo remonftrance ?–Does Hot Dion feettt to fey, 1. liitv p. 648, B., that fli& was, notwithftaKding Tiberius fo ftvenuoufly oppb- fed h, deified, when Ihfc received fuch a profufion of other hon&rs? – He tliefe fays that Caius mt only beftowed on his departed fifter Dru fillaw///4 *Mker ftanots thtit ftad Ixe vb'ted to* ZiV/abut alfo immortality

""Untt M Vlh T *tMvx,* frz Attudc teSaro *ut$urflf H. atl nat o&alstttttAn,* xat

tor t *ffufnntfHn yym* v'n'fli).-='Ahd does not Tacitus himfelf teem td intimate that the Senate did actually confecrate her, by observing that file had *prtefls* of her own-, as, Prudentius alfo feemfe to teftffy by. the following lina–Adjecere facrum fieret quo Livia Juno.-Claudius, we have ihdefed juft feen, is fai-d by SenecA and others, to haVe had the credit of having Caulfed her cohfecration, but may it riot be doubted whether he did any thing more than revive the dorrnant decree ' – Has not Seneca himfelf given us fordething like a reafon to doubt it by naming her – -. Drt/dt Auguftam–in the very beginning of the fentence wherein he fpeaks of her deification by Claudius?

As then it appears by the evidence of Suetonius and Dion that Tiberius oppofed the deification of his mother, as he had before that of himfelf – and – that he oppofed the former at his mother's requeft, but hotVvithflanding all the oppofition which he made to it he could

t

not prevent it, ought not Tacitus to have acquainted us with this ? – Inftead of doing fo, he has, we find, informed us that Tiberius refufed all honors (which, we find, by the report of Suetonius and Dion, was not tfue,) jftot, indeed, abfolutely, but, optionally – fie illarn

I. iu SjtTratach. p. 25!..

Why Tiberius did not see Ms dying mother.

maluiffe.- – As then this feems to have been the cafe – aad-ne coeleftis teligio – does not well comport with either the refufal of honors, or, with her option, fuppofe we endeavour to make this diflbnant fentence to be more in confonance both with what precedes and foltews. – What then if we read *ni* for *ne* ?-r-And what if his meaning had been this TT-Tiberius, who, in the year before had propofed it *to* the Senats to authorife the worfhip of Chrift, and had the mortification to fee his propofal rejefted, declared that it was his mother's laft command that but few of the honors, which the Senate intended to decree to her memory, fhould be accepted, *ui,* untafe they would, at the fame time, decree celeftiai religion-that is-decree that Chrift fhoutd1 be worfhipped.

Tiberius then, we have feerj, did not, out of any difrefpeft to his, mother, refufe the honors decreed to her, but, in compliance with, her own injun&ion. – Why then fhould we be expected to believe that he voluntarily neglected to fee her in her laft illnefe or,, to attend her funeral? – Why, as he complained to the Senate, a few months before, that his enemies had a clefign on his. life, mould we. not think that the fear of being aflaffinatjed is much more likely to have deterred, him from going to Rome to Tee her ? – and to attend her funeral? – But why Ihould fo good a prince, who, as Suetonius fays, Hi. 67 v had the title of Pater Patripe voted him by the Senate, in the very beginning of his reign – ut imperinm, inierit – and who, as Tacitus fays, A. i. 72,. had the fame title often given, hjm, by the people – a populo. faspius ingeftum – who had, for his paft fervices

often received the thanks of the Senate – who had, by their permiffion,

. .
. .1 -.'.. '

The ut of *ni for ntst* is very common with Tacitus – in the reign tiberini. *q$j.* ff. ofteft SCe it – Se A. 30, 64.

Why Tiberius did not see his dying mother.

been every where worfhipped – who had, but the year before, been, both by the Senate and the people, thanked for his beneficence – and who ufed to go any where alone. – Why fhould fuch an one have been afraid of what his enemies could do to him? – Unlefs, indeed, he, as Tacitus remarks, afte having done fo much good, artfully contrived to introduce a moft (as he alfo fays) grievous evil, or, execrable fuperftition – that is – as we imagine, an ineftimable good, or, the belief of the divinity of Chrift, and, thereby caufed that internal alarm, which, fays he, was far worfe than *the revolt of a war like people,* and, perhaps, that rage for accufing, which, as Seneca fays, was *worfe than any civil war,* and more deftruftive to the Romans. Now if Tiberius did introduce Chriftianity into Rome, and much oppofition was, as both Seneca and Tacitus feem to fay, and, as Clemens, of Rome, expreffly fays, made to it, at the very firft, by unbelievers, and, as Tertullian fays, even by a majority of the Senate – for Tiberius, he fays, firft propofed it to them to admit the worfhip: of Chrift at Rome, and that they, inftead of acceding to the propofak; ordered all Chriftians to leave Rome, and, of courfe, Tiberius hinv felf, (for he, it feems, as the fame writer fays, remained ftill of the fame perfuafion,) and, by that means, fupprefled it, as Tacitus fays, for the prefent. – If, fay we again, Tiberius did really introduce Chriftianity into Rome, and was, thereby, the caufe of fo much dif- cord, how are we to be fure that he may not have been afraid of fomc of the adverfaries of Chriflianity, and of moft of the Senate ? – Does not all that Tacitus fays, iv. 74, of the internal alarm – of the means which the Senate took to remove it – viz – the religious adulation of

Suetontus, iii. 30, *JVunquam* curiam nisi solus intravit: lectica, &c. – 40, potestatem omnibus adeundi sui fecit; tanto magis, &c. – Tacitus, iv. 22, Non cunctanter Tiberius pergit in domum, fisit cubiculum: &c. – Dton, I. lvii. p. 609, B. C. D.

Why Tiberius did not see his dying mother.

Tiberius – of the many petitions, which they, in the midft of all this confufion, fent to Tiberius to requeft him to return to Rome – of his refufing, contrary to his ufual praftice, to comply – of their going, while Rome was ftill agitated with terror, in a body, with the knights and the commonalty, to the coaft of Campania for the fole purpofe of feeing him – of the grievous exit that awaited thofe cheerful few who had been favored with a fight of Sejanus; – does not all this feem to indicate that Tiberius was afraid to truft himfelf with them ?

.- .
. i. *i* .: .. .
t ! /t '".'i ... *i* !; ,. v
- i–'ii .'! Dd CHAPTER IX.

Why and when Tiberius forbad instant executions.

J. T was ever the praftice of the Romans, till the reign of Tibe. rius, to execute thofe who had been condemned for any fort of crime as foon as fentence had been puffed on them. Tiberius, we are informed by Suetonius, iii. 75, Tacitus, iii. 49, and Dion, 1. 57, p. 616, 617, was the firft who put a flop to this praftice. The occafton, fay they, was this – Lutorius Prifcus, in the 8th year of Tiberius, u. c. 774, wrote a copy of varfes againft Drufus, while fick; and the Senate, without confulting Tiberius, who was at the time abfcnt, on the point, profecuted him on his own confeffion, for the defamation, and found him guilty of the crime, and, almoft unanimoufly, condemned him to fuffer death for the offence, and, as ufual, in- ftantly ordered him to be executed. All this was done without the knowledge of Tiberius. As foon as he was informed of the tranfac- tion, he, who, as Suetonius fays, ufed to refer all matters to the Senate, who was contented to have fome matters decided againft his

Why and when Tiberius forbad instant executions.

will, immediately, fays Dion, 1. 57, 617, A., exprefled his, difappro- bation of tite proceeding, and ordered the Senate to pafs a decree – *ttnTtfixto-t re avrots, xt* Soy/xz *n trxfxSoQmxt* ttXtwrf – that no condemned perfon fhould, from that time, be executed within ten days after fentence had been pafled upon him.

Tiberius then, we find, is allowed by thofe three hiftorians to have been the fole caufe of this new regulation, and, by two of them, to have been fo in the 8th year of his reign. But though both Tacitus and Dion allow, that Tiberius was, in the 8th of his reign, the caufe of paffing this moft humane decree, and, that he caufed it to be pafled, becaufe the Senate had, almoft unanimoufly, put a man to death for faying that he had libelled his fick fon, without bringing him acquainted with it; – yet, we find, that they both appear to fay that it was, about fix years after, violated, by putting a man to death, on the accufation of four of their own body, for only *jpcaktng* certain unknown words, which were drawn from him, in favor of Germani- cus, who had then been dead nearly nine years, and againft the pride, the cruelty, and the expeftations of Sejanus, and fome others about Tiberius. – Tacitus alfo adds, that Tiberius himfelf pretty clearly – haud obfcure – ordered the Senate to do it, and, feemtngly, *immediately – nee* mora, quin decerneretur.

Let us confider what Tacitus fays of this matter a little attentively. He relates moft of the particulars of it A. iv. c. 68, 69, 70.

He begins the 68th with the names of tlte confuls for that year, and then immediately proceeds to fay how filthy – fcedum – the beginning of the year was rendered by the unexpefted imprifonment of an illuftrious Roman knight *for his attachment to the family ofGermanlcus.*

Why and when Tiberius forbad instant executions.

And in the fcquel of the chapter he fays who were his accufers – viz – four expeftants of the enfuing confulfhip – and – how they, in order to ingratiate themfelves, not with Tiberius, but with Sejanus, (for by him they all hoped to obtain that office,) contrived to accufe him of having fpoken treafonable words. – Their contrivance was, fays, he, this – one of them got acquainted with him in the ftreets and drew him into converfation about his departed friend and about his family, and, by appearing to commiferate them, obtained the confidence of Sabinus, (for that was the name of this knight.) – Having fecured this point – they next agreed that his pretended friend fhould invite him to his houfe, and take him into a certain clofet in the upper ftory, which was fo near the roof, that any thing which was faid there could be diftinftly heard – over this clofet the other three agreed to take their ftation. – All things being thus contrived, Sabinus was, by his pretended friend, condufted to this clofet, where they firft con- verfed – not about the family of Germanicus, and then about the cruelty, the pride, and the expe&ations of Sejanus, not even fparing Tiberiqs – ne in Tiberium quidem convicio abftinet – but about what had recently happened – recens cognita – then the converfation turned on what might be Ihortly expefted – inftantia – which, it feems, was a copious fubjeft – quorum adfatim copia – and, laftly, a great deal was faid of *new terrors* – ac novos terrores cumulat – the fubftance of this converfation thofe four confpirators confidered as treafonable, and contrived to report it, in that light, to Tiberius, then at Capreae. No fooner was this known, than all the city was in the utmoft con- fternation, as if the fame thing which had happened to Sabinus might

How can four candidates for an office, that was discharged by two only, be supposed to have entered into such a conspiracy – especially so soon after the election was passed ?

Why and when Tiberius forbad instant executions.

happen to every individual, howerer humble. – Non alias magis anxia et pavens civitas, egens adverfus proximos, congreflus, colloquia, notae ignotaique aurai vitari; etiam muta atque inani.-na, teftum, et parietes circumfpeftabantur. – But what ? – Were the people indeed fo terrified at the cxpeftation that the fame thing might happen to any of them ? – What fays Pliny of the feelings of the people on this occa- fion?

– He fays, viii. 40, that the body of Sabinus was, after his execution, tumbled down the Geraonios – and that his dog, which had followed him all the way to the place of execution, ftill kept clofe to him, howling, as if for grief, to the admiration of *a great number of people* – magna populi romani corona – fome of whom procured fome meat for him, which he inftantly offered to his dead matter. – The body was then thrown into the river, and the faithful dog, to the no little furprife of the *[urroundmg multitude* – effufa multitudine ad fpec- Undam ammalis fidem – fwam after it and endeavoured to bring it out. And, laftly, Tacitus, in the 7oth chapter, relates how Tiberius, after having fet on him *the majl di/filute of the libertines* ordered him to be tried not for writing, but for uttering thofe complaints concerning the times, and to be immediately executed. – His own words – Sed C; cfar folemnia incipientis anni kalendis januariis epiftola precatus; vertit in Sabinum corruptos quofdam libertorum, et petitum fe arguens, ultion- emque *haud obfcure* pofcebat. – Now how could Tiberius have pre- fumed, on the evidence ftated by thofe four fenatorials, to affirm that he was, any other way than with foul words, attacked by Sabinus – and, that he was the principal objeft of his obloquy ? – If Tiberius, by petitum fe arguens, meant to affirm that Sabinus had entered into a treafon- able converfation againft himfelf, he, it feems, muft have deriTed that

N. B. He is said, by Philo, p. 786, F., to have disliked Hclico for being a kuare.
Why and when Tiberius forbad instant executions.
information, not from thofe four candidates for the confulfhip, for they did not charge Sabinus with any thing more than with having fpoken difrefpeftfuUy of him, but, afterwards, from thofe proffigate libertines. But how was it that Sabinus, knowing their charafters, fhould, after having fuffered fo much, through a pretended friend, fuffer himfelf to be again inveigled into a like converfation by Caefar's own creatures ? However, he, it feerns, demanded, in a manner not to be mifunder- flood, the immediate execution of him, and his demand was, by the Senate, immediately, on the firft day of the year, aflented to – for Sabinus exclaimed, on the way to the place of execution – Sic inchoari annum, &c. – The city, fays Tacitus, was again panic ftruck – fuga, vaftitas: deferi itinera, fora: et quidam regrediebantur, oftentabantque fe rurfurn, id ipfum paventes, quod timuiflent. – After the execution of Sabinus, fays Tacitus, Tiberius returned thanks to the Senate for having punifhed an enemy to the republic – and added that his life was in danger – that his enemies, whom he would not name, had a defign againft it: but, fubjoins Tacitus, though he would not fay who thofe enemies were, nobody doubted but that he meant Agrippina
and Nero.

Tacitus then fays, that Tiberius himfelf, within fix years after he had caufed the Senate to pafs this celebrated decree (which it fhould

This it appears by what Tacitus had previoufly said, iv. 67, and, by what D'ion says, I. 58, init., must have happened very shortly after Tiberius went to Capreap – and – but a few months, as Tacitus also says, 62, 63, 61, after the two disasters happened at Fidenae and at Home – on *the former* of which he, says Suetonius, iii. 40, at the request of the friends of the sufferers (who, il ttems, vere mostly of Rome) went from Capreae to FideniE, and while he was there permitted any person to have access to him; – and, on *the lalter* he, says Tacitus, iv. 64, behaved so beneficently that he received the thanks of both the Senate and the people.

Why and -when Tiberius forbad tnstant executions.

be remembered he did becaufe they had prefumed to execute a man for only writing a few verfes on his fick fon, and, which was never annulled) afted in defiance of it – 'or, rather – caufed them to aft in defiance of it. – But, admitting that he encouraged the bafe defign of thofe four fenators, and, that he employed thofe vile libertines to fecond what thofe fenators had begun, can it alfo be ftippofed that he would have ordered the Senate to aft in defiance of his own decree ? And when Sabinus had only fpoken certain unknown *words,* and thofe in reply to fome obiervation of a fuperior ? – But have we not fomething like a reafon to queftion this whole report of Tacitus concerning Sabinus, when we confidervvhat Pliny fays of his profecution in the t4th year of Tiberius? – He fays, viii. 40 – Sed fuper omnia, in noftro aevo aftis populi romani teftatum, Appio Junio et P. Srlio Cofs. cum animadverteretur *ex cauffa Neronis,* Gerrnanici filii, in- Titium Sabinum *et fervitia ejus.* – Titius Sabinus then was, in the 14th year of Tiberius, by the report of Pliny, who lived at the time, and who appealed to the Afta P. R., involved, together with his dependants, in fome treafonable affair with Nero, the fon of Germa- nicus, and was, on that account, tried by the Senate. – Pliny, it fhould be obferved, fays nothing of the interference of Tiberius, norofSabi nus having been both imprifoned and executed on the firft day of the year – he only fays that it happened in the confulfhip of App. J. and P. Sil. – Had it happened on the ftrft day of that year would he not have noticed fo remarkable an occurrence? – Dion, however, who, we find, alfo pafles by thofe circumftances, fays, that Sabinus was, on *the fame day – xvQnff. tfot* – put to prifon, and that he was executed *uncomdemned – axftrwf –* which laft remark, is, we have feen, contrary to the report of Taciju, . wkp fays – nee tnora quin decernerehir.

and when Tiberius forbad instant executions.

But what occafion have we to acquiefce in the report of either of thofe contradiftory and therefore fufpicious hiftorians, when we are afiured, by the unanimous evidence of four moft credible hiftorians, who lived in the reign of Tiberius, that one of his provincial praefefts did, in the fame year, much againft his own will, and without con- fulting 'Tiberius, confent to the *immedtate* execution of the moft exalted, beneficent, and inoffenfive perfonage that ever came into the world. – The four hiftorians above meant are the four Evangelifts – all of whom, we find, fay that our" Lord was accufed by the rulers of the Jews, before Pilate, of having faid that he was a king, and, of having been a ring-leader of fedition – and, that he was, on the fame day, pronounced guilty, and *immediately* executed.

Now can it be fuppofed that Pilate, who difliked the Jews and their religion, who had, on their complaint, been twtce reprimanded by Tiberius, who was glad to refer the hearing of the charge to Herod, as being the governor of the country where the alledged crime was faid to have been committed, who, after having heard Herod's report on the cafe, called the rulers of the Jews together to let them know that neither Herod nor himfelf had found any fault at all in him, who faid to them, the third time, on their refolutely demanding his crucifixion – Why ? – What evil hath he done ? – Who ftill perfifted in refufing to comply with their demand till a tumult was likely to enfue, who was importuned by his wife to have nothing to do with him, who warned his hands of the guilt of his condemnation – and, who was required, every year, to make a return of his official conduct. – Can it be fuppofed that Pilate would, after all this, have fuffered himfelf to be compelled to aft in defiance of this decree without authority – efpecially, as he knew, that Tiberius would not permit any of his

Why and when Tiberius forbad instant executions.

fefts to be guilty of injuftice, and that our Lord had fo many followers all over Judea and Galilee ? – Or, that the rulers of the Jews, who protefted that they would have no king but Tiberius, would, if that decree had been then pafled, have demanded the immediate execution of our Lord fo vehemently, and in the name too of Tiberius ?

This celebrated decree then clearly appears to have been pafled not till after the crucifixion of our Lord, and, as Sabinus is faid to have been put to dfeath in the beginning of u. c. 781, feveral months at leaft after his death. – As then this appears to be fo very clear – let us proceed to enquire whether it may not have been pafled before the death of Sejanus – for, notwithflanding he was, by the Senate, executed on the fame day in which he was apprehended – and – as Dion would have it thought, in compliance with the prefumed intimation of Tiberius, yet, why, if as both Tacitus and Dion fay, that decree had then been pafled, fhould it have been prefumed that he, after having caufed the Senate to pafs it, expefted them to execute his prime rolnifter fo foon, and, as Dion fays, without trial.

We are informed by Dion, 1. 58, that Tiberius, in the beginning of the 18th year of his reign, confident of the co-operation of the Senate and of the people, determined to crufh Sejanus – and – that he, in order to accomplifh his purpofe, wrote a very prolix incoherent letter to the confcript fathers. – This letter, fays he, p. 626, E., was, by Macro, delivered to the confuls early in the morning of the day in which Sejanus was executed. – It, continues Dion, did not contain any exprefs order for the execution of Sejanus – *wrixpvs yap airaQya-xtit avnt a Tit[ios 5* irfoo-sT$i – and of courfe not for his *immediate* execution, but only here and there glanced at him. – No fooner, fays he, p. 627, D., had this incomprehcnfible letter been read than the Senate,

Be- -

Why and when Tiberius forbad instant executions.

without in the leaft endeavouring to get at a right underftanding of it, (fo far were they from being difpofed to make any attempt of the kind, that they, one and all, immediately loaded him with reproaches,) and without any trial, (for Regulus, he fays, fearing a tumult would, as Sejanus had fo many friends and relations, enfue, if he was to proceed to try him, after having afked one only what Ihoqld be dons with him, and prefuming that he faid in reply – bind him and put him to prifon, immediately proceeded to do it) – andw on the fame day, as Dipn proceeds to fay, p. 628, A , executed him.

Now if Tiberius wrote thus obfcurely of Sejanus, and did not fpecify any charge againft him, how could he have expedted that he would be tried ? – And if he gave no order for his execution, efpecially his immediate execution, does it not imply that the Senate muft have afted arbitrarily, if not in defiance of his decree ?

Again – Tacitus has, vi. 18, mentioned another itiftance of immediate executions – he there fays – and the fprmar fears returned w)th the accufation of Confidius Proculus, of high-treafon, whom the Senate feized, while he was celebrating a birth-day, condemned and killed. – Dein redcunt priores metus, poftulato majeftatis Confidio Proculo: qui nullo pavore diem natalem cefebrans, raptus in Curiam pariterque damnatus interfeftufquc.

Before we take our- leave of this inftancc of th readincfs of th Senate to punifh, with immediate death, thole who were accufed ef high-treafon, it may not be amifs to attend to what both Tacitus and Dion fay happened a little before in the fame year.

Great complaints were, fays Tacitus, c 16, made by accufers againft ufurers, who were fo powerful that Gracchus, the praetor, thought it right to take the fenfe of the fathers on the point. – The

Why and when Tiberius forbad instant executions.

fathers afraid to decide on it, defired Tiberius to direft them how to proceed in the bufinefs – with their requeft he inftantly complied. – This is nearly the film of the Contents of this chapter. – In the next – viz – 17, he fays, thata great fcarcity of coin enfued – Hinc, &c. – which, he fays, Was partly oecafitmed by the praftice of ufurers, and partly by the fale of the effefts of condemned perfons, the produce of which had been placed either in the exchequer or treafury.-Qefar, fays he, again ftept forth and lent a large fum of money to the public, without intereft, for three years – or, as Dion fays, *l*. 58, p. *6$fa* E., lent it to fenatorial men that they might diftribute it, without inter- eft, to the public – *n, re TtfUfpa* To *xarit r'ot,* Siivar/J. Ta *iptrfmfv, xai Ii. yyjixs Kxi iretraxofiics fiVfixiSas ra* mi//ria toWcv, *ti avrxs wii cevipifii*

ftaturvt anxn ibis Siocsvbir r *rfix trti tx$ami6Qwai.* – -*To* this Dion immediately fubjoins what feems to be quite unconnefted witli the foregoing – viz – that Tiberius ordered all the principal accufers to be executed in one day – -*ras n titiGwinvaras rut ras* xariyojxxs *iro'tafj. ciu amQonin i pta -sa tx&ivm.* – Now who can be fuppofed to believe that any prince would, immediately after having done two fuch noble afts of beneficence in favor of the Roman people, as Tacitus has recorded – and, after having removed thofe terrific pefts of their repofe – accufers, have permitted any one to accufe another – or, an accufed perfon to be condemned without trial – and to be immcdiately executed, and in defiance of his decree forbidding fuch hafty executions ? And yet Tacitus, we find, fays – that he did both know of the proceeding and permit it to take place – and, moreover, that he, by fo doing, caufed the former fears of the Romans to return – Dein, redeunt priores rnetus, poftulato iriajeftatis C. Proculo, &c.

Why and when Tiberius forbad instant executions.

The next inftance which it may be proper to adduce on this point, is that of Afinius Callus, an aged fenator, and the father of feveral confulars, who was brother-in-law to Agrippina, by marrying Vip- fania the firft wife of Tiberius, and who, as Tacitus fays, 5v. 71, had moved the Senate, immediately aftef the affair of Sabinus, that a petition fhould be prefented to Tiberius requefting him to make the ground of his fear known to them, to the end, that they might, if they could, remove it. – This aged fenator was, fays Tacitus, vi. 23, in the year 786, no doubt – baud dubium – ftarved to death – but whether voluntarily, or by necerfity, no one, fays he, could fay – iiicertum habebatur. – Caefar, fays he, was defired to fay whether he would permit him to be buried – and was not amamed to fay that he had no objeftion to it – and to lament his hard lot in being taken off before he was tried, as if, in the courfe of three years, he could not have cauſed him to be tried. – This is nearly the whole of the account which Tacitus gives, iv. 23, of the death of this aged ſenator – an account which ſeems to be intended to convey a pretty ſtrong refleſtion on Tiberius. – But, of what nature, we cannot perceive. – Neither can we, others may ſay, nor how this ſtory any way tends to illuſtrate the queſtion of immediate executions – for, Tacitus, it ſeems, is ſo far from ſaying that Gallus was condemned that he even complains that he was not tried. – True. – ButJet us attend to what Dion ſays of this fame Afinius Gallus.

Dion ſays, 1. 58, p. 622, B., that the Senate, the knights, and the commonalty of Rome uſed, in the year 782, to ſend deputations, from each of their ranks, to Tiberius, at Capreae – and – that Afinius*Why and when Tiberius forbad instant executions.*

Tacitus says, vi. 25, that Gallus had committed adultery with Agrippina, -tu; had then been a widow nearly 15 jears.

Gallus, who had been very forward to make motions tending to ia- creafe the honors of Sejanus, vvas, in the year 783, ambitious of being employed, by the Senate, as one of their delegates. – Tiberius, ſays Dion C., received him very kindly – xx 1 *"natn avnv tluapsy"D4.* – But in the mean time, he, ſays Dion, had ſent an epiſtle to the Senate ac- cuſmg Gallus, *among other things,* of having, regardleſs of his own intimacy with Syriacus, envied Ttberius the friendſhip of Sejanus. – The Senate, continues he, proceeded, without delay, to confider the charge, and, without further evidence, and, without even hearing Gallus in his own defence, and, on the fame day – H Tt *aun* t/*/*i – paſſed ſentence of death on him, and ſent a prxtor to app-rehend him and to execute him. – The praetor, continues Dion, (not without a remark that the whole affair was quite paradoxical and novelj found Gallus regaling himſelf with Tiberius and drinking with him cups of mutual love. – And did this praetor prefume to take Gallus away from the buſineſs of his embaſſy, and from his love feaſt, to execution immediately ? – So, we find, ſays Dion. – And would Tiberius permit it to be done? – No, he would not, even though Gallos himſelf defired it – but he bade Gallus to be of good courage, and detained him as a priſoner at large, till he himſelf Ihould return to Rome. This, ſays Dion, was done by confuls, or, during the confulſhip of Tiberius, by prartors, for three years, not indeed to keep him from eſcaping, but from laying violent hands on himſelf. – During which time, he, ſubjoins Dion, was not permitted to ſee any body but the perſon whoſe buſineſs it was *to force him to eat.* – So that we perceive by this that Gallus was not permitted to ſtarve himſelf, as Tacitus ſays. – On the contrary, Dion ſeems to ſay, p. 636, B., that he was, with many others, put to death.

Dion, I. 58, p. 6S2, D. – *xxt ts ip*u?, axw *ms afsytt us ware rot*
Why and *"when Tiberius forbad instant executions.*

In ſhort – that this decree was not paſſed till after the death of our Lord is plain – and, that the proceeding of the Senate, with reſpeſt to the execution of Sejanus, cannot be adduced as a proof that it was not paſſed nearly four years after his death, is not Ids plain.

10

SECTION 10

CHAPTER X.

W hen and "why did Tiberius abolish all the asyla in the empire ?

SUETONIUS tells us, *ill.* 37, that Tiberius abolifhed all the afyla in the empire – Abolevit jus moremque afylorum quae ufquam crant. – Now when did he do this, and why did he do it ?

That Tiberius fhould have thought of doing it is a matter of no little aftonimment, becaufe Tacitus, we find, fays iii. 60, that he, in the year 775, permitted the Senate to take cognizance of the *Grectan* afyla, and to fupprefs thofe that had been abufed. The account which Tacitus gives of this affair is very remarkable, and de- ferves our particular attention. And not only the account itfelf is very remarkable, but alfo the manner in which he introduces it, for by the manner in which ho introduces it, we fhall be enabled to perceive, that he permitted the Senate to take cognizance not of the Grecian afyla only, but, of all foreign afyla. – -He introduces his account of this matter, with telling us, that Tiberius, by way of confirming his defpotifm, ordered all hjs provincial preefe&s to make,*When and "why did Tiberius abolish all the asyla in the empire ?*

every year, a return, not to himfelf, but to the Senate, of the memorable occurrences that had happened in the year preceding, as they ufed to do in the days of the republic. –

THE HISTORY OF THAT INIMITABLE MONARCH TIBERIUS. John Rendle **125**

His own words are thefe – Sed Tiberius, vim ftbi principatus firmans, imaginem antiquitatis fenatui praebebat, poftulata provinciarum ad difquifitionem Patrum, mittendo. – And can he have meant this as the introduftion of what concerned the Grecian ftates only? – Does it not feem that the provinces in general were to make their complaints to the Senate? – If Tiberius made this new regulation, by way, as Tacitus fays, of confolidating his fovereignty, would he have ordered the Grecian ftates only to make thofe returns ? – Would not a partial reftoration of an ancient privilege have tended only to remind them of how much more power they were ftill deprived ? – Befides – who would have thought that he could, by the general terms – poftulata provinciarum – have meant only the complaints of the abufes of the afyla in the Grecian ftates? If we were to confine our attention to what immediately follows – viz – Crebefcebat *tntm* Graecas per urbes licentia et impunitas afyla ftatuendi – we mould be led to think that he muft have meant thofe complaints only – but if we extend our enquiry though the whole of the fequel, we fhall, perhaps, perceive that we feem to have no little reafon to think that he evidently meant all foreign afyla.

But for what reafon, does he fay, thofe numerous unchartered afyla were inftituted all over the Grecian ftates? – fcil – complebantur tcmpla peffimis fervitiorum : eodem fubfidio obaerati adverfum credi- tores: – but were thofe unauthorifed Grecian afyla the only receptacles for fuch fort of wretches ? – Were not thofe at Rome, even by the evidence of Tacitus, iii. 36, abufed in the fame manner ? – And were fuch wretches only fhut up in thofe Grecian afyla? – No – Tacitus fays immediately after – fufpe&ique capitalium criminum recepta*When and why did Tiberius abolish all the asyla in the empire?*

bantur. – Having told us that thofe Grecian afyla were receptacles of (late delinquents, he fubjoins – Nee ullum fatis validum imperium erat coercendis feditionibus populi, flagitia hominum ut caeremonias Deum protegentis. – *lyttur,* continues he, that is, feemingly, for this latter reafon only – placitum ut mitterent civitates jura atque legatos. This, then, feems to be the firft and the only ftep which the Senate took in confequence of the renewal of their loft privilege.

Thus far he feems to have conftned himfelf to a detail of the abufes praftifed in the afyla of the Grecian ftates only. – Some of which, he fays, voluntarily relinquifhed their ufurpations – Et quaedam quod falfo ufurpaverant fponte omifere. – But in all the fequel he feems to have extended his view of the fabjeft to confederate ftates, and tributary kingdoms, if not to thofe allies whofe religion they could not comprehend – Magnaque ejus diei fpecjes fuit, quo Senatus majorum bene- ficia, *fociorum pafla, regum* etiam, qui ante vim rotnanam valuerant, *decreta,* ipforumque numinum religiones introfpexit. – As a concjufion to all this, and to the chapter, he adds – that the Senate were ftill permitted to proceed in the enquiry – libero ut quondam quid linuutel mutaretve.

In the two next chapters – viz – 61, 62, he proceeds to mention feveral Afiatic ftates that then appeared to prove the prefcriptive rights of their afyla. – In the 6tft he mentions the Ephefians, and the Ephe- fians only. – In the 6id he places firft the Magnates – then the Aphro- difienfes – then the Stratonicenfes – then the Hierocaefariences – and, laftly, the Cyprians. – Thefe are all he mentions by name.

But befides the deputies from thofe Grecian and Afiatic ftates for the rights of their afyla, there were alfo fome from ftill other ftates on

When and why did Tibsrius abolish all the asyla in the empire?

the fame bufinefs – for he, we find, begins the next chapter – viz – 63, with faying – Auditae *aliarum* quoque civitatum legationes. – But what other ftates, fent deputies, he does not fay – nor can we conceive, unlefs the Jewifh was one of thofe ftates. – They were, it feems, fo many, that he fubjoins – Quorum copia feffi patres, et quia ftudiis certabatur, *confulibus* permifere, ut perfpefto jure, et fi qua iniquitas involveretur, ran integram rurfus *adfenatum* referrent. – By which it feems to appear more clearly that the Senate confidered themfelves as the proper judges of fuch matters – that they had a further hearing on them – and, that they expefted further information from the confuls.

In the following year – viz – 776, he fays, iv. 14, that the deputies from Samos and Coos petitioned to have the ancient rights of their afyla confirmed. – And again, in the next chapter, he fays enough to convince us that Tiberius did not, in that year, revoke his late conceffion, he there fays of the Senate, that they, *even then,* difcufled every thing – apud quos, *etiam tum,* cunfta traftabantur – and fubjoins a moft remarkable inftance of it, in the cafe of Lucilius Capito, the praefeft of Afia, whofe accufers Tiberius exhorted the Senate to hear.

By the evidence of Tacitus then, in thofe two chapters of the fourth book, it appears that the Senate had a further hearing of fome of the afyla deputies the following year – and, that they were, even then, poflefled of the power of difcuffing all points. – How much longer they exercifed this privilege let us proceed to enquire.

That Tiberius is not likely to have revoked his voluntary conceffion before the end of the year 778 is plain, by what Tacitus fays, iv. 43, of the decifion of the Senate concerning the difputed right of the *When and why did Tiberius abolish all the asyla in the empire?*

temple of Diana Limenatidis – De jure templi Dianae Limenatidis.– – The difpute, it fhould be obferved, arofe between the Lacedaemonians (who, Suetonius fays, iii. 6, were under the proteftion of the Clau- dian family,) and the Meflenians – but, notwithflanding that, the Senate decided in favor of the Meflenians.

Again – That Tiberius is not likely to have revoked his voluntary conceffion to the Senate, before the year 779 – or, juft before he retired from Rome, is plain from what Tacitus fays, iv. 55, 56 – viz – that the Senate took it upon them to decide in what municipality of Afia the temple, decreed two years before to Tiberius, fhould be built. – This, it fhould be obferved, they did, though Tiberius had, in the mean time, refufed a fimilar requeft from the people of Spain.

Laftly – That Tiberjus could not have abolifhed all the afyla in the empire before the end of the year 780 is plain from what Tacitus fays, iv. 67 – viz – that Tiberius was reported to have fet feme to perfuade Agrippina and Nero (who, as Paterculus and Plinyf fay, were in cuftody for endeavouring to raife a fedition at Rome,) to take refuge at a famous ftatue of Auguftus in the forumj – ultroque ftrue- bantur, qui monerent perfugere ad Germaniae exercitus, vel celeber- rimo fori effigiem divi Augufti amplefti, populumque ac fenatum auxilio vocare.

ii. iso.

' . '. i '

+ viii. 40.
,
.
$ That this statue of Augustus -was, by Tiberius, allowed to protect delinquents, late in his reign, may be inferred from what Suetonius says, iii. .5H – viz – paullatim hoc genus caluraniae co processit, ul haec quoque capitalia, esseut: circa $imulgcrum Auguti servum cecidisse, &c.

When and why did Tiberius abolish all the asyla in the empire?

Let us now hear what the fcriptures fay of this matter – Mofes, fays the old teftament, eftablifhed afyla – now, whatever he eftablifhed was, as Jofephus informs us, fecured by mutual compaft at the de- pofition of Archeluus, when the Jews voluntarily requefted to bft governed, in political matters, by the Roman laws – their religious laws were preferved ever after by Auguftus and by Tiberius inviolate. They were alfo indulged by the Romans with the moft extraordinary privilege of demanding yearly, of their Roman governor, the releafc of a notorious malefaftor, though (as Tacitus obferves of thofe delinquents who were protefted by moft of thofe other afyla,) a ftate pri- foner, who had caufed a fedition and in it had committed murder This privilege they always enjoyed under Pilate, and, in the I4th year of Tiberius, they compelled him to do as he had ever done, and, to releafe to them one whom he had imprifoned as the leader of fedition, and in preference to one who, Pilate was convinced, was quite innocent of any crime. – Confequently as this privilege of th moft dangerous tendency was then continued, why fhould we not conclude that Tiberius had not, when our Lord was crucified, abolifhed all the afyla in the empire ?

Let us now, in order to obtain a little more futisfaftion on this point, confult Suetonius:

Suetonius, we have obferved, fpeaks of the abolition of afyla in the 37l1l chapter. – In the *preceding* part of that chapter he fpeaks popular tumults, and of the great care which Tiberius took to fupprefs them – viz – by ftationing guards all over Italy – and, by collefting the body guards at Rome – and, in the part following, he fpeaks of the inhabitants of Cyzicum being deprived of their freedom of Rome. – Now Dion, we find, has, 1. 57, p. 619, D., placed thofe two events in the year 777. – In this then either Suetonius or Dion*When and why did Tiberius abolish all the asyla in the empire?*

appears, by what has been already faid of this matter, to be wrong. Again – Suetonius, we obferve, in the 36th chapter, mentions the cxpulfion of the Jews, Egyptians, and fuch like feftaries from Rome- why then mould we not fuppofe that the expulfion of the Jews, &c. preceded, and but a Ihort time, the abolition of the afyla ?

Let us now then look out for a period before which it feems likely that Tiberius muft have done it.

The Talmud of Jerufalem, we find, fays, that judgment was taken from Ifrael in the 16th year of Tiberius, that is, as is commonly fdpi pofed, all power of life and death, but, as we fuppofe, only that of ftoning the Jewifh believers, as blafphemers. – Now if Tiberitis, in the" 16th year of his reign, forbad the Jews to ftone thfcir believing brethren, as blafphemers, why fhould we not fuppofe that He did, before he took from them this imagined right, revoke what Was only a gratuitoufly conceded privilege ?

– Would it not have been altogether unaccountable, if Tiberius fhould have permitted the Jews to retain any indulgence, efpecially one of fo extraordinary a nature, and fo dangerous to the Roman ftate, after they had prefumed to ufurp fo ftrange a power as that of ftoning to death their believing couritry-
men.

t Tiberius then appears to hare abolifhed all the afyla between the

14th and t6th year of his reign – that is, about the time when he ordered condemned criminals not to be immediately executed – and, about the time when the Senate expelled from Rome the Jews and
fuch like feftaries.

t

Having now endeavoured to fatisfy ourfelves concerning the year in which Tiberius abolifhed all the afyla – let us next, as was propofed, endeavour to fatisfy ourfelves alfo why he did it.

When and why did Tiberius abolish all the asyla in the empire?

As then Tiberius appears, in the year 775, to have permitted the Senate to enquire into the privileges of the afyla in mod of the eaftern countries, and to correft the abufes to which they were perverted, (of which the chief was, as Tacitus fays, the proteftion of ftate delinquents) – and to continue the exercife of their ancient right till the year 781. – Why fhould he, who, as Tacitus fays, was for nothing fo anxious as to let every thing remain as it was; and, who, as Jofephus fays, would hardly take the trouble to order a man, who had been accufed of confpiring againft him, to be imprifoned, have, without fome very cogent reafon, prefumed to revoke an indulgence which he had freely granted to the Senate, and, as Tacitus fays, by way of confirming his own defpotifm; and then to abolifh all thofe afyla which the Senate had eftablifhed, not excepting even the Jewifh indulgence? – If indeed, he reftored this privilege to the Senate, as Tacitus fays, by way of confirming his defpotifm, would he, without a fufficient provocation, have prefumed to take it from them again ? Would it, in that cafe, not have been better not to have reftored it ? Did he then notice fome very great abufe in any of them which the Senate ought to have correfted f – If fo what could that have been, but the abufe of the Jewifh, in the cafe of our Lord? – when, we find, a feditious perfon and a murderer was fuffered to efcape with impunity, and an innocent perfon put to death in his ftead.

But if Tiberius, after having permitted the Senate to take cognizance of the abufes to which the afyla were generally perverted, found him- felf compelled, by their connivance at the greateft poffible abufe of an afylum, to revoke his former conceffion, does it not feem to imply that fome difagreement took place between them from that time ? – And, efpecially, if Tiberius, at the fame time, and for the fame reafon, forbad immediate executions? – This we hope to afcertain in the next chapter.

11

SECTION 11

CHAPTER XI.
Why and when Tiberius was afraid to enter the Senate,
JTRABO, who it appears by what he fays, vi. p. 199, wrote in the year 772 – and, by what he fays, vi. p. 199, juft before the death of Germanicus (for Germanicus and Drufus, he there fays, were ftill the lieutenants of Tiberius – *U7tapyarrn)* – and therefore in the 5th or 6th year of Tiberius, after having told us, in the preceding part of the laft mentioned paflage, how much more peace and plenty mankind enjoyed after they came under the dominion of Auguftus, than they did, at any time, before, proceeds to fay that they enjoyed the fame under his fucceflor Tiberius, *who followed all the rules of government*
   hrefcribed by Allgujlus. – *Qv$t wori* yv EtwropSjo-ai *roo-avrw tifsns xai afQottas ayaQut mnift Pufmxiois, xai rois* o-r/A/Axj$oiJ *Avtw,* Ootjv Kaio-ap rc o *iGmos irapcrctr o.$ e wxpAxvi ryt s%uyiav avmretiri, xai m o* SjoEa$tivor *t/os txtitot, irapixft TiGtfios, Kxvovx rys* Sioikho-ewj, xai *rut irfisxyfiarut iroiactos saiHmi* x *aurot ot inoii$is avm, Tippatixos re xai Apvovs, virapyutrts ru irarfi.* –
   And thofe rules prefcribed by Auguftus, we may fuppofe he followed, till the end of Strabo's days – that is. at leaft, as we are informed by
   Why and when Tiberius was afraid to enter the Senate.

Cafaubon, his interpreter, till the 12th of Tiberius. – And, if we may believe Tacitus, Ann. i. 77, ii. 65, iv. 37 – and, again, in his life of Agricola, 13, Tiberius never after deviated from the line pointed out by his predeceflbr – excepting only in refufing divine honors himfelf – and, in aboliihing all the afyla in the empire.

Seneca, in his Confol. ad Marc., 15, which he wrote after the death ofCordus, who died u. c. 778, reckons Tiberius as not inferior to Auguftus, or, rather as the greateft of great men. – And, in his de Benef., ii. c. 7, he fays, that Tiberius affifted feveral paft praetors, whofe income was not fufficient to enable them to live refpeftably, with money fufficient for that purpofe. – And, iii. 26, he fays, that, at the time, when the rage of accufing was fo very great – that is, as we fuppofe, u. c. 781, the Senate encouraged accufations againft thofc who, in compliance with his own decree, refufed to worfhip him; and even fat in judgement on Paullus, a praetor, though he was accufed of nothing more than of having, when intoxicated, polluted an effigies of him which he wore on his ring.

Patereulus feems to intimate, ii. 126, that the Senate had, either before, or, in the year 783, difagreed among themfelves – and, that Tiberius was then fo far from being difpofed to widen the breach, that he had been the means of reconciling their mutual animofities –

and, of increafing their dignity – fummota difcordia curia acceffit

fenatui majeftas. – And what does Patereulus feem to fay was th& refult of this pacific difpofition of Tiberius? – fcil – Such an uniterfal and profound peace as was never known before – Quando, fays he, a little after, pax laetior ? – Pax Augufta in omnes, &c. – He alfo fays, c. 129, that Tiberius had, before the i6th year of his reign, enabled many fenatorials to recover their dignity – Quotiens populum congia*Why and when Tiberius was afraid to enter the Senate.*

tlls honoravit, fenatorumque cenfum, *cum id fenatu auffore facere Jtotuit,* quam libenter explevit; ut neque luxuriam invitaret, nequc honeftam paupertatem pateretur dignitate deftitui ?

V. Maximus fcems to fay, ix. 11, that the fame undifturbed manner of tranfafting public and private bufinefs continued both before and after the death of Sejanus. – Itaque Hat pax – valent leges – fincerus privati ac *publtci officti tenor* fervatur.

Philo fays, p. 769, that the profound peace which prevailed every where on the acceffion of Caius was the refult of the prudent government of Tiberius – and, p. 780, F., that no king or autocrat was more venerable in his old age – and again, p. 783, F., that he enjoyed the bleffings of peace to the end of his days.

To the evidence of thofe feveral cotemporary writers on this point, may be added that of Suetonius, and Jofephus, and Dion.

Suetonius has related feveral things which tend to imprefs us with the idea that no caufe of difagreement could, at any time, have exifted between Tiberius and the Senate. – But of any notorious difagreement between them he fays not a word. – Chapter 28, 29, he relates what he faid, on feveral occafions, of the freedom of debate – and, laft of all, what he faid to all the fenators on this fame point – Dixi et nunc et faepe alias P. C. bonum et falutarem principem, quem vos tanta et tam libera poteftate inftruxiftis Senatui fervire debere, et univerfis civibus fepe, et plerumque etiam fingulis: neque id dixifle me poenitet, et bonos et aequos et faventes vos habui dominos, et adhuc habeo. – – Chapter 47, he reluftantly acknowledges what Paterculus, we have juft feen, aflertsTiberius often did for reduced patricians. – And, chap. 67, he alfo informs us that he cautioned them not to be forward to

Why and when Tiberius "was afraid to enter the Senate.

fwear to obferve the future afts of any one – Similem fe femper fui futurum: nee unquam mutaturum mores fuos, quandiu mentis fanae fuiflet: fed exempli caufa cavendum, ne fenatus in afta cujufSam obligaret, qui aliquo cafu mutari poflet. – -Chapter 31, he fays, that Tiberius was, on two or three queftions, outvoted – and, that he was hot, in the leaft, difpleafed at it – ne queftus quidein eft. – Chap. 33, he, it muft be confefled, feems to apprife us that Tiberius controled the debates of the Senate much, and, that he even annulled one or two of their decrees – for he there fays, that he, *atfirjl,* only annulled their decrees when they were manifeftly wrong – Ac *primo* eatenus interveniebat ne quid perperam fieret. *Itaque* et conftitutiones quaf dam fenatus refcidit. – which, furely, feems to imply that he, afterwards, took much greater liberties with the Senate. – But where does Suetonius fpeak of the liberties which he took with the decrees of the Senate ? – May we not expeft to find, in the fequel, fome account both of the liberties which Tiberius took of this kind, and of the re- monftrances of the Senate ? – Not a word, can, we perceive, has he faid of either of thofe points – unlefs, he may be fuppofed to have alluded to the former by what he fays, 37, of the abolition of all the afyla – and, 26, . of the refufal of Tiberius of divine honors. – Laftly, chapter 37, he fays how careful he was to preferve the public peace from being difturbed by either domeftic or foreign enemies.

Jofephus, A. xviii. 4, defcribes him as having been ready to oblige a fenator at any time before the expulfion of the Jews – and, as having been, after that time, remarkably inattentive to the moft intercfting concerns – and, alfo, as having, when he might have lived in quiet, dift rafted himfelf about futurity.

Dion, 1. 57, p. 606, B. C. D. E., relates how very modeftly Tiberius behaved, on all occafions, and efpecially in the Senate, till the death

Why and when Tiberius was afraid to enter the Senate.

of Germanicus – and, p. 607, A., how he would not fuffer them to addrefs him by any other appellation than that of prefident, and, how

often he ulcd to lay – Aeuronir /i *Tm $itut avroxfarup St rut fariuruf rat* St Sn XonrSv *foxfirts tifti.* – Again, he fays, 1. 57, p. 608, B. C., that Tiberius expended very little on hirnfelf, very much on the republic – much on foreign flutes and individuals – and that he enriched many fenators who were reduced to poverty – *rm psy"D4 guteurZt mix. ias itnttwHe*

tat piaan nSt jSaXmit oi Tbt' *iQ&otrxs, nrarini.* – Dion alfo fays, 1. 58, p. 623, B., that the Senate, in the year 782, or the i5th or i6th of Tiberius, ufed to fend delegates to him from their body – and, C., that he, in the next year, 783, received their delegates, headed by

Gallns, with the greateft cordiality.

On reconfidering what thofe feveral writers have faid of the con- duel of Tiberius, in various parts of his reign, towards the Senate, and of his endeavours to preferve the peace of the republic, both internally and externally, who can think that he, at any time, difagree J greatly with moft of the Senate and for no affignable reafon –

and, efpecially, during his refidence at Capreae ? – And, when he was overcome with exceffive grief? – And yet Tacitus, we find, who fays, that he was particularly revered by the Senate till the beginning of 781, alfo fays, that he did difagree with the Senate in that year, and molt inconceivably, and without acquainting us with the reafon. – He moreover feems to fay that this difagreement continued till the death of Sejanus.

Let us be a little careful in noticing what Tacitus fays of the behavior of Tiberius and the Senate towards each other, immediately before this breach happened, in hope of being able to difcover what may have been the caufe of it.

Why and when Tiberius was afraid to enter the Senate.

He, we find, has recorded feveral inftances of the mutual amity of Tiberius and the Senate, in the courfe of the year 780. – Tiberius, he fays, was, in that year, all beneficence, and, the Senate all gratitude. He alfo lays, that Tiberius, in the former part of that year, Ihewed not the leaft fign of fear or fufpicion, for when the fire had confumed a great part of Mount Coelius, Tiberius, fays he, quite unfolicited, fent for the fufferers and relieved them – famaque apud populum, quia fine ambitione, aut *proximorum ptecibus,* ignotos etiam et *ultra accitos* munificentia juverat. – By a fubfequent report of Tacitus (67) Tiberius muft have returned from Campania to do this – but, by that of Suetonius, iii. 40, he muft have returned from Capreae to do it. – However, in either cafe, he, it feems, muft, at that time, have been quite un- difturbed by any apprehenfion for his fafety. – Towards the conclufion of that year he, fays Tacitus, iv. 67, having finifhed all that he had to do in Campania, retired to Capreae, full of fufpicions, and of a temerity to believe. – Why, if the people and the Senate had been fo recently obliged by him, and had exprefled their obligations fo openly, he Ihould have tormented himfelf with fufpicions of any kind, we cannot conceive – and, what he could have meant by a temerity of believing we do not attempt to difcover. – Tacitus feems to hint that thofe fufpicions and this temerity of believing had fome fort of a reference to the conduft of Agrippina and Nero, whom, he feems to fay, Tiberius had then imprifoned. – But Paterculus, who wrote at the time, and addrefled his work to one of the then confuls, who, a little more than five years after, married Julia, one of the daughters of Agrippina, informs us, iii. 130, that Tiberius was compelled to grieve, to be indignant, to blufh, on their accounts. – And Pliny, riii. 40, feems to render his report credible.

Tac. Ann. vi. 13.

Why and when Tiberius was afraid to enter the Senate.

Again – In the beginning of the year following – viz – 781, Tacitus relates another remarkable inftance of the devotednefs of the Senate to Tiberius – aninftance, which, if true, as he reports it, muft render it ftill more furprifing that Tiberius fhould, at the time, have entertained any fufpicions about the difaffeftednefs of any of his fubjefts. It is the ftrange ftory of the miferable end of Titius Sabinus, a knight, and the almoft only remaining adherent of the family of Germanicus, who, in the year 777, had been, with C. Silius, a man patronized bjr Tiberius, arraigned for treafonable praflices, in favor of that family. This Sabinus, fays Tacitus, had been again fo imprudent as to fuffer himfelf to be decoyed into a repetition of his former offence. – Four of the Senate, fays he, fufpefting his difloyalty, contrived to draw him into a converfation about Tiberius and his treatment of the family of Germanicus, and, taking the advantage of what

fell from him, lodged an accufation of treafon againft him. – The reft of the Senate, on hearing the charge, immediately proceeded to pafs fentence on him, and, on the fame day, to execute him. – Tiberius, fubjoins he, thanked them for what they had done, and complained that his life was in danger, that he fufpefted the confpiracies of his enemies – adjefto, trepidam fibi vitam, fufpeftas inimicorum infidias. – And what if he was afraid his life was in danger, and that he fufpefted the confpiracies of his enemies? – Why fhould he have complained of it to the Senate ? Had he not, as Dion fays, 1. 57, p. 606, C., privy counfellors ? – Who could have thought that Tiberius would, fo very foon after his voluntary trip from Capreae to FidenEC, and there making himfelf fo very acceffible to all, have uttered fuch a complaint? – Or, after having rendered himfelf fo very popular to all the people of Rome, and to the Senate, by his beneficence to the fufferers by fire on Mount
Coelius?
Paterculus ii. ISO.

Why and when Tiberius was afraid to enter the Senate.

In the courfe of the fame year, fays Tacitus, iv. 74, the Senate, on account of fome unaccountable internal alarm, (which he reprefents as having been infinitely greater than that caufed by the revolt of the Frifii) fought to obtain, *by adulation,* the interference of Tiberius. – But what was the caufe of this internal confirmation he, it feems, though he complains of a want of materials to write about, does not fay. – He only leaves us to conclude that Tiberius himfelf, an exile as he then was, and the flave of indolence and vice, and worn out with age and grief, could alone counterast it. – But what caufe of internal alarm could have terrified thofe who fmiled at all terrors ? – And, at a time too, when only the extremity of the empire was dif- turbed ? – Or could have been of fuch a nature as to make the confcript fathers think of nothing elfe but of offering incenfe to a woe worn old man, who had retired from the buftle of government in difguft, and and was then living far away in obfcurity ? – And then, on finding that he did not perceive the fragrance of their precious oblation, as to make them think of fending petition after petition to him to requeft an interview? – Not at Rome, but, ifheqhofe, far off on the coaft of Campania ? – -And then again, finding their petitions difregarded, as to make them refolve on fending a deputation to him, confiding, not of one or two of the principal people of Rome, but of men of all ranks, and moftly of the commonalty – of whom a large party attended – magna pars plebis. – Thofe were all the partifans of Sejanus – anxii erga Sejanum. – And this laft ftep, our hiftorian'intimates, the Senate took, without being fure whether thofe delegates would be permitted to have accefs to him, though that, it feems, was to be their grand objeft – crebrifque precibus *effZagitabant,* vifendi fui co- piam facerent. – This numerous motley partyf fays he, proceeded from Rome, in commotion as it then was, and uncertain as it then was what was the objeft of the commotion, without any aflurance of

Why and when Tiberius was afraid to enter the Senate.

being permitted to fee Tiberius, or even their idol Sejanus, and with- 9ut any hope of accommodation for the night, to the coaft of Campania, – When they arrived there they remained *a Jay and a night* in the open air, when they were given to underftand that all their endeavours to obtain an interview would be of no avail, and that it was expefted they would remain there no longer. – This made moft of them return, as, it feems, they went, in trepidation. – Some few, however, were, it feems, permitted to have a tranfitory fight of, at leaft, one of their objefts, but whether Tiberius or Sejanus he does not fay. Thofe few, fays he, were fo mal-apert that they (notwithftanding the fcene of mifery which they had juft left, and to which they were immediately about to return,] rejoiced at their fuperior good hick. – But, fubjoins Tacitus, they foon paid dear for their ill-timed exultation.

This is the account which Tacitus, who complains that to record What happened in the reign of Tiberius, was, as it was fo very barren ef interefting events, but an inglorious tafk, has thought proper to give us of this, as he fays, internal pavor, which, he fays, difturbed fo unexpeftedly and fo unaccountably the peace of Rome, and of that city only, after the execution of Sabinus, in the I4th year of Tiberius. A confternation f which Caius, the fucceflbr of Tiberius, if we may believe Suetonius, does not feem to have been aware – for he, fays Suetonius, iv. 31, complained that his reign was not likely to be rendered memorable by any remarkable occurrence, as thofe of his two predeceflbrs had been – that of Auguftus having been rendered memorable by the defeat of Varus – and that of Tiberius, not by this internal terrific phenomenon, but the fall of the Amphitheatre at Fidenae. And a confternation which feems to have afrcfted neither Seneca nor

Male alacre.
Why and when Tiberius "was afraid to enter the Senate.
Pliny in any remarkable degree – for the former, though he has taken notice of the death of Sabinus, yet he fays not a word of the internal alarm which took place at Rome immediately after. – And the latter, in his Confol. to Marcia for the lofs of Cordus and Mctilius, which, it feems, he wrote *three entire yean* after the death of Cordus, who, Tacitus fays, iv. 34, died no one knows how long after the year 778 was begun, and therefore, no one knows how long after the year 781 was begun, but before the death of Livia, fays – that fhe had not feen any public or private calamity – nulla publica clades confpicitur, nulia privata.

As this report of Tacitus then feems, by the manner in which he has related it, to be not a little queftionable – and, by the account of Caius, Pliny, and Seneca the elder, to be not very credible. – Let us proceed to enquire if he may not, by his acknowledged prejudice on a certain point, have been induced to make a falfe reprefentation of a moft notorious event which happened in the courfe of this very year.

It mould be recollefted that he had, before Ann. i. 73, as good as promifed us to let us know how Tiberius had, with exquifite craft, favored the irruption of a moft grievous peft – and how it had been fhortly after reprefled, by, no doubt, fome other power – and, how it then again blazed forth, notwithftanding all oppofition, and hurried away every thing – and, all this, he promifed to let us know in the cafe of two Roman knights. – Have we not then fomewhat like a reafon to fufpeft that he means here to fulfill his promife ? – In what of year the reign of Tiberius can we think it likely to have happened, if not in this ? – What but this moft grievous peft could have caufed this moft extraordinary pavor ? – And what could this moft grievous peft have been but the execrable fuperftition, which, he fays, A. xv, was alfo, *for the prefent,* reprefled ? – And then burft forth, not only *Why and when Tiberius was afraid to enter the Senate.*

in Judea, but in the city too ? – Does not Seneca, the elder, appear to advert to this very thing in his work againft fuperftitlon, by fpeak- ing of the praftice of that moft impious of people, who had, after they had been conquered, vanquifhed their antagonifts ? – And does not his fon too appear to allude to it both in his cviii. epiftle and in his work de Benef. ? – In the former work, he, we have feen, fpeaks of the facred rites of foreigners being difcufled – and, in the latter, of the frequent and almoft public rage of accufers having, in the reign of Tiberius, wafted the Roman flate worfe than any civil war.

By comparing this account of Tacitus with thofe other two in the fame work (the laft of which evidently defcribes the bad effcfts which followed the introduftion of the Chriftian religion into Rome,) and with thofe of the two Senecas, why fhould we not fufpeft that they all allude to the fame event – viz – ths introduftion of Chriftianity into Rome, which, we have found, began to be preached in the i4th year of Tiberius – the very year in which, Tacitus fays, this unaccountable panic feized the inhabitants of that city.

As this then appears to have been, in all probability, the faft, let us attend to what one or two early Chriftian writers fay of the year when the faith of Chrift was firft publiihed at Rome, and of the reception which it then obtained there and a year or two after. ?

Clemens, of Rome, fays, in each of his works – viz – in his Recog., his Horn., and his G. P., that the report of our Lord's miracles and refurreftion reached Rome in the fpring of the year in which he fuffered – that frefh accounts continued to arrive every day – that what they had heard was, at laft, rendered certain by the arrival of

Why and -when Tiberius was afraid to enter the Senate.

duly accredited witnefles. – This, it fhould be obferved, is no more than what might be expefted, as Luke, we find, fays, Afts ii. 10, that there were at Jerufalem, at the Pentecoft, next after the afcen- fion, " ftrangers of Rome, Jews, and Profelytes" – and, as, we find, he alfo fays, Afts vi. 9, that there was a fynagogue appropriated at Jerufalem to the ufe of the libertines. – Clemens alfo fays, and in each of thofe works, that the faith was, in the courfe of that fummer, preached at Rome, in the forum, by Barnabas, and that fo great was the oppofirion which was made to him, on that account, that he was, before the winter came on, obliged to withdraw from Rome, and to retire into his own country.

This moft remarkable event then, in the I4th year of Tiberius, Tacitus, if he does not mean to allude to it by this internal panic, which he fo obfcurely and unfatisfaftorily defcribes, entirely overlooks. As then this event appears to have happened in the I4th year of Tiberius and to have been the caufe of much diflention, among the populace, in that year, how are we to be fure that it may not have been the caufe of pretty nearly as much between Tiberius and the Senate ? And, of courfe, of the retirement of Tiberius to Caprex, and of that immenfe cavalcade to the coaft of Campania, in order to get a fight of him – and of his refufing to grant them an interview ? – What other event could have made him, who, but the year before, haftened from Campania, if not from Capreae, to Fidenae and Rome, to affift the fufferers in each of thofe places, (and thofe of Rome un-alked,) and who had accepted the thanks of the Senate and of the people for his very beneficent conduft on thofe two occafions, to be fo very deaf to all their fupplications now ? – Efpecially if any thing like a tumult was likely to enfue ? – Are we not told by Suetonius, c. 3, that he, in. the loth year of bis reign, took all poffible care to prevent tumults. *Why and when Tiberius was afraid to enter the Senate.*

by ftationing the praetorian cohorts at Rome? – And are we not told, by the fame writer, c. 65, that he was, even after the death of Seja- nus, fo fearful of tumults, that he even ordered fome veffels to be in waiting to take him to fome other country ? – In fhort – what other event but this, could, if the Senate and the people were fo very ob- fequious to him, on two occafions, in this very fame year, have made him afraid of his enemies ? – That this very event did, foon after it took place, make a very wide breach between Tiberius and the Senate, why mould we not conclude from what Tertullian faid in the apology which he delivered to the emperor Severus, in favor of the Chriltians of his days, chapter 5.

In that apology Tertullian fays – " There was an ancient flatutc, " that no God mould be confecrated by the king, unlefs the Senate " confented to it. Marcus jEmilius applied to them about his idol

" Alburnus Tiberius therefore, in whofe reign the name of

" Chriftians was firft known in the world, on a report being made to " him, from Paleftine, of this deity, communicated it to the Senate, " in fuch a manner as to convince them that he was prejudiced in " favor of the deity; but the Senate, not approving it, rejefted the " propofal; but he remained of the fame perfuafion, threatening *fttri-* " *culum* to the accufers of Chriftians." – Now if the Senate had not encouraged the accufers of Chriftians, why mould Tiberius have

- Dion says, I. 57, p. 619, D,, that Tiberius, u. c. 777, in order to overawe the people of Rome, collected the guards, which before that time used to be dispersed all over Italy, into one body at Rome. – i"? v *ra rete 0* TiCc- *ftos* Tw Tm Soffofxa *yvtJ. tainen Tois PuttTaus, unrtf xytaum m ttrtauZtt, wtws* xi ffoXXtu *o-tyats xju tffupttas* M&tnff f/. A?, s auron Tacitus, iv. 8, Says nearly the same.

Why and when Tiberius was afraid to enter the Senate.

thought of threatening them with any fort of punifment ? – Some of our moderns have thought that Tertullian muft have erred in this matter, fo incredible does his report appear to them! – That he mould have adopted this report on mere rumour is not likely – efpecially, if, as Eufebius fays, Eccl. hift. ii. 2, he was a man moft learned in the Roman laws, and othei wife famous, particularly for his knowledge of Roman concerns. – That he mould have aflerted it at Rome, before an emperor, in the courfe of the fecond century – and, on fuch an occafion, if it was not a well-known faft, is what nobody can believe; and, that he fhould have recorded his having aflerted it on that occa- lion, if it was not an acknowledged faft, is what no Chriftian will believe. – Why then mould our moderns not believe it ?

In what year of Tiberius this diflention, concerning the dignity of our Lord, and oppofition concerning his followers, took place between Tiberius and the Senate, Tertullian does not fay; but that it took place before the expulfion of the Jews from Rome – that is, as Philo fays, before the death of Sejanus – or, before the expiration of the I7th year of Tiberius, why mould we doubt?

Prefently after the death of his mother, this fuperannuated monarch, fufpicious of his enemies, as, Tacitus fays, iv. 67, he always had been, and fearful of any attempt on his life, as, he alfo fays, iv. 71, he then was, and fo, as Suetoniqs fays, 65, continued to be three years after; no longer, fays Tacitus, v. 3, adhered to thofe very excellent meafures of policy, which he had, till then, religioufly followed; but, as if re- leafed from reftraint by the death of his mother, began to be lawlefs and oppreffive – Ceterum ex eo, praerupta jam et urgens dominatio – to the great aftonifhment and terror of all ranks of people, no doubt. But though Tacitus tells us that Tiberius, after the death of his mother, began inftantly to be fo very lawlefs and oppreffive, yet he *Why and when Tiberius was afraid to enter the Senate.*

alfo, we find, and, to our no little aftonifhment, tells us, v. 2, that Fufius, one of the then confuls, who had been patronifed by Livia, ufed, immediately after her death, to divert the confcript fathers with farcaflic failles againft Tiberius – is gratia Augufbe floruerat aptus alli- ciendis feminarum animis; dicax idem, et Tiberium acerbis facetiis irridere folitus, quarum apud praepotentes in longum memoria eft. – But what have we here? – Fufius, the conful, who had been fo much indebted to Livia for his preferment, notwithftanding he knew what had happened to Saturninus ar. d Sabinus for a fimilar offence – notwithftanding he had been fo terrified but a few months before by the internal alarm, and had been obliged to return from Campania in trepidation – notwithftanding he knew how domineering and oppref- five the government of Tiberius was become – notwithftanding he could not have been conful but by the favor of Sejanus – notwithftanding all this, ufed to make the confcript fathers, who, but a year before, had exprefled their gratitude to their prince, who, but a few months before, could not extricate themfelves from their political terror without his help, and, who, then were obliged to return from Campania, in trepidation, merry, when they were ailembled on bufi- nefs, with laughing at him, though he had always been fo good a prince! though he then was fo aged!! and fo deprefled with grief!!! Can this have been poffible ? – And in the beginning of the year too after thofe very fathers had, and by the evidence of four of their own body, put to death a knight for only fpeaking againft him – and, had, but a few months before, judged it neceflary to have recourfe to adulation, in order to prevail on Tiberius to remove from them the caufe which had fo terrified Rome internally.

Immediately after the interment of Livia, a letter of accufation, fays Tacitus, v. 3, againft Agrippina and Nero, was fent by Tiberius to the

Why and -when Tiberius was afraid to enter the Senate.

Senate, in which, fays he, there was no charge againft them of any attempt at innovation – the only thing with which they were each charged was, fays he – *he* of juvenile love and immodefty – *-JJic* of being haughty: this charge, fays he, the Senate heard with dread and filence. – A few, at laft, of the fervile party, propofed that they fhould enter into a debate on thofe articles. – Great altercation enfued on the propofal, when, at laft, Junius Rufticus, who was appointed, by Caefar, as a fort of recorder of the a&s of the Senate, and who was therefore fuppofed to be acquainted with his private views, either by a fatal im- pulfe – fatali quodam motu – or, with a bad defign – feu prava foler- tJa – unmindful of imminent danger and fearful of what might not happen, put an end to further debate by advifing the confuls not to propofe the queftion – and the reafon which he gave for his advice was this – diflerebatque brevibusmomentisywwa *vertl /taffe,* dandum- que interftitium pcenitentiae fenis – v. 4. At the fame time, fays Tacitus, the populace furrounded the houfe – and nothing fad was perpetrated – patratum – that day. – At the fame time Sejanus, who was reported to have been the onfetter of all this, with indignation exclaimed that the Senate held the *grief* of their prince in contempt – that the people were become difaffefted – that new *conciones* were heard and read – new *confulta /tatrum* – *that* nothing now remained for them but to fly to arms, and to arrange themfelves under the command of thofe *whofe Jlandards they bore.*

Tiberius, not at all difcouraged by all this unexpefted oppofition from the Senate and the people, repeated his charge againft his daughter-in-law and her fon – reprimanded, by an edift, the populace – complained to the fathers that his imperial majefty had been publicly difobeyed by the finefle of one man – and, demanded the entire exercife of his prerogative. – Nor did-they deliberate any further,

Why and token Tiberius was afraid to enter the Senate.

left they Ihould decree, not indeed the extreme, for that was forbidden, but left they Ihould teftify that they, who were prepared for revenge – ad ultionem – were hindered by the power of the prince- Nee ultra deliberatum, quo minus non quidem extrema decerne- rent, id enim vetitum, fed paratos ad ultionem vi principis impediri teftarentur.

Here then we perceive was fomething like the beginning of an open war between Tiberius and the Senate fupported by the people. Whether it was then fuppreffed and whether it continued any time our enigmatift has not been permitted to afford us any information. – But if we attend to what Dion fays, 1. 58, p. 622, A. B., we mall think that we have reaibn enough to conclude that this political confab was loon ended – for he there fays, that the Senate were, before the end of that year, (782) difpofed to adulate both Tiberius and Sejanus, as they did to procure their mediation when the internal

panic feized them – *a-ftirGtis Tt,* j5x *pet* ytfsom, *iSia* St *at tirirtis,* To, *n Ti/. y6os ix ft rut SyfJ. xpxiur* xa *ex rut ayofoHOfAxii rut o-Qtrefut Trfos aforifas* vrr EWi/xiro *xai* Wjohto *vaif xJXiTr opoius,* xai *sduov, xiiti* Tij *TojQM avrut*

On the whole – as the writers, who lived under Tiberius, fay not a word of any difagreement between him and the Senate, and Paterculus affirms, pofitively, that the Senate had, before the i6th year, differed among themfelves, and that Tiberius had, before that year, reconciled them to each other – as Suetonius does not fay that any difagreement took place between, him and that body, before the i6th, and that Tiberius, after the fire on Mount Ccelius, gave up all concern for the republic ; and, as Dion fays, pofitively, that the Senate were, in the i. jth year, all adulation – as all this is faid, – why fhould we be ex*Why and when Tiberius was afraid to enter the Senate.*

pefted to believe with Tacitus, that a difagreement between him and them began in the I4th year, and was, by the oppofition of the Senate to fome important aflair, widened in the 151!! year, and continued, no one knows how much longer, after that ?

12

SECTION 12

CHAPTER XII.
Tlie worship of Tiberius enforced against his will.
JLJlON fays, 1. 57, p. 607, B., (in which page he continues to treat of the tranfaftions of the laftyear of Auguftus – viz – u. c. 767,) that Tiberius was, in every thing, very popular – *xai aru ye* &a Wxto *Oimius SviMrixos m* – and, in particular, becaufe he would not permit any thing extraordinary to be done on his birth-day, (i6th November) nor any one to fwear by his fortune, and if any one was accufed of having fworn falfe by it he took no notice of it. – This he fays in the former part of that page, and, in the latter, he, after having repeated how popular he was, proceeds to give a ftill ftronger inftance of his moderation, or, rather of his reverence for the Gods – *TSurx* & Ju/xo- *rus livtav, xai* Ot. – For thofe two inftances juft mentioned he obtained popularity, and for this alfo – 'he would not permit any fane – npiwapue – to be *then* erefted to him – *nri ye tripmo-Qy* – nor any ftatue to be fet up in honor of him; and moreover, continues Dion, *heim-*
The worship of Tiberius enforced against his will.
mediately, ftriftly forbad – *xtnxpvs yxp irxfafp. x attyofncn* – any city or private perfon to do it – /jte Wxej //. jit' *ilium ran mitit* – to this prohibition he, fays Dion, fubjoined this exception – " *Unlefs I Jhall permit it"*

– TTfoo-rflxt *p. n yap Th airoffwrei on – eu ft. y tyt i tirtrfriju* – to all Wiiicll he, continues Dion, fuperadded – " *And that I never will*" – *aavnitt* Ss *on* – Bx *iwiTftu*. – This prohibition, Dion, it has been obferved, feems to intimate, Tiberius publifhed before the confulihip of Sex. Ap. and Sex. Pomp, expired, and therefore it feems to imply that the worfhip of Tiberius was, in the year 767, pretty general. – After having faid all this, Dion proceeds, immediately after, to tell us what we did not expeft to hear – viz – that Tiberius, though popular in every thing, was, by fome, treated contumelioufly – and, by others, irreverently – and, by others, again worfhipped in defiance of his prohibition ; and, what we ftill lefs expefted to hear, that thofe who treated him with irreverence were profecuted for it – and that he took not the Jeaft notice of either the one or the other – *i. mi -n yc* v? prfti *itfos nnt,* xat

i irfos ritos (xytGtiat Tc yxp iiSii xai To *roiarot atof/Ofati,* xai Sixr *es*

ioyyn) mrx wfoa-ETroiTiro. – Dion not only fays all this, but he ftill proceeds further to fay that Tiberius would not receive any written accufation of this fort from any one – s er *i n rua roivrm tip mvru yfa(fyi itfoaiatra.* – And all this he feems to fay, as Tacitus alfo does, ii. 50, Tiberius did out of refpeft to Auguftus – *uuirif roi Avyaot xai* Ev *ram npavti*. – Dion, at laft, concludes this paragraph with this remark – viz – that though Tiberius was, at firft, fo tolerant of fuch offences, yet, in procefs of time, he deftroyed many on that account

– to *p. n yaf itfuTfot tsStva* aS(*rut tir ivttta Tita atriat &xGnrut atoaftv,* a?. X *xai* iyxXiifirvTai *rnas, us* xa *iiriufioiwTas* Tw *rvyyn auru, airttm : irfoiomr* Sr Tb *X(oi xat iran*

Damnarique si qua de Angus to irreligioie disisscti: In te jacta nolle ad col nitionem vocari.

The worship of Tibtrius enforced against his will.

Dion, then we find, here informs us that Tiberius, who, at firft, was very popular in every thing, and efpecially for having forbidden divine honors to be paid to him, was, notwithftanding his great popularity, calumniated – and, that he paid no attention to it – he alfo informs us that, notwithftanding he had forbidden any one to worfhip him, many perfifted in doing it – and, ftrange to fay, that even thofe who, in compliance with his order, would not worfhip him, were profecuted for it – and, that, in procefs of time, he himfelf caufed very many of thofe who fwore falfely by his fortune, or, of thofe who treated his majefty with irreverence, to be put to death for it. – Now when does Dion fay Tiberius himfelf began to profecute for this offence ?

He informs us, 1. 57, p. 615, E., that Tiberius, as foon as he had been, by the death of Germanicus, releafed from all reftraint, became, fuddenly, as bad as he had before been good ; and, among other afts of cruelty, profecuted many for doing or faying any thing againft himfelf or his mother, as well as againft Auguftus, as deities – Ta *n //*

aXX *affuas* uf $t lean *tattt Ttts ato-eGetas* Sikw, 1i *ns & oo-ot ts rot* Auysf *xat ts &urot txtttw 7W Ti Ijwti(a oatru Wfa%as n tt Kui uvut* vftr:rJ; Sfiov

But what? – Did the Romans begin to worfhip Tiberius almoft as foon as he began to reign – and fo generally that he thought it necefTary to forbid the praftice publicly? – And, did they perftft in fo doing, notwithftanding he fo exprefUy forbad it ? – If they did fo, muft they not, all over the empire, have confidered him as an object of

great reverence ? – And for what could they have looked up to him as a God but, as Philo obferves, for his moft eminent vir-
The worship of Tiberius enforced against his will.
tues ? – And, did this moft eminently virtuous emperor, after having rendered himfelffo very popular on all accounts, and, efpecially, by forbidding any one to worfhip him – did he, after having done this, in procefs of time, fuffer many to be profecuted and punifhed for obeying his own mandate? – And a few years after, put thofe who treated his majefty with irreverence to death? – So Dion, we find, fays here. – But what fays he, 1. 57, p. 617, B., of a praetor, who was, in the courfe of the third year after – viz – 775, accufed, by fome perfon or perfons in the Senate, of having been guilty, *eit&er by word or deed,* of irreverence towards Tiberius? – He there fays that the praetor im mediately left the houfe, and divefted himfelf of his robes of office, and then returned again, and pleaded to the accufation as a private perfon. – And what fays he of Tiberius? – Does he fay that he put this praetor to death ? – He fays, that Tiberius, who was prefent, was *ex tremely forry for It,* and that he would hear no more of it – *Iwtis n rtrpiav,* i 8xET *avra* 4. ro. – This Dion fays in page 617, B., and in the next page 618, D., he fays, that Tiberius himfelf, before the conclufion of the fame year, ufed to punifh others for neglefting his worihip, when he, at the fame time, ufed to negleft it too – *xax ram ewiCaim Avtu, Irixstix re iwia, tf ois riss* aXA. r *us* xai *aircGarras cuoatv, i'i* – but does he

Htoi *irxuns u Txn Six rots* vTTHfy/AEvar *ivtpyiyias tQavpMa-tlyyCH,* x' *en tvt QavfJ. atyvrai , xai* ritTao-/xS *ri xati rut aturoraru* r/xaI *y%iu&nyai,* – Philo, ad C. 177, D.

ras 9' *itptxs rm Atyuirriut xeti Xx?* latitis, Kxi *pMyns, o-otyia rivt SiaQipotrxs rat* aAAwx, *iyifAOvias xai rifws Tvyamv irafa Tois irfo tifiLott aru* Se *xai ron Bitiv na txarw rui j-mnpZ-i* rivor EUfsriiv yeo/ntvot, Ti/x. ayflai. – Strabo, i. 16.

1 Tacitui sa; s, iii. 70, that 1. l-'unins, a knight, was accused, in this same year, of having melted down a silver *effigies* of Caesar, to make common utensils of it. – And, that Tiberius would not permit the Senate to consider it as injury to the republic.

The worship of Tiberius enforced against his vaill.
fay that Tiberius punifhed them with *death?* – No, finely. – He only fays – *us* xt *anGatrxs* txox$sv – he chaftifed them as being impious towards himfelf. – This inconfiftency, continues Dion, led fome people to think that he was befide himfelf – p t &t xi *ttmutat ma aurov* Tv Wow *vnovTtto-xv* – but in this, fubjoins he, they were miftaken, for, he did almoft every thing elfe well – r *yaf* xx vi trav

In the next book (1. 58) there occur two other paflages illuftrative of this point – they refer to the events of the year 784 – or, to what happened juft before the death of Sejanus, for, in that year, Sejanus was put to death. – Let us attend to them too.

In the firft which occurs, p. 623, D., he fays, that the Senate facri- ficed to the ftatues of Sejanus, as they did to thofe of Tiberius –

xat reXof *nan Thus tnuunv xvra, utrrrtf xxt tout ra TtGtfta tQtor.* – And having faid this, he abruptly proceeds to fay that many *other* eminent men were deftroyed – tp0pwv – but for what he does not fay. – Among them, he fays, was C. Rufus Geminius, who had been conful three years before – this perfon, he fays, was accufed of irreverence towards Tiberius – *xo-sCnats yaf tt rot* Teflot tyxu0tis – and, like the namelefe praetor before-mentioned, in the Senate, though without the knowledge of Tiberius. – Rufus, by the way of exculpating himfelf, produced his will, and -me wed them that he had left Tiberius one of his executors. – But how could he, by fuch evidence, difprove the charge which was brought againft him ? – With it, however, the Senate feems to have been fatisfied. – For, fays Dion, he was then attacked on the fcore of effeminacy – xi p, aXaxtr *xtnaQets* – and, before fentence was pafied on him, he went home, and hearing the quaeftor coming with it, he deftroyed himfelf.

The worship of Tiberius enforced against his will.

By this then it appears that Tiberius was, notwithftanding his edift to the contrary, worfhipped by the Senate – and, that they, without confulting him, profecuted others for not worfhipping him. – And, notwithftanding all this, he, fays Dion, p. 630, A., refufed to go amongft them, even though protefted by a party under Regulus.

Let us now then attend to the laft paffage in which Dion mentions human deification – it occurs, p. 626, B., where he fays, that Tiberius fent a letter to the Senate concerning the death of Nera, whom he had, three years before, accufed, in the Senate, and whofe caufe, (notwithftanding he, as well as his mother, had, as Paterculus fays, ii. 130, been the occafion of much grief, fhame, and indignation to him,) had then been, as Tacitus alfo fays, v. 4, in fpite of Tiberius and the Senate, by the populace, vindicated with flying banners. – In this letter, he did not, as ufual, mention Sejanus with any term of refpeft; and, in it, he, glancing at the deification of his prime. minifter, and, perhaps, that of the Senate too, forbad them to facrifice to any *man* – *xan Vfoo-tn* xt *titttn Iwt at&futrav rm QvtrQat.*

By this evidence of Dion then, as well as by that adduced firft, it appears that Tiberius forbad, not only the worfhip of himfelf, but that of any *man.* – And it almoft appears, from the cafe of the praetor and of Rufus, that the Senate took it upon them, feveral times, to enforce the worfhip of him, contrary to his own. inclination. – That this was probably the cafe, appears to be rather likely from what Dion

fays followed in that letter – viz – *pure cm rv tavrx Ttpn n* j$fn/K. aT/$io-fli, Sioti woXX Fxfjvoi tJ/tpttro. *run yatf myoftvn* fv xat *trfonfov, rore* Se S/

Tov Zwwot *atsvtuo-Mro.* – To all this Dion fubjoins this remark of his own – Tiberius would not permit that to be done to another which he would not to himfelf. – But, notwithftanding this prohibition, they, as Dion fays, p. 629, D. E., prefently after voted him feveral things,

The worship of Tiberius enforced against his will.

which he always refufed – viz – the title of father of his country – the celebration of his birth-day with ten hoife races – and a fenatorial banquet. – All which he again refufed, and again forbad them to vote him any fuch thing.

Let us now hear what Suetonius fays of the time when Tiberius forbad any worfhip of himfelf.

He fays, iii. 58, that Tiberius foon after the death of Auguftus, and therefore feveral years before the death of Germanicus, was very ftrift in punifhing any irreverence fhewn to the divinity of Auguftus – but of his punifhing any one for an offence of that kind againft himfelf he fays not a word; on the contrary, he fays, iii. 26, that Tiberius, *after he was delivered from the fear of competitors,* and, therefore, we prefume, after the death of Germanicus, forbad the Senate to decree him temples, priefts, and flamens. – What? – Does he, indeed, fay that Tiberius, *after the death of Germanicus,* forbad any one to worfhip him ? – If fo he flatly contradifts what Dion, as we have juft feen, fays, at p. 615, E., for Dion there fays that he then profecuted many for doing or faying any thing either againft himfelf or his mother, as well as againft Auguftus, as deities. – Which then are we to believe ? – Dion, who fays, that Tiberius, in the year 767, forbad any worfhip of himfelf, and that he, in the year 772, profecuted many for not worfhipping him ? – Ot, Suetonius, who fays, that he, in the year 772, forbad the Senate to decree him any thing of a religious nature ? – Let us attend to all that Suetonius fays of this matter, in order to fatisfy ourfelves whether he does really aflert that Tiberius began to forbid any worfhip of himfelf exaftly at the time when Dion fays he began to profecute others for not worfhipping him.

Does not this imply that Tiberius did not, as Tacitus says, *A.* i, 72, behave disrespectfully to his mother.

The worship of Tiberius enforced against his

In the former part of chapter 25 he points out the caufes which made Tiberius hefitate to begin his reign ; and then mentions the way in which he contrived to fraftrate the expeftations of Germanicus, who from expefting to be his fucceflor, expefted to be his colleague – Simulavit et valetudinem, quo aequiore animo Germanicus celercm fucceffionem, vel certe focietatem principatus opperiretur. – And, in . the latter part of that chapter, he proceeds to fay how he quelled the feditions and defeated the machinations of Clemens and Libo. – Having premifed this in the 25th chapter, he begins the 26th witk thefe words – *Verum liberatus metu* – which evidently refer to what he had been faying in the 25th, as may be made to appear ftill more clearly by adverting to the evidence of Tacitus and Dion; the latter of whom fays, in feveral places of l. 57,! that Tiberius flood in awe of Germanicus, as long as he lived, and, after he was dead, did every thing that was bad.

Suetonius then by – *Verum liberatus metu* – evidently means that he did the feveral things mentioned in this chapter after the death of Germanicus. – Having now fatisfied ourfelves on this point, let us attend to what follows. – Firft, he prefaces his account as Dion, we have juft feen, does, with an eulogium on his extreme popularity – and then, a little after, he fays, that the Senate were inclined to decree him temples, flamens, and priefts – and, that he oppofed it – that they would have placed ftatues and images to him among thofe of the Gods – and, that he would not permit it to be done. – Verum liberatus metu, civilem admodum inter initia ac paullo minus quam privatum egit. Ex plurimis maximifque honoribus, prater paucos et modicos non recepit. Natalem fuum, plebeis incurrentem circenfibus,

A. vi.

+ p. 606, B., 610, K., 615, D. /

The worship of Tiberius enforced against his will.

vix unius bigae adjeftione honorari paflus eft. Templa, Flamines, Sacerdotes decerni fibi prohibuit: etiam ftatuas, atque imagines, nifi permittente fe poni: permifitque ea fola conditione, ne inter fimu- lachra Deorum, fed inter ornamenta aedium ponerentur.

The fame line of conduft, it appears by what Suetonius fays in the next chapter, Tiberius purfued till the year 775 – the 8th or gth of his reign. – He begins that chapter thus – Adulationes adeo averfatus eft, ut neminem Senatorum aut officii aut negotii caufa ad lefticam fuam admiferit: confularem vero fatisfcientem fibi, ac per genua orare conantem ita fuffugerit, ut caderet fupinus; atque etiam, &c.

Suetonius and Dion then, we find, appear to difagree in their reports concerning the time when Tiberius forbad people to pay him divine honors, moft materially. – Suetonius fays that he did it when Dion fays he began to profecute people for not doing it – and Suetonius alfo feems to fay that he continued to difapprove of the praftice a long while after.

Let us now fee whether Tacitus appears to agree with either of thofe hiftorians refpefting the time when Tiberius prohibited this praftice to be continued.

Tacitus, neither fays, with Dion, that Tiberius, in the firft year of his reign, forbad any one to worfhip him – nor, with Suetonius, that he did fo, in the fifth or fixth. – On the contrary, it appears, by what Tiberius faid in the Senate, in the i ith year of his reign, when delegates from further Spain applied for permiffion to ereft a temple to him, as thofe of Afia had done the fecond year before, that he had not then forbad any one to worfhip him; for if he had, would he not,

The worship of Tiberius enforced against his no ill.

inftead of adverting to the motives which then induced him to ac- quiefce – viz – obedience to the example of Auguftus, and refpeft to the will of the Senate, have much rather have adverted to his prohibition ? – And as to the many inftances of compulfion, which, Dion fays, he ufed to make people worfhip him, Tacitus, we find, as well as Suetonius, is entirely filent. – On that occafion, Tacitus, we find, fays, that he, who had before been mighty to defpife honors, and who longed for an opportunity to combat the infinuutions of thofe who imputed his acquiefcence in the praftice to ambition, publicly, in the Senate, deprecated a continuance of the praftice in the following fpeech:

" *I know, confertfit fathers, that I am generally accufed of inconftancy,* " *for not having oppofed the cities of Afia when they petitioned for this* " *very thing,* – *I //tall now therefore acquaint yon why I was then jilent,* " *and fay what I mean to do for the time to conie.* – *As the deified* " *Auguftus did not oppofe the founding of a temple to himfelf and to the* " *city of Rome, at Pergamos, I, who conjider all his deeds and fay ings* " *as laws, followed a precedent all eady approved, and, the more willingly,* " *becaufe to the worfoip of me was annexed that of the Senate* – *quia* " cultui meo veneratio fenatus *adjungebatur"* – And was not his worfhip to be connefted now with that of the Senate ? – This, we have already obfenred, feems, by the account of Tacitus, not to have been thought of, for he only fays – Tiberio matrique ejus. – Tiberius continued his fpeech thus – " *But as my acceptance of that honor once may be excufable.* " *fo to be adored in every province, as a deity, favors of pride and am-* " *bition: bejides* – *the rendering this honor common would be to detraft "from that of Auguftus.* – *I acknowledge, confcript fathers, that I am " mortal and of like frame as other men. – I wiflt you to teflify, and " pojlerity tt remember it, that I think it enough to hold the chief place*

The worship of Tiberius enforced against his will.

" among you. – Thofe who come after me wtll, I hope, believe me to have " been worthy of my ancejlors, careful of your affairs, unmoved by dangers, " regardlefs of offences for the public welfare. – Thefe are the temples " which I would raife in your breajis – thefe the be/1 and moji lajitng "tmages – effigies. – As for the temples and jtatues of ftone, if pojterity " reprobates the condufl of thofe to whom they are dedicated, they are " defpifed as their fepulchres. – I therefore implorf eur allies and citizens, " all the Gods, befeeching thefe to grant me, to the end of my life, a mind " undijlurbed, and a thorough knowledge of the laws, human and divine; " and thofe to celebrate, whenever my diffolution comes, my afJions with a " kind remembrance."

Such is the report which even Tacitus has made of the fpeech of Tiberius, when delegates from further Spain applied to the *Senate* for leave to build a temple to him *and to his mother,* in the year 778. – A fpeech which evidently implies that the praftice of worfhipping both Tiberius *and his mother* was then extended all the way from the weftern coafts of Spain to Afia Minor – and, that the Senate fanftioned it – and, ofcourfe, that Tiberius was then in the higheft repute all over the empire, though fome, it feems, by the preamble of it, wondered that Tiberius permitted it. – A fpeech which implies that he had not before, notwithftanding both Suetonius and Dion affirm that he had, forbad the praftice, and, which does not imply, in any part of it, that the Senate were included in the petition of thofe Spaniards.

To this fpeech of Tiberius, on this memorable occafion, Tacitus fubjoins an aflertion of his own – an aflertion which, if true, deftroys both his own teftimony in the fequel of his hiftory. as well as that of Dion, which we have been juft confidering – viz – and he perfifted

The worship of Tiberius enforced against his will.

ever after – pofthac – even in his private conventions, to exprefs his contempt of fuch a worfhip of himfelf – to which aflertion he adds the feveral opinions of the people on the fubjeft – fome, fays he, attributed his refufal to *modejly* – many to a fpirit of *oppojttion* – fome to *littlenefs of mind* – but, amongft all, it is not a little remarkable that he does not fay that any one derided the abfurdity of worfhipping fuch a monfter of luft and cruelty – nor, that fome thought him deficient in his ufual conftancy, by having neglefted hitherto to put a ftop to it, a rcmark which, Tacitus fays, he made in the very beginning of his fpeech. – After having obferved-what thofe three clafles of the people thought of his conduft in this affair, onr hiftorian proceeds to prove, by a few examples, how preferable the opinion of thofe who imputed his refufal to *littlenefs of mind,* was to either of thofe of the other two. – And to the whole narrative, he, in the laft place, fuper- adds a moral refleftion, of no doubt his own too – viz – Contemptu famse, contemni virtutes. – By which, if he did not, in oppofition to thofe, who, as Tiberius himfelf obferved in the beginning of his fpeech, thought him deficient in his ufual conftancy for having negleft- ed fo long to put a flop to it, mean to convey an indireft cenfure on the conduft of Tiberius for having, on this occafion, oppofed it, it is not eafy to fee what he meant. – But inftead of anfwering his defign, does it not appear to imply that Tiberius began, about the t tth year of his reign and 66th of his age, to defpife virtue ?

From this fpeech of Tiberius to the Senate, on the application of the Spaniards for leave to erect a temple to Tiberius and his mother, u. c. 778 – and, in the nth year of his reign, we learn that to his worfhip the Afiatics had annexed not only that of the Senate, but that of his mother too – and, that he then difclaimed, in the Senate,' the leaft pretenfion to divine honors, if not that fome blamed him for

The worship of Tiberius enforced against his will.

not having oppofed the worfhip of himfelf before – confequently, why fhould we not infer, from the former point learnt, that he, as he appears to have objected only to his own worfhip, had no objection to that of his mother – and, from the latter, that he flatly contradifts what both Suetonius and Dion fay of the time when he firft oppofed his own deification. – And, by the fubjoined aflertion of Tacitus, we alfo learn, that Tiberius crer after perfifted, even in his private con- verfations, to exprefs his contempt of the worfhip of *man*. – Confequently, why fhould we not infer from this, that Tacitus flatly contra- difts not only what Dion fays of the numerous profecutions which he inftituted againft people for not worfhipping him ; but alfo what he himfelf fays, as we fhall come to fee prefently, in the end of this and the next book. – And, laftly, from what he fays of the opinion of one clafs of people out of three, we further learn, that he oppofed it out of *modefty,* that is, as appears by his fpeech, out of reverence to the deity, as, it feems, his friends alfo thought. – Aad confequently why fhould we not fuppofe that his mother, three years after, objected to her own confecration or immortalization, out of the fame motive- namely – *modefty.*

But what effect does this fpeech feem to have had on the minds of the Senate and of the people ? – Do they appear to have been deterred by it from thinking this mortal man entitled to divine honors? – Would the Senate confent to have their partnerfhip in divinity diflbl- ved ? – If not, how were thofe to act who thought that the refufal proceeded from a fpirit of oppofition?

In the fpring of the year following that in which Tiberius objected to the requeft of the Spaniards, and, feemingly, but a few days before he went into Campania, that is, in the fpring of the year 779, he, fays Tacitus, 55, attended the Senate conftantly – and, for many days

The worship of Tiberius enforced against his will.

– plures per dies – heard the claims of the inhabitants of feveral cities of Afia, who could not agree among themfelves where the temple, to the Senate, to himfelf, and to his mother, which they had, three years before, obtained permiffion to build, ought to be built. – And did the cities of Afia contend for the honor of giving a fcite to this temple the year after Tiberius had fo publicly exprefled his difpleafure at the being worflupped ? – And in his prefence ? – If they did fo – may we not fuppofe that the Senate, who feem to have claimed the ex- clufive privilege of deciding in fuch cafes, encouraged, if not the application, at leaft, the tedious litigation ? – And did Tiberius, for fo many days, fit ftill and Men to fo contemptible a litigation ? – So fays Tacitus, who has taken care not to let us know what he faid on that occafion – though he has taken care to let us know that he attended fo conftantly to obviate fome report, and, if we miftake not, a report that had gone abroad that he intended to deflroy

Agrippina privately. What mould have induced Tiberius to think of going conftantly to the Senate, for the purpofe of obviating fuch a report, we cannot imagine.

In the following year – viz – 780, Tacitus fays, A. iv. 64, that the fenator Junius had an effigies of Tiberius in his houfe – and, that that effigies was fuppofed to have ftopt the rage of the fire on Mount Coelius. – It alfo appears, from what Tacitus fays further in that chapter, that the Senate and Tiberius were, at that time, on the beft of terms; and, from what Paterculus fays, ii. 130, that Tiberius and all the other ranks of the people were on exaftly the fame terms. – Is it not then rather ftrange that the fenator Junius mould have had an effigies of Tiberius in his houfe, when Tiberius had, at the time, thrice prohibited it, and once publicly ? – And ftill, as Tacitus fays, continued to exprefs his contempt of it ? – And is it not ftill ftranger that the Senate fhould have decreed then that the part of the city *Tlie worship of Tiberius enforced against his will.*

which was then burnt Ihould be called Auguftus – and, that the facrednefs of the place, in which the Gods had manifefted fo much honor to the prince, fhould be increafed. – Did this proceed from extreme deference or extreme oppofition ?

In the next year – viz – 781, Tacitus, we find, fays, iv. 74, that the Senate were terrified with the apprehenfion of fome very great undefcribed internal political evil, which, he feems to infinuate, was worfe than the revolt of a warlike people, and which, he feems alfo to intimate, it was in the power of Tiberius, who was then refident at Capreae, and afraid to appear at Rome, to remedy, and that they therefore came to a refolution of trying to procure his interference by *adulation.* – What? – The Senate came to a refolution of trying to obtain the interference of Tiberius by adulation! ? – Was he ever before known to be negligent in his duty ? – And did they not know how offenfive adulation ever was to him? – And what fort of adulation did they think would be moft acceptable to him ? – fcil – They, though engaged in the difcuffion of other points – Ita quanquam diverfis fuper rebus confulerentur – decreed effigies to him and to Sejanus around the altar of Clemency and that of Amity. – And did the Senate really decree effigies to him and to Sejanus, too around the altars of thofe deities, and perfuade themfelves that it was a fpecies of adulation which he was moft likely to relifh ? – Had they, as well as Tacitus, forgotten that he had ordered them not to decree him flatues or images ? – That he difapproved of the worfhip of himfelf but two years before ? – Has not Tacitus before faid that he *ever* exprefled his contempt of the worfhip of himfelf? – They furely muft have intenJed to infult him.

Dion, I. 58, p. 623, I!., seems to say, that Sejanus was not worshipped till the year 784, when the Senate discovered by the very respectful expressions which Tiberius had lately used concerning him how much he valued him.

The worship of Tiberius enforced against his will.

In the beginning of the year 785, fays Tacitus, A. vi. 3, the people of Rome, having lately difcovered the flagitious praftices of Livia, proceeded to vent their indignation againft her effigies and memory – or, perhaps he meant to fay, her effigies which were intended to perpetuate her memory. – But what Livia could he have meant ? – If Livia the mother of Tiberius, the Senate appear to have confecrated her in defiance of Tiberius. – But of what flagitious praftices could me have been guilty? – And as to Livia the daughter-in-law of Tiberius, does not Dion inform us, 1. 58, p. 628, D., that Tiberius put her to death, in the year 784, for being concerned in the murder of her huſband ? How then can any one ſuppoſe that he would have permitted effigies to be be ſet up in remembrance of her.

The laſt evidence which we mall adduce from this author is from A. vi. 47, where he relates the ſtory of Albucilla, a woman infamous for her manifold amours – multorum amoribus famoſa – having been, in the laſt half of the laſt year of Tiberius, accuſed of impiety, and ſeemingly before the Senate – defertur impietatis – not to any God or Goddeſs – but of impiety to the prince – impietatis in principem. – A woman, infamous for her manifold amours, accuſed of impiety ? – Moſt ridiculous! – And of impiety to that vicious old goat Tiberius ? And before the Roman Senate too ? – Moſt contemptible! – And would the conſcript fathers attend to ſuch a charge ? – And, after the emperor had publicly proteſted againſt the praſtice of paying divine honors to himſelf, or, to any other perſon ? – Why was me not accuſed before any particular magiſtrate ? – This it ſeems me was not, but before the Senate. – But in what did her impiety confiſt ? – In doing, or, not doing – in believing, or, not believing ? – Who were her accuſers, if more than one ? – What penalty could the Senate inffift on her, in oppoſition to the will of the prince, againſt whom alone the impiety *is* ſaid to have been committed ? – And laſtly – had me any accomplice?

The toorship of Tiberius enforced against his will.

Her accuſer, Tacitus ſeems to ſay, was her own huſband – cui matrimonium cum Satrio Secundo *conjurationis* (obſcrve, and not *im- /ttetatts*) indice. – Albucilla then was married, and, ſeemingly, to a ſenator, for, if not, why mould her huſband have thought of accuſing her in the Senate ? – S. Secundus then muſt be ſuppoſed to have been a worſhipper of the prince – that is, of Tiberius, though he had, as Tacitus himſelf ſays, vi. 38, been, but a little more than a yeartefore, repreſented by Trio, as an old dotard; and, as Suetonius ſays, iii. 45, been ridiculed, on the ſtage, as an old goat. And ſo muſt the Senate too, though he had, as Tacitus ſays, v. 2, been derided, in their pre- fence, by one of the conſuls, to the great diverſion of the higher orders; and, as Dion ſays, l. 58, p. 633, A., been expoſed by Lucius Sejanus, the pnetor, on the 4th of the kal. of May, next after the death of his kinſman, who, in the Floralia, employed, in the day time, none but bald men; and, in the night, ordered all the link boys, of whom there were 5,000, that attended the theatre, to be Ihaved.

But did the impiety of Albucilla end in any conſpiracy againſt Tiberius ? – So, it ſcems by the expreſſion which Tacitus has uſed, we are left to imagine. – If it did, ſhe muſt have had accomplices. Who then were her accomplices ? – Tacitus, in this chapter, mentions three – viz – Cn. Domitius, V. Marſus, and L. Arruntius: thoſe, ſubjoins Tacitus, were men of the greateſt rank – that is, patricians. – Thoſe he mentions as having been conneſted with her, though not as accomplices with her in impiety to the prince, but only as conſpirators and adulterers – conneſtabantur ut conſcii et adulteſi ejus. But of thoſe it ſecms, Tiberius himſelf had no fuſpicion – nullaeque in eos impera- toris littera e fuſpicionem dabant. – Indeed Tacitus ſeems to intimate

The worship of Tiberius enforced against his will.

that Tiberius, their deified prince, was then *infirm,* and, it may have been, even ignorant of the offence of thoſe noblemen if not of that of Albucilla – invalido ac fortaſle ignaro.

But could it have been poffible that the Roman Senate, or any officer belonging to that body, could have thought fuch an offence cognizable in a woman infamous for her manifold amours, efpecially after the emperor had publicly exprefled his difpleafure at the pra&ice, and had continued fo to do in private, and had even ordered that no human being mould be worfhipped. Had they not before permitted one of their own body to deride him in their pTefence ? – And had not fome of them fignified their approbation of it afterwards by treafuring up his farcafms in their memories? – And who, if Tiberius was ignorant of the matter, was the prefident of the committee appointed by them to take cognizance of the imputed offence? – fcil – Macro, the praefeft of the city – Sed teftium interrogation!, tormentis fervorum Macronem praefedifle, commentarii ad fenatum miffi ferebant. – What ? – Was Macro, who was the commander of the life guards, appointed by the Senate prefident of the committee who tried Albucilla for impiety towards his fovereign ? – And did he, in order to prove her guilty of the offence, torture her fervants? – Does not Tacitus fay, in the next fentence, that Macro was a known adverfary to one of her accomplices – viz – Arruntius ? – -And does he not alfo feem to fay that moft of the things (for it feems there were many) laid to his charge were without foundation ? – And even forged by Macro ? liftaque ob inimicitias Macronis notas in Arruntium?

But if Satrius Secundus was the informer, muft there not have been fomething like a confpiracy between him and Macro, againft Arruntius, if not againft the whole party ? – And a confpiracy too about we know not what ? – And why were the flaves to be tormented on this *The worship of Tiberius enforced against his will.*

occafion ? – Whofe flaves were they, if not thofe of S. Secundus ? – And if they were his, what neceffity was there to torment them for evidence againft his own wife ? – But what fentence was pronounced on Albucilla and her three impious accomplices or adulterers ? – Of the fentence of Albucilla he fays nothing – at leaft, in this chapter: and of the fentences of her paramours he alfo makes no mention. He only feems to intimate that their lives were in imminent danger – and, that Arruntius, fearing what might enfue, put an end to himfelf – Igttur Domitius defenfionem meditans, Marfus tanquam inediam deftinaviflet, produxere vitam. – Arruntius was perfuaded by his friends to procaftinate, but refufed to live any longer – and why ? – Was he afraid of an ignominious punifhment ? – This does not feem to have been the caufe of his deadly refolution. What then was the caufe of it? – fcil – it was then pretty well underftood that Caius, who had received the worft education – peffimis innutritum – would foon fuc- ceed Tiberiusf – and, that Macro, who was worfe than Sejanus, would then have more power. And could this confederation have arifen in the mind of one accufed of having committed adultery with an impious common woman ? – And, efpecially, if he had been then likely to fuffer for his having denied the divinity of Tiberius? – Bcfides – was it true that he had received fo bad an education ? – Or, was it then known, that he was to fucceed Tiberius ? – What fays Suetonius and *The worship of Tiberius enforced against his will.*

Suetonius says, iv. 10, that Caius lived with Livia till she died, ami then with Antonia till he was 20 years old.

1 Tacitus says, vi. 46, that Tiberius had not, a little before his death, fixod on his successor. – Suetonius says, iv. 19 – Sed avum meum narrantem puer audiebam,

causam opens ab interioribus aulicis protlihun, quod Thrasvllus Mathematicus, anxio de successore Tiberio, et in verum nepotcm proniori, affirmasset – Kon magis Caium imperaturum, quam per Bnjanum sinum equis discursurum. ,

Jofephus on the former point? – And what fays Suetonius and Tacitus hhnfclf on the latter ? – Suetonius fays, iv. 10, that Caius ever remained with his mother till her banifhment, then with Livia till her death, and then, with his grand-mother Antonia, till he was 20 years of age, when he was fent for to Capreae, and foon after – viz – in the 21 ft of his age, (t9th of Tiberius) was married to Junia Claudilla, the daughter of M. Silanus, one, as Suetonius, iv. 12, and-Dion, 1. 59, p. 646, A., fay, of the moft noble men at Rome. – Jofephus fays, A. xix. 2, *t.,* that he received the beft education, under Tiberius, and afterwards made a bad ufe of it. – Stxpt . *fxf vxt'Sas tltt ytyamn* Ti$tft, $

fs ytttrat /-tyx xtxyxafm tratnas avTt%ur&at, 8 To *nxt xvros ut* ij *narofQut tatfrfnntv, xat ovvtftttcast rattos, inytltas n ati(os tnun tvir0, atts, tvfunvo-t re* Tuv xr' anrot troXiTnv, 8 *Imt attrnrtt ta n lytvtro attru r tx nts vaiiuas* o-uXXtysvTa y9 *trfos* rov ttX9otT oXtflfav

avro wo *rw tl-ttcnats.* – And as to the other point – Tacitus himfelf has, only the chapter immediately before that in which he begins to relate this ftory of Albucilla, (46) faid that Tiberius, after a long while deliberating about a fucceffor, finding himfelf unable to determine, left it to fate. And Jofephus, we know, fays, A. xviii. 7, *Q.,* that he, juft before his death, ordered Euodius to bring his grandfpns to him in the morning, with a refolution to appoint him who fhould be brought firft.

But what fentence was pafled on Albucilla for her impiety to her prince, and for her numerous adulteries ? – viz – fhe was, *by the Senate,* ordered to prifon, after having attempted to kill herfelf. – Albucilla irrito iftu femet vulnerata, juflu *Jenatus* in carcerem fertur. And was his the whole of her punifment? – If it was, fhe feems to have fuf- fered a lefs fevere punifhment for her impiety to her prince, and her infidelity to her hufband, than her paramours expefted to receive for having been too familiar with hen

The worship of Tibsrius enforced against his will.

But were the three before-mentioned the only partakers of her impiety, or, rather iniquity? – In the next chapter – viz – the 48, he enumerates two or three others – viz – Grafidius Sacerdos, and Pontius Fregellanus, and thofe two, he fays, were men of the greateft rank; for Grafidius Sacetxlos, he fays, was a *prator,* and Pontius Fregellanus, a man of fenatorial rank. – But neither of thefe, it feems, by what Tacitus fays, was an accomplice in any other fort of impiety than in fornication – Stuprorum ejus miniftri. Confequently, this Albucilla, who was accufed of impiety againft the old goat Tiberius, muft, as Tacitus has, in the beginning, intimated, have been, what we call, a common ftrumpet.

And what punifment, does he fay, was inffifted on thefe miniftcrs of her lewdnefs? – fcil – Grafidius Sacerdos, was, *by the Senate,* banifhed to an ifland – and Pontius Fregellanus was expelled from their aflembly.

Such is the unintelligible and ridiculous account which Tacitus, the prince of hiftorians, (as he has been, by our illiterate Literati, ufualty called,) has given of this affair. – An account which, at leaft, implies that certain perfons, if not moft of the

Senate, ftill wor- Ihipped Tiberius – and, in defiance too of his edift to the contrary – and of the contempt which he always ufed to exprefs of thofe that worihipped him; and which alfo implies that they did not confider him fuch a monfter of luft, and cruelty, and irreligion as Suetonius reprefents him to have been. All this, this account pretty clearly implies, if not, that the offence of Albucilla was of a very different nature from that commonly meant by adultery or impiety to Tiberius.

We find then that thofe three hiftorians – viz – Tacitus, Suetonius, and Dion agree in acknowledging that Tiberius did, in fome part of his reign, prohibit the worfhip of himfelf, but in what year he did it,

The worship of Tiberius enforced against his will. no two of them arc agreed. We alfo find that Tacitus and Dion fay

that the people continued to worfhip him notwithftanding his prohibition, and notwithftanding he, ever after, exprefled fuch contempt of the worfhippers of man; and, that the Senate appear to have profe- cuted many, even when he was afraid to truft himfelf among them, for not worfhipping him – and, among them, a notorious adulterefs of' rank and her fenatorial paramours, who were confpirators with her not againfl his earthly throne but againft his heavenly.

Having now eftablifhed thofe three important facrs – viz – that Tiberius was, in his life time, worfhipped by moft of his fubjefts – that he, both publicly and privately, condemned the praftice as being moft abfurd and impious – and that the Senate, after all, perfifted in making the people worfhip him. Let us now proceed to enquire what one or two other writers fay of their continuing to worfhip him. And firft let us hear what Seneca fays of the praftice of profecuting folks for not worfhipping him.

Seneca, de Ben. 1. iii, c. 26, fays, that as a man of prartorian rank, named Paullus, was once partaking of a certain fupper – caenabat in convivio quodam – he had a ring on his fmger with an image of Tiberius on it in relief. With this ring on his finger he was, by a well- known informer, obferved to take an urinal in his hand, in a ftate, as appears by the fequel, of intoxication. Of this Maro, a notorious informer, who happened to be of the party, took notice, and immediately went and informed againft him as having been guilty of impiety towards Caefar, and cited the reft of the company in fupport of his charge. This moft ridiculous ftory, Seneca relates as an inftance of the inconceivable mifchief which informers did under Tiberius.*The worship of Tiberius enforced against his will.*

Hott Maro, a notorious informer, happened to be of *One* of this praeto- rian party, Seneca has forgot to tell us.

A ftory which appears to be rendered not a little queftionable by what Tacitus fays, iii. 70, of the conduft of Tiberius when L. Ennius, a Roman knight, was, in the year, 775, profecuted, in the Senate, for a fimilar offence. Tiberius, fays he, objefted to his being profecuted on fuch a charge – but Atejus Capito, zealous for the divinity of his fovereign, contended that the Senate had a right to proceed – that Tiberius did wrong by endeavouring to Hop the profecution – that fo great an inflance of *maleficence* ought not to be permitted to pafs uu- punimed – that Caefar might do asi he pleafed in cafes which concerned himfelf only, but that this was one which concerned the Roman people. All this, fays Tacitus, Tiberius heard, but ftill would not give up the point.

We have now examined what Dion and the Roman writers have faid of the worfhip of Tiberius, and we feem to have difcovered that they have given an unfatisfaftory, if not a contradiftory, account of it, but an account which tends to make us apprehenfive that the Romans mufl have held him in the greateft veneration, and that he had too much good fenfe to be pleafed with it, if not an account to induce us to think that fome moft extraordinary change of a religious nature muft have taken place in him. Let us now hear what Philo fays of his worfhip.

Philo, in his leg. 769, B., fpeaks of the very unufual happinefe which overfpread the whole world at the death of Tiberius – this happinefs, he fays, 769, G., continued during the firft 7 months of Caius – in the 8th month, fays he, Caius was taken dangeroufly ill: on his recovery, fays he, 770, E., there was an univerfal rejoicing – but, fays he, F., this did not continue long, for, fays he, 776, D., he, foon after, murdered the young Tiberius, Silanus, and Macro – and the two laft for giving him wholefome advice. After he

Tlie worship of Tiberius enforced against his -will. had murdered thofe three he afpired to be a God – sx *in* !

Having taken this conceit into his head he, E., inftantly got the people to acquiefce in the fuppofition that he was a God – firft of an inferior order, and then of the firft order. Philo then proceeds to fhew that his aftions were neither like thofe of a Demi-God, nor, like thofe of a God, *becaufe the aflions of all Gods were fuppofed to have bcnefitted mankind,* p. 777, D ; whereas Caius, he aflerts, had done nothing but to make them miferable, F. ; thereby confefling that the very unufual peace which overfpread the world at his accef- fion, did not originate with him, but with Tiberius. But what ? – Was Caius not the fole caufe of the moft profound and univerfal peace which pervaded all mankind at his acceffion, and was he the fole caufe of this moft afflifting reverfe in the happinefs of the whole world? – And by afpiring to be a God? – If he was, for this fole reafon, the caufe of their mifery – may we not conclude that it is very likely, that Tiberius was, for the oppofite reafon, the caufe of their exceffive happinefs? – Philo, having premifed all this, proceeds, at 780, D., to fubjoin that the Jews were the principal fufferers, for fays he, p. 780, E., all the reft of the world had, though very reluftantly, fubmitted to adore. The confequence of this infubmiffion of the Jews to his Godfhip, fays he, p. 781, A., was that a moft deftruftive and an undeclared war was carried on againft our nation – *piyws* a *ttin axtfUKros* Xi/or *titt ru* flej owtx/aTTo – which, fays he, B., as foon as the *Alexandrians* (who, fubjoins he, had long wifhed for the opportunity) perceived, they, *as if a fling by the authority of the emperor,* proceeded to perfecute the Jews in the moft cruel manner. And, as he fays, p. 782, E., by the connivance of the governor, who could alone have put a ftop to it in an hour – *Ufa* ..

The worship of Tiberius enforced against his will.

Now when does Philo appear to fay this perfecution of the Jews of Alexandria happened, if not, as we have already feen, he himfelf pretty clearly feems to fay, foon after the murder of Silanus and Macro ? – That is – in the year 792, or, before the 2d year of Caius was ended. Early in that year, fays Dion, 1. 59, p. 652, C., he revived pro- fecutions for impiety – Faior *n, ravrx tiiruv, xai Tv aa-ienas iyxypara nrotiayxyvi* – which, he had, asDionalfo fays, p. 642, D., before prohibited. And who was then the governor of Egypt, but, as Philo fays, Flaccus ? – Let us attend to what he fays of the perfecution of the Jews of Alexandria under Flaccus.

Philo fays, p. 761, D., of Flaccus, that he was fix years the praefeft of Egypt – viz – from 785, when Severus was removed, till 7914 and of thofe fix years, he fays, p. 748, D., that he was nearly five under Tiberius; and, that he was, during the life of Tiberius, not only by far better than any of his predeceflbrs, but really very excellent. – Philo alfo fays, that Flaccus permitted a perfon, named Lampoon, who, he feems to fay, p. 749, F. i was the head of one of the feveral parries that perfecuted the Jews of Alexandria, to be profecuted for irreverence to his patron and friend Tiberius – and, that he not only did fo, but that he permitted the perfecution to be continued two years

– Aa/xiraIv fuv *aureSiots lit TiGifnt Kaurotpa* Sixbv *o-ti, xai eVi* ftsnv Tio'i/trv ra *vfttyttivros tnnip)xois.* – A. nd did Flaccus, who was fo incomparable a governor, who, as Philo fays, p. 761, A., 764, D., was one of the chief friends of Tiberius, and who therefore muft be fuppofed to have heard him often exprefs his contempt of fuch worfhip, and alfo to have heard, before he went to Egypt, that he had commanded that no man fhould be worfhipped; (for, according to Dion, Tiberius for-

If Tiberius be thought to hate countenanced this proceeding how is it that he left the world in 50 profound a peace?

The worship of Tiberius enforced against his 'joilL

bad the worfhip of any man u. c. 785,) did Flaccus, indeed, after all this, permit fuch a perfecution, and in Egypt above all places r – And before the death of Tiberius? – And did he alfo permit it to be continued two years? – Did he not know, as well as Philo, that Tiberius had punifhed feveral of his praefefts for their mifconduft in their refpeftive provinces ? – And that all the reft had taken warning by it? – Why then did not Flaccus ? – Philo alfo fays, p. 749, D., that Flaccus was, after the death of his beft friend Macro, and in the courfe of the year 791, the fecond of Caius, quite broken-hearted and unfit for bufinefs, and that the enemies of the Jews, who, he fays, were claffed under feveral heads, (among whom he, it fhould be obferved, fays, were the followers of Lampoon and Taraxipolis,) taking advantage of this paralyfis of Flaccus, prevailed on him to permit them to perfecute the Jews, p. 750, A. Soon after, fays Philo, p. 750, B., Agrippa paffed through Alexandria in his way from Rome to Paleftine to take pofleffion of his uncle Philip's tetrarchy, where he was groflly infulted by the populace, and, without the leaft interruption from Flaccus. Encouraged by the paffivenefs of their governor, fays Philo, p. 752, the enraged populace rufhed early in the morning into the theatre, and there tumultuoufly agreed to ereft ftatues in the oratories of the Jews. And what, as the Jews were protefted by the laws, could have difpofed them to think of committing this outrage ? Efpecially as Agrippa, the favorite of Caius, was then prefent, and, as Philo fays, p. 758, $., undertook that Caius mould be brought acquainted with the whole proceeding ? – fcil – they pretended to do it

tmot yaf xat mt Ttftfm xat nrt ra xarfos aura Kxtrafot rut dtfovnuv rats smxfaTf-tatt, Tnt ffftptnxt Juki trfofxatxt su vvxnxt "' ntfomtox y. cQzfpoo-xfAtM, Tsls jxfas fvfvXjTav xaxajv avxfraiVf o&'fodoxJaKf &ftroty&tft xaTaotxatt Tut /v x.'v ttmnt xat *fwvZH,* Tsiv Suvarwv *atxftrots atattfunv, us fiurot* Tov *f3""* Tt)1 fX,, *tTJJtiEQ-tra! etf Puy. rn,* 0i *xvroxfarofts* Xoyov xv/ v *trevfaypttzt* Itbv, *xat px.* urff oTTorat *trftffGvffxttTo at . s.* – Philo, in Fl. p. 578, F. 9. A.

'Dte worship of Tiberius enforced against his will. out of refpeft to Cxfar, becaufe he could not be profecuted. – *x*

T;-. tx.".'ultx TTotno-xfAttot, a wfoo-atrTto Ti *rut ttrxtnut a Qtlunt.* B – But would they have prefumed to commit fo flagrant an outrage in the name of Cfar, if they had not, by fome means, been informed that it would be agreeable to Caefar ? – What fays he in his Leg. on this point ? – He there fays, p. 783, F., that the Alexandrians were the moft inveterate enemies of the Jews, and, that when they heard that Caius had commanded people to worfhip him they were emboldened to profane the fynagogues of the Jews – that they erefted in them ftatues to Caius, and in one of them a flatue fet in a chariot, to which were joined four horfes of brafs, which had formerly been dedicated to the great-grandmother of the laft Cleopatra. A praftice, continues he, to which they were, above all people, always addifted. It was therefore out of zeal for the worfhip of Caius that the Alexandrians proceeded to profane the oratories of the Jews. And confcquently Caius muft have ordered himfelf to be worfhipped in the fecond, year of his reign, and before Agrippa went to his kingdom, as Jofephus alfo attcfts, A. xviii. 7, *tx.*

The worfhip of Caius then was, by the account of Philo, inflantly attended with the moft grievous perfecntion of the Jews, and profanation of their oratories at Alexandria; why then, if Tiberius had enjoined the worfhip of himfelf, was not that alfo attended with the profanation of their places of worfhip at Alexandria alfo ? – That Tiberius was not worfhipped by the Alexandrians, notwithftanding what Philo fays of the profecution of Lampoon, is plain both from what he himfelf fays immediately after, in the fame work, and from what he. in the fequel, reprefents Agrippa as having faid to Caius.

The worship of Tiberius enforced against his will.'

He fays, immediately after – perhaps they, that is, the Egyptians, will fay, that as the Csefars are greater than the Ptolemies, fo tis but fair that the former Ihould be honored more than the latter. A moft ridiculous reafon' For why then had not Tiberius, to whom Caius was indebted for every thing, the fame honors paid to him? – A prince, who, after a reign of 23 years, did not leave any thing like the appearance of war, either in Greece or Barbary, but lived in the con- flant enjoyment of the bleffings of peace till he died. And yet Tiberius, after all this, *was net fa honored.*

In the fequel, Philo reprefents Agrippa, p. 799, F., as obfeiving in a deprecatory epiftle to Caius, when he was afraid to appear in the prefence of his offended Godfhip, that Tiberius had, through the whole courfe of his reign, maintained the temple fervice – and, that he had, in particular, continued the oblation of a bull and two lambs. But of Caius having obferved in reply how many he had profecuted for not worfhipping him, he fays not a word.

Laftly – Jofephus fays of this fame Agrippa, A. xix. 7, y,, that he was a remarkably zealous obferver of the law. And Philo, in his Leg. fay?, that he was overcome with horror when he heard from Caius, his pupil in the fyftem of tyranny, for whofe fake he had been im- prifoned, and by whom he had been liberated, that he had given orders for his ftatue to be fet up in the temple. But if his religious notions would not permit him to appear in the prefence of fo impious a charafter, would not the fame principles have kept him from begging to be permitted to vifit Tiberius,' if he had claimed divine honors and had profecuted many for not paying them ? – Jofephus, we find, fays, A. xviii. 7, S., that he, on his return to Italy, fent to Tiberius, then

Does not Philo, by this, seem to deny that divine honors were erer paid to Tiberius.
The worship of Tibsrius enforced against his will.

at Capreae, to know if he had any objeftion to fee him – that Tiberius, with all kindnefs, inftantly defired him to come, and, when he arrived, received him with all imaginable cordiality – gave him apartments in the palace, and defired him to undertake the inftruftion of his grand- fon. Now as Agrippa was fo fcrupulous an obferver of the law, would he, if Tiberius had pretended to an equality with God, have deftred to be admitted into his prefence ? – Would he not have been deterred from refiding in his houfe by the fear of being prefled to partake of things offered to idols? – If not of other things forbidden by the law?

13

SECTION 13

CHAPTER XIII.
Tiberius why and when lampboned,
T V E have feen, CHAP, vi, that Tiberius was, notwithfianding what Suetonius, Tacitus, and Dion fay of him, moft eminently exemplary, great, juft, and humane, till he went to Capreae. And we have alfo feen, CHAP, xii, that he was, always, almoft univerfally worfhipped for his beneficence to mankind – and, at' laft, contrary to his will. If then he was fo excellent a prince as to have been thought worthy of divine honors, and fuch honors were conftantly paid to him during the whole of his reign, and in the latter part of it in oppo- fition to an edift which he publifhed forbiding it to be done – who would expeft to hear any writers fay that he was vilifyed by any of his cotemporaries? – And for his cruelties and unnatural luft? – Efpe- cially, as not one of his cotemporary hiftorians, Roman, Jewim, or Chriftian, has made the leaft mention of his having been lampooned, or, of his having, in the leaft, deferved it. We are informed by Tacitus, iv. 11, that mod of the writers who lived after the days of*Tiberius taliy and when lampooned.*
Tiberius, fought for every thing fcandalous to fay of him. – Neque quifquam fcriptor tarn infenfus exftitit, ut Tiberio objeftaret, cum ornnia alia conquirerent, intenderentque. – Now what thofe writers, whofc works are loft, may have faid of

Tiberius, we know not; but of this we feem to be pretty fure, that neither Jofephus nor Juvenal, who had both very good means of being well acquainted with his charafter, have faid any thing to lead us to fuppofe that he did any thing reprehenfible. Indeed if he had done any thing very reprehenfible, would not Juvenal have taken care to fatyrize him for it? – Have we not then fome reafon to queftion this report of Tacitus ? – And the more fo, as, we find, he himfelf acknowledges that the government of Tiberius was very good till the ninth year, or, till the death of Drufus – and, as we have alfo feen, that he himfelf allows that Tiberius left Rome, according to his own predetermination, and, that he remained at Caprea e voluntarily.

That moft of his predeceflbrs then were fond of afperfing the cha- rafter of Tiberius appears to be not true. But Tacitus himfelf, we find, and one or two others have, to our no little aftonifhment, aflerted that he was commonly lampooned; and, to our inconceivably greater aftonifhment, he himfelf fays, that the praftice of lampooning h!ru was continued during almoft the whole of his reign. – Lotus attend to what Tacitus and each of thofe other two fay of this moft unufual praftice – of the perfons who did it, of the time when they did it rnoft, and of the reafon or reafons why they did fo – and, for the purpofe of fatisfying ourfelves whether their accounts appear to agree or to difagree. And firft let us attend to what Tacitus fays on thofe points.

The firft inftance which occurs in the hiftory of this writer is A. i. 72, in the end of which chapter he fays – Tiberius was exafperated by fome verfes, made by fome anonymous authors, lafhing his cruelty, his *Tiberius why and when lampooned.*
pride, and his contentions with his mother. – Hunc quoque afperavere carmina, incertis au&oribus vulgata, in faevitiam fuperbiamque ejus, et difcordem cum matre animum. – In the beginning of the chapter he, it Ihould be obferved, had faid – that the people had *often* offered him the title of " *father of his country"* – and, that he had as often refufed it – and, that he ufed to fay, on fuch occafions, that all things in this life are uncertain, and, that the more he had, the greater was his danger. – Nomen Patris Patriae Tiberius a populo fepius ingeftum repudiavit: neque, &c.: – cunfta mortalium incerta, quantoque plus adeptus foret, tanto fe magis in lubrico diftans: non tamen ideo fidem faciebat civilis animi. – As then Tiberius was, after he became a monarch, even by the evidence of Tacitus himfelf, i. 12, eminently exemplary in private life – and was, in the eourfe of the year following, fo frequently importuned by the people to take the title of " father of his country," and expreffed himfelf with fo much diffidence on thofe occafions. And as Tacitus alfo fays, i. 80, continued afterwards to hate vice. Why Ihould we be expefted to believe that he was, even then, both cruel and proud? – And that, even then, anonymous verfifyers took the liberty of lafhing him for thofe vices? Does not Tacitus himfelf fay, iv. I, that in the beginning of the 9th year he began either to be cruel himfelf, or to give others the power of being cruel ? – And does he not again fay, iv. 57, that he retired to Caprex on purpofe to conceal his cruelty? – And, as to his pride, does not Tacitus himfelf fay of him, iv. 38, that he refufed the moft refpeftful title that could be conferred on him – and, that he refnfed it again and again ? – And, does he not inform us that the people were, every where, fond of deifying him ? – Not for his bad qualities, furely, but for his good. And does he not alfo inform us, iv. 38, that he pbje&ed to his being deified – and, that fome attributed his refufal to *Tibertus why and when lampooned.*

Philo says, Legal, p. 777, D., that the beneficent only were deified.

modefty, iomc to *difftdence* ? – If he was fo very proud, would he, as Dion fays, 1. 57, have been fo very popular ? – And, as he alfo fays have continued fo till the death of Germanicus ? – And, as he moreover fays, highly extolled – *ptaus* xt wfonfot *nrxtvnlf. tm.-* – And, had that been the cafe, would Suetonius have faid of him, iii. 26, that he, even after the death of Germanicus, lived, in all refpefts, like a private citizen. Out of the very marly and the very great honors offered to him, accepting only few and the leaft. – Verurri liberatus metu, civilem admodum inter initia ac paullo minus quam privatum egit. Ex plurimis maximifque honoribus, prater paucos et modicos non recepit, &c. Nothing then can have been more untrue than that Tiberius was fo foon both cruel and proud – and, as to his dif- agreements with his mother have we not already, CHAP, viii, had fufficicnt proof that there is not the leaft foundation for the charge ? – But, befides thofe feveral inftances of mifreprefentation already noticed, there remains ftill one, if not two others – viz – his prefu- med irritability at feeing the contents of thofe libellous publications, grounded on the prefumed faft that he did fee them. Tacitus himfelf fays, in feveral parts of his hiftorjr of the reign of Tiberius, that he was fo far from being moved at thofe anonymous publications, that he not only took no notice of them but even defptfed them ; f and that this appears to be true, why may we not conclude from this undeniable faft that no writer has told us that he endeavoured? by the means of accufers, to difcover the authors. And as to the prefump"

That Tiberius continued of the same disposition to the end of his days, who can doubt, that knows what Suetonius says, 29, of his affability – 40, of hi accessibility – and, 76, of his choice of witnesses to bis will.

t See note, $. at p. 84.

Tiberius why and when lampooned.

tJon of his having condefcended to read them, by whom were they, as bookfellers were not then in fafhion, conveyed to him ? – As then every one of the particulars contained in this infamous report appears, by the evidence of all preceding writers, and even of Tacitus himfelf, to be untrue; what reafon have we to believe either Tacitus or his numerous learned admirers in other cafes – efpecially concerning the graviffimum exitium. mentioned in the very next fentence, as introduced by the art of Tiberius? – Let us proceed to fee what Tacitus fays of the defamers of Tiberius in the three next books.

He fays, ii. 50, that Apulcja Varilia was accufed of having fpoken difrefpeftfully of Auguftus, Tiberius, and Livia – and, that Tiberius would not luffer her to be tried for what fhe was faid to have fpoken againft himfelf; – In fe ja&a nolle ad cognitionem vocari.

Again–he fays, iii. 49, that Lutorius Prifcus (who, it feems by the account of Dion, was. a fenator,) was, in the end of the year 774, and in the former part of the 8th of Tiberius, while he was ab- fent from Rome, accufed, before the Senate, of having faid that he had written fome verfes on Drufus, while fick, for which, if that prince were to die, he Ihould be better rewarded than he had before been for thofe he had written on Germanicusand, that the Senate, without the knowledge of Tiberius, attended to the charge, and condemned him. Tiberius, on hearing of this precipitate proceeding, was very much difpleafed, and ordered, that, for the time to come, no condemned perfon Ihould be executed within ten days after condemnation.

We meet with, in this same book, c. 57, 65, 70, three other instances of the zeal which the Senate manifested for the credit of Tiberius – and in the next c. 47, 69, two more.

Tiberius why and when lampooned.

In the next year – viz – 775, Tacitus does not mention any inflance of a fimilar nature – but Dion, we find, has, among the events of that year, mentioned a moft remarkable inftance – viz – of one lius Saturninus, who, from his name and from his having been tried in the Senate, appears to have been aperfon of great if not the greateft rank, having been caft headlong from the Capitol for having written fome fcurrilous verfes on Tiberius. – Let us then leave Tacitus, for a while, and attend to what Dion fays of this ./Elius Saturninus.

Dion fays, 1. 57, p. 618, C. u. c. 775, that Elius Saturninus was, after the death of Drufus, (that is, after the 9th year of Tiberius was pretty far advanced, for he, fays Tacitus, iv. 8, was, in that year, poifoned by Sejanus,) and before the commencement of the loth year, accufed of having written fome, not fuch as they Ihould be, verfes – *tin rlia Uk* ewTiSii – againft the emperor – that he was, in the Senate, tried for the offence, and found guilty – but what his fentence was he does not fay – he only fays, that Tiberius himfelf, who, as Dion had before, 1. 57, p. 607, E., faid, never before regarded what any one fpoke or wrote againft him, and efpecially againft his divinity – who, as Suetonius fays, (28) ufed, even in the Senate, to deprecate the cognizance of fuch offences – and who, as they both fay, had felefted twenty privy counfellors from among the firft families at Rome – caufed him to be precipitated from the Capitol.

But was it poffible that any one, knowing how fevere the Senate had been towards Lutorius Prifcus, and how nobly Tiberius had behaved on that occafion, could, in fo fhort a time, have written againft him ? – Does not Tacitus fay that he was an excellent prince till the death of Drufus ? – And that he from that time only began to be*Tiberius why and when lampooned.*

cruel? – And does he not fay, iii. 59, iv. 8, that when Tiberius, the year before, mentioned the infirmities of his age, and his paft fervices, as an excufe for not attending the Senate, they acquiefced in that ex- cufe? – And does he not, moreover, fay, that Drufus, who was then become, by age and experience, qualified to tranfaft all public bufi- nefs, died ? – - And does he not fay, iv. 15, that Tiberius, before the end of that fame year, fuffered two other grievous lofles – viz – that of his grandfon Drufus and his long tried friend Lucilius Largus ? – For the lofs of his only fon, he, fays Jofephus, A. xviii. 7. ., grieved fo very much that he was not able, for a long time, to bear the fight of any of his fon's companions. And, continues that fame writer, for that reafon, Agrippa, who had been one of the mod intimate of them, was obliged to leave Ttaly. If now Tiberius was fo much affefted at the lofs of his only fon, may we not well fuppofe that he was not a little more affe&ed by the lofs of that fon's fon, and of his long tried friend, in the courfe of that fame year ? – How then can it be fuppofed that any one could, in that fame year, have been fo unfeeling as to aggravate his misfortunes r – And efpecially as he does not appear to have given any proof of his depravity ? – Or, that he would, in that year, have put any one to death only for writing a few paltry verfes – and, efpecially one who appears to have been related to two of the mod noble families in Rome, if not to Sejanus ?

However if it be true that Saturninus was, by the order of Tiberius, precipitated from the Capitol, for having written verfes againft him, may we not fuppofe that no one attempted to write verfes, or, to do any thing elfe to offend him after the execution of Saturninus? – Efpecially, as Tacitus, we find, fays, that, in the 9th year of his reign, he began to be either a cruel tyrant himfelf – or, to depute pthers to be his vicegerents in tyranny – faevire ipfe, aut faevientibqs*Tiberius why and when lampooned.*

vires praebere ? – And yet Dion, we find, not only fays that fuch was the fate of Saturninus for having written verfes againft him, he alfo fubjoins – " *I could enumerate many more* who were put to death *for the fame Offence."* – rioXX S'av xat aX?. rotaTtffo-rrx yfoupew to/li, tt trmrct Tbto Tf Bv H Ktfyixatiu ufno-Qta, Oti wygtot St ra rotavroc vtr aura

leaving us to think that thofe many were executed after the horrid affair of Saturninus, and before the commencement of the loth year of his reign. Dion fubjoins that Tiberius profccuted many, not only, for what they wrote, but, for what they faid, and even, for what they *thought.* And from this very circumftance fome, fays he, fuf- pefted that he (and not thofe fatyrical fcriblers) was befide himfelf. – p a Sn xat f$truxevan *nvts avnt rut tpftvut vwo-nvo-av.* – But notwtth- ftanding fome, from this circumftance only, thought that it was fo, others, fays Dion, obferving moft other things that he did, thought that he was not fo, for, fays he, he, who after the death of Germani- eus did fcarce any thing well, now again did almoft every thing well – T *yaf* xt *xau trmv troHTx Htovrots Stuxtt* – of which general rcftitude of conduft he immediately fubjoins two moft remarkable inftances.

But, could a prince, who did almoft every other thing well, have been capable of putting many, for fuch triffing offences, to death ? – And, were many others indeed fo infatuated that they would not take warning by the fate of Saturninus? – But continued ftill to write againft their often acknowledged common *father?* – Who but madmen would have thought of writing againft the father of their country, when he did almoft all things well ? – And efpecially after he put only one to death for it ?–Now if it be true that, not only Saturninus, but many others were put to death for writing, fpeaking, and thinking reproachfully of Tiberius, may we not expeft to find that Tacitus has mentioned a few of thofe executions, and efpecially that of Saturninus?

Tiberius ixhy and when lampooned.

Let us now then proceed in our fearch of what Tacitus fays of this matter in the remaining part of the reign of Tiberius.

Tacitus does not relate this fhocking ftory of the execution of Satur- ninus for writing a few fcurrilous verfes on Tiberius, which Dion, we have feen, fays, happened in the year 775, neither does he fay that any one was profecuted for writing againft him in that or the following year; but in the year 777, he fays, iv. 31, that C. Cominius, a knight, made fome verfes on Tiberius, and that Tiberius, at the re- queft of his brother, who was a fenator, forgave him. But what ? – Did this knight, only two years after fElius Saturninus had, for writing againft Tiberius, been thrown from the Capitol, prefume to write againft him? – And was he, after all, forgiven by Tiberius ? – And at the requeft of his brother, who was a fenator? – Had not *JElms* Saturninus any friend who could intercede for him – fcil – Saturninus who, as Jofephus fays, A. xviii. 4, §., was the friend of Tiberius, and procured the expulfion of the Jews – or, Jilius Sejanus ?

Again – -he fays, iv. 34, that Cremutius Cordus was, in the year 778, accufed of having faid, in his annals, that C. Caffius was the laft of Romans – and, that he made an animated defence, and, then went and (to our no little aftonifhment) ftarved himfelf.

By the three preceding inftances quoted from the third and fourth books of the annals of Tacitus, it appears that Tiberius was not at all fond of punifhing his flandcrers – and, efpecially with death. – What then had Cremutius Cordus to fear from Tiberius ? – Seneca indeed, Confol ad Marc., acquits Tiberius of having any thing to do with this affair, and lays all the blame on Sejanus. – So far, indeed, is he from faying that Tiberius was the caufe of the death of her father, that he propofes to her, when almoft inconfolable for-the lofs of her fon, the*Tiberius why and when lampooned*-

example of Tiberius when he had loft his only fon. Now would he have recommended the example of Tiberius to her if he had been the caufe of the death of her father ? – Befides – he fays, that Marcia was moft intimately acquainted with Livia, and Livia, we know, Tacitus fays, A. v. 3, was the only *ferfuge* in fuch cafes.

Again – Tacitus fays, iv. 42, that Votienus Montanus was, u. ct. 778, accufed of having fpoken contumelioufly of Caefar – that Tiberius was prefent, and heard all that was faid of him in private – that he was much agitated, and could fcarce be reftrained from immediately entering into a defence of his conduct – (which furely implies that he was ftill concerned for his charafter, and therefore that he had not begun then to defpife virtue,) and, laftly, that Votienus was found guilty of high-treafon – but, that he was punifhed with death, Tacitus does not fay.

In the two following years Tacitus does not mention any inftance of this kind, but, in the year 781, he relates that incredible ftory of Sabinus who, Pliny, viii. 40, feems to fay, was executed, not for fpeaking againft Tiberius, but, for afting againft him, and, with Nero, who, even Tacitus admits, iv. 67, was, but in the end of the year before, in the cuftody of a guard, and, was advifed either to efcape to Germany and to place himfelf at the head of the army in that country, or, to take refuge at the ftatue of Auguftus in the forum – and who, as Paterculus fays, ii. 130, had in the courfe of the two years preceding the t6th, been the caufe of inexpreffible uneafinefs to Tiberius. The words of Pliny, in the place above referred to are thefe – Sed fuper omnia, in noftro aevo aftis populi romani teftatum, Appio Junto, et P. Silio Cofs. cum anirnadverteretur ex cauffa Nero- nis Germanici filii in Titium Sabinum, et fervitia ejus.

Tiberius why and when lampooned.

Again – Tacitus intimates, v. 2, that there was fomething in the charafter of Tiberius, at the death of his mother, very ridiculous – and, that Fufius, one of the confuls, foon after her death, ufed to make it his bufinefs to expofe it publicly – and, even before the Senate – and, that the fathers, who, in the courfe of the two preceding years, had manifefted the moft abjeft fubferviency to the will of Tiberius, were fo far from being offended at the liberty which he took, that they ufed to enjoy it. But if Tiberius continued till that time to be a moft excellent prince, (as we have feen CHAP. vi. he did) and, but a year or two before, had, by his folicited and unfolicited beneficence and affability endeared himfelf to all ranks of people, what writer would have thought of mentioning his fingularities at this junfture efpecially ? – And as having been expofed by any one at any time – and efpecially by one of his moft trufty fervants, and before his chief council ? – What can we think of a conful who took this liberty of amufing himfelf with expofing publicly the defets of his fovereign, efpecially of one fo good and fo venerable ? – And at a time too when he had juft loft his fuperannuated mother ? – Or, what can we think of the chief council of any realm who could fit and with pleafure liften to the farcafms of any of their own body when levelled either at the perfon or private qualities of their forereign ? – Efpecially of a fovereign fo fituated as Tiberius then was ? – Or, rather, what can we think of an hiftorian who would endeavour to make us believe that the chief council of any realm, who had, during 14 years, been all fubmiffion to their fovereign – who had, but two years before, deferred the hearing of a matter of importance till his return – who had afterwards rendered him their thanks, in the moft flattering manner, for his exceffive beneficence – who, but the year before, manifefted their fubferviency to him, by putting the only furviving adherent of *Tiberius "why and -when lampooned.*

the family of Germanicus, in the moft unjuftifiable manner, to death – and who had, but a few months before, taken the moft extraordinary trouble of going, in a body, a journey of two or three days in length, in order to get a fight of him, if not to proftrate themfelves before him, would have fuffered him to be fo expofed in their prefence ? – And yet our enigmatift, we find, not only fays that this ufed to be the cafe, but that Junius Rufticus too, a creature of Tiberius, took, at the fame time, the liberty not only of advifing the Senate not to attend to the complaint of their aged fovereign, concerning the conduft of Agrippina and Nero, (though every body, he admits, knew that he confidered them as his mortal enemies,) but alfo of fpeaking of his patron with extreme difrefpeft. Tacitus alfo adds that even confulars took, at the fame time, pretty nearly the fame liberty with Sejanus. And all this, Tacitus alfo adds, and to our no little furprife, Fufius, Rufticus, and thofe confulars did at the very time when the government of Tiberius, by the inftrumentality of Sejanus, became, as he fays – praerupta et urgens.

Again – Tacitus fays, vt. 29, that Mamercus Scaurus, who was of the /F. miliaii family, and therefore a man of the firft rank, and an orator, but, of a bad cbarafter – vita probrofus – was, in the year 787, again – rurftim – charged, and, feemingly by Macro, who purfued, as he fays, the fame arts as Sejanus, but more privately, of having, regardlefs of the fate of Saturninus, written a tragedy, in which he had afperfed the charafter of Tiberius. To this, he fubjoins, that he was aHo charged by Servilius and Cornelius, profefled accufers, of having been guilty *of adultery wtth Livia,* who, if not married to Sejanus, muft have been a widow nine years before fhe died, and eleven years before

Tiberius why and when lampooned,

the accufation of Scaurus – and, of having attended the facred rites of Magi. For which of thofe offences he was tried, Tacitus does not fay – he only fays, that he anticipated his condemnation – damija- tionem anteit – that is we fuppofe, killed himfelf.

Let us now then again leave Tacitus, for a while, and attend to what Dion fays of this Scaurus.

Dion, who atfo records this matter among the tranfaftions of the fame year, fays, I. 58, p. 636, D. E., that the praenomen of this Scaurus was not Mamercus but Marcus -/Emilius, and, that the tragedy, which he wrote, was like one of Euripides, called Atreus – and that the part of it which gave offence was an exhortation to the people to bear with the inconfideratenefs, or, unadvifednefs of their prince – iv *mt ra xfxruvros* ? txv *ftf.* – Now if this tragedy, conr- pofed by Scaurus, contained no other refleftion on the conduft of Tiberius than this, how can that prince be fuppofed to have been fo much offended at it, as to have caufed him to deflroy himfelf ? – And if a profecution had then been commenced againft Scaurus for having alluded to Tiberius in any part of this tragedy, why fhould Tiberius be faid to have worried him to death before his trial ? – Why would he not permit him to live till after his trial ? – when he might have precipitated him, as, this fame writer, we have found, fays, he did Saturninus, a few years before, for nearly the fame offence, from the Capitol? – Dion, however, affures us that Tiberius did behave fo, offenfively to him, as foon as he had heard of the comparifon between

himfelf and AtreUS – /flvtv St *ran x TtGtftos,* tp' *txvru ron ro ttros ttfwrQeu tfn Arftts* Jta Tuv fuaif ovtav *ittou vftxnrotfto-aff. ttos' Kati vtrtttrut or!,* Ki ty. v rot AiavTv *aunt mmffu, avvyxr. t 0i trfonynyn attrettnt ctvofao-Qat.* – 'But UlOil

does not fay that Tiberius was induced to behave fo offenfively to Scaurus merely becaufe Scaurus had covertly advifed folks to bear*Tiberius why and when lampooned.*

with his unadvifednefs. – Dion fays, that he was induced to behave fo towards Scaurus becaufe he had alluded to Come impious homicide, or, rather perhaps feaft which Tiberius was fuppofed to have made of a murdered perfon. And yet after having pofitively faid fo, he, imme- mediately after, feems to fay enough to make it queftionable – viz –

(Ml xi *Phi* T8T4I xTV5i)fl, XX *ins* Tiiv AniXX. w *p. ip. oitvxvs.* – "This, We

affirm, appears to contradift what he had faid before, for by this it appears that he, as Tacitus, we find, fays, was accufed for his offence before fome magiftrate. Now if he was accufed of this offence, and not of this only, but of having committed adultery with Livilla, why would Dion have us to think that Tiberius anticipated his condemnation by forcing him to become an Ajax to himfelf ? – that he would not fuffer his guilt to be made rnanifefr. ? – . when he might have put him to death publicly, either to that of Saturninus, or, to that of Sabinus.

But why fhould Scaurus be faid to have been accufed of having committed adultery with Livilla ? – Was Livilla then alive ? – Had Ihe not then been dead more than two years? – And, had fhe not been a widow nine years, at her death ? – And does not Tacitus fay, iv. 3, that Sejanus was, before her hufband was dead, too familiar with her? Dion not only fays that Scaurus was profecuted on this account, but that *many others* were punifhed on the fame account – Tomoi *vf sv*

xa t a. ti JJ *avriit, m* f *It?* aXsfluasi, *0i Hc* ix *o-mtfatrtias,* ExoXoo-i. –

But if many had been punifhed on that account, did not Sejanus know it, and, of courfe, how very common Ihe was ? – Why then d; d he apply to Tiberius, in the year 778, that is, two years after the death of Drufus, for leave to marry her? – And why does Suetonius fay, Hi. 65, that he continued his fuit till he was made conful – that is, till *Tiberius why and when lampooned.*

the year 784, when Tiberius, it feems, ftill gave him reafon to hope that his defire would foon be accomplifhed ?–And when if we may believe Tacitus, v. 6, vi. 8, it was accomplifhed. Will it be faid that her infamous conduct did not come to light till the beginning of th year 785? – -That is, as Tacitus fays, vi. 2, fome time after fhe was dead ? – Thofe many then muft have been punifhed, for having been too familiar with her, after the beginning of that year.

Scaurus then was, by the account of both Tacitus and Dion, ac- cufed, in the year 785, not only of having reflecled, notwithdanding the fate of Saturninus and Sabinus, on the conduft of Tiberius, his then fuperannuated fovereign, in a tragedy, which Dion fays, he entitled Atreus, but of having been guilty, with many others, of adultery with Livia or Livilla, who, Dion fays, 1. 58, p. 628, D., was, two years before, by the order of Tiberius, at the requeft of her own mother Antonia, put to death,

Tacitus alfq fays, that Scaurus was accufed of having attended the facred rites of the Magi, who, he fays, ii. 32, had, with the Mathematicians, been, in the year, 769, by the Senate, expelled from Pome. – Of his having attended thofe, Dion fays not a word.

Thofe feveral charges then feem to have been of a very different jjature from each other. – The firft was of a political nature – the fecond of a moral – and the third of a religious. – A ftrange mixture to have been thought to be in one who undertook to reprobate the atrocity of his fovereign! – Let us proceed to enquire if they really were of three diftinft forts – and, whether they may not be made to appear to have been of pretty nearly the fame.

Firft, let us enquire who was this Atreus, and what tragical event his hiflory furnifhes:

Tiberius why and when lampooned.

Atreus, we are told, was the king of Mycenae, and, as Strabo feems to intimate, i. 16, made fo for his fuperior knowledge of the motions of the heavenly bodies. He was alfo, we are told, the hulband of Europa, and the brother of Thyeftes, who, we are alfo told, feduced Europa, and had children by her, one of whom Atreu killed, and, having drefled the limbs, placed them in a difh before Europa and Thyeftes, at an entertainment. But how could Scaurus have contrived to refleft on the conduft of Tiberius in a tragedy of which fuch was the argument ? – Had Tiberius ever committed fuch like atrocity? Was he not very much affefted at his family loflcs ? – And does not his kinfman Clemens fay that he wept very plentifully at the recovery of Fauftus and Mathilda? – And did he not, both before and after, feel for the diftrefles of his fubjefts ? – In what then could the fimi- larity between thofe monarchs have confided? – In order to enable our- felves to form a conjefture as to the nature of this fimilarity let us confult Athenagoras, an early Chriftian writer. He, in his apology for Chriftians, p. 4, C., fays – there are three charges, which are ufuallymade againft us – viz – atheifm, *Thyejlean banquets,* and CEdo- podean connexions – T tvptyuwi / fyiAyp. arx, aQnoryTx, psy"D3ws-tja *Stitrex,* aWoStjsi /x'| i. – Now if Thyeftean banquets was one of the charges againft the early Chriftians what but the communion of the body and blood of Chrift could have been the ground of that charge? Had then Tiberius attended that communion ? – If fo, why may not Scaurus be thought to have fancied fome kind of a fimilarity between the imagined atrocities of thofe two monarchs? – Of this, more pre- fently, when we come to confider what Suetonius fays.

Again – Tacitus fays, vi. 38, that Fulcinius Trio, in the year 778, indignant at the increafing prevalence of accufers, left in his laft will *Tiberius why and when lampooned.*

De gestis P. chapter 143.

feme fevere refleftions, not only on Macro and the more diflblute of Caefar's freedmen, but on Tiberius himfelf, who, he alfo fays, chap. 30, Bad, but the year before, difcouraged accufers, accufing him, not as a monfter of cruelty and 1 nil, but as a dotard, and as an exile. – Tiberius, fays Tacitus, caufed his will to be publifhed, and thereby proved himfelf to be a defpifer of his own mame.

Laftly – Tacitus fays, in the next chapter, 39, that Paconianus was, for fome verfes which he, *while in prifon,* made on Tiberius, ftrangled.

Let us now hear what Suetonius fays of thofe fatyrical pieces pub- liihcd againft Tiberius.

Suetonius fays, iii. 45, that Tiberius, when old, and after his debaucheries were known, and therefore after the death of Sejanus, when he was, as Tacitus fays, moft cruel and lewd, expofed for his lewdnefs in an Atellane exode, and that the attack on his charafter was received with applaufe.

Again – chapter 59, he informs us that Tiberius did (not by any deputy, but by the impulfe of his own favage temper,) many things fo cruelly and atrocioufly, *through an affeflatwn of gravity, and byway ef correcting tc /mbltc manners,* that fome farcaftic poetafters made the following verfes on him: –

AS PER et immitis, breviter vis omnia dicam ?

Difpeream fi te mater amare poteft.

Non es eques – Quare ? non funt tibi millia centum;

Omnia fi quaeras et Rhodes exilium eft.

Suetonius, iii. 61.

Tiberius why and when lampooned.

AUREA mutafti Saturni faecula Caefar:

Incolumi nam te, ferrea feuiper erunt.

FASTIDIT vinum, quia jam fitit ifte cruorern,

Tam bibit hunc avide, quam bibit ante merum.

Afpice felicem fibi, non tibi Romule Syllam

Et Marium fi vis adfpice, led reducem.

Nee non Antoni civilia bella moventis

Nee femel infeftas adfpice coede manus.

'Et die Roma perit: regnabit fanguine multo,

Ad regnum quifquis venit ab exilio.

Now what punifhment did he infffit on the authors of thofe verfes, (for Suetonius feems to fay that they were written by more than one.) Did he tear them limb from limb, and -make a Thyeftean feaft of them ? – Not he indeed. Far, far from it. He did not make the leafl attempt to difcover the authors. At *fiji* fays Suetonius, he would have it thought that the authors of them did not mean what they faid, that they were difaffefted to him and impatient of his government. – And, that he ufed to fay often –

let such hate me, if the rest do not. And then, says Suetonius, he gave proofs of what they had said.

Now when, if those verses were made at the same time, can we suppose that they were published ? – When did Tiberius, by attempting to ameliorate the manners of the Romans, change the golden age into iron ? – And when did he, by the same attempt, cause a civil war at Rome like that of Antony?

Those verses seem to have been written by three different persons and at three different times. – For, the writer of the two first pairs addresses Tiberiui himself as an unfilled person. – The writer of the tliird pair addresses him as Ctesar. – The writer of the remaining four addresses, not Tiberius himself, but a third person.

Tiberius why and when lampooned.

We have already seen, CHAP, vi, that Tiberius was, for some time of his reign, accounted, by every body, a most excellent prince, and that he was, by no other writers but Tacitus, Suetonius, and Dion, said to have been, at any time in his reign, a bad prince – and, we there also saw that these three writers are by no means agreed as to the time when he began to be a bad prince – and, lastly, we there saw that Suetonius himself says that he . was not a bad prince till after the disaster at Fidenae – and, that he became, soon after, totally depraved and totally cruel. – What else then can we think, than that Tiberius must, after he retired from Fidenae to Capreae, and before he became so totally depraved and cruel, have attempted to correct the dislblute manners of the Romans? – And that those verses were published in that interval ? – Now if this was the time when he made this attempt it must have been made after the end of 780, or in 781, or 782 – or, as Paterculus says, ii. 130, while his mind was so overcome with grief. But would he, who, as Tacitus says, iv. 57, retired thither for the purpose of concealing his own vices – who, as Suetonius says, iii. 41, had no sooner returned to Capreae, than he became totally inattentive to the concerns of the republic, have given himself the least trouble about the manners of the people of Rome ? – If he then became himself totally depraved and totally cruel ? – What says Paterculus of his conduct at the time? – He says, ii. 126, that Tiberius had, in 783, habituated *all* to do what was right, either by his example, or, by his authority – recte faciendi *omnibus* aut incusla voluntas, aut impofita necessitas – facere recte cives suos Princeps optimus faciendo docet.

We have now seen that the golden age of Rome is said by those libellers to have ceased about 781 or 782, and that the iron then began. – We have also seen that this change is said by Suetonius to have been effected by the efforts of Tiberius to correct the manners of*Tiberius why and when lampooned.*

the Romans. We are moreover told by the same persons that Tiberius, by his severity in correcting the manners of the Romans, caused a civil war like that of Antorty. Now in what year of Tiberius did this civil war happen?

Suetonius himself, we find, though he in one chapter, 37, mentions the care which Tiberius took to prevent *seditions,* and the severity with which he punished popular *tumults,* takes not the least notice of this civil war. And, though he says that Tiberius, more than once, undertook to correct the manners of the Romans, yet he does not say that any tumult arose on that account. On the contrary, he seems to admit, 33,

34, 35, that the people fubmitted quietly to all his regulations for that purpofe. What Suetonius here feems to admit, Tacitus, we find, exprefily affirms, iv. 62, where he fays, that the people of Rome, were, in the year 780, contented to go to Fidenae (that is, as Strabo fays, v. p. 159, about 4 or 5 miles from Rome,) to "fee cruel fports, becaufe Tiberius had forbidden fuch fpeftacles to be exhibited at Rome – Adfluere avidi talium, imperitante Tiberio procul voluptatibus habitis, virilis ac muliebris fexus, omnis aetatis, ob propinquitatem loci effufius.

The civil war then, alluded to in thofe verfes as having been caufed by the rigour of Tiberius, in his extreme zeal to correft the manners of the Romans, appears to have happened, if at all, after the year 780. Again – as the fecond verfe feems to imply that Li via was alive, when thofe verfes were written, they muft have been written before the year 782, and therefore in the year 781. – Befides – what popular tumult happened at Rome in the reign of Tiberius, on account of his feverity in correfting the manners of the people, that could be faid to b? at*Tiberius why and when lampooned.* "

all like the civil war caufed by Anthony, but that caufed by the re- preffion of the moft grievous peft, introduced by the artifice of Tiberius – or, that caufed by the, we know not what, foon after the death of Sabinus – or, that caufed by the repreffion of the execrable fuper- flition? – or, that caufed by the prevalence of accufers, which Seneca reprefents as worfe than any civil war ? – and which he feems to intimate, by the fubjoined flory of Paullus, was caufed by religious accufers ? – Now all thefe we have ihewn to have been the fame, and to have happened in the year 781. That Suetonius himfelf muft have meant that it happened in this very year why fhould we not conclude, as, we find, he fays, iii. 37, that Tiberius moft grievoufly fuppreffed popular tumults, and took particular care that they fhould never happen again ? – Populares tumultus exortos graviffime coercuil; et ne orirentur fedulo cavit.

Having now feemingly afcertained the year when thofe verfes were written let us next proceed to examine the fcveral charges contained in them.

The writer of the firft two pairs reproaches him with having been fent to Rhodes for afpiring at the fovereignty. – The writer of the third pair accufes him of having been the author of an amazing change of the times. – The writer of the remaining four accufes him of having been, by his cruelty, the caufe of a civil war, which cruelty he feems to have imputed to his *banljhment.* But with what propriety could the fecond writer have faid that Tiberius, while Caefar, and in fafety, caufed fo amazing a change in the times ? – And, with what propriety could the third writer have faid that he, by his cruelty, caufed a civil war at Rome, and that his cruelty was owing to his baniment ? – that is, furely, to Rhodes. How could his cruelty have been imputed to his fcfidence at Rhodes, whither he, we have feen, went in*Tiberius why and when lampooned.*

the year 749 – that is, more than 30 years before? – Was it, as we have already hinted CHAP. ii. p. 16, caufed by what then happened in Judea ? – Of this more prefently. The third writer, we find, fays that he defpifed or hated wine. Now when did he, who, for his immoderate love of wine, ufed to be nick-named Mero, begin to defpife it ? – and, for this reafon – becaufe he now thirfls for blood ? – quia jam fitit ifte cruorem. – What blood had he wantonly fpilt before the beginning of the year 782 ? – Have we not feen, CHAP, vi, that he was a moft excellent prince till after the difafter at Fidena ? – And did not Paterculus remark to Vinicius, in the year 783, how he had, for the three years before, been laboring under the preflure of extreme grief? – And yet, he muft, if the following words – viz – Tam bibit hunc avide, quam bibit ante merum – have been underftood rightly, have fpilt it profufely. – But who ever heard of any tyrant drinking blood? – To thirft for blood is what we fometimes hear: but further than this the metaphor is never ufed. And after having difturbed our imaginations with all thofe fuppofed butcheries and blood-bibings, he begs us to take notice how happy he was – Afpice felicem ftbi.

How then fhould thofe verfes be underftood, fo as to make them have the appearance of veriiimilitude, and to remove that horrible pifture which one of them prefents to our imagination of a truly cyclopian repaft ? – Suppofe we once more refleft a little on the nature of one of the three charges which Athenagoras told the Emperors, M. Aur. Antoninus and L. Aurel. Commodus, the early unbelievers ufed to make againft believers – viz – a fondnefs for Thyeftean banquets – psy"D3xtnt Stnrvot – and then we mall, probably, be no longer in doubt about the meaning of thofe verfes. We fhall be inclined tq*Tiberius tvlty and when lampooned.*

think that thtfy may be a little metaphorical – that the "blood which Tiberias was fo fond of quaffing was no other than the blood of *tnx* Lord. If our conjecture be approved of by any, fuch may be dilpofed to think that Tiberius was charged with having learnt to be cruel while he was at Rhodes, becaufe he, as we have already hinted, was there firft brought acquainted with the arrival of the wife men from the eaft at Jerufalem – the fummoning of a council on that account – and, the confequent maflacre of the infants at Bethlehem.

Again – Suetonius, chapter 62, enumerates fome of the more atrocious cruelties which Tiberius ufed to infflit on fuch as were obnoxious to him, not any where, but at Caprea;, and, as he feems to intimate, after the death of his two grandfons Nero and Drufus, of whom Drufus, the furvivor, was, fays Tacitus, vi. 23, ftarved to death in the year 786, and therefore after Agrippa, Herod had been readmitted into the family of Tiberius. Suetonius having faid all this in the 6zd chapter, begins the 6jd with telling us how the people, *in the mean time,* hated, and detefted, and reviled him, and in what prae- trepidation he, who, but two or three years before, was happy ra him- felf – felix fibi – lived – Quatn vero inter haec non modo invifus, ac deteftabilis, fed praetrepidus quoque atque etiarn *contumelils olnott-ms* vixerit, multa indicia funt. – But, if he had, four years before, m braced the faith of Chrifl, can we wonder that he was fo hated and calumniated by his unbelieving fubjefts now ? – If he was fo detefted by his fubjecls in general, why mould V. Maximus have told us that the people of Rome were ready to crufh Sejanus, late in the year 784, and that the fame good order was continued, Bo one knows how long -after that ? – Why does Philo tell us that the Jews continued his beft friends, and that no potentate was more honorable in his old age ? – Why did Agrippa refide in his faniily, the laft three years of his reign,

Tiberius why and "when lampooned.

and, fpeak fo refpeftfully of him to Caius ? – And why does Jofephus fay that Tiberius might have lived in peace if he had not troubled himfelffo much about futurity?

Laftly – Suetonius fays, chapter 66, that reproaches, from all quarters, fcorched or burnt his anxious mind – and, that, among the reft, every one of the condemned perfons openly upbraided him to his face, or, by means of libels (luck up in the

Orcheftra," with his multifarious mifdeeds – Urebant infuper *anxlam* mentern varia *undique* convitia, nullo non damnatorum omne probri genus *coram,* vel per libellos in *'Orcheflra* poiitos, ingerentc. – And did even the condemned perfons too join in the general outcry againft the multifarious mifdeeds of their fovereign and father, did they, after having by their offences forfeited their lives, dare to revile him *to his face,* and, to expofe catalogues of the feveral forts of his mifdeeds in the *Orcheftra ?* – Has it not been ever allowed to be intolerable prefumption for any on to publifh libels agaift thofe in power, efpecially againft his fovereign ? – How then is it that thofe condemned perfons were pec- mitted to employ the few days which remained, and for which they were tndebted folely to the humane interpofition of Tiberius, in reviling him, moft excellent as he had been, and aged as he then was? – Were they the proper perfons to correft his faults ? – Why are they Kid to have been more forward than others to expofe them? – Could all this tiave been tWe ? – Has it not, at leaft, fomething like the appearance of "being incredible ? – Was ever an old tyrant, hackneyed in the habits of cruelty and profligacy of every fort, known, as long as tte was continuing in the purfuit of his darling courfes, to fuffer him*Tiberius why and when lampooned.*

How those damnati found means to see him, espectally if he was then at Capreae – and, how they found means to fix their pasquinades ip the Orchestra we are at a low to conceive.

kif to be impeded by the general outcries of his fubjefts ? – efpecially of thofe who had forfeited their lives? – or, to fuffer remorfe for his deeds ? – How then can Tiberius be fuppofed to have fuffered himfelf to be reviled for his manifold enormities by *all his fubjefls. ?* – and, by the moft depraved amongft them ? – who had forfeited their lives, and were, by his clemency, only permitted to live ? – How did this old, decrepit, deformed, exiled, hated, detefted, blood bibing, quaking, anxious, credulous tyrant behave on this occafion ? – Would he fuffer thofe numerous publications of his evil courfes to pafs unnoticed ? – and, the authors of them to efcape with impunity? – this Suetonius has taken care not to fay; – he only fays – quibus quidcm diverfirfime afficiebatur – but, had he not before faid that the anxious mind of Tiberius was fcorched or nettled by the varia undique convitia? – How then is it that he was fo very differently affefted by thofe libels – libclli – of the condemned perfons ?

Let us, laftly, enquire when this general defamation of Tiberius took place.

That it could not have happened before the decree, forbidding immediate executions, was pafled – that is, as we have feen, CHAP, ix, before the crucifixion of our Lord, or, before the year 781, is plain. That it could not have happened before the end of the year 783 is not much lefs fo, becaufe Dion allures us, I. 58, p. 623, C., that deluded and *believing* perfons, in the end of that year, erefted, *every where,* to Tiberius and Sejanus, *jlatues of brafs,* and procured their *likenejjes,* and placed *thrones of gold* for both of them in the

Theatres – *rums Sv* oi *atQpumi airartifam xai itirivotris, aitat re avrois xat rsit ypxtyaiis avnypatpov, $i$ftts ri nr%pvo-tts i:*

. – And that it is not likely to have happened*Tiberius why and when lampooned.*

before the end of the year 784 why fhould we not conclude from what Suetonius himfelf fays, chapter 61 – viz – that the more atrocious of his crimes were committed after the death of Sejanus, who was put to death in Oftober in that year.

14

SECTION 14

CHAPTER XIV.
Tiberius ever fond of Jews and of their religion.

JL O any one who confiders that Livia, the mother of Tiberius, was intimate with Salome, the fifter of Herod, before the death of that prince – that fhe is faid to have made many coftly prefents to the Jews for the fervice of the temple – that Auguftus and Agrippa were both attached to Herod, and contributors to the fervice of the temple – that Antonia, the fifter-in-law of Tiberius, was alfo intimate with Berenice, the mother of Herod Agrippa – that Herod Agrippa appears to have been fo named from Agrippa, the friend of Auguftus – that he was educated with Claudius, the nephew, and Drufus, the fon of Tiberius, and continued his intimacy with the latter till his death – that he then left Italy, and refided in Judea, becaufe Tiberius could not endure to fee any of his fon's intimates – that, after a few years, he returned to Italy, and was received by Tiberius with open arms, and requefted to remain with his family. To any one who confiders

Strabo says of Augustus, xvi. p. 526, that he honored Herod and all his family – *Kato-af* St *xat rus* y *tnpnfft ra* HfaSs, *xat m*
rxvrts
Tiberius ever fond of Jews and of their religion.

all this – the attachment of Tiberius to the Jews muft appear to have been very great. But this is not all the evidence which may be adduced in fupport of this point. Strabo fays, xvi. p. 463, that Tiberius was educated by one of the two Athenodorus's, of Tarfus – that the one who inftrufted him was the fon of Sando, a *Canaanitt – Aitif*

S'tl *oivrrit* (Tarfus) yeyoao-j *Tut* (e *iiuiuv AmiraTfot rt xai* Apj$'Sa/xor, *xat* Nifwf *en y* AvfltvoSwfoj Syo $v o /xrv KopSrXwv xaXityuvor, o St Ta 2avuwvor, ot *nai KataHirnr yxo-i aira X. Up. ns ritos, Kitttrapos x-xQ-riyio-aro, Xmi ntis trvjff t. tyx&is,*

He feems, by the evidence of Suetonius, to have been, when he was about 40, fond of attending to the inftruftion of Jewifh doftors – viz – Diogenes, and Theodoras, of Gadara – the former of whom ufed, as Suetenius himfelf fays, iii. 32, to lefture on *ihzfabbaths* – and the latter, as Quinftilian and Senecaf fay, was a famous leader of a feft.

Let us proceed to enquire on what terms he and the Jews were during his monarchy.

- Quinctilian, iii. 1, p. 127 – Praecipue tamen in se converterunt studia *dpollodorus Pergamenus,* qui proeceptor Apolloniae Caesaris Augnsti fuit: et, *Thcndnrus Gadareus,* qui se dici maluit Rhodium; quem sludioso audisse, cum in earn insulam secessisset, dicitur Tiberius Caesar. Hi diversas opiniones tra- diderunt, appellatique iode *Apollodorei* el *Tlieodorei,* ad morem certas in philosophic *sectas* sequendi. Sed Apollodorei praecepta mag-is ex discipulis cognos- ca. Flura scripsit Theodorus.

- ' v. 13, p. 278 – Ideoque miror *inter duos divcrsarum sectarum vetut duces* non mediocri contcntione quaesitum, s'lDgulisne quaestioaibus subjiciendi essent loci, ut Theotloro placet; an prius docendus judex quam movendus, ut prxcipit Apollodorus.

- r – ii. 1 1, p. 94 – Alius percontanti, Theodoreus an Apollodoreus esset. Ego, inquit, parmularius sum.

Strabo, xvi. p. 522, Ex St Twv *ToSapm o Qm$upos o naff*

+ Seneca, Ix. p. 103 – Contr. – Primum non apud eundem pra&ceptorem studnimiis. Tu Apollodorum habuisti, cui semper narrare placet : ege Theodo- rum cui non semper. – Syriacus to Niger.

Tiberius ever fond of Jews and of their religion.

John the Evangelift informs us that the rulers of the Jews faid to Pilate, when our Lord was crucified – that is – in the I4th year of Tiberius – " Whofoever maketh himfelf a king fpeaketh againft Caefar," – " We have no king but Caefar."- – Now can it be thought that the rulers of the Jews would have faid fo, by way of influencing their governor to comply, on this occafion, if they had not found the government of Tiberius very mild till that time ? – That they had found it fo till that time is plain from their having ben indulged with that moft extraordinary privilege of demanding every year, at the paflbver, the releafe of a criminal, however atrocious his crime ; and that they muft have found it fo for two or three years later, who can doubt, that confiders that they were, till the churches had reft, indulged with the privilege of fending to *jlrange cities* for tranfgreflbrs of the law – a privilege which, as Jofephus fays, B. i. 24, /3., was granted to no other people. Now as this latter privilege was, as Jofephus alfo fays, granted to the Jews by Auguftus, why fhould we not fuppofe that the former privilege was, in all probability, granted by him ? – If then thofe two moft extraordinary privileges were granted to them by Auguftus, may we not conclude that he had the greateft veneration for the objeft of their vvorfhip ? – This indeed is, we find, attefted by Agrippa, Philo, and Jofephus, each of whom fays of him that he was ever zealous for the honor of the moft high God – Tor nt irror psy"D3Eor – and the two

> Sttral-atro yatf tx rut tStut TTfo&aSxt atxyarQxt Qvo-tats txr&cts
> "TO Ti'IZTn psy"D3En *xatS1* txaptv *nptfxv, 0. i xat (U-j/t vn nrtreatrat, aftts uo-t* . St.'o *x. at raM(m.* p. 801, F.
> XX *enxs uo-ttaro tnft Tx vptnfa, an fwot a vatwn. ns* avafiiiftao-/ *xu To ufot Viauv* txoojtxno-s, *vfoo-atas xat S/' mutes* avaytxflatt *Quo-tas* ft-
> XX"J aXoxaT8r xfl' txarnv *vptfxv tx rut t&ut vfoo-ol*
> psy"D3En *at t xat ptxft nt mtnmrat, xat tts anrxt t*
> *rfoTTut otrus avroxfaroftxut.* p. 785, E.
> Josephus, A. xvi. 6. *0. y.* S.-e. *s.* $
> *Tiberius ever fond of Jews and of their religion.*

laft mentioned fay that he was favorable to his people, every where. So zealous for the honor of the moft high God, and fo kind to his chofen people, every where, was Auguftus, that the Jews of Judea, with probably Joazar, the high-prieft, at their head, in conjunftion with 8,000 of thofe at Rome, (who, we take it for granted, were libertines) petitioned him, foon after the acceffion of Archelaus, to deliver them from their allegiance to their lawful prince, and to take them under his immediate proteftion,

Suetonius fays of Auguftus, ii. 93, that he had the greateft veneration for all thofe foreign modes of worfhip which were ancient and received – Peregrinarum caeremoniarum veteres ftudiofiffime coluit.

Now as Auguftus was fo very partial to the Jews, on account of their religion, and, as Paterculus fays, ii. 123, on his death bed, earneftly defired Tiberius to adhere to the fame fyftem as had already been purfued by them, and as Tiberius, Strabof and others fay, religioufly followed all the ways of Auguftus – and, was, as Tacitus fays, A. ii. 65, for nothing fo anxious as to let every thing remain as*Tiberius ever fond of Jews and of their religion.*

Philo, in Flac. p. 755, D., calls Augustus the *savtor* and the *benefactor* of the *Jews* – *'Tvis yatf nptnfas, tn o rumf xat tttfytns ZtGaros.*

Philo, p. 785, F., says, that Augustus was so very favorable to the Jens of Rome, that all nations, even those that disliked them, behaved respectfully towards them. Josephus, contra Ap. I. ii. 5, gays – Nos autem maxiino Caesare utiinur teste auxilii atque fidet quam circa eum contra Egyptios gossi- mus: necnon et senatu ejusque consultis, et epistolis Ca; saris August!, quibus nostra merita comprobanlur. – Those letters, continues he, Apion should have read, and not those only, but those also, written by the greatest Roman emperors – amongst whom, he surely reckons Tiberius.

t Strabo, vi. sub ftne *Km* vtiv *o Stxexti. ttos t/os txstm, ototxninus, xau fut TrfOSOtyffLaTut vatalattn; txtttn xxt* JCfrov *at Kxtes aura, it xat &fvins, wnymns ru*

it was, and, as he alfo fays, H. v. 9, kept the Jews quiet all the time of his reign, why fhould we not think that he was equally favorable to them? – Of this, at leaft, we are afiured, and by the Evangelifts, that the afore-mentioned two moft remarkable indulgences were by him continued – the *farmer* till the crucifixion of our Lord, and the *latter,* till, at leaft, two or three years later- – and if Tiberius did not then deprive them of it, no doubt, till the end of his reign. Can we wonder then that the rulers of the Jews fhould have been fo ready to reply to Pilate, on the former occafion – " If thou let this man go thou art not Caefar's friend." – " Whofoever maketh himfelf a king fpeaketh againfl Caefar." – " We have no king but Caefar," – efpecially if Tiberius had, as Jofephus fays, A. xviii. 4, ., then reprimanded Pilate, fo feverely, for having attempted to pollute their holy city.

This continuance of thofe two privileges, it will furely bq allowed, feems to prove that Tiberius muft have treated the Jews with the greateft indulgence, till the crucifixion of our Lord – or rather, till we know not how long after. How then is it that many, if not moft divines, among whom, we perceive, one or two fuper-eminent pro- feflbrs have thought that the power of inflifting capital punifhments

Michaelis, vol. iii. part. 1, ch. 8, . 4, says, that Stephen *ltar tlly* suffered martyrdom before Pilate was recalled from the government of Judea, (viz – - *tSS, A. D. 41,) far under Ptlate the Jews had not the power of tnfltcttng captttal puntshments.* Jf, says he, this be true, Saul's conversion must have happened likewise after Pilate's recall – (that is – probably after the death of Tiberius, who died March 22d, T90.)

Marsh, his equally learned annotator, after having taken it for granted that *the Jews certatnly had not the power of stontng blasphemers under Ptlate –* and, observed that Pilate was recalled early in the year (as he says) 37, says – it is Dot improbable that the Sanhedrin obtained from his successor a privilege which *they dtd not enjoy under Ptlate:* And, if they did, they, of course, took the earltest opportunity of making use of it.

Tibertus ever fond of Jews and of their

was, before our Lord fuffered, taken from the Jews ? – On what evidence can they have perfuaded themfelves that their opinion was grounded ? – fcil – On the prefumed incontrovertiblenefs of that affirmation of the rulers of the Jews to Pilate – " It is not lawful for us to put any man to death." – But if this affirmation fo clearly and undoubtedly means that it Was not lawful to ftone blafphemers or adulterers, &c. why, it may be afked, has John fubjoined that explanatory inter-locution – this is to be underftood of the nature of the death he was to undergo. Bafides – why would they prefer the evidence of men, who were fo bafe, as to fuborn falfe witneffes againft perfet innocence, to that of him who catne into the world for the fole pur, pofe of bearing witnefs to the truth ? – What faid our Lord who was that truth? – He, fays Matthew, v. 18, and Luke, xvi. 17, declared unto the Jews – " Verily I fay unto you – till heaven and earth pafs, one jot or one tittle fliall in no wife pafs from the law, till all be fulfilled." – And when was all fulfilled? – Not furely before his death, as fbme would perfuade us, but at his death – when he faid – " It is finifhed." – Did not the Jews make this declaration to Pilate after they had fought to put Jefus to death for blafphemy – and, when they had ace u fed him as a mover of fedition? – If they had not the power of putting any one to death, why fhould they have offered Judas fo hand- feme a reward for his bafenefs? – And how could his offence have been fo very heinous as fome ot thofe very perfons contend? – Had not thofe very rulers previoufly fought to ftone him ? – And had not this been the caufe of his retiring from Judea into another country and there concealing himfelf ? – And did they not, but a little before, " take counfel to put him to death5" – And, not Jefus only but Lazarus alfo? – All this happened before the death of Jefus. – And why, if they had been then deprived of the power, are they faid to have ufed it fo often in the courfe of the two next years ? – Why did

Tiberius ever fond of Jews and of their religion.

the Sanhedrin take counfel to flay the Apoftles ? Afts, v. 33. Why are the libertines faid to have *fuborned* men to accufe Stephen of having fpoken againft God and agaiuft Mofes ? – And why did the Sanhedrin take cognizance of his offence ? – And when he faid, before them – " Behold, &c." – why did they inftantly ftone him ? – Why would thofe D. Ds. and S. T. Ps. overlook this evidence of the Evan- gelifts, and not only this, but alfo that of Agrippa to Caius, and that of Philo, and that of the Talmud of Jerufalem ? – Agrippa, in his letter to Caius, p. 799, F., fays, (after having extolled the reverence of Auguftus and Agrippa towards the molt high God) – " And as to ' your other grandfather Tiberius was not he entirely of the fame " difpofition towards our temple, as the two juft mentioned ? Did he " not, through all the twenty-three years of his reign, preferve the " holy fervice entire, as it was at firft?" – Thus faid Agrippa to Caius only three years after the death of Tiberius. And Philo, we find, fays, in his life of Mofes, p. 508, A., that his law alone had remained, as it was at firft, to the prefent time, firm, unmaken, unaltered, fealed with the impreffion of nature – and, that it was his hope that it would remain fo as long as the fun, the moon, the heavens, and the whole univerfe mould remain – that the Jews had not fuffered a letter of it to be altered though they themfelves had undergone many viciffitudes.

fat i? t *rara* Jiovh (3tCi, *xffafavnc, axfaaxvrx, xaQantf xQfzylT. tyuo-sus a:rr. , pttu tfxytxt at"$ n! nlixfas t-/fxQn it. t./Jt tvv, xxt trpt rot tmtra* ta/Asvto tAtrn *aura atmx wffftf aQavara, tus at* t)Xio. t xai Ctf?, h) *xau* o

ftor *n xxt Mso's n.* – Laftly – the Talmud of Jerufalem aflerts that the power of puni. Tting capitally was taken from Ifrael, not before the death of our Lord, but about two years and three or four months after that event – or, about the time when the perfecurion which followed the death of Stephen ceafed – or, when Paul returned from Damafcus to Jerufalem and the churches had reft. – It aflerts

Tiberius ever fond of Jews and of their religion.

that it was taken from them forty years before the deftruftion of Jerufalem, now Jerufalem was deftroyed on the loth of Auguft, in the fecond year of Vefpafian, which began on the 2d of July, 823. – If then this power was, as Lightfoot fays, taken from them precifely forty years before the deftruftion of the temple, it muft have been taken from them Auguft the loth, 783 – or, about the beginning of the t 7th of Tiberius. But perhaps the Talmud only meant to fay that this power was taken from them in the courfe of the fortieth year before that event – or, in the courfe of the I7th of Tiberius. However if *all* power of punifhing capitally was taken from Ifrael, before our Lord fuffered, as thofe divines would perfuade us – or, in the year 783, as the Talmud of Jerufalem pretends, who but Tiberius can be thought to have done it ? – And if he did, muft not the Jews, who, as Jofephus fays, A. xvii. 15, B. ii. 6, ., fent ambafladors to Rome, to requeft, (on condition, that their hierarchy might be continued as before,) to be taken under the government of Rome in all other matters – and, becaufe Archelaus had trangrefied the law, by marrying the widow of his brother Alexander, when his brother had left children by her – and, becaufe he had alfo polluted the temple, on a folemn feaft, by flaying many of the congregation – who, as he alfo fays, A. xv. 7, n., would not permit the leaft innovation to be made in their religious affairs – who, a few years after, procured the recall of Pilate becaufe he offered an infult to the moft high God – and who flew to arms as foon as they heard of the blafphemous intention of Caius – if Tiberius, repeat we, took from the Jews the grand fupport of their religion, and without the leaft provocation, can we fuppofe that they, who ever manifefted fo much zeal for their law, would have fubmitted to it, and without even the appearance of oppo- fttion ? – That they muft have been fo unaccountably paffive is plain by what they faid to Pilate – " If thou let this man go thou art not*Tiberius ever fond of Jews and of their religion.*

Caefar's friend." – " Whofoever maketh himfelf a king fpeaketh againft Caefar."- – " We have no king but Caefar." – And, by what Tacitus fays of them, hift. v. 9, under Tiberius the Jews had reft – Sub Tiberio quies – not fo under Caius – for they flew to arms as foon as they knew that he was about to place his ftatue in the temple.

But is it not ftrange that Tiberius, who pleaded the caufe of Arche- laus, when Auguftus was again petitioned to depofe him, and of courfe knew that the chief reafon which induced the Jews to apply for his removal was of a religious nature – and alfo, that the fole objeft of the compaft then entered into between the Jews and the Romans was to fecure their religious eftablifhment – who held all the afts of Auguftus as facred – who was for nothing fo anxious as to let eVery thing remain as it was – who continued the indulgence granted to the Jews by Auguftus 16 years after his death – or, it may have been, till the Chriftian churches in Judea had reft – even when he knew that they were abufing it to the purpofe of trying their brethren of other countries, who believed in the divinity of Jefus Chrift, as blafphemers – and who continued, to the end of his reign, the daily oblation direfted by Auguftus – is it not, fay we, ftrange that fuch an one ihould, without the leaft provocation, have, in the interim, taken from Ifrael the power of inffifting capital punifhments? – Or, in other words, is it not moft unaccountably ftrange, that he, who knew and did all this, fhould not have permitted them to punifh any one with death for oflences which Mofes faid expreflly fhould be punifhed with death, and, at the fame time mould have permitted them to fend to ftrange cities for prefumed capital offenders – that is, for thofe who believed in one of whom Mofes and the prophets fpake, and who was greater than Mofes, for the purpofe of punifhing them with death? – and, that he fhould not have permitted *the former* and have permitted

Tiberius ever fond of Jews and of their religion.

the *latter* at the very time when he was fo overcome with grief that his life was a burden to him ? – and, when he was fo afraid of his enemies, as to think it prudent to defift from attending the Senate, and even from entering Rome ? – If not when his mother, who was a friend of Jews and a promoter of the temple fervice, had, by interfering in the management of public matters, driven him from Rome ?

That the tradition, recorded in the Talmud of Jerufalem, appears, as it is tranflated, to be very queftionable – who will deny ? – No one furely who knows what Philo fays, ad C. p. 785, F., and in the next fentence, p. 786, A. – In the former page he fays that Tiberius was very careful, till the death of Sejanus, to preferve the Jewifh hierarchy entire as it was at firft – and in the latter page he fays that the Jews were, till that time, more attached to him than any other people. – Now what can have been the caufe of their greater attachment to him, but the confideration of that beneficence which he had always extended to their whole nation on account of their religious tenets? – Docs not Philo feem to fay fo immediately after, where he tells us of the circular letter which he fent to all his foreign *ordained underlings' – xttftretoliutotf* nrafotf – charging them to behave kindly to the Jews in their refpeftive departments – to make no alteration in their cuftoms, and to refpecl the Jews themfelves as peaceable, and their laws as conducing to peace. As now, Philo fays, that fuch was the concern of Tiberius for the fufety of the Jews and for the prefer- vation of their law, after the death of Sejanus, that is, In the beginning of the 18th year of his reign, who can think that he deprived them of the power of putting any one to death any time before, and, efpecially, only the year before, and, it may have been, in the cpuric

Tiberius ever fond of Jews and of their religion.

of the fame year ? – Would the Jews, in that cafe, inftead of being exafperated to madnefs at the unjuft and unprovoked privation, have continued to be, above others, attached to him ? – And, if fuch was his Concern for them and for their law, fo foon after their expulfion, who can think that the Jews confidered him as being the caufe of their expulfion?

Having now difcovered, by the evidence of the Evangelifts, Agrippa, Philo, and Jofephus, and even that of Tacitus, that Tiberius feems to have been a friend of the Jews, and on account of their religion, till the year 784 was pretty far advanced, or, till the beginning of the 18th year of his reign; – let us now make it our bufinefs to inform ourfelves whether he behaved himfelf towards that people during the remaining four or five years of his reign as he did in the preceding part of it.

We have juft feen that Philo, ad C. p. 786, A., fays, that Tiberius, immediately after the death of Sejanus, wrote to all his ordained minifters abroad, that they fhould behave, kindly to the Jews under them, in confideration of their fober behaviour, and the peaceable fpirit of their law. And in his next work againft Flaccus, he leaves us to conclude that the governor behaved moft impartially towards thofe of Alexandria, from the expulfion of thofe of Rome by Sejanus, to the perfecution of thofe of Alexandria, in the next reign, by Flaccus. – And Jofephus, we perceive, A. xviii. 5, 6, 7, and in one or two other places, confirms this report of Philo.

In the 7, *t.*, he fays, that Agrippa, who had been brought up at Rome with Drufus, and had, at his death, been obliged to leave Italy, becaufe he could not appear in the prefence of Tiberius as ufual, re-

Tiberius ever fond of Jews and of their religion.

turned to Italy, before the death of Pifo. f who died in the year 784, and, as Tacitus fays, vi. 10, in the latter end of the i8th year of Tiberius, or, in the beginning of the igth. As foon as he arrived at Puteoli, he, fays Jofephus, A. xviii. 7, i., fent a letter to Tiberius, tjien at Capreae, to beg permiflion to wait on him – and, that Tiberius, without delay, fent him a moft benevolent anfwer; and, when he arrived at Capreae, received him in the moft affeftionate manner. Now if Tiberius, in the year 784, deprived the Jews of the power of punifhing any one with death – that is, of the power of inflifting the capital penalties prefcribed by Mofes – and, had, in the courfe of that fame year, expelled the Jews from Rome, and treated the libertines fo much more barbaroufly than any other of the reft, and thofe who en- lifted worfe than thofe who refufed to enlift – if he, in that year, did all this, would Agrippa, who fainted away on hearing of the impious intention of his coufin Caius, and, who told that prince, that he would rather fuffer death than fee the temple polluted, have, in the year following, been fo ready to wait on Tiberius at Capreae – and, as it mould feem, to accufe Herod of having been concerned in the con- fpiracy of Sejanus ? – Or, would Tiberius have been fo overjoyed to fee him, and fo ready to requeft him to remain at Capreae, and to undertake the care of his grandfon.

Josephus says, B. ii. 9, i., that the object of Agrippa's visit to Rome, this time, was to accuse bis uncle, the tetrarch, but of what, he does not there say; but as he says, A. xviii. 7, (3., that he had just before quarrelled with his uncle – and, A. xviii. 8, &., that he afterwards went to Rome to accuse him, to Caius, of having been concerned in the conspiracy of Sejanus why should we not suspect that this is likely to have been his object now, – Tiberius, it howerer seems, paid Do attention to it.

t A. xviii. 7, s.

Tiberius ever fond of Jews and of their religion.

In the 5th chapter, /3., he fays, that Vitellius, on the petition of the Samaritans, fent Pilate to Rome, to anfwer for his conduct towards that people – or, rather, as he fays, a few lines after in the fame § –

irfos a xaryyofoiti lu$$ioi iSavTa *rot eivroxfarofa* – that, it- may be, IS – to the emperor for inftructions as to what the Jews might be permitted to accufe.

In the fame chapter, ., he fays, that Vitellius (in the 2 ift year of Tiberius) went up to Jerufalem at the paflbter, and then, by the order of Tiberius, no doubt, granted to the Jews two favors – viz – a remiffion of the tribute on fruit fold at Jerufalem – and, a permiffion to the priefts to have the cuftody of the high-priefts ftole and ornaments, of which they had been deprived by Hyrcanus, A. xv. n, S.

In the next chapter, 6, ., he fays, that Aretas and Herod were at war with each other – that Aretas defeated the troopsof Herod – that Herod complained of it to Tiberius – and, that Tiberius was very much offended at the news of it – and, laftly, that he, notwithftand- ing what Agrippa had faid of him, inftantly wrote to Vitellius to affift Herod.

In the fame chapter, /3., he fays, that Vitellius marched with hie forces to join thofe of Herod ; and that when he would have palled through Judea, with his army, the rulers of the Jews went to meet him and to defire him not to think of doing it, becaufe the admiffion of Roman ftandards into their country was confidered as illegal – that Vitellius immediately complied with their requeft, and ordered his

Ayfiiriras t/ts HpS *ra &aa-iius xarwyofos HfuSu ru rirfofa* sv Pupy St/xTi *viro TiCifiu.* Epitome xfotwv, p. 268, Aon. Tib. K. *(90)* Galba and Sjlla Cost.

N. B. la the Cliron. Can. this is placed in the K. A. of Tib. p. 189.

Tiberius ever fond of Jews and of their religion.

troops to take another route, while he and Herod went up to Jeru- falem to facrifice – there he was honorably received, and there he remained three days, and then was informed that Tiberius was dead.

Again, xix. 5, &., he relates how Claudius, in the beginning of his reign, publifhed an edict in favor of the Jews of Alexandria, in which he notices the favors conferred on them by Auguftus, and the perle- cution of them under Caius; but of their having been forbidden, by Tiberius, to punifh any one with death, for having tranlgrefled the law of Mofes, or of their having been otherwife difturbed by him, he fays not a word.

Laftly – in his work againft Apion, 1. ii. §. 5, he fays, that the care of the Nile, &c. which had been, by the Ptolemies, entrufted to the Jews, had been continued to them by all the emperors.

15

SECTION 15

CHAPTER XV.
Tiberius did not expel the Jews from Rome.
O any one who has read the chapter of this work immediately preceding, or, the epiftle which Agrippa fent to Caius to deprecate the ereftion of his ftatue in the temple, it muft feem very ftrange that any writer fhould have faid that the Jews were, at any time, in the reign of Tiberius, for any reafon, expelled from Rome. And to any one who has read what Strabo has faid, xvi. 526, of the intimacy of Herod with Antony and Auguftus, and what Jofephus has faid, A. xvi. 2, of his intimacy with Agrippa, and what Jofephus has alfo faid, A. xvii. 15, of the petition of the Jews to be releafed from their allegiance to the family of Herod, and to be taken under the immediate dominion of the Romans, (provided only that all the powers of their hierarchy might remain as they were) – to any one who has read this, and who confiders that all the powers of their hierarchy were religioufly fupported by Auguftus, as long as he lived, not only in Judea, but in every other country, and even in Rome itfelf, it muft feem unaccountably ftrange that any one fhould have faid that the Jews of Rome were, at any time, in the reign of Tiberius, expelled
Tiberius did not expel the Jews from Rome.

from that cityr and from that city only, for exercifing thofe very rites which his predeceflbr had folemnly agreed they mould always exercife unmolefled at Rome, as well as at any other place, efpecially as Dion fays, 57, p. 607, C., that Tiberius, after his acceffion, not only fwore himfelf to obferve all the afts of Auguftus, but that he compelled others to do fo too. And, again, to any one who recollefts what the rulers of the Jews faid, in the year 781, to Pilate – or, how intimate Livia is faid to have been with Salome, till that year – and how intimate Antonia is faid to have been with Berenice, it muft feem ftill more ftrange that any one fhou'. d have faid that they were expelled before that year. And, laftly, to any one who knows how reverently Strabo fpeaks of their religion, xvi. 523, what can be more aftonifh- ing than to hear that they were expelled, at any time, for holding fuperftitious opinions and praftifing profane rites ?

The expulfion of the Jews from Rome, in the reign of Tiberius, is however noticed by four early writers – viz – by two Jewifh and by two Roman: but though thofe four writers are agreed as to the faft of their expulfion, in that reign, yet as to moft other points they all, more or lefs, difagree – and, as to fome of the more important ones, not a little, the Jewifh as well as the Roman. Scarce two of them agree as to the caufe of their expulfion – the year when it happened – the perfon by whom they were expelled – or, the confequence, the period for which they were expelled. And, what is flill more remarkable, they all, we perceive, feemingly, carefully avoid to tell us that thofe Jews, who acknowledged their belief that Jefus was the Chrift, were alfo expelled, notwithftanding they muft, by the account of two of thofe writers, have, at that time, been very numerous, and had, by the account of one of them – viz – Tacitus, been, above other Jews, kept in awe at Rome, and had, by that of three early Chriftian writers, been alfo expelled in the fame reign.

Tiberius did not expel the Jews from Rome.

Let us next proceed to examine each of the accounts which thofe four writers have given of this matter. – And, firft, let us attend to what Tacitus fays of it.

Tacitus informs us, A. ii. 85, that in the year 772, T. 5 or 6, the Jewifh or Egyptian rites, for fome reafon which he does not affign, excited the attention of, not Tiberius, but the Senate – and, that a decree was then made, by the Senate, that thofe who pracHfed Jewifh or Egyptian rites fiiould no longer remain at Rome, or in Italy – that is, unlefs they would, by a fixed day, relinquifh their fuperftitious cuftoms. He moreover informs us that the Senate, not content with this enormous ftretch of power, ordered (and without affigning any reafon for it) 4,000 of fuch libertine youths as had been infefted with that fuperftition to Sardinia (a province, at that time, as Strabo and Dionf fay, under their jurifdiftion) – not merely as a place of confinement, but to fupprefs the pirates, or, it may have been to perifh. His own words are – Aftum et de facris aegyptiis judaicifque pellen- dis: faftaque patrum confultum, ut quatuor millia libertini generis, *ea fuperftitione infefla,* queis idonea aetas, in infulam Sardinian! vehe- rentur, coercendis illic latrociniis, et fi ob gravitatem coeli interiflent, vile damnum: ceteri cederent Italia, nifi certam ante diem *profanos* ritus exuiflent.

And did the Senate indeed prefume, contrary to their ufual praftice, to take, in the year 772, cognizance of the religions of other ftates, and even of a people who had, as Jofephus fays, J been allied to the Romans more than a century and a half, as well as that of a conquered people, whofe religion was more ancient than their own, if not old enough to have been the parent of it ? – Were not the religions of the conquered nations always tolerated ? – Had not that of the Jews

I. xvii, p. 578. t J. 53, p. 503, D. $ A. xii. 10, *s.*

Tiberiusdid not expel the Jews from Rome.

been not only tolerated, but even refpefted by each of the Caefars ? – And had not that of the Egyptians been introduced, by the Triumvirs, into Rome ? – If they did prefume to do fo, do they not appear to have forgotten the oath which they had, as Dion, we have juft feen, fays, taken a year or two before, to obferve all the afts of Auguftus ? And do they not, in that cafe, appear, even by the account of Tacitus himfelf, A. iii. 60, to have ufurped a power which did not then belong to them, and which, he fays, Tiberius did not concede to them before the year 775? – Tiberius, he fays, then, by way of confolidating his power, afforded the Senate a fhadow of their ancient rights, and they, he fays, in purfuance of their revived privilege, proceeded to enquire into the abufes of the foreign afyla, and, by way of doing it effeft- ually, proceeded to examine the pretenfions of the Deities wormipped by their allies. If now Tiberius did not concede the ancient privilege of enquiring into the religious affairs of the provinces till the year 775, why Ihould we fuppofe that the Senate, in the year 772, pre- fumed to enquire into the religious concerns of foreign ftates, and, efpecially of thofe of the Jews and Egyptians only? – What provocation could thofe two ftates have given them ? – And why fhould they have pronounced their religions to have been indifcriminately fuper- ftitious ? – If the religion of the Jews was fo very fuperftitious, why did Cyrus behave fo very kindly towards them, and particularly towards thofe in captivity? – And why did Alexander, in his way to the eaft, behave fo refpeftfully to their priefts, and afterwards treat thofe in Egypt as Macedonians, efpecially thofe who inhabited his new- founded city Alexandria? – Why did Ptolemy Philadelphus, a few

Tov /v *at wtavrw* (711) *ravrx* re *Htus tTnttxrat, xat* vewv *ru n*

t *-n linSt fTtf'3-attro.* Dion, I. 47, p. *336,* A.

Tiberius did not expel the Jews from Rome.

years after, defire to have a tranflation of the laws which they ufed, and why did he offer for it the redemption of 120,000 Jewifh captives, &c. &c ? – Why did Seleucus Nicator, after the example of Alexander, grant to them the fame indulgences, as he did to the Macedonians, in all the new-built cities of Afia and Syria, and efpecially at Antioch ? Why did Antiochus the Great write to all his praefefts fpecifying what favors he willed them to beftow on the Jews, for their fervices ? – Afl this Tacitus appears, by what he fays, Hift. iv. 8, to have overlooked, for he there fays – while the Aflyrians, the Medes, and Perfians pof- feffed the eaft, the Jews were the moft contemptible Slaves – Dum Aflyrios penes Medofque et Perfas Oriens fuit, defpeftiffima pars fer- vientium – and immediately after he adds – under the Macedonians, Antiochus would have civilifed that moft favage people and removed their *fuperfthion,* but was prevented by the breaking out of the Parthian war – poflquam Macedones prsepotuere, rex Antiochus demere *fufur- jlitionem,* et mores Graecorum dare adnixus, quo minus teterrimam gentem in melius mutaret, Parthorum bello prohibitus eft. But though Tacitus does not feem to have been aware of the great favors which Cyrus, Alexander, and his fucceffors conferred on the Jews, yet how could he have contrived to overlook what two of the firft and two of the fecond Triumvirate did for them, efpecjally what Pompey did, immediately after the reduction of Jerufalem ? – Cicero, he ought to have known, fays of that conquerorf that he took nothing from the temple, though Tacitus himfelf fays, Hift. v. 8, it contained an im- menfe treafure – Cn. Pompeius, captis Hierofolymis, ex illo fano nihil attigit. Jofephus indeed informs us, A. xiv. 4, $., that it, at the time,

How differently does Josephus, A. xii. 3, i?., and xiii. 8, p., speak of tie conduct of two other princes of this line towards the Jews.

i Pro Ffecco.

Tiberius did not expel the Jews from Rome.

contained, befides the facred veflels, two thoufand talents. And Agrippa, and, after him, Vefpafian and Titus, he ought to have known, though importuned by the adverfaries of the Jews to withhold from thofe of Afia and Syria their ancient privileges, refufed to comply. Now who that confiders all the evidence in favor of the religion of the Jews can help being aftonifhed at hearing Tacitus fo confidently aflert that it was fo intolerably fuperftitious as to make the Senate think it neceflary to order all the Jews to leave Rome ? – In what did their exceffive fuperftition confift ? – Seneca, we find, fays, Ep. 108, p. 635, that when the facred rites of the provinces were, in the reign of Tiberius, and in his own youthful days, fcrutlnized, one of the arguments of fuperftition was, the abftinence from certain meats – and that he himfelf, for a year after, conformed to that fuperftitious praftice, and found himfelf the better for it. Strabo fays, xvi, p. 524, that the fucceflbrs of Mofes continued, for a great length of time, to follow his direftions, in truth worfhipping God and doing what was I'ight – SjxiotT(iayoTEr *xai Qeoa-iGiis* wr x0J? *oirts.* – and that, in procefs of time, fuperftitious perfons, who recommended abftinence from certain, forts of animal food, found means to introduce that practice generally among them, which, fays he, is followed at the prefent time – *u, -ntf wi iQs trtt avnis avtxfo-Qai.* – Now if the fuperftition of the Jews and of the people infeAed with it confifted chiefly in abftaining from certain forts of meats, and even Seneca thought it not amifs to conform to their praaice, why fhould the Senate have prefumed, for that reafon chiefly, to expel them from Italy, ought they not to have expelled Seneca too ? – Efpecially, as, we find, he fays, that he continued to follow the praftice a year after the Senate took the liberty of prying into the facred rites of foreigners ?

Tiberius did not expel the Jews front Rome.

But were the religions of the Jews and Egyptians, indeed, fo very like ? – Does not Tacitus himfelf fay, Hift. v. 3, that Bocchoris, the king of Egypt, expelled the Jews from that country, as being a fet of wretches whom the Gods hated – ut invifum dels – rand does he not fay again, chapter 4, that Mofes, after they had been expelled from thence, enjoined them, by way of fecuring to himfelf their allegiance, t; o adopt rites which he had devifed, and, which were not like thofe praftifed by any other people – Mofes quo fibi in pofterum gentem firmaret; novos ritus, contrariofque ceteris mortalibus indidit. – And, does he not, immediately after, proceed to inform us that the Jews liot only praftifed rites totally different from all thofe praftifed by the. Romans, but that they *facrificed fame of thofe very animals which the Egyptians adored?* – Profana illic omnia, quae apud nos facra: rurfum concefla apud ijlos, quae nobis incefta. Effigies animalis, quo mon ftrante errorem fitimque depulerant, penetrali facravere: caefo ariete yelut in contumeliam liammonis. Bos quoque immolatur, quern JEgyptii cqlunt. – –And does he not again, in the next chapter, endeavour to convince us that *the religious notions and praflices of the Jews were totally different from thofe of the Egyptians ?* – JEgyptii pleraque animalia effigiefque compofitas venerantur. Judaei men. ta fola, unum- que numen intelligunt: Prqfanos, qui deum imagines, mortalibus materiis, in fpeciem hominum effingunt: Summum illud et aeternum, neque mutabile, neque interitunlm. Igitur nulla fimulachra urbibus fuis, nedum templis funt. – AH this Tacitus himfelf fays in the v. book of his hiftory – why then mould we be expefted to believe what he fays in the ii. book of his annals of the identity of the jewifh and egyptian fuperftition ? – And as to what he fays of Mofes, how diflerent is jt from what Diodorus and Strabo, who each lived in Egypt,*Tiberius did not expel the Jews from Rome.*

And yet he had, but just before, told us – Effigies animalis, quo mon-, . itraute errorem sitinique depulerant, penetrali sacravere. – See chapter 9.

fay of him? – Diodorus, it feems, by his own report i. book, obtained this account of him from the Egyptian priefts – viz – that he was the moft ancient and therefore the firft lawgiver – *fitra* yji r *taatai ra*

xar *Aiyvirrov 0m xarxfyo-it* Tx /ufloXoyei/MW *ytna&ai em Qiu xai* pwwv,

xai ru &iu ixaiurarot nfMnoyLtiat . – And, a little after, Diodorus, enumerating ancient lawgivers, places Mofes before all of them, then four egyptian lawgivers, and *Bocchoris* as the fourth. And of Mofes, he fays, that he was, by the Jews, entitled a God, both becaufc they expefted that his wonderful and divine mind would benefit pofterity – and, becaufe people are apt to look up, with admiration, to the fuper- eminence and energy of thofe who could devife laws – na l *rn*

ladxmis Mio-)v *rot J..', . l;:ij. i-i-:s @to, cm QavfAXfnt xxi Qtiar ous ttmeu tHai xpnot.*

ns Tn *iMxa*

li. it Tut tvpuv

3; A"ovros'A ..... *reraprot* e *tyxrt* vo/xoETiv lytyvo-j BoxXofiv To

By this extraft, then we find, that Diodorus contradifts Tacitus both with regard to the time when the Jews left Egypt, and, with regard to the legiflation of Mofes. And, we alfo fiad, that Strabo, who alfo lrefided in Egypt a long while, contradifts him with regard to the ljeafon which induced Mofes to depart from Egypt and with regard to bis charafter as a legiflator, for he, we find, fays, 1. xvi. p. 523, that he was an egyptian prieft, and, that he, being difgufted at the fuper- ftitious ways of the country, left it, and, with him, many who feared

the dfiity – 'MwaiiJ yp *ns Tvt A. iyvttritti etfiut* eXw *n p. ipos rys xaup. mr %fufas, ornifM ixim tiQiiSt Sua-sfa1its ro, xaQirvTa, xm yliti.'fjifxt avru* 1roXXoi *ripmrts* To fltiiy. – Strabo having thought it neceflary to introduce his account of the Jews and Judea with this preliminary account of Mofes, proceeds then to relate what that lawgiver himfelf faid – viz – " He, fays Strabo, affirmed and taught that the Egyptians, who affimi*Tiberius did not expel the Jews from Rome.*

" lated the Deity to wild beafts and cattle, had not proper notions of " him – that the Libyans had not – that the Greeks too erred by re- " prefenting him in a human form – that the Deity was that one being " which contains all the race of man, and the world, or, as we fay, " the heavens and the earth and all nature, whofe image no wife " perfon would undertake to exhibit by any objeft of fenfe. – What " rational being would think of reprefenting fuch a being by any ob- " jeft that he fees? – All animal reprefentations of him being there- " fore irrational, they that would confecrate any acceptable inclofure " or fane to him would not think of giving it any particular form – ' that he fignifies his approbation of the upright by good dreams for " themfelves and for others – that fuch as live foberly and uprightly " may expeft from him fome compenfation and fign of his ap- " probation – that others may not." – Eh yp *etams xai* E&Wxnr, *ur ax*

ofdtis pfoatnv *Oi Aiyuirrioi (tyfiois tixaotnv, @oo-xyftari n Qtio* sS' *Oi AiGvts ax w y* S' *Oi* Exxws-, *o. fyumtiftpas mratrn, K. r.* X. – By preaching fuch doftrine he, continues Strabo, prevailed on *not a few ivell-dif/wfcd ftcr- fans* to follow him to Jerufalem, where the temple now ftands. Here he promifed them the proteftion of that Deity, and fuch a form of worfhip as would be attended neither with expenfive ceremonies, nor with extravagant raptures, nor with unfeemly actions. All this, fays Strabo, happened according to promife, which when all the furround- ing races perceived, they placed themfelves under his government, which, by thofe aceffions, was rendered refpeftable. His fucceflbrs, proceeds Strabo, continued to purfue the fame courfe, doing what was right, and worfhipping the Deity in truth – *ixaiswfayrc:,* flro&ii r X9wr Otk. – Notwithftanding Strabo here fays that the fucceflbrs of Mofes continued to follow his fteps, yet it is rather remarkable that he, in the courfe of the fame page, alfo fays that they afterwards did

See p. 559.

Tiberiuf did not expel the Jews from Rome.

not follow his fteps – and, that Come of the feparatifts laid wafte both Judea and the neighbouring country – *Tcmns* SE nVw xai *i* Mw,

i3. iiixu.!ioi txtivot rxr pit PXiXS -*Ga?* ts aiAar *enrfttirofJxtoi* S' Eot To *Jif"* 0i /a. iv yap apr/voi Tfl ;$a'fa Exoskbv, xai aiirv xai Tv *ytimua-xt.* p. 54-

The evidence of Diodorus and Strabo, as to the time when the Jews left Egypt, and the religious tenets of Mofes, are then, we find, con- tradiftory of that given by Tacitus on the fame points. What reafon then have we to acquiefce in what he fays of the fuperftition of the Jews? – If they were, at any time, fuppofed to have adopted fuper- ftitious notions, why fhould we not conclude, from what Strabo fays immediately after, that their fuperftition confifed not, as Strabo fays, *in circumcijin and excijion*, but in abftaining from certain forts of animal food? – A praftice which, one fhould have thought, could not have given offence to any one, and which Seneca, we find, fays, was beneficial to him. And as to the fuperftition of the Egyptians he fays not a word, on the contrary, he fays enough to convince us that the religious ceremonies of the Egyptians were not then thought to be at all fuperftitious. In the firft book, p. 16, (which book, it may not be amifs to obferve, he is thought to have written b&fbre the end of the year 772, and feveral years after Tiberius fucceeded Auguftus,) he tells us that the Egyptian priefts were, by thofe *who prececkd him,* held in the higheft eftimation – *ras ff npixs rut Aiyuirrut x*

s, o-otyia Tin SiapifoTts Tut aut, '/E/Aotiat *xai* Ti/xiji

. – And again, in ihe xii, he tells us, firft at p. 541, that they were, on account of their knowledge of philofophy and aftronomy, converfant with their kings – *a ff nftis x . amtyiat wntit ai* as/xio/xa, *ifinrai rc rut I3x-riiu vo-at* – laftly, he, at p. 554, tells us that Plato and Eudoxus were faid to have fpent 13 years in Egypt with the priefts, and, that the Grecians derived their knowledge of aftronomy

Tiberius did not expel the Jews from Some.

from the Egyptians. In Ihort – how could the fuperftition of thofe two nations have been the fame, when as Tacitus himfetf fays, Hift. v. 5, they had contrary notions about heavenly things – caeleftium contra *r*

Befides – Tacitus and Juvenal, we find, reprefent the conduct of thofe two nations, towards their own countrymen, to have been totally different. – Tacitus fays, Hift. v. 5, of the Jews – Necare quen- quam ex agnatis, nefas: – Juvenal tells us, xv. 33, that the antipathy that exifted between two neighbouring egyptian clans about religion, was fo great that they not only killed each other, but even devoured the carcafes of the flain:

Inter finitimos vetus atque antiqua fimultas
Immortale odium, et nunquam fanabile vulnus
Ardet adhuc Ombos et Tentyra. Summus utrinque
Inde furor vulgo, quod Numina vicinorum
Odit uterque locus; cum folos credat habendos
Erie Deos, quos ipfe colit, &c. '

Philo, befidei telling us how very fuperior the religion of the Jews was to thofe of all other people, alfo tells us, de vita M. p. 508, C. D., how little regard all the reft of the world had for the religious inftitu-

tions of each Other – rwv *xarat m* E? tXaSa *xat @xfGxfov, u$- frros enrut,* sSe/tta woXir *tft, v rx trtfot! Vo/ulax ny.* Z, /AoXu Se *xat Tut avrw ttast tnftstrat, vps fa! tut xattfut xat rut trfayp, xrut* /nsflaf/-oiJo/Asvt) *rftwets. AOsxttot x. r.* X. –

He alfo tells us, in Fl., how the Alexandrians, within a few months only after the death of Tiberius, petitioned Flaccus for leave to per- fecute the Jews of that city for their religion. And, laftly, Jofepbus, in his difpute with Apion, ii. §. 6, p. 1367, reprefents that adverfary of the Jews as attempting to prove that the Jews of Alexandria could not be free of that city, as the natives were, *becaufe they did not wofjlnjt*

Tiberius did not expel the Jews from Rome,

the fame God. – Sed fuper hoc: quomodo ergo, inquit, fi funt cives, eofdem Deos, quos Alexandriai non colunt ? Cui refpondeo: Quomodo etiam, cum vos fitis ./Egyptii, inter alterutros praelio magno et fine faedere *de religions* eontenditis ? – Now as fo many writers, three of whom lived in Egypt, atteft the difcrepancy between the jewifh religion and every one of the egyptian, and of the egyptian between each other, why mould Tacitus have aflumed it as granted that all the religions of the Egyptians were the fame, and precifely like that of the Jews?

But, after all, had the religions of thofe two people been precifely the fame, how will it be made to appear that their religion was more fuperftitious than that of the Romans? – Had not the Romans derived the worfhip of fome if not of moft of their Deities from the Egyptians ? At leaft does not Strabo fay, xvii, that fome of the Egyptians were worfhippers of Jupiter, fome of Apollo, others of Venus, and others again of Pallas, &c. ? – And does not Dion fay, 1. 48, p. 336, that the Triumvirs, in the year 711, that is, before Egypt was made a Roman province, erefted a temple to Serapis and Ifis? – And as to the 4,000 young men, citizens, who, he fays, were, for their fuperftition, by the Senate, fent, 'as foldiers, to Sardinia, (admitting that Sardinia then belonged to them) what right had they to pvmim them fo much more feverely for their fuppofed fuperftition ? – Whether they were previoufly inlifted or not, what right had they to order them any where, efpecially as they belonged to provinces confefledly under the control of the emperor ? – Tacitus tells us that they were fent to Sardinia to prevent piracy – coercendis illic latrociniis; – but do not Paterculus and Suetonius inform us that Tiberius was himfelf very induftrious to prevent piracy? – Paterculus fays, ii. 126, that Tiberius

Tiberius did not expel tlie Jews from Rome.

had, before the i6th year of his reign, entirely fupprefled piracy- pax augufta per omnes terrarum orbis angulos a latrociniorum metu fervat immunes. – Suetonius fays in the beginning of the chapter next after that in which he fpeaks of the expulfion of the Jews, &c. that Tiberius put an entire flop to the depredations of pirates – Imprimis tuendae pacis a graflaturis ac latrociniis feditionumque licentia curam habuit.

Laftly – Tacitus fays, that all the reft were ordered – that is, in the year 772, to leave Italy, unlefs they would, by a fixed day, relinquifh their profane rites. But if all this took place in the year 772, it muft have happened before the death of Drufus, who, we find, by Jofe- phus, was ever fond of the company of Agrippa. How then is it that Agrippa had no intereft at court, to prevent this general expulfion of his countrymen? – How is it that he was permitted to remain at Rome till the death of Drufus ? – Did he top renounce his religion ? – How is it to be accounted for that Tiberius, at the requeft of the Jews, rebuked Pilate fo feverely for having prefumed to introduce the Roman flandards into Jerufalem ? – How happened it that Paulina, the wife of Saturninus was, as Jofephus fays, in the year 783, a votary of Ifis ' – and that, that Goddefs had, in that year, a temple at Rome? – How was it that Fulvia too . was permitted to become *a profelyte?* – Ho. w was it that thofe four, jewifh vagabonds, mentioned by Jofephus, found admiffion at Rome ? – And, laftly, how is it that Luke tells us that there were at Jerufalem, in the year 781, " ftrangers of Rome, Jews, as well as Profelytes ?" /

Befides – how is it that no other roman pr jewifh writer has mentioned this expulfion? – Even Philq and Jofephus appear not to have been aware of this expulfion of their countrymen. They ech appear to deny it. Philo fays, leg. 785, F.. that the Jews were, even at Rome,*ftberius did not expel the Jews from Some.*

as quiet all through the reign of Tiberius as they had been under that of their benefaAor Auguftus, excepting only when Sejanus obtained kave to difturb their repofe to prevent their taking up arms in aid of Tiberius. Jofephus not only fays that even Fulvia, on whofe account the Jews were expelled from Rome, juft before the death of Sejanus, was, before fhe was deceived by the jewifh outcafts, a profelyte, but that fhe thought it no new thing to be expefted to give fomething towards the fupport of the temple.

On re-confidering all -that Tacitus fays of this matter why fhould we not conclude that he appears to have been quite ignorant of the jewifh religion, if not of the egyptian too – and, that he appears to have been almoft as ignorant of the affairs of his own country, by faying that the Senate (who, he himfelf fays, often afked and followed the advice of Tiberius on extraordinary matters,] took the liberty of prying into the religious concerns of other countries, and efpccially of the Jews, which he ought to have known were fecured by compaft – and, of fending thofe 4,000 libertines (who, as being Jews and Egyptians, muft have been fubjeft to the emperor,) to Sardinia, as foldiers. And, on comparing what he here fays, with what he fays, iii. 60, why mould we not conclude that he appears to have antidated this event not a little, if not that he appears to have contradicted himfelf?

Let us now attend to what Suetonius fays of tins event:

Suetonius fays, c. 36, that Tiberius, notwithftanJing he was, as we have feen in the laft CHAP., ever fond of Jews and of their religion, notwithftanding he, as Strabo fays, vi. p. 199, followed all the rules prefcribed by Auguftus, notwithftanding he, as Dion fays, 1. 58,

Tta

Tiberius did not expel the Jews from Rome.

p. 607, C., fwore to obferve all the afts of Auguftus, (who, as Sue- tonius himfelf acknowledges, ii. 93, had the moft profound reverence for all ancient religious inftitutions,) and compelled the Senate to do fo too, and, notwithftanding he, as Suetonius himfelf acknowledges, iii. 41, 69, cared nothing about the republic, or about religion, and the Gods – notwithftanding all this evidence to the contrary, Suetonius, we find, tells us that Tiberius forbad the continuance of jewifii or egyptian rites at Rome – that he compelled all who were addifted to *that fuper/iition* to burn every veft and utenfil neceflary for the performance of its rites – that he difperfed the *jewljh youth* all over the *unhealthy* provinces – that is, furely, the imperial provinces, and therefore not Sardinia, unlefs he had then exchanged fome other for it – that he did it *per fpeclem facramenti* – that is, we are told, as foldiers – and, that he ordered all *the reft of the fame nation,* or, the *like feflarles* to leave the *city* – and, that he threatened them with perpetual *fervltude* if they would not obey. – His own words are – Exter- nas caeremonias, aegyptios judaicofque ritus compefcuit: coaftis qui fuperftitione *ea* tenebantur, religiofas veftes cum inftrumento omni comburere. *Judteorum* juventutem, per fpeciem facramenti, in pro- vincias gravioris caeli diftribuit: reliquos ejufdem gentis, vel fimilia feftantes, urbe fubmovit, fub paina perpetuae fervitutis, nifi obtempe- raflent. – All this Suetonius fays Tiberius did, and pretty clearly, after the fpring of the year 781 – for then the rulers of the Jews faid to Pilate " We have no king but Caefar," – and then they poflefled the privilege of demanding the releafe of any ftate delinquent – and, after Midfummer in that year, for a little before, there were, fays Luke, at Jerufalem, devout ftrangers of Rome, Jews, and Profelytes – and, c-

Per speciem honoris, iii. 65. – Under a pretence of conferring honor ou Sejanu.

+ Does not this seem to imply that these Jewi of Home were libertines.

Tiberius did not expel the Jews from Rome.

after the beginning of 782, for then there were at Jerufalem jewtih libertines, fays the fame writer – and probably when the year 783 was pretty far advanced, for in that year they ftill poflefled the privilege of fending to ftrange cities for tranfgreflbrs of the law, and, as the Talmud of Jerufalem fays, the power of putting any one to death – that is, feemingly, the year after the facred rites of foreign nations were fcrutinized, for then Seneca fays, that he, in compliance with the requeft of his father, ceafed to follow the *fuperftition of* feme of them, in abftaining from the food of certain animals.

Let us next hear what Jofephus fays of the expulfion of his countrymen from Rome: Jofephus, after having given us an account, A. xviii. 4, y., of the works &c. of our Lord, proceeds, in the next §. v,, to fay how *another difafttr* AXo n Sttvot about the fame time – Kt *wo res vrat yj/mas* – befell the Jews. But though he raifes our expeftation in this unufual manner, he does not immediately proceed to gratify it. Before I, fays he, proceed to give an account of this other difafter which, at this time, befell the Jews, I requeft your attention to an irrelevant anecdote concerning Ifis, the Goddefs of the Egyptians, her temple at Rome, and her priefts. f And having indulged himfelf with this digref- fion, in the end of that §. he fays again – Kt *res %fins rurat.* – He then proceeds, in §. *t.,* to relate the expulfion of the Jews.

Fulvia, fays he, the wife of Saturninns, a Patrician, and one of the friends of Tiberius, had embraced the jewifh religion. After me bad become a profelyte to it, me placed herfelf under the inftrucUon of a

Those who contend that Josephus did not record the previous account of our Lord, are desired to tell us what he means by *another* disaster.

t By this it appears that the Egyptian! had, at that time, a temple, &c at Rome – and, that they Wcfc not expelled.

Tibsrius did not expel the Jews from Rome.

certain Jew, who, for fear of the punifhment which he deferved for tranfgreffing the law, and for his total depravity, had fled from his country ; but who, notwithftanding his tranfgreffion of the law, pretended fo be an interpreter of it. This noble lady, fays he, not fatis- fied with the inftruftions which fhe received from this wicked would be doftor, attended likewife thofe of three or four other vagabonds, in all things as bad as her firft teacher. By thofe four outcafts fhe was perfuaded to fend coftly prefents to Jerufalem, which they took care to apply to their own ufe. Saturninus, (and not the Jews of Rome,) fays Jofephus, complained of this fraud, not to any magiftrate, but to Tiberius, then at Capreae, immerfed in indolence and vice, and totally indifferent about the republic, or religion, and the Gods. Tiberius, our hiftorian proceeds to fay, on hearing of this fraud, inftead of punifhing thofe four impoftors, ordered every thing jewifh – *n laSaixo,* – that is, we fuppofe, the Jews, and, at leaft, their profelytes, if not then- believing countrymen, to be driven from Rome. The con- fuls, f fubjoins he, at the time making a levy,! tok 4iooo of them and fent them not, as Suetonius fays, 'into the unhealthy provinces,

ififti Se *xai mi ras axs twQpu7rus Oyoi rot Kjjjx. avruv, xatiirif* oXXotftui *otns,* $)X307. Diou, 1. 37, p. 87, B.

t w *rut* Xojirav avflponrw *ts rc ra x'f.. x ra irifi rm*

It *tnttw, xeti* fuXia8' *on rut fui o. ut Qiu* sStJ! *nxo-i, wo.* Se *rtto. signs'.* B. C.

t This event, we shall see presently, he appears to have placed iu the year 783, when M. Vinucius Uuartiuus and C. Cassius Longinus were consuls.

+ Palerculus says, ii. 130, that Tiberius made this levy, and, that he made it without causing the least disturbance – Quanta cum quiete hominum, rem perpetui prtccipuique timoris, supplementum, sine trepidatione dilectus, pro
 vidit ?

Tiberius did not expel the Jews from Rome.

but to Sardinia, and . punifhed moft of the reft for refuting, in obedience to Mofes, to enlift. All thefe were, for the one offence of thofe four impoftors, fo punifhed and expelled from Rome. . .

Now as this jewifh impoftor found it neceflary to leave Judea on account of his having tranfgrefled the law of Mofes, why mould we not fuppofe that he had done fomething to deferve death ? – For what other crime mould he have thought it neceflary to leave his native country ? – If then this jewim tranfgreflbr had been obliged to leave Judea to avoid a capital pumfhmeat, and foon after the crucifixion of Jefus, does it not feem to imply that Ifrael had ftill the power of in- flifting capital punifhments ? – But whether he had or had not done fomething worthy of death, if he fled for having tranfgrefled the law of Mofes, why, if the Jews had then the privilege offending to flrange cities for tranfgreflors of the law, did they not fend to Rome to apprehend him ? – Efpecially if, as Jofephus fays, he had aggravated his former tranfgreffions by embezzling the voluntary oblations of this honorable, profelyte to the fupport of the fervice of the temple ? – For, in that cafe, he muft have been guilty of a breach of thofe fix edifts publifhed by Auguflus, Agrippa, &c. and recited by Jofephus, A. xvi. 6, (3. y. 3. f. *s.* $., which edifts, Tiberius, who, as Dion fays, 1. 57, p. 607, C., had fworn to obferve all the afts of Auguflus, and had compelled the Senate to do fo too, mufl be fuppofed to have flill enforced. And if the privilege offending to ftrange cities for tranf- greflbrs of the law of Mofes was then alfo taken from them, why did jhey not complain of his having afted in defiance of thofe edifts ? – Tiberius, furely, would have caufed them to be enforced. – But inftead of telling us that the Jews took any flep to punifh thole vile tranfgreflors of their law, he would have us to believe that Sutur-

Does not thit too seem to imply that those Jews were libertines.'

Tiberius did not evftel'the Jews from Rome.

ninus, who, no doubt, knew that his wife was a profelyte, and, that it was expefted of profelytes to make prefents to the temple, went him- felf to Capreae, and complained of the fraud to Tiberius. And what faid Tiberius? – Was he not offended at Saturninus for interrupting his repofe with fuch a filly complaint ? – efpecially if he had, as Dion fays, then furrendered the management of every thing to Sejanus? – Or, did he give orders to try them ? – Not he indeed. Inftead of doing fo, he, fays Jofephus, not only ordered every thing jewifh – *wo. n inlaixm* – that is – two or three myriads of Jews, with their profelytes, if not believers and unbelievers, to leave Rome – but likewife 4,000 jewifh libertines to be fent to Sardinia! as foldiers, and punifhed moft of the reft of the *libertines* for refufing to ferve. And all this, as Jofephus would have us to believe, for the offence of this felf exiled wretch and his three accomplices.

So replete with incredible particulars is the account which this prince of facerdotal hiftorians has had the afTurance to recommend to our notice – and, as attefted by Agrippa, the younger. – An account never objefted to by learned interpreters, though calculated only for the initiation of the illiterate! And an account in which there is much more falfhood than any one can well eftimate without attending to the particulars. Let us endeavour to make ourfelves acquainted with them.

How could this Saturninus, if he was any way related to Saturninus mentioned by Dion as having been, for writing verses against Tiberius, praecipitated from the Capitol, six years before, have presumed to trouble Tiberius with any complaint, and especially with so silly an one against his friends the Jews!

i He begins V 5. thus – And about the same time – *Kat wo ms avrac yjpm* – (the resurrection of Jesus) another sad disaster befell the Jews of Rome. – And, he ends it thus – I now proceed to relate what happened to the Jews of Rome, at this time – xara runt rot jviai,

Tiberius did not expel the Jews from Rome.

In the firji place, he, it mould be obferved, has not told us the names of thofe four Iranfgreflbrs of the law, nor the nature of their tranfgreffions, nor why, as the Jews then poflefled the privilege of fending to ftrange cities for fuch tranfgreflbrs, thofe four Ifraelites were, not only, not apprehended, but permitted to live unmolefted at Rome, and to fet up for interpreters of that very law which they had tranfgrefled – an occupation which they could not follow in private nor in public, unlefs they had been of the tribe of Levi. *In the next place,* he fays, that this execrable wretch found means to ingratiate himfelf with this noble lady, (who, he fays, was before a profelyte,) and not only he, but three others as worthlefs as himfelf. *In the third place,* we perceive, he does not fay that they taught any thing contrary to the law. Indeed as Fulvia was before a profelyte to its fpirit, and muft, of courfe, be fuppofed to have been, in a great lneafure, acquainted with its precepts, it cannot be fuppofed that me would have liftened to them, if they had attempted to inftill tenets into her contrary to thofe received by other profelytes. – *In the fourth /dace,* he informs us that this worthlefs gang contrived to obtain from her valuable prefents, in addition, no doubt, to her accuftomed oblations for the temple, which they took care to apply to their own ufe – and, without reminding us of thofe feveral edifts which, he had before faid, were publifhed by Auguftus, and Agrippa, &c. threatening punifhment to fuch offenders. – *In the fifth place,* we find, he would have us to believe that Fulvia did not complain of this facri- Jegious fraud to Sejanus, though that minifter had, as Dion fays, found means to recommend himfelf to the efteem of all the noble married ladies of Rome, and for the purpofe of difcovering the fentiments and aftions of their hufbands, and had rendered them fubfervient to his views, but to her hufband, who, and not the Jews of Rome, complained of it, (not to any magiftrate,) but, to Tiberius, then rellding

Tiberius did not expel the Jews from Rome.

at Capreae, and totally inattentive to all political affairs, (even to the internal pavor,) if not overcome with grief. – *In the jixth fllace,* he fays that Tiberius, who, as Agrippa told Caius, p. 800, D., was, though by no means apt to be irritable, enraged when he heard that Pilate had prefumed to introduce his ftandards into the holy city – and, who, as the fame writer told the fame prince, p. 801, F., continued, at the very time, the daily oblation of a bull and two lambs – and, who, as Jofephus himfelf fays, A. xviii. 2, *y.*, was intimately acquainted with Herod, the tetrarch – and, who, as he again fays, 7, S., was glad to hear of the return of Agrippa to Italy, a year or two after – notwith- ftanding all this, he afiures us, that Tiberius, on hearing of the facri- legious fraud, inftead of punifhing thofe unprincipled Ifraelites, according to the tenor of the edifts publifhed by his two fathers-in-law, inftantly ordered every thing jewifh, or, the Jews, believing and unbelieving, and their profelytes (among whom we, furely, may reckon Fulvia) to leave Rome. – *In the loft place,* he fays, that Tiberius, who, as Philo fays, p. 783, F., always lived in peace – who, as Paterculus fays, ii. 126, was, at no time, more blefTed with it than in the t6th year – who, as Tacitus fays, iv. 74, was totally unconcerned at the revolt of the Frifii – who, as Suetonius fays, iii. 37, never undertook any expedition afterwards, not content with all this feverity towards twenty or thirty thoufand Jews, and their profelytes, for this fingle offence of three or four wretches, for which the roman as well as the jewifh laws had provided a punifhment, ordered the confuls to enlift mod of *thetr libertines,* and (though Paterculus remarks, ii. 1 30, with*Tiberius did not expel the Jews from Home.*

Philo, ad C. p. 785, C., says, that the Jews of Rome occupied a great part of the city – and, that they were mostly freedmen. – *vus $v tttSttro Tnv Tt TtGtftus troratf. x ptyatm rns Pw/xnr atroroptn, tn ax vyvoft*

xat Oixb/ajvijv trfos yaf axfittns tts

how little inconvenience to the public he had, jufl before, raifed a levy,) to punifh thofe who refufed to enlift, and to fend 4,000 of thofe who did enliit to Sardinia, one, as Paufanias fays, of his own provinces, there, as Tacitus and Suetonius, we have feen, fay, to perifh by the inclemency of the climate. – And, all this he fays, without telling us why thofe libertines were treated worfe than others – and, why thofe who did enlift were treated worfe than thofe who did not – and, without telling us how long this feverity lafted.

Of thofe feveral moft incredible particulars does this jumble of falfehoods confift. And though any one of common fenfe may fancy that he fees the enormity of the component parts, and, confequently of the whole – yet to view it as a folitary monfter of jewifh fiftion, will not be enough – it will be neceflary to place it in contraft with an egyptian of fomewhat the fame caft.

In the feftion immediately preceding (S) Jofephus relates how Decius Mundus wanted to feduce Paulina, the wife of *Saturninus,* who, not- withftanding the expulfion of the Egyptians, as Tacitus fays, feven or eight years before, happened to be a votary of Ifis. Paulina refifted his overture. Mundus then applied to the priefts of Ifis, who, on being well rewarded, went, to Paulina and told her that the God Anubis would be glad to have a night's lodging with her: this made her vain, and – &c. This Saturninus alfo made his complaint to Tiberius. – And what followed? – Were the Egyptians all expelled from Rome? – No fuch thing, though Suetonius, we have juft feen, fays, that they were. – What then? – Tiberius ordered all the priefts to be crucified, the temple of Ifis to be demolifhed, and her ftatue to be thrown into the Tyber.

Kai tfavQtfor a tXtfut pn)rv *airatruv,* aW. ayw *itfor* Swaov *irowrap, Etos re* Sw *yap fm wen ir rot pairx ivftxtpwa atn* EXXaSoi o-ipio- vtj-

Fausan. p. 428.

Tiberius did not expel the Jews from Rome.

Jofephus, it fhould be obferved, does not precifely mention the year when this expulfion of his countrymen from Rome happened. – He only fays that it happened after the death of our Lord. – And for the reafons before adduced by us, in examining the report which Suetonius has made of this affair, it cannot be fuppofed to have happened before the year 783. – Some indeed may be almoft inclined to infer this, from the confideration that Jofephus has afterwards, vii. r., mentioned the confpiracy of Sejanus, in which moft of the libertines were concerned – and, from this, that he fays that it was the confuls – *at vtrarot* – who punilhcd the jewifh libertines for refufing to enlift. – In his account of the expulfion of the Jews he does not intimate that the confpiracy of Sejanus then took place – nor, in his account of the confpiracy of Sejanus, does he fay that the expulfion of the Jews then took place.

Let us, in the lad place, enquire what Philo fays of the expulfton of the Jews from Rome:

Philo, in tvo of his works – viz – in Fl. and ad C., feemingly alludes to their expulfion.-r-In his work, ad C., after having told us how very kind Auguftus always was to the Jews of Rome, he proceeds to tell us how Tiberius behaved to them in the fame manner, till juft before the death of Sejanus: when he, till the death of that minifter, difturbed the repofe of all thofe in Italy. The ftrift verfion of his own words is nearly this – and under Tiberius it was exaftly the fame, excepting only the agitation of thofe in Italy, when Sejanus was fabricating the

tmpOlltlOn – *Xki mt TtGtftu li. ttrot* ρov *avrot rfotrov, xatlrot rut ct Iroctx wafz-xmv8trruv, wx* Ini'atos- *unvuftt mt* emflto-tv. – By which it appears that not only the Jews of Rome, but thofe of Italy, were in commotion when Sejanus was fabricating his impofition, but, for what reafon, it does not appear, unlefs it was becaufe they not only knew that Sejanus was

Tiberius did not expel the Jews from Rome.

fabricating his impofition, (which, furely, would imply, according to the report of Juvenal and Dionf of this affair, that the Jews all over Italy knew more of this matter than the inhabitants of Rome,) but, that his impofition would affcft them. But were it indeed fo, what reafon had they, as they were fo thoroughly convinced that Tiberius was their friend, to be, alarmed on that account ? – In how very different a manner does Philo, V. Maximus, and Juvenal fpeak of this fuppofed plot of Sejanus! *Philo* fays, that the Jews only or chiefly would oppofe it, and that Sejanus, on that account, prevailed on Tiberius to expel them. *V. Maximus* fays, that Sejanus intended to maffacre all the people of *Rome,* that the peace of the *whole world* would have been difturbed. *Juvenal* fays, that the people of Rome did not know, even after the death of Sejanus, for what crime he had fuffered. Of what nature was this impofition that it could have affeft- ed all the Jews of Italy fo much more than the people of Rome ? – Was it an impofition that was likely to affeft the fovereignty of their great benefaftor the emperor5 – If it was, muft not the Jews have, not- withftanding they, as the Talmud of Jerufalem fays, had, in the year 783, been deprived of the power of inffifting capital punifhments, and of the privilege of demanding the releafe of any prifoner every year, been very much attached to his government ? – But if fuch was the attachment of all the Jews of Italy to the perfon and government of Tiberius, how is it that Jofephus affures us, A. xviii. 8, (3., that Herod, the tetrarch, was, by his brother-in-law Agrippa, accufed to CaiusJ of having been concerned in it? – Do not Philo and Jofephus feem to dilagree, not a little, in their evidence on this point ? – Let us how-

Sat. x. 69, &c. Scd quo, &c. t Dion, 1. 58, p. 624, D.

Josephus says, B. ii. 9, *t.*, that Agrippa went, before the death of Piso, to Rome to accuse Herod of something to Tiberius – and, that he took no notice of it.

Tiberius did not expel the Jews from Rome.

ever proceed to hear what Philo fays followed, immediately on the fall of Sejanus, this commotion of the Jews of Italy.

He continues thus – " Immediately after whofe death, Tiberius, " knowing that the things lie had faid, againft the Jews of Rome, " were falfe and invented by himfelf, and that he aimed at injuring, ' not only thofe of Rome or thofe of Italy, but, the whole nation, as " being aware that, befides their engagement to defend the life of the " emperor, they would be the firft, if not the only people, to oppofe " his impious intentions and aftions, enjoined his ordained miniflers, " every where, to comfort thofe that were refiding in heathen cities, " but to reprimand only the culpable, who were not many – and to " make no alteration in their cuftoms, and to hold, as a depofit, their " perfons as peaceable, and their laws as conducive to regularity."

– iyv /xtT *rni txtitH reiorm, on Ta mxTiyoftiQetrot rut uxtntorai rii t Pufan v,*]euie *Tia-xt $ixSoai,* irto/a!T *2yiatu* To *cQvos atapmxa-iti QsoTos,* (xovot, /xa. if i /jBAiii *annals xai irfai, ri a-ir$rlariftmi, mip* r ai xjvJuti-aror *aunxparofos, xat Tois itaiTayiai ti'fontois wxp. ois* iirjo-x4ji, *irafayifyo-at put rat itara irotis rut airo rS tQus,* XX *nn (riTXTtti) ttinai ras airias, oiyei* St *y&CH,* xii? o-ai St *fioi* Ss *rut c% cQss,* aXXas xai 5rafaxaTaflnx iXe" Ti l ri at"fxs " "f""r *rxs tyvaiis, xai* T *topifj. ae af a. tlpinra. irfos cufaQtioH .* f

But what? – Does Philo here indeed affirm that Tiberius, foon after the fall of Sejanus, knew that Sejanus had accufed the Jews to him of feveral things falfely – that he knew that he did fo in order to deftroy the whole nation – that he alfo knew that the Jews would be the firft,

!*miv,* ifl8t rj/itafo/xssr *ras* says the margin. – But, what if we suppose that rir is only a part of the verb nririMio-ari ? – Would it not correspond a litlle better with

t Does not this last clause seem to be a plain contradiction of the Talmud of Jerusalem? – At least, if it is to be understood of capital punishments in general.

Tiberius did not expel the Jews from Rome.

if not the only people, to rife in his own defence, and, to oppofe the impious *Intentions* and *deeds* of Sejanus ? – That he does indeed mean to affirm, at leaft, that Sejanus fought to deftroy the whole nation of the Jews is rendered pretty evident by what he fays in the beginning of his work againft Flaccus, where he fays, p. 747, that Flaccus -was the next after Sejanus who confpired to injure the Jews – not the whole race, as Sejanus had done, for he had not fo much power –

AETTEPO2 M- rj. 2iaiot 4iX:txxor *AyilAios* 5XsEr. i *rm Xxtx rut laSaitit iiri* 3Xv, *yvitisai* /Atu aSlxijyi To *iQms uo"iref ix'iitos a SvinQtis, tarrys* yap *lii ras*

us rar aQofpat. – By this then it appears that Philo meant to affirm that Sejanus formed a confpiracy, not only againft the Jews of Rome or thofe of Italy, but againft *the whole race* – that is, furely, againft thofe who believed in Jefus Chrift, as well as againft thofe who did not believe in him, and, for the purpofe of carrying into efleft, it fhould feem, the impofition – and, that he had the addrefs to perfuade Tiberius to let him difturb thofe of Rome and Italy. But how could any prime minifter have thought of injuring a whole nation, and fo difperfed as the Jews were, and by accufing them to his sovereign, and to a sovereign so attached to them as, we have seen, Tiberius then was? – Of what could he have accused a whole nation, especially one so dispersed and divided as the jewish nation then was ? – Philo, and he only, tells us that it was to effect, some imposition. Now if that imposition confided in any project against his sovereign, why did not Sejanus, as he so far succeeded as to get the greatest obstacle removed, proceed to accomplish it? – However, if Tiberius did really order all the Jews to be expelled from Rome, in consequence of the charges alledged against them by Sejanus, and was, immediately after the fall of that minister, so convinced that the charges alledged against them were false, and, that they only, or chiefly, would have opposed Sejanus, and have defended himself, ordered all his praefefts to treat those in

Tiberius did not expel the Jews from Rome.

Gentile cities with kindness – why did not Agrippa mention it in his epistle to Caius? – In that epistle, he, we find, speaks very highly of the protestion which Tiberius *always* afforded the Jews, and of the respect which he manifested for the service of the temple, and though he, in it, adverts to the, as he was pleased to call it, severe treatment which he himself experienced from him, just before his death, yet he never alludes to expulsion of his countrymen from Rome. If we may believe Josephus this same Agrippa, went to Rome to accuse Herod of having been an accomplice with Sejanus in that conspiracy, which, if true, proves, surely, that Sejanus could not have conspired against *all* the Jews, at least, if not that he could not have conspired against any of them – and, that all the Jews were not well affected to Tiberius. Josephus too, though he speaks both of the expulsion of his countrymen, and, of the conspiracy of Sejanus, says, not that Sejanus was the cause of their expulsion. And of the conspiracy of Sejanus, he says, that he was supported by the Senate, by the *freedmen,* and by a great part of the army, and (if the charge of Agrippa against Herod was, as he says, true) by him also. And he further says, that the discovery of it was made to Tiberius by Antonia, the mother of Livilla, who was, at last, by the consent, no doubt, of all parties, shortly to be married to him. f

Suetonius says, Hi. 48 – . Militi nihil nnquam largitus cst, proeterquam siagula millia denariorum praetorianis, *quod Sejano te non accommodfssent.* – Now as Sejanus was the commander of those praetorian cohorts, how can it be thought that other divisions of the arm; would support him, if bis own would not ? – Suetonius subjoins – et quaedam munera Syriacis legionibus quod *sola:* nullam Sejani iraaginem coluissent. – And again, 65, he says – Aptatis etiam navibus ad quascumque legiones meditabatur fugam.

t As Dion says, I. 58, p. 623, A., that Sejanus contrived to ingratiate himself with all the honorable married ladies of Rome, and, that he, in order to obtain the secrets of their husbands, promised them marriage, how can we be expected to believe that every one of them, knowing he was abo'ut to disappoint them by marrying Livilla, still concealed his treachery?

Tiberius did not expel the Jews from Rome.

Having now endeavoured to make ourselves acquainted with what Philo says of the commotion of the Jews of Italy, while Sejanus was fabricating the imposition, and what he appears to say of the different manner in which Tiberius behaved towards most of those in Gentile cities, and towards some of them immediately after the death of Sejanus. Let us in the laft place attend to what he may be underftood to fay of the year when Sejanus fabricated the impofition, and thereby fet the Jews of Italy in commotion.

In the year 782, fays Tacitus, v. 4, 5, 6, when the Senate and the populace of Rome appeared to be ready for rebellion, Sejanus was very forward to oppofe them. In the year 783, fays Paterculus, ii. 127, 128, he was the obedient affiftant of the emperor – and fo, we may conclude, from what Juvenal fays, S. x. 92, continued till his death. But if we may believe Suetonius, iii. 65, he was, before he was made conful, or before the year 784 began, meditating a revolution – and fo long before the commencement of that year, that Tiberius had, before the year began, been apprifed of it. – Sejanum res novas motientem vix tandem et aftu magis ac dolo quam principal! auftoritate fubvertit. Nam primo ut fe per fpeciem honoris dimitteret, collegam fibi in quinto confulatu aflumpfit, quem longo intervallo *ob id i/ifum* fufceperat. – Now if Tiberius knew that Sejanus was, even while he wus at Capreae, plotting a revolution, and, was fo confident of his own fuperiority in the art of counter plotting, as to fend him to Rome to be his colleague in the confulfhip for the year 784, for the purpofe of deftroying him, how can we think that he, who, as Philo fays, ad C. p. 772, A., knew mankind better than any one, either before or afterwards, permitted his prime minifter to perfuade him that the Jews, whom he, furely, knew, as well as Philo, to be a*Tiberius did not expel the Jews from Rome.*

much attached to himfelf as they were hoflile to Sejanus, had done certain things for which they ought to be expelled from Rome and Italy ?

If we may believe Dion, 1. 58, p. 623, A., Sejanus began, in the year 783, when he found that Tiberius had fent Drufus (who Tacitus fays, iv. 36, was, in the year 778, praefeft of the city,) to Rome, to be fearful that a change might take place, in the mind of Tiberius, and, for that reafon, prevailed on Caffius Longinus, the colleague of Vinicius, (who, in the year 785, married'Julia, the fifter of Drufus,) to accufe him of fomething – χρυρ. ario-ai n Xt' avrn. – And in the fame page, B., he fays, that Sejanus contrived, but a little before the beginning of the year 784, to keep his future colleague Tiberius (cunning as Suetonius fays he was) in ignorance of every thing then tranfafting at Rome. But in p. 625, A., he fays, that Sejanus was fo vacillating between exceflive pride and exceffive fear that he could not refolve on attempting any thing. And again, at the bottom of that page, at E., he fays, that he, when he found that Tiberius had made Caius (who, as being the fon of Germanicus, was the darling of the people, and who had, as Suetonius fays, iv. 12, been lately married to Junia Claudilla, the daughter of M. Silanus,) a prieft, in the room of his brother Drufus, as well as himfelf and his fon, *gave up all thought of making a revolution.* Confequently if, as Philo fays, Sejanus, in order to accomplifh his impofition, perfuaded" Tiberins to expel the Jews from Rome, it feems pretty clear, by the evidence above adduced, that he muft have done it, at leaft, many months before he was put*Tiberius did not expel the Jews from Rome.*

Non ita multo post Jnniam Claudillam M. Silani nobilissimi viri filiam duxil uxorcm. *Deinde* augur in locum fratris sui D1usi dcstinatus, priusquam uiauguraretur, ad Pontificatum traductusest: insigni testimonio pietatis atque indolis: cum deserta desolataque reliqnis subsidiis aula, Sejano vero tune ms- pecto, mox et oppresso, ad spcm successionis paullatim admoveretnr.

to death, if not in the preceding year – viz – 783. Indeed when we confider what Dion fays, 1. 58, p. 625, D., – viz – that Tiberius would not permit him to come to Caprele, we fhall have the greater reafon to acquiefce in the above conclufion.

The fum of what Philo fays of the commotion among the Jews of Rome and Italy, in the reign of Tiberius, is this – Sejanus, in the year 783, (the very year in which the Talmud of Jerufalem fays the power of inffifting capital punifhments was taken from Ifrael, and the yea; before he married Li villa,) meditated fome remarkable impofition. – What this impofition was he does not fay – he leaves us to conjefture by the fequel. – This impofition, he intimates, Sejanus was aware the Jews at large (that, we fuppofe, is, believers and unbelievers,) would, if not alone, at leaft chiefly, oppofe, partly from attachment to the interefts of Tiberius, partly from oppofition to his own wicked projefts and feats, and therefore accufed thofe of Rome to Tiberius ot feveral things, but, as he himfelf fays, falfely ; and, by fo doing, prevailed on Tiberius to let him ufe, not only thofe of Rome and Italy, but the whole nation, believers as well as unbelievers, unjuftly. – All this Philo fays of their oppreffion, in the year 783, and, in the year following, till the death of Sejanus. After whofe death, that is, nearly a year, if not more than a year after, (for Sejanus was not put to death till Oflober,) Tiberius convinced that the feveral things, of which Sejanus had, the year before, accufed them, were without foundation, inftantly enjoined all his manually appointed fub-niiniftcrs to comfort thofe in Gentile cities, and to reprimand or to punifh thofe who wore *culpable,* who, it feems, were, as Philo fays, but few. – To make no alteration in their cutloms, but to refpeft them for the fake of their law.

Tiberius did not expel the Jews from Rome.

This, we take it, is very near the fum of what Philo fays of the injury done the Jews of Rome and Italy, in the year 783, by Sejanus, and of what he fays that minifter intended to do the Jews every where, and, of courfe, believers as well as unbelievers – for the believing Jews were not then denominated Chriftians. The effects of which injury, he would have us to believe, Tiberius, about a year after, endeavored to alleviate, by enjoining all his praefefts to treat thofe of the difper- fion well, and to reprimand only the culpable, who, he confeffes, were a few – that is, we fuppofe, in each of their diflrifts. But amidft all of it, he, we perceive, fays not a word of the cotemporary privation of Ifrael, of the power of putting any one to death, though the Talmud has been underftood to afTert it, nor of demanding yearly the releafe of any ftate criminal.

Having now paid due attention to the feveral reports of Suetonius, Jofephus, and Philo concerning this tranfaftion, let us proceed to enquire how far they appear to agree or to difagree.

They appear to difagree in this – that Tiberius either expelled them himfelf, or, permitted them to be expelled – and, in this, that he expelled them in the year 783, the very year in which the Talmud of Jerufalem fays Ifrael was deprived of the power of punifhing with death. – In all other particulars they difagree not a little.

Suetonius, who, v. 25, calls Chriftians Jews, fays, that Tiberius, of his own accord, expelled his beft friends the Jews, and with them the Egyptians, from Rome, and from that city only; and this he, we, to our no little furprife, find, fays, Tiberius did, at the very time when he cared nothing for the republic, nothing for religion, or the Gods,

If those two remarkable events happened by the order of Tiberius, and tn the same year, how is it that neither Philo or Josephus mentions the one, nor the Talmud the other?

Tiberius did not expel the Jews from Rome.

and had even quarrelled with Apollo and had attempted to deftroy all his oracles near Rome, for exercifing their profane rites. Suetonius alfo fays, that he fent the jewiftt youths, and them only, into the unhealthy provinces, and, that he did it – per fpeciem facramenti – that is, furely, not as foldiers, for all the other Jews, befides the 4,000, fent to Sardinia, refufed, as Jofephus, we fhall prefently find, fays, to ferve – but, as Suetonius again fays, iii. 65, of the miffion of Sejanus to Rome – per fpeciem honoris – under a colour of a, or the facrament. And, laftly, he, by faying that the reft of the fame nation, (that is the jewifh) and thofe of a like religious perfuafion, were threatened with perpetual fervitude if they did not obey, feems to intimate, that they were roman citizens, if not that they were never permitted to return.

Jofephus, we find, fays, that Tiberius expelled every thing jewiflt from Rome – and, that he did it, on the complaint of Saturninus againft the jewifh impoftors, for applying to their own ufe his wife's coftly oblations to the temple. He alfo aflerts that the Egyptians were not then expelled. He further fays that the confuls enlifted 4,000, and fent them to Sardinia – that the reft would not enlift, and that the confuls therefore punifhed them.

Philo, who fays, that the conduf t of Tiberius towards the Jews in general was, till the year 783, the very fame as that of their great benefaftor Auguftus had ever been, and that the Jews were, for that reafon, as much attached to him, as any people, if not more; fays alfo, that Sejanus was, in that year, fabricating the impofition, and, that he, in order to carry it into effeft, fought to injure the whole nation – that he accufed thofe of Rome and Italy of certain things to their friend Tiberius, and thereby caufed a commotion. – And, laftly,

Tac. tv. 19, Proprium id Tiberio fait, scelera nuper reperta priscis rer- bis oblegere.

Tiberius did not expel the Jews from Rome.

that Tiberius, being, not immediately, but feveral months after, (viz – on the death of Sejanus) convinced that the charges were falfe, enjoined all his manually ordained fub-minifters to comfort thofe that were in Gentile cities, and to reprimand, or, to punifh only fome few, in each of their feveral diftrifts, who were culpable – and, to fhew the fame refpeft for their law as they had before fhewn – but, of reftoring to Ifrael the power of floning blafphemers, &c. he, it mould be ob- ferved, fays not a word.

It is not a little remarkable that thofe three hiftorians have attributed the expulfion of the Jews from Rome to three widely different caufcs, neither of which has the leaft claim to verifimilitude. Suetonius fays, that they were expelled for praftifing fuperftitious rites. – Jofephus fays, that they were expelled becaufe three or four worthlefs Ifraelites intercepted a religious lady's prefent to the temple at Jerufa- lem. Philo, who does not tell us in what the impofition, which fet the Jews of Rome and Italy in commotion, and which, he fays, they were fo ready to refift, confifted, fays, if he meant that they were expelled, that they were expelled becaufe they were, more than any other fet of men attached to Tiberius. And, it is not lefs remarkable, that not one of thofe writers appears to have noticed (unlefs Suetonius may be thought to have alluded to it by – fuperftitione *ea* – or, by – per fpeciem facramenti – or, by- – fimilia feftantes – and, Jofephus, by *ita1* To luSa/icot) the expulfion of Chriftians from Rome about the fame time, though the two Senecas and Tacitus feem to have pretty plainly intimated it; – the elder Seneca, by fpeaking of the prevalence of the ufage of that mod wicked of all people, after it had been dif- continued – and, of the facraments of the Jews – and, the younger, by faying, that when the facred rights of foreigners were difcuffed, the abftinence from certain forts of food was reckoned as the chief evi-

Tiberius did not expel the Jews from Rome.

dence of fuperftition; – and Tacitus, by faying, that the execrable fuperftition, or mod grievous peft, which crept in, was fuppreffed; – and, though feveral early Chriftians writers, among whom, we find, two of the fecond century, aflert it – and, that they were expelled, after the year 782. Neither is it lefs remarkable than either of the two forementioned particulars, that not one of thofe three writers has noticed any attempt which thofe exiled Jews made to repel the unjuft attempt to difturb their repofe, and to evade fuch unheard of barbarity. Who can think that any people, who had been in alliance with another city nearly two centuries – who had been permitted to fettle in the metropolis of that other for more than one – and who, while there, had been indulged with extraordinary favors and exemptions – and who had been admitted to the rights of citizenfhip, would, without the leaft remonftrance, have tamely confented to be expelled, and for no reafon ? – And who can think that any monarch would have confented to the expulfion of twenty or thirty thoufand of his beft fubjefts for any reafon? – And, efpecially, without hearing what they had to offer in their own defence ? – And who can think that that moft eminently juft and humane monarch Tiberius would have confented to the expulfion of any defcription of roman citizens, efpecially of his favorites the Jews, and for a reafon fo abfurd as thofe affigned by the two roman writers, or fo unjuft and fo irreconcileable with his juft and fagacious charafter, as thofe affigned by the two jewifh.

Before we take our leave of this enquiry let us endeavour to fatisfy ourfelves whether the Jews alone were fet in commotion by the im- pofition of Sejanus – or, whether the Romans in general (of whom fome, we find, by the report of V. Maximus, were extremely attached to Tiberius,) do not appear to have participated in the agitation. – That the Jews fhould alone have known what Sejanus intended to do, and have been alone diflurbed by it, is not a little extraordinary.

Tiberius did not expel the Jews from Rome.

Suetonius, we have feen, relates the expulfion of the Jews and of others of the like religious modes of worfhip in the 361!! chapter; the 37th he, we fee, begins with *Imprimis* – an odd way of beginning a chapter it muft be allowed, if the contents of it were not connefted with thofe of the preceding. But what follows this *tm/vrinus* – fcil – tuendae pads a graflaturis ac latrociniis *feditionumyte licentia,* curarn habuit. – If now there was not any appearance of fedition, why does he fay that Tiberius attended to them above any other concern ? – And if there was, why mould he have increafed the number of malcontents by the expulfion of fo large a body of his beft friends, and without any caufe ? – or rather for a moft unjuft caufe ? – And why fhould he have fent his moft loyal troops to the unhealthy climates, or to Sardinia ? – Suetonius next proceeds to fpecify the difpofitions which he made in order to preferve the public tranquillity – Stationes militum per Italiam *follto frequentiores* difpofuit. – And was not this enough to preferve peace ? – Aye. But was he fure by fo doing of preferving the peace of Rome ? – Romae, fays he, caftra conftituit, quibus Praetoriarae cohortes *ante id tempus vagts* et per hofpitia dif- perfae, continerentur. – And was it neceflary to take fo much precaution at Rome ? – Which, as Paterculus, V. Maximus, and Dion fay, abounded, in the i6th and i7th years, with his friends? – And after he had expelled one-third of the inhabitants ? – Were the Romans too inclined to be feditious? – Populares tumultus, he fubjoins, exortos graviffime coercuit – and not only fo – et ne orirentur fedulo cavit. – And notwithftanding all this precaution, the populace of Pollentia, it feems, contrived to make a riot, and under a very licentious pretence. This, however, he quickly ftopt by fending two cohorts, one from *the city* and one from a neighbouring kingdom on the Alps, and fo contriving it that they mould enter Pollentia at the fame time at oppofite gates. After having related all this under the head – *Imprimis – and* as

Tiberius did not expel the Jews from Rome.

having happened nearly about the fame time – *id tempus* – he goes on to fay – *Abolcmt et jus moremque afylorum qua ufquam erant.* And what are we to underftand by this, if not that the abolition of the afyla, was, fome how or other, connefted with thofe riots, if not with the expulfion of the Jews, and of the iimilia feftantes, and with the tranf- portation of the jewifh libertines to . Sardinia ? – Now the abolition of the afyla, we have feen, happened, after the death of our Lord, or, rather, in the year 783. Why then Ihould we not fuppofe that thof riots happened about the fame time ?

SECTION 16

CHAPTER XVI.
The Senate, u. c. 783, expelled believers as Jews from Rome – and, Tiberius then protected them.

the chapter immediately preceding, we difcovered that there is not the leaft reafon to fufpeft Tiberius of having expelled his beft friends the Jews from Rome – and, in that fame chapter, we alfo perceived, that there is no little reafon to fuppofe that by Jews, Jofephus, Suetonius, and Tacitus meant believers and unbelievers, with their refpeftive profelytes, or, Jews and Chriftians. Let us now proceed to enquire when the gofpel was firfl preached at Rome – and, endeavour to difcover why the Jews and Chriftians were expelled from that city – and why the libertines were treated worfe than the other Jews – and why 4,000 of them were fent to Sardinia – and, alfo, by whom thofe two fecls were expelled – whether they were expelled by the fame power – and, laftly, why Philo fays, that Tiberius, immediately after the death of Sejanus, fent to all his foreign manually ordained fub-miniflers to check the culpable few Jews in their refpeftive departments.

The Senate, u. c. 783, expelled believers as Jews, S$c.

Clemens of Rome, who, we find, was, by his own account, at Rome when our Lord was put to death – and, who, we alfo find, and, by his own account too, was related to

Tiberius, f fays, in three of his works, J that the death, refurreftion, and afcenfion of our Lord were publicly announced at Rome a few Weeks after the laft mentioned event – that many (among whom, there, no doubt, were not a few jewifh, frequenters of the temple fervice, and among thofe a pretty large party of jewifh libertines,) arrived in Italy, from Judea, foon after that event – and that they were all full of the news of. the wonderful works, which, he, for feveral years, had been performing. – Clemens alfo fays, that every body at Rome was occupied in nothing elfe but in hearing thofe reports, and in talking of what this new mcf- fenger from God had faid and done – that every day frefh intelligence arrived – that frequent meetings were held, in every part of the city, to enquire about the defign of his miffion – that the vague rumours of what he had faid and done were foon confirmed beyond a doubt, § not only by the arrival of the Jews who dwelt at Rome (who, it feems, were moftly libertines) and their roman profelytes, but by that of *mamfejl* (that is, perhaps, ftate) meflengers, who, probably, brought a full account of the matter from Pilate. – Clemens moreover fays, that, before the fummer was ended, a man named, not Peter, obferve, but Barnabas,! who had been one of the followers of this wonderful meflenger from God, and who, we prefume, was the vile outcaft mentioned by the vileft of all vile wretches Flavius Jofephus, flanding in

the moft public place of the city – urbis loco celebcrrimo – attefted

Recog. I. i. tait. – Horn. I. i. init. – de G. P. init. t R. vii. 8. – Horn. xii. 8. – de G. P. c. 46. + R. H. de G. P.
)
§ R. i. 7. J Horn. t. 6. – de G. P. c. 6.
The Senate, u. c. 783, expelled believers as Jews, $c.

the truth of the fafts, of which they had he. ard fo much from fo many others, and, that he even appealed to the teflimony of many among his hearers, who had heard and feen thofe things, which he himfelf attefted, for the truth of themand, that he offered, in the name of that meflenger from heaven – *eternal life* to thofe who would become his followers. – Clemens next fays, that he himfelf then became a convert to the preaching of Barnabas, and, with him, moft of the multitude – cum reliqua multitudine – and, that Barnabas was, by fome of the hearers, derided and fcoffed at, for what he had faid, fome of whom were even proceeding to commit a&s of violence on his per- fon, when Clemens, to fave-his inflruftor from their fury, defired him to take refuge in his own houfe – and, that Barnabas, unwillingly, accepted the offer. – Barnabas, adds Clemens, was fo fhocked at this outrageous attempt made on him, that he, before the autumn was ended, returned to Judea – evidenter indicans, injuriae fe horrore per- culfum.

Now why, as thofe things had been reported by fo many witnefles, and even by meflengers of the irate, before Barnabas arrived at Rome, fhould fo much oppofition have been made to his teflimony concerning them, unlefs he had announced the divinity of this meflenger from God? – But by whom was the preaching of the gofpel at Rome chiefly oppofed ? – Was it oppofed by the idolatrous inhabitants – or, by the Jews ? – If we may believe Tacitus, it muft have been oppofed either by Tiberius, or, by the Senate – for, of that execrable fuperftition, chriftianity, he fays, that it was reprefled –

and, of the graviffimum exitium, he alfo fays, that it was reprefled. But would any of the idolatrous inhabitants have oppofed any teacher of morality or fcience? Have we not reafon to fuppofe, by confidering what Luke fays in the Afts, that the Jews – that is, not the Jews indifcriminately, but the libertines, or, thofe that had been made free of Rome, were the chief

The Senate, u. c. 783, expelled believers as Jews, $c.

oppofers of the faith ? – He there informs us that the libertines had a fynagogue of their own at Jerufalem – that they were the very men who, a few months after, difputed with Stephen. Now about what could they have difputed with him but about the dignity of our Lord' If it was not about that point, why mould they have thought of feizing him, and taking him before the Sanhedrin? – And why mould they have borne fuch teftimony againft him as caufed him to be ftoned as a blafphemer ?

Let us next attend to the teftimony which-a Jew has adduced concerning the oppofite conduft which Tiberius and the Senate followed on hearing of the refurreftion of our Lord. The Jew, to whofe record of it we mean to refer, is Mofes, the Chorenenfian, who, it feems, wrote the hiftory of Armenia, in the language of that country – , a writer very little known, and not thought worthy of notice, even by thofe who have the cuftody of his work, though it has been tranf- lated into latin by William and George Whifton, the fons of the learned William Whifton, of Sidney Suflex College, Cambridge. The teftimony which this writer has adduced is not his own – it is that of no lefs a perfon than Tiberius himfelf, who, he fays, having received a letter from Abgarus. f the king of Edefla, concerning the moft won-

A copy of this curious work is said to be in the library of Ex. Coll. Oxf.

+ In the letter of Abgarus to Tiberius the following sentence occurs – viz – nomenque ejus omnibus locis ctiamnum pcrdUcipulos ipsius niiracula maxima perficit id quod in me demonstravit – vix – by healing him.

Now wheu -was Abgarus healed? – If we may believe Eosebius, Eccl. hist, i. last chapter, he was healed in the 340th year of the aera of the Selcucidae – *titfay(Qy rxurx fiyirapaxofu xai Tfiaxzyiw* Etei – which aera began at the autumnal a? quinox, in the first year of the 117th olympiad; therefore the 340th year of it, or, 85 olympiads must have tallied with the first year of the 202d olympiad – or the beginning of the 340th year of the Edessenes, must hate about three months after that of the tfOVId olympiad – or with the last half of o. c. 782.

The Senate, u. c. 783, expelled believers as Jews, Sgc.

clerful works of our Lord, the total darknefs of the fun while our Lord was fufpended on the crofs, the earthquake that happened while he was in the grave, and his refurreftion from the dead, and which letter that prince concluded with this remarkable fentence – " Jam itaque " novit majeftas tua, quid de Judaeorum populo imperandum fit, qui " haec perpetranmt, ftatuendumque per totum orbem *ut Chrlftum co-* " *lant tanquam verum Beum.*" Vale. – returned the following anfwer: " Tiberius Romanorum Caefar, Abgaro regi falutem. – Lefta fuit " coram me epiftola amicitiae tuae, ob quam gratia a nobis tibi haben- " da eft, quanquam et a multis hoc ipfum prius audiveramus. Miru- " cula ejus luculenter etiam expofuit Pilatus, eumque, poftquam e " mortuis furrexit, a multis pro Deo fuifle habitum. Ac propterea, " volui ipfe idem facere, quod tu cogitafti; fed cum Romanorum con- " fuetudo fit, ut, Imperatoris modo auftoritate, neminem in Deorum " numero reponant, dum a Senatu tentatus fuerit probatufque, ideo " rem ad Senatum retuli; refpuit autem Senatus, quod ab ipfo " primum quaeftio de eo non fuerat habita. *Net autem unicuique, qui " volet permijimus, ut Jefum in Deos recifiat, mortemque Hits minati " fumttf, qui Chriftianos criminari pergant.* De Judaeorum autem " populo, qui eum temere aufi funt cruci fuffigere, quem ego noa " cruce, fed honore et veneratione dignum fuifle audio, ubi a bello*The Senate, u. c. 783, expelled believers as Jews, &; c.*

This probably happened before the death of Livia, for then, it seems, he refused the apotheosis of her, ni coclestis religio decerneretur – and therefore it must have happened either in the latter part of 781, or, in the beginning of 782.

If the Senate refused, in the ycar 781 or 782, to permit the worship of Christ – why did they, in the years 782, 783, 784, permit the worship of Sejanus? – For so Dion tells us, 1. 58, p. 622,)!., p. 626, B., they did: and, p. 625, B., that Sejanus used to sacrifice to himself?

In a subsequent letter of . Abgarus he hints that it would be proper to recall rilate, and be, we bae seeu, was recalled, and died on his voyage.

" *cum Hif/taals, qui a me deftes re,* otium naftus fucro, re explorata iis " pro meritis retribuam." – Mofes has fubfcribed the following memorandum – " Abgarus depofited a copy of this, and his own letters, in " the archives of Edefla." – Haec fcripfit Abgarus, atque epiftola e ejus, ut et cxterarum, exemplum in Tabulario Edeffeno repofuit.

The teftimony of Clemens, the Roman, then feems to agree pretty nearly with that of Tiberius himfelf, as related to us by Mofes, the Chorenenfian. But is their's the only evidence on this moft interefling of all points which we can obtain ? – Has not any early roman writer noticed this interference of Tiberius in behalf of Chriftians? – Tacitus, we know, fays, that he, with exceffive art, contrived to introduce the graviffimum exituuu into fome place, moft likely into Rome, but then he feems to have faid that he did it o. c. 768. But may not the elder Pliny have alluded to this afrair in his Nat. hift. ? – He, we find, there, xxx. t, tells us that the cuftom of offering up a human iacrifice was, in the year of Rome 657, by the Senate, interdifted, and, that *their* Druids were, in the reign of Tiberius, extirpated – and, moreover, that nobody can conceive how much praife the Romans deferved for extirpating thofe who could think it a very religious aft to kill a man, and a very falubrious one to feed on his flefh. Now in order to have a proper notion of what he here means, let us attentively confider what is his drift in this chapter.

The title of it is, we find, this – De origine magicae artis, quando et a qisibus coeperit, et a quibus celebrata fuerit – et reliquae ex ani- malibus rnedicin. In the courfe of that chapter Pliny fays – Eft et alia magices faftio, a Mofe et Jamne et Jotape, Judaeis pendens, fed multis millibus annorum poft Zoroaftr'em. Tanto recentior eft Cypria 657, demum anno Romae Cn. Corn. Lentulo, et P. Licinio Craflb, Cofs. Scnatus – confultum fa&um eft, ne homo immolatetur, palam*The Senate, u. c. 783, expelled believers as Jews, 8fc.*

que in tempus illud facra prodigiofa celebrata. Gallias utique pofle- dit, ct quidem ad noftram memoriam. Namquc Tibcrii Caefaris prin- cipatus fuftulit Druidas eorum, ct hoc genus omnc vatum medico- rumque. Sed, continues he, quid ego haec commemorcm in arte? – Oceanum quoque tranfgrdTa, et ad nature inane pcrvefta.

Britannia hodieque earn attonite celebrat tantis ceremoniis, ut deduTe Perfis videri poffit. Adeo ifta toto mundo confenfere, quanquam difcordi fibi et ignoto. Non fatis aeftimari poteft, quantum Romanis debeatur, qui fuftulere monftra, in quibus hominem occidere religiofiffimum erat mandi vero etiam faluberrimum.

Pliny, we here find, takes it for granted that magic was fome kind of art, and, that it was well underftood what that art was, and alib, feems to intimate, that it was, fomehow, connefted with animal medicine, and, laftly, that it well underftood what that medicine was. – Of the origin of this art he propofes to treat and to mew when and by whom it had been, as he fays, celebrated, and alfo, of the origtn of the reft of animal medicine, &c.

After having mentioned the origin of this, as he calls it, art, he fays, there *is* another magic, not art, obferve, but faftion, which, feveral thoufand years after Zoroafter, depended on Mofes, and Jamnes, and one or two other Jews. Now whom could he have meant by Jamnes? – Did not Paul tell Timothy, 2d ep. 3d c., that Jamnes withftood Mofes, and, not unlikely, about fotne truth ? – Belides – do we not read of Mofes that he, in Egypt, contended with, and overcame, the magicians of that country ? – How then can he be fuppofed to have fupported any magic art or fa&ion ? – Does not Straba tell us, xvi. p. 524, that the fucceflbrs of Mofes continued, for fome ttme, to do what was right, and to worfhip the Deity in truth ? – Does he not alfo lay, immediately after, that, in procefs of time, fome of his fuc*The Senate, u. c. 783, expelled believers as Jews, &; c.*

ceflbrs deviated from his inftitutes, and introduced fuperftitious tenets, fuch as the abftaining from certain forts of animal food ? – And does he not, in the fame page, fay, that the Magi of Perfia and the tyr- rhenian Arufpices of the Romans were nearly of the fame refpefta- bility 33 Mofes ?

That Zoroafter, the king of the Baftrians, was faid to have been the inventor of the magic arts, is, we find, attefted by Juftin, i. t, who there fays, that Zoroafter invented (not the praftice of immolating men, but) the magic arts, of which the principal, he feems to fay, was the fcience of the principles of the world and the motions of the heavenly bodies. – Poftremum illi bellum cum Zoroaftre rege Baftrianorum fuit, qui primus dicitur artes magicas invenifle, et mundi principia, fide- rumque motus diligentiffime fpeftafle. – Befides faying this, Juftin alfo fays, that the Jews derived the knowledge of the magic arts (not from Baftriana, but) from Egypt – and, not lefs, if we may believe the facred writers, than three hundred years before the Jews, under the influence of Mofes, left Egypt. – Juftin moreover fays, that the firft Jew who learnt thofe arts in Egypt was, not Mofes, but Jofeph, who he, to our no little aftonimment, affirms, was *fix father of Mofes*. – Of the ikill of this Jofeph, in both human and divine affairs, Juftin then pro '- ceeds to give the following account – " For he was very fagacious in the meaning of prodigies, and the firft that could explain the fcience of dreams: and there feemed to be nothing, either of divine or human jurifprudence, that was unknown to him: fo that he forefaw, many years, any deficiency of crops: all Egypt would have perifhed by famine, if the king had not, by his recommendation, commanded the Egyptians to lay up flores for many years; and fo great were the proofs which he gave of his wifdom, on all points, that they feemed to be

The Senate, u. c. 783, expelled believers as Jews, fyc.

the refponfes of a God rather than of a man." – A quibus deportatus (Jofephus) in gyptum cum magicas ibi artes folerti ingenio perce- piflet, brevi, ipfi regi percarus fuit. Nam et prodigiorum fagaciffimus erat, et fomniorum primus intelligentiam condidit, nihilque divini juris humanique ei incognitum videbatur; adeo, ut etiam fterilitatem agrorum ante multos annos provident; periifletque omnis fEgyptus fame, nifi monitu ejus rex edifto fervari per multos annos fruges juf- fiflet; tantaque experimenta ejus fuerunt, ut non ab homine, fed a Deo refponfa dari viderentur. – Such is the account which Juftin gives of Jofeph, who, he fays, was the firft Jew that learned the magic arts, not in Perfia, but in Egypt. – An account which fatisfaftorily proves that Jofeph was greatly in favor with the Deity, and confequently that he could not have praftifed any fuperftitious rites, much lefs that of immolating human viftims. – After having given us this account of what Jofeph learnt in Egypt, and of the amazing good which he, by his forefight, did the Egyptians, he immediately proceeds to tell us how his fon Mofes was the heir of his father's pre-fcience – and that he was not only fo, but that his perfon was remarkably graceful – Filius ejus Mofes fuit, quem praeter paternae fcientia e hereditatem, etiam forma e pulchritudo commendabat. – He next proceeds to fay, that the Egyptians, by divine monition, expelled him becaufe he was infefted with a contagious diforder, and with him all thofe whom he had infefted – that Mofes contrived to fteal their facred rites – and, that therefore, the Egyptians inftantly purfued him, till they were, by a tempeft, that is, we prefume, by the Deity, obliged to defift. – In the end of the fame chapter, he furthermore tells us that the defcendants of Mofes (among whom he, in the firft place, names Aaron) religioufly avoided all intercourfe with all neighbouring nations, and, with what incredible firmnefs they united by mixing juflice with religion.

The Senate, u. c. 783, expelled believers as Jews, Sfe.

This Juftin fays of the unfociable religion of the Jews, and therefore what reafon have we to think that any nation learned the magic arts from them, and, efpecially the Cyprians ? – And of one of the pofterity of the Magi, in the original country, he fays, xii. 1 3, that, as Alexander the Great was haftening to Babylon, he predifted that if he proceeded thither he would die there. – What reafon then have we to think that the Magi had any rites that were offenfive to the Gods ? Strabo, in feveral parts of his work, gives, we find, pretty nearly the fame account of the Magi as Juftin, and, book xvi, fays, that they were as refpeftable a fet of priefts as any in the world, not excepting even Mofes and his fucceflbrs, of whom he fpeaks in the higheft terms – of their manner of facrifking, he, we find, gives an account, xV. p. 503, 504, an account the more to be relied on becaufe, he fays, that he himfelf was an eye-witnefs of their proceedings in Cappadocia, in which country, he fays, that there was a very great multitude of them, and that Amafea, the place of his birth, was near it – but of their offering human viftims, he fays not a word.

Let us now endeavour to difcover the period in which he appears to have written his xvi. book, for which purpofe let us confult the xii. xiii. xiv. – in thofe only we hope to find data enough to point out the year very nearly.

In the xii. Strabo fays, of Cyzicum – " and it is free till the prefent time" – *xai cm ttvQtfa t,* ;. p. 396. – And what can he have meant by adding – *ptxfi n.* – Was it not enough to have faid – and it is free ?

Xenophon, we find, says of Cyrus, chap. viii. – *Ovru fEv ra irtfi Tbs Vias p. aiM. ot nri$tixmtit layrot txirotatra* sv *Tutu ra ivSaiocyifos m. Ka t rori irftirn xaTe? aQyo-x at tuvyoi vu, vuv ri at i apM rv ras Qeas, xai Qvtit I* txarnv /xepav *ois Oi fjMyoi* fltoi *tiiroitr. OvTu* $ *ra* ror: ! *in titi nt* Siayi *tteifa* Tw *ati nn, fixyifoT.* , T. X.

The Senate, u. c. 783, *expelled believers as Jews,* Sfc.

Does he not feem to have intimated that it was expefted that Cyzicum would fhortly forfeit its freedom ? – A little after, in the fame book, he fays, of Magnefia, Sardes, and other neighbouring cities that they had lately been deftroyed by an earthquake – and, that Tiberius had, at his own expence, rebuilt them – K yli *w rin*

xaTtfa. ot *awrfa(, ffi'm. y. xai Xcfoin xai Tut a. ui ras tTr tuyn* SiiXu/iwtro, *iiratvfQvn* S' o yi/xnT *jjyara mi$us.* p. 39' 399.

In the xiii. he, we find, repeats what he had before faid of Magnefia

– *Km ravTyt cxaxua-xt 0i* yeo/oj *o-tio-p,psy"D4* – p. 47' – And of the haerefy of Apollodorus he fays, p. 430 – Ei *ns iror ent.-A. nd,* in the next p. 431, he fays, of Afia, that it had been alfo deftroyed by an earthquake, and rebuilt by the beneficence of Tiberius – Jew?-j Mto C-iio-/xmv wECXt iroXAn

ns Mammas n St Tb *TiGifiu irfotoix Tu* xfl' *sS. s vytfJ. wiis, uai ravrm* (Afia) *xai rai* axx5 *ovixs* atsXaCr *ratt tvipytiriais* – p. 43 1- – And again, towards the end of this book, he fays, p. 443, of the diftrift where the cities An- tioch and Cybara the Great were fituated, that it had fuffered much by earthquakes – *tvmris* St x *arts* sr' *Toitos.*

In the xiv. book, he, p. 441, fays, of the afylum at Ephefus –

p. mi To itfat xai tl xi *irforifor, Tys* Si *ayvias Tus opas* aXXy? ai *i maais* .... *Aurutia* St *in. yyiayatros Turu, xai evpmp* iXatoiros Td

- *p. ifos* Ti *rys* woXta; r, eawi St r$ro fXaCEfsv, *xat cTtt roTs xaxupyois* T)v *iroiv, us T' tixvfuo-iv o*

Now as Strabo muft be fuppofed to have written his xvi. book after the xii. xiii. and xiv. – and, in that book, has borne teftimony to the refpeftability of the Magi, why Ihould we not conclude from the date of fome of the events mentioned in thofe preceding books as having then happened, and, as about to happen, that he bore this teftimony of the Magi after the cities of Afia had been rebuilt, and juft about . the time when the afyla were abolimed, and the Cyzicenians were deprived of their liberty.

The Senate, u. c. 783, *expelled believers as Jews,* $c.

But – how many cities were deftroyed – and, were they all tieftroyed in the fame year ?

Tacitus tells us, Ann. ii. 47, that twelve of them were deftroyed An. u. c. 770. He alfo tells us, iv. 13, that Cybaritica was deftroyed An. u. c. 776. In the intermediate time one other was, as we are informed by Eufebius, Nicephorus, and others, deftroyed by the fame caufe. Now how long can we fuppofe thofe twelve cities were building ? – It took Herod, we find, by Jofephus, at leaft ten years to rebuild Caefarea? – Can we then think that thofe twelve cities were built in a period lefs than that? – Would the revenues of Tiberius have enabled him to rebuild thofe twelve cities only in a lefs period ? f – However when Strabo wrote his xii. and xiii. books they had beenTe-built – and, how long we know not. – Let us hear what ancient infcriptions fay of the year when thofe twelve cities are fuppofed to have been completed.

The bafis of a column erefted at Rome, by the people of Alia, to the memory of Tiberius, on, as 'tis thought, this occafion, is faid to be ftill extant, on which is the following infcription : –
Ti.
DIVI. AUGUST!. F. DIVI. JULII. N.
AUGUSTO. PONT1F. MAXIMO.
Cons. iv. Imp. viii. Trie. Potkstat. xxxii,
AUGUSTALES RESPUBLICA RESTITUIT.
Other chronologists say, that this earthquake happened a -year or two later. – A greek chronologist says that tt happened in the 2d year of the 199th olympiad.

t Phlegon says, that Apollonius, the grammarian, spoke of this earthquake; of the re-building of the cities he says – *us vnfot o TtGtftos* Oixfj& *xvxn*

The Senate, u. c. 783, expelled believers as Jews, %c.

Now Tiberius was a fourth time conful in the year of Rome 774, confequently he could not have re-built thofe twelve cities before that year. But, confidering what Jofephus fays of the number of years which the re-building of Caefarea alone took, and of the vaft expence which it coft, thofe twelve cities cannot well be fuppofed to have been completed in lefs than ten years, and if, while thofe were re-building, Cybaritica was demolifhed, we may well fuppofe that its inhabitants alfo contributed to the expence of the ereftion of this column. But in what year of Rome did the 32d of his tribunitial power happen? – If he, as we have fuppofed, chapter ii, was firft inverted with that power in the year 748, and was in pofleffion of it ever after, he muft, in the year 780, have been poflefled of that authority 32 years.

To this it may be objefted, that if Strabo meant to fay that thofe cities were re-built about the year in which the people of Gyzicum loft their freedom – and if, as Tacitus tells us, Ann. iv. 36, the Cyzi- cenians were deprived of their liberty in 778, Tiberius could not, as Suetonius affirms, have enjoyed the tribunitial authority, without intermiffion, fince 748. Who then has been inaccurate in this matter ? Has Strabo, who appears to fay that the cities were re-built before the Cyzicenians were deprived of their liberty ? – Or, Tacitus, who, fays that the Cyzicenians were punifhed with the lofs of liberty in the year 778? – We cannot fuppofe that Strabo has made a miftake in this matter, becaufe thofe events muft have happened before he died. – Has then Tacitus antidated the difgrace of the Cyzicenians more than a year ? – We know that in feveral inftances he has not been fo attentive to chronological pointsf as he ought to have been – and, we alfo

Suetontus, tii II, seems to say that he was not. t E. G. He has anfidated the time when Tiberius introduced the gravissi-

tvt

mum exittum. – When the Senate expelled the Jews from Rome. – He says that the Amphitheatre at Fidenae fell before Tiberius rettred to Caprex.

The Senate, u. c. 783, expelled believers as Jews, f$c.

know that he fays, iv. 13, that there was a decree pafled, at the recommendation of Tiberius, in the year 776, to affift the inhabitants of Cybaritica, in Afia, and thofe of ./Egira, in Achaia, when their cities were deftroyed by earthquakes. – But lot us confult Suetonius on this point.

Suetonius fays, iii. 37 – Abolevit et jus, moremque afylorum quaj ufquam erant. – This we have fhewn is not likely to have happened till after the death of our Lord, nor before the year 783. – And in the next fentence, he fays – Cyzicenis in cives Romanos, violentius quae- dam aufis, publice libertatem ademit – Suetonius then, we find, places the privation of the Cyzicenians, immediately after the abolition of the afyla.

In the next place, Pliny fays, that there is a Cyprian branch of this magic faftion, and feems to intimate, by ufing the prefent tenfe of the verb fubftantive, that it was exifting in his days. – And who ever heard of the Cyprian branch of the Mofaic magic faftion ? – Strabo, we know, who gives us an account of Cyprus, fays not a word of it. – After mentioning thofe two branches of the magic faftion, he then proceeds, immediately, to inform us that the praftice of immolating a man was continued till the year 657, and that it was then, by the Romans prohibited – (which, by the bye, feems to imply that he thought the Magi, jewim and cyprian, ufed to immolate men) that is, furely, in thofe countries then become fubjeft to Rome, and therefore neither in Judea nor in Cyprus.-r-He next takes a rapid ffight to Gaul, which country, he feems to fay, the magic faftion ftill poflefled, that is, in his own time.. – He, laftly, pretends to affign a reafon why it was not continued later – Namque Tiberii Caefaris principatus fuf- tulit Druidas *eorum,* and not only *their* Druids, but – et hoc genus vatum medicorumque – where, by, *Druidas eorum,* he could not have*The Senate, u. c. 783, expelled believers as Jews, f$c,*

meant the Druids of the Gauls, becaufe he had not before fpoken of the Gauls, but only of their country – Gallias utique poffidet – and therefore he muft have meant the Druids of thofe on whom the other magic faftion, afterwards denominated the Cyprian, depended – fcil – of Mofes, &c. – But how could Mofes be faid to have had any thing at all to do with people who facrificed a man, unlefs by being the author of that religion which Chrift came to eftablifh ? – And how could the Magi be faid to have been extirpated by Tiberius, when, we are informed by Tacitus, vi. 29, it was objefted to iicaufus u. c. 787, that he had attended their rites ?

After having told us that the cuftom of immolating a man , was abolifhed, and having, feemingly, intimated that this was a druidical praftice, he proceeds to fay that this art, as he calls it, after all, found means to crofs the fea, and that, when he wrote, it ftill exifted in Britain, and with as much fervor as if it had originated in that ifland. – He concludes the whole with this remarkable encomium on the humanity of the perfon or perfons who put an entire flop to the praftice of not only immoJating a human viftim, but of eating his flefh, out of conceit that it was moft falubrious – nobody can conceive how much praife the Romans deferved for having extirpated the monfters who thought it a moft religious aft to kill a man, and a moft falubrious one to eat his flem.

And did the magic faftion prevail in Britain after the praftice of facrificing *men* had been interdifted, and after the Druids had, in the reign of Tiberius, been removed ? – Even till Pliny wrote ? – And did the Senate, in his days, remove, not only the praftice of offering human viftims, but even the monfters, who thought it an aft of the greateft piety to offer fuch prodigious facrifices, and the moft falu- brious to feed on the flefh of thofe viftims? And did they, by fo

The Senate, u. c. 783, *expelled believers as Jews, $$e.*

doing, merit the greateft praifc? – If they merited fo much praife for it, did not Tiberius deferve, at leaft, a part of it? – If not almoft all of it? Could the Senate have, without either his command or confent, pre- fumed to interdift the praftice? – What had they to do with the religions of other countries, efpecially with that of Gaul or Britain ? – Is it not much more likely that Tiberius himfelf put an end to this moft inhuman praftice, at leaft in Gaul and Britain ? – And if he did, was not all the praife, inconceivable as it was, due to him ? – How is it that no writer has noticed either his humanity on this moft extraordinary occafion, or the praife which Pliny fays he deferved for it, or any of the confequences that may be fuppofed to have followed the prohibition of fo inveterate, fo univerfal, fo inhuman a fuperftition ? And how is it that two or three later writers fay that he, who extirpated the race of cannibals all over the empire, was liknfelf afterwards the greateft of all cannibals ? – And that he, who cared nothing for the Gods or religion, and was himfelf fo remarkably impious, and a fatalift, was fo much concerned about the fuperftition of the Druids?

And how did the people who followed this fuperftitious mode of worfhip behave on this occafion ? – efpecially they of Gaul ? – where, as Caefar fays in his commentaries of the Gallic war, the Chief part of the nobles of that country were Druids. – Did they too, like the Jews, fubmit quietly to the fuppreffion of their fuperftitious praftice? – And after they had been permitted, by both of the two former Caefars, Julius and Auguftus, to exercife it, for fo many years, without the leaft reftriftion ? – If, as Julius himfelf fays, vi. p. 224, one-half of the leading men of Gaul were Druids, and the Druids, as he alfo fays, regulated all the principal concerns of the religion, and learning, and polity of that country, would they too fubmit, and without the leaft oppofition, to any innovation in the rites of their religion? – Were they, in the reign

Aaa

Senate, u. c. 783, *expelled believers as Jews, $c.*

of Tiberius, known to have refifted the Romans, before or after the year 774? – And what does Tacitus fay was the caufe of that rebellion? Does he fay that it was excited by any attempt of Tiberius to hinder them from immolating men ? – Does he not fay, iii. 40, that the Gauls were then, by the exaftion of heavy taxes, irritated to rebel ? – Does he not fay that they complained of the magnitude of their debts, and of the *cruelty* and the pride of their rulers? – And does he not fay that Sacrovir then endeavoured to perfuade them, that the opportunity of recovering their loft liberty was at laft arrived ? – Eodem anno (774, T. 7, 8,) Galliarum civitates ob magnitudinem seris alieni rebellioncm cceptavere: cujus exftimulator acerrimus inter Treviros Jvjlius Florus,

apud ./Eduos Julius Sacrovir Igitur per conciliabula et ccetus

feditiofa diflerebant, de continuatione tributorum, gravitate fcenoris,

favitia ac fuperbia praefidentium egregium refumendae libertati

tempus, &c. – This Tacitus fays was the caufe of the Gallic infurrec- tion in the year 774, which, he feems to fay, c. 47, was no fooner begun than ended.

The following year – viz – 775 was, fays Tacitus, iii. 52, undiftmbid by external foes – Inturbidus externis rebus annus. Confequently why fhould we not fuppofe that the Senate did not make this alteration in the fuperftitious rites of the Gallic Druids till after that year ?

This peaceable ftate of affairs feems, by the account of the fame writer, to have continued till the year 777 – for, in that year, he complains that he had nothing of importance to write about – that the public peace was undifturbed, or, at rnoft, but flightly ruffled – Im- mota quippe aut modice laceffita pax.

Paterculus, we alfo find, confirms what Tacitus fays of the difturb- ances in Gaul, in the year 774, under Sacrovir, and of the continuance of peace till 777. And he not only fays, with Tacitus, that

The Senate, u. c. 783, *expelled believers as Jews,* $c. -

every thing remained in a tranquil ftate till that year, but he even feems to intimate that the fame flate of tranquility remained till the year 783. – For after having remarked with what celerity the Gallic war was ended, he, in the year 783, exults in the refleftion that peace had then taken pofleffion of every part of the world.

There is not then the leaft reafon to think that the Druids of Gaul were at all difcompofed at the queftionable decree. Indeed, if we attend to what- Strabo and Suetonius fay of them, we fhall be inclined to think that they were, before the reign of Tiberius, in part, if not altogether, induced to difcontinue this horrid praftice, but whether, by their long intercourfe with the Romans, as Strabo feems to fay, or, by the edift of Auguftus, as Suetonius fays, we need not endeavour to afcertain.. – Strabo fays, iv. p. 136, that the Romans, by their intercourfe with the Gauls, induced them to relinquifhyrA *modes affacri- ficing as were contrary to thofe which they themfelves followed – xai rurut* o' *iirxva-at auras PaiAaiiv, xai rut Kxtx Qvyias Kai Fj, ohtcixs wiritxtnus roi s irap up'* vo/xj/4u. – Arid, in the fequel, he proceeds to point out what thofe rites peculiar to the Gauls were – *-for,* fays he, they ufed to facrifice a man, and to divine from the palpitations of the viftim – 0pw7rot yap

a!TEr7rti7l Aivot iraiaauiru *tis* oitov *paaifa, cp. au/rcmtro tx ra* o-paSaaTS, (flta 5e Bk *ana* fyu&w *xai* x. T. X. – Now if the Gauls were, by their long intercourfe with the Romans, in a manner humanized, early in the reign pf Tiberius, if not before, why fhould we not prefume, on the authority of the fame writer, immediately preceding, that almoft all the inhabitants of Britain were alfo, as early, humanized ? – For, of that ifland, he fays – " Now indeed fome of the princes of that ifland, by " embaffies and fubmiffions, feek the favor of Cafar, and make coltly " prefents to the Capitol, and have rendered almoft the whole ifland

The Senate, u. c. 783, *expelled believers as Jews, fyc.* " dependent on the Romans .... fo that they need not maintain

' any great force thef C." – Nuw /xeytoi Tw W,-wv *rms rai avro it Tv Kxiriruiu, Kx. i otxtiat o-sSot irxpiTxEvxrxt Tois Vux-ois o/.* w Tdv sift /xioi Stiv *ffSfas Tvs mm.*

By the evidence of Strabo and Suetonius, as well as by the preceding of Tacitus and Paterculus, it appears to be far from clear that this decree was pafled in the reign of Tiberius.

Let us then, in order to obtain more fatisfaftion on this point, proceed to enquire in what year of Tiberius this moft remarkable decree eould have been pafled. – And in order to do it the more effeftually let us make the enquiry firft on the fuppofition that the Senate alone, without the concurrence of Tiberius, did it – and, fecondly, on the fuppofition that Tiberius ordered it to be paſſed or confented to the paſſing of it. ,

If Pliny meant that the Senate, of their own accord, put a ſtop to this barbarous praƈtice, he muſt have meant that they did it after Strabo wrote, for, at that time, it ſeems, by what he ſays, iii. p. 106, the Luſitanians continued, as uſual, to immolate men. . Now Strabo wrote, as it is ſuppoſed, about the year 772 – when, as Tacitus ſays, (though, as we have proved', erroneouſly) the Senate expelled the Jews and Egyptians from Rome and Italy for exerciſing their profane rites. At which time, we may ſuppoſe, this barbarous praƈtice had not been prohibited. Did they then do it in the year 775 ? – In that year, ſays Tacitus, iii. 60, Tiberius conceded to them the privilege of hearing the populates or complaints of the provinces, and they, immediately, made it their buſineſs to enquire into the abuſes of the aſyla, and to infpeƈt the modes of religion followed by their allies, but that they then ſcrutinized any of the rites of the Druids, or interdiƈted the prac-

The Senate, u. c. 783, expelled believers as Jews, c.

tice of offering human ſacrifices, he does not ſay. – Beſides, Tacitus ſays, iii. 65, that, in the ſame year, the Senate was all ſubmiſſion to the will of Tiberius – Ceterum tempora ilia adeo infeſta et adulatione ſordida fuere, ut non modo primores civitatis, quibus claritudo fua ob- ſequiis protegenda erat; fed omnes conſulares, magna pars eorum qui praetura funcƚi multique etiam pedarii ſenatores certatim exſurgerent, foedaque et nitnia cenferent. – Again, if the Senate put an end to this inhuman praƈtice, before the year 777, why did Tacitus complain, *iv.* 32, that he had nothing of importance to write about? – Efpecially if, as Pliny ſays, nobody can conceive how much credit the Romans deſerved for doing it, why ſhould Tacitus have thought it not worth the recording ? – Was the ſuppreſſion of ſo prodigious, ſo horrid a' ſuperſtition, ſo generally received and ſo long praƈtiſed, of leſs importance than the prohibition of immediate executions, or of the innocent ſuperſtition praƈtiſed by the Jews and Egyptians, or than that of the abuſe of the Grecian aſyla? – Laſtly, was it done before the year 783? – In that year Paterculus, we know, finiſhed his hiſtory, and concluded it with an eulogium on Tiberius and Sejanus, but though he ſays what has been by the conductors of one of our principal fem-maries for claſſtc education pronounced adulatory, yet he, we find, ſays nothing of this moſt humane decree. In ſhorr, if the Senate did not do it when the ſacred rites of other nations were, as Seneca ſays, difcuſled, we know not when they did it, or, if they did it not when the execrable ſuperſtition was repreſſed, we cannot conceive when they did it. And yet we cannot think that it was done at either of thoſe times – for, at the former time, ſays Seneca, epiſt. 108, abſtinence from certain forts of animal (obferve, but not human) food was confidered as the chief argument of ſuperſtition – and, at the latter, the ſuperſtition blazed forth again and overcame everything, v

The Senate, u. c. 783, expelled believers as Jews, $c.

Let us now proceed to enquire when this decree could have been paſſed, on the fuppofition that Tiberius himſelf ordered it to be paſſed or confented to the paſſing of it.

If it was paſſed by his order or confent, it ſeems to have been paſſed before the difagreement between him and the Senate took place, about which time, ſays Tacitus,

v. 3, his domination began to be exceffivc and arbitrary – that is, before he became fo very cruel, and fo very carelefs about the worfhip of the Gods, and the interefts of the ftate, and before he went to Capreae to conceal his cruelty – and before he began the praftice of ifluing edifts, to the deflruftion of innocent per- fons – and before he began to be cruel, or, to make others the agents of his cruelty – that is, before he employed Sejanus as his prime minifter, or before the year 776 – or, laftly, (if as Tacitus feems to fay, i. 72, 73, he, in the year 768, introduced the graviffimum exi- tium into Rome, and, in that year, was, by anonymous authors, faty- rized for his cruelty,) it may be, even before that year – or, before Strabo wrote.

We have now been as attentive to this fubject as can be expefted, and we cannot find the leaft encouragement to think that this decree was pafl"ed in the reign of Tiberius – we alfo cannot perceive that any other author was aware of it, and we, on the contrary, obferve that even V. Maximus, who wrote on religious and moral fubjefts only, and dedicated his work to Tiberius, fays nothing of this decree – and this is the more obfcrvable' as he propofes, v. t, in the firft place, to relate the moft humane and the moft clement afts of the Senate- Ante omnia autem humaniffima et clementiffima fenatus afta referam and as he, in ix. 2, (which chapter is on cruelty) fays nothing of this barbarous praftice, though he concludes it with this moft remarkable

Cxtcrurn ex eo prerupta jam et urgcns dommatio.

The Senate, u. c. 783, *expelled believers as Jews,* c.

fentence – Sicut illi Barbari, quos ferunt maftatarum pecudum iutef- tinis, et vifceribus egcftis, homines inferere, ita at capitibns tantum- modo emineant, atque ut diutius pcenae fufficiant, cibo et potione in felicem fpiritum prorogare: donee intus putrefafti, laniati fint anima- libus, quae tabidis corporibus innafci folent- Queramur nunc cum natura rcrum, quod nos multis et afperis adverfae valetudinis incom- modis obnoxios efle voluerit habitumque coeleftis roboris humana e condition! denega- tum molefte feramus, cum tot cruciatus fibimet ipfa mortalitas impulfu crudelitatis excogitaverit.

Now as we find that Maximus, on the one hand, profefles to relate, in the firft place, all the moft humane decrees of the Senate, and yet takes not the leaft notice of this, the moft humane of all others – and, as we alfo find, that he, on the other hand, has, in the chapter in which he treats of cruelty, omitted to notice the praftice of immolating men! thofe two difcoveries may, with the help of the foregoing difcoveries, help to convince us that the praclice of offering human facrifices is not likely to have been continued in the days of Tiberius.

But Pliny, it feems, would not only have us to believe that it was, in the reign of Tiberias, a common praftice to offer fuch facrifices – but, if we underfland him rightly, he would alfo have us to believe that it was as common a practtce, at the fame time, to feed on the flefh of fuch viftims. The exiftence of which pra&ice, in the reign of Tiberius, is, we find, alfo denied by Strabo, for he tells us, iv. p. 139 – " Of the people of Ireland I have nothing certain to fay, but that they " are more uncivilized than the Britains, being both cannibals and " gluttons. – This, I find, *is faid* of them, but *by no credible witneffes."* risfi *Ris* (lEPNH) Ssv tx0'" XfYii o-?' ww *an, aypiurifoi rut inr&fXtsyH* 0J xaroixSmr *eturw, an9fvmfxiyot Tt orris xai Kai roitroi* S' *ttru .* iyorv nr *vv. tyjnris a$nmut*

The Senate, u. c. 783, expelled believers as Jews, $c.

Now as Pliny appears to have given fo quteftionable an account of the magic faftion, and to have affected, of both, that they were abo- lifhed, in the reign of Tiberius, as having been obnoxious to the Senate by following the barbarous praftice of offering up human viftims and feafting on the fle. Tt of thofe viftims. – And, as we find, by the evidence of feveral hiftorians, (two or three of whom were cotemporaries with Pliny) that his aflertion was not true – why mould we not fuf- peft that it is very likely that he may have had fome covert meaning – efpecially as, we find, mention made in feveral authors of the early difcontinuance of this horrid praftice. – Suetonius, we find, who takes not the leaft notice of the praife which Pliny fays the Romans, in the reign of Tiberius, acquired for having abolimed it, aflerts, in his life of Claudius, v. 25, that the Roman citizens were prohibited by *Auguftus* from following the rites of the Druids, and that Claudius entirely abolimed that fuperftition – Druidarum religionem apud Gallos dirae immanitatis, et tantum civibus fub Augufto interdiftam, penitus abo- levit. – This teftimony of Suetonius is, we find, fupported by that of Pomponius Mela, who fays, that though the praftice had then been abolimed, yet the veftiges ftill remained, excepting that they ab- ftained from offering up human viftims. – Apud Anthropophagos ip- *fx* etiam epula e vifceribus humanis apparantur. Pomponius Mela, l. ii. c. t, p. 27. – Manent veftigia feritatis jam abolitae, atque ut ab ultimis caedibus temperant, ita nihilominus, ubi devotos admovere, delibant. – Habent tamen et facundiam fuam, magiftrofque fapientiae Druidas, l. ii. 2, p. 49. – And the evidence of Petronius Arbiter, in the end of his Satyricon, will, if attended to, be found to be pretty nearly of the fame tendency. – He there humoroufly reprefents Eu- molpus as propofing, at his death, to leave the inhabitants of Croton a legacy, on condition that they mould cut his body in pieces and eat it in public – and, as obferving, by way of lulling any qualms*The Senate, u. c. 783, expelled believers as Jews,* &c.

of confcience they might have at the idea, that, in fome countries, it was ftill a praftice (not, obferve, to immolate a man and to feaft on his remains, but) for the friends of a deceafed perfonto devout him – and, as inftancing, not the Druids of any country, but the people of Saguntum, when befieged by Hannibal, and thofe of Peta- vium, and the mothers of Numantia, when taken by Scipio–a plain proof that he could not adduce any recent inftance of the praftice. – The people of Croton, continues Petronius, perceiting that Eumolpus only meant to laugh at them, Ihortly after facrificed him – and how does he fay they did it ? – fcil – as the people of Marfeilles ufed to do formerly. And how was that ? – It was, it feems, as little underftood - by the people of Croton, in thofe early days, as by any of us, for he immediately proceeds to explain it – they fed him a year at the public expence, and then led him through the town, attired like any other viftim, and then loading him with curfes, precipitated him from a rock. – Another plain proof that the praftice of immolating men was very little known when Petronius wrote – that is, not improbably, in the days of Tiberius.

That Petronius Arbiter wrote his Satyricon in the reign of Tiberius appears from his often calling the then emperor Agamemnon, by which name Tiberius was, as Dion fays, l. 59, p. 654, D., called by Antonia – and, that he wrote after the year 775, appears from the ftory which he relates of the miraculous mender of broken glafs, for

Dion, who has alfo related the fame ftory, 1. 57, p. 613, E., places the performance of that wonder in the year 775 – that he wrote after the conful- ihip of the twins – that is, after the year 782, appears from that epic poem which, he fays, Eumolpts made on the civil war, for, in that poem, he fays –

Quid tarn parva cjueror: *Gefriino cum einfule,* Magnus Ille, &c.
Bbb
; N

The Senate, u. c. 783, expelled believers as Jews, S$c.

Soon after Eumolpus had written this pigmy poem he entered Croton, where he, a few days after, made his will, in which he gave the people of that city all his effefts, on condition that they would eat his flcfh.

But though Petronius feems to deny that it was in the reign of Tiberius the prafticc of the Romans to eat human fldh, yet he, we find, reprefents Eumolpus as fpeaking, in the fame poem, of the applaufe which a perfon who drank human blood received from the Romans. Ut bibat humanum, populo plaudente, cruorem.

But what could Eumolpus have meant by this poem and the feveral circumftances which he introduces in the courfe of k? – On-wh'at oc- cafion was it written.'

He, we find, prefaces it with this remark – that' whoever undertakes to write a poem, *on the great fubjefl 'of the civil war,* muft, unlefshe was poflefled of much literature, neceflarily fink under the burden. For, fnbjoins he, the occurrences of it had better be recorded by an hifto- rian than by a poet. But, continues he, a free Ipirit is to be praeci- pitated through intricate windings, aftd the miniftration of the Gods, and a fabulous torture of fentences, fo that it may rather appear the prediftion (vaticination) of phrenfy, than the faith of a religious oration attefted by witnefles.

Ecce, belli civilis ingens opus quifquis atrigerit, nifi plenus litteris, fub onere labetur. "Non enim res geftfe verfibus compreheridendc funt quod longe melius Hiftorici faci- unt; fed per ambages, iDeorum- que minifteria, et fabulofum fententiarum tprmentum pt-aecipitandus eft liber fpiritus, ut potius furentis animi vaticinatio appareat, quam religiofae orationis fub teftibus fides; tanquam fi placet his impetus,
L "" "
etiamfi non recepit ultimam manum.

It consists of tiO mere than 296 lines.

The Senate, u. c. 783, expelled believers as Jews, S$c.

But what are fome pf the principal features of this poem ? – Let us make it our bufinefs to enquire.

He, we perceive, begins it with obferving that Rome had arrived at the fummit of glory, power, and luxury, and, prefently after, he tells us, that fhe was, not long after, deprefled to the lowed flate of mifery, fo that no efforts of found reafon could make her endeavour to raife herfelf.

Hoc merfam coeno Romam, fomnoquc jacentem
Qua poterant artes fana ratione mpvcr, e.

But when, in the days of Petronius, could Rome be fai. d to be Fo funk ? – and to be fo afleep ?

He next introduces Dis or Pluto as complaining to Fors. or Fortune that his infernal fubjefts had been commanded to expeft heaven – Inferni manes coelum fperare jubentur.

He then introduces Fortune as declaring that fhe had done every thing for Rome, and, that the fame Deity who had, at firft, raifed her up, would now deftroy her:

deftruet iftas

Idem, qui pofuit, moles Deus, et mihi cordi.

She then, immediately after, affigns the reafon for it:

Quippe cremare viros, et fanguine pafcere luxum.

She then foretells what wars . were fhortly about to take place. She next proceeds to advife Pluto to throw open his parched domains, and to receive frefh fouls, and, not only fo, but to get, inftead of a boat. a fleet to tranfport them.

, Vix navita Porthmeus,

Sufficiet fimulachra virum traducere cymba

Clafle opus eft.

The Senate, u. c. 783, expelled believers as Jews, $c.

Laftly, Ihc adds, that the whole world is about to be fent acrofs the Styx by thofe proceedings.

Scarce, fays the poet, was the conference between thofe two imaginary Dieties ended, when all the other Gods, of the fame clafs, bore teftimony to the truth of it.

Continue clades hominum venturaque damna

Aufpiciis patuere Deum; namque ore cruento

Deformes Titan vultus caligine texit. -

Civiles acies jam turn fpirare putares.

Having fpoken of the moft flourifhing ftate of Rome and her fubfe- quent downfall, and given this terrific account of the conference between Fortune and Pluto, and obferved that their determination was aflented to by the reft of the Gods, he, in the end of the firft half of his poem, prefents us with three or four moft unexpefted and feeraingly moft unconnefted images – for firft, he fays, that a torch, accompanied by new ftars, was the leader of this conflagration. Fax ftellis comitata novis incendia ducit.

And then he fays that Jupiter defcended fuddenly in a fhower, not of gold, as formerly, but of blood.

Sanguineoque repens defcendit Jupiter imbre.

Next he fays, that fome anonymous God, in a Ihort time, unfolded thofe tokens.

Haec oftenta brevi folvit Deus.

And, laftly, he, moft abruptly, introduces Caefar as, without delay, and aftuated by a love of vengeance, throwing away the Gallic arms, and, ftrange to fay, as taking up *civil arms.*

- . Exuit omnes

Quippe moras Caefar, vindiftaeque aftus amore

Gallica projecit, civilia fuftulit arma.

The Senate, u. c. 783, expelled believers as Jews, S? c.

Now of what Caefar does he here fpeak, and what can he have meant by faying that he took up *civil arms,* and, at the time when he caft away the Gallic ? – Of whom, but Tiberius, can he be fuppofed to have fpoken ? – And if he did mean him what civil war happened in his reign but that on account of the introduftion of Chriftianity into Rome ?

And where does he fay Caefar made ufe of thofe civil arms ? – fcil – on that part of the Alps from whence he could obtain a profpeft
of Spain ?

Haec ubi calcavit Caefar juga *milite lee to*
Optavitque locum, fummo de vertice mentis
Hefjteria campos late profpexit.

On this exalted flation Caefar poured forth a complaint to Jupiter, &c. that he had been *driven from his city.%* But why, if the fubjeft of this poem be the civil war, and Caefar was driven from his city, can he be fuppofed to have taken his ftation on that part of the Alps which overlooks Spain? – But at what time of the year did Caefar take this exalted ftation ? – fcil – In the depth of winter. And when does he appear to have quitted it ? – fcil – After the thaw commenced. Sed poftquam turmae nimbos fregere ligatos, Et pavidus quadrupes undarum vincula rupit, Incaluere nives, mox flumina montibus altis Undabant modo nata; fed haec quoque jufla putares.

Quanta cum quiete hominuro, retn perpetui precipuiqne timorcs, sup- plemcntum, sine trepidatione delectus provide! ? – Paterc. ti. 130.

f TJhi a bello cum *Htspants,* qui a me defecere, ottum nactus fuero, &c. Tib. ad Abg.

$ He afterwards sajs, p. ISO, that Czsar fled from Rome.
Senate u. &. 783, *expelled, believers as Jews,* %c.

And whithe/r did Carfax move- next ? – Towards Spain ? – Or, did. he content himfelf wjilfa only, taking a peep at it? – He does not fay. – This only he fays – ? that Caefar, before the froft had entirely difap- peared, defcended into fome more tillageable country.

Nondum Caefar erat: fed magnam nixus in haftain
Horrida fecuris frangebat greffibus arva,
Qualis, &c.

And what, does he fay, followed ? – fell – As foon as it was known that he had defcended, Fame flew quickly to aftonifhed Rome. Dum Caefar tumidas iratus deprimh arces Interea volucer, mods conterrita pennis Fatna volat, fummique petit juga celfa Palati: Atque hec Romano attonite fert omnia iigna:

But why mould the people of Rome be faid to have been aftonifhed at his defcent from the Alps ? – What ftep did they take in confe- quence of their aftonimmeqt ?

Anna, cruor, caedes, incendia, totaque bella
Ante oculos volitant: *ergo* pulfata tumultu
Peftora per dubias fcinduntur territa caufas.
Hule fuga per terras, /-///- magis unda probatur
Et patria eft pontus jam tutior: *eft magis arma*
Qul tentata velit: fatifque jubentibus aftus,
Quantum quifque timet, tantum fugit. Ocior ipfs,
Hos inter motus populus, miferabile vifu!
Quo mens ifta jubet, *defend dvcitttr urle.*
Gaudct Jtomafuga, debellattque Qpirites

Rumorh fonitu marentia tefla rdinquunt.
Hie manu trepida natos tenet: ille *Penates*
Occultat gremio, deploratumque relinquit
Limen, et *abfentcm vatis interjtcit hojlsm.*
The Senate, u. c. 783, expelled believers as Jews, Sfc.

Having thus defcribed this general dereliftion of Rome, becaufe report had faid that Caefar had defcended from-the Alps, he, a few lines after proceeds thus –

Quid tarn parva queror? *Gemino cum Conftde* Magnus
Hie tremor Ponti, faevi quoque terror-Hydafpis,
$t piratarum fcopulus: modo quem ter ovantem
Jupiter horruerat, quem frafto gurgite Pontus,
Et veneratus erat fubmifla Bofphorus unda,
Proh Pudor! *Imperti deferto nomine fugit,*
Ignavaque fuga *Romam famamque relinquit,*
Ut fortuna levis! Magni quoque terga videres.

And can he have meant to affirm this of the fame Caefar, who had, in the depth of winter, afcended the Alps, artd thence taken a peep at Spain .' – And whofe reported defcent had caufed fuch a. panic at Rome, and fo total a defertion of that city ? – If he does, what can he have meant by the lines immediately following? – viz –

Ergo tanta lues Divum quoque numina vidit;
Confenfitque fugae coeli timor. Ecce per orbem
Mills turba Deum, terras exofa furentes
Deferit, atque hominum damnatum avertitur agmen.

And what by thofe again immediately following –

Pax prima ante alias, niveos pulfata lacertos
Abfcondit olea vinftum caput, atque relifto
Orbe fiigax Ditis petit implacabile fegnum.
Iluic comes it fubmijjja Ftdes et crine foluto
Juilitia, *ac ma-rens Jacera Coneordta paila.*

And, to crown the whole, he, a few lines after, fays, that there was as much diilenfion among the Gods as among the Romans.

The Senate, u. c. 783," expelled believers as Jews, S$c.

Scntit terra Decs, mutataque fidera pond us
Quaefivere fuum: natnque omnis Regia coeli
In partes didufta ruit.

The evidence of thofe three writers then fcems to prove that the praftice of immolating human viftims feems to have been difcon- tinued, by Roman citizens, in the reign of Auguftus, and every where elfe, foon after, if not early in the reign of Tiberius.

Now what fhould hinder us from fufpefting that the fuppreffion of thofe druidical rites, here mentioned by Pliny, may have been no other than the repreffion of the execrable fuperflition of ChrifHans mentioned by Tacitus ? – Or the expulfion of the fimilia feftantes, mentioned by Suetonius3 – Or of the trav To Ib&ixov, mentioned by Jofephus ? – And that it may have been voted when the fa(cred rites of other nations were, as Seneca fays, difcufled ? – And that it may have been, as he alfo fays, enforced by the rage of accufers ? – Has not Pliny himfelf, by obferving that a fort of phyficians were expelled with them, afforded us fomething like a further reafon for cherifhing this fufpicion ? – What could he have meant by faying that a fort of phyficians were expelled with them ? – Were the Druids too phyficians? – Were not the elders of the church a fort of phyficians – at leaft, were they not required to pray for the fick ? – Whxt elfe could he have meant by the latter part of the title prefixed to this chapter – de origine reliquae ex animalibus medicinae.

The Chriflians then feem, by the evidence of Pliny, to have been expelled from Rome, by the Senate, and for what offence, unlefs it was for feafting on the body and blood of Chrift, as conducive to eternal life – and, for praying for the fick members of the church? – Are we not informed by feveral of the firft champions for chriftianity that the eatly Chriftians labored under the imputation of being cannibals?

The Senate, u. c. 783, expelled believers as Jews, $r.

Befides the teftitnony of Athenagoras, on this point, already adduced, that of Juftyn Martyr, both before a roman emperor and an ephefian Jew, and that of Theophilus, the patriarch of Antioch, which he produced againft the calumniators of Chriftians, might be appealed to. – The former afked the roman Senate – *nt yf* piXuVw *n xxfams xat*

XMt tofatv *ayxvot nyufiuos ovvxtrO ctt Vxvxtov x-zTza-to-Cxt, ovus Tuv*

tfnQv ; – and of Trypho he, in the firft place, demanded whether he really believed that the Chriftians feafted on human flefh

– *rum* SI triv o *ft. sya, pn xat vfAtts vttnftvxtarc tnft Nfauv, on* Sn tsdto/- sv *ew&futTHv, xxt Iutx ift tt)xmtm atrotrGtmtotns ras* XuvBf, *Qto'pott fJ. tco- Ht!xvtofsQx; – r-* and the latter fays, 1. iii, of the Syrian adverfaries of chriftianity, that they entertained the fame ridiculous notion – *tpxa-natTut us* Xhv

xtras rott yvvatxaf nptav, xt duttyofu futt %vv0tras, tn /xfv *xat This itxts , xat To aQturarot xat upatatrot, Vxo-ut o-afxar xtQfuwttut t*

Having now difcovered, by the evidence of an Apoftolic Chriftiaa writer, that great oppofition appears to have been made to the firft preaching of the gofpel at Rome foon after the afcenfion of our Lord, both by jewifh libertines and by prejudiced heathens – and by that of Tiberius, that the Senate refufed to admit the worfhip of our Lord, and, that he threatened death to the accufers of Chriftians – and, by that of a cotemporary roman writer, that the Chriftians of Rome appear to have been expelled from that city in the reign of Tiberius, and for worfhipping Chrift. – Let us ne, xt proceed to enquire what other early Chriftian writers have faid of their expulfion by the Senate, and of" jhejr proteftion by Tiberius.

See Mimitius Felix in Octavio.

Ccc

The Senate, u. c. 783, cupelled believers as Jews, $c.

Tertullian, who, as Eufebius fays, E. H. ii. 2, was a man moft learned in the roman laws, and otherwife famous, particularly for his knowledge of roman concerns, fays, in the apology which he delivered to the emperor Severus, chapter 5 – " There was an ancient ftatute " that no God mould be confecrated by the king, unlefs the Senate

" confented to it. Marcus milius Tiberius therefore, in

" whofe reign the name of Chiftians was firft known in the world, on " a report being made to him, from Paleftine, of this divinity, refer- " red it to the Senate, as if he had a right to vote firft on the occa- " fton:, but the Senate, not approving it, reje&ed the

propofal. Cæsfar, " however, continued of the fame perfuafion, and threatened *ftericu-*
" *lum* to the accufers of Chriftians." – Vetus erat decretum, ne qui Deus ab imperatore
confecraretur, nifi a Senatu probatus. Scil. M. fEmilius de Deo propitius efle debebit.
Tiberius ergo, cujus tempore nomen chriftianorum in feculum introivit, annunciata
fibi ex Syria Palaeeftina. qua illic veritatem iftius divinitatis revelarunt, detulit ad
Senatum cum praerogativa fuffragii fui. Senatus, quia non ipfe proba- verat, refpuit.
Cxfar in fententia manfit, comminatus periculum ac- cufatoribus chriftianorum.

This, Tertullian afferted at Rome, before the then emperor, in the courfe of the
fecond century, in defence of the faith of Chriftians – and, afterwards recorded it.
And, we find, it is ahnoft a tranfcript of the letter of Tiberius to Abgarus. The only
thing in which it differs from that letter is this, that he ufes the word *danger,* whereas
Tiberius ufes the word *death*

Let us hear what Eufebius and Jerom fay of this matter:

Eufebius, we find, in two of his works – viz – his chronology and his E. hift. ii. 2,
mentions this interference of Tiberius in behalf of ac- Par this difference we hope to
account in the nex-. two chapters.

The Senate, u. c. 783, expelled believers as Jews, $c.

cufed Chriftians, and, in each work, as the report of Tertullian, in each too as
unobjeftionable. But though he has, in each work, acknowledged that he derived his
information from Tertullian, it is ob- fervable, that he, in each work, fubftitutes the
word 0vrov for peri- culum. In his chronology (moft of which, it may be right to
obferve, he borrowed from Africanus, who was a cotemporary with Tertullian) he has
mentioned the year in which he fuppofes this event took place – viz – xxii. of Tiberius.
In his hiftory he devotes a chapter to the relation of this moft remarkable occurrence.
But though he has, in the laft chapter of the firft book, given us copies of the letters
that pafled between Abgarus and our Lord, yet, it is not a little obfervable, that he
does not fay any thing of thofe letters which paffed between Abgarus and Tiberius,
and which, Mofes Chorenenfis informs us, were depofited in the fame archives.

Jerom alfo mentions this imerpofition of Tiberius in behalf of Chriftians, and on
the authority of Tertullian, in his chronology. – ' And of that work, he, in his epift.
to Vincentius and Gallienus, fays, he partly tranflated, partly compofed. What he
compofed, he adds, is moftly in the roman hiftory. Now in that chronology he not
only fays, with Eufebius, that the punifhment which Tiberius threatened was death
– he alfo adds a circumftance or two omitted both by Tertullian and Eufebius, and,
one, at leaft, of a moft remarkable import, and which may fairly be fuppofed to
have provoked the emperor's threat – viz – that the Senate decreed that all Chriftians
fhould be expelled from Rome. Indeed Jerom, both in his former and latter, book,
lias expreflly affigned this as the reafon. For he fays in each – Verum quum ex confulto Patrum Chriftianos eliminari Urbe placuiiTet, Tiberius per ediftum accufatoribus
chriftianorum comminatus eft mortem.

The Senate, u. c. 783, expelled believers as Jews, $c.-

Now can it be fuppofed that Jerom would not only have faid, with Eufebius, that
death was the punifhment threatened by Tiberius – but have alfo added, that the Senate
firft decreed that all Chriftians fhould depart from Rome – and that the emperot iflued
another decree " ediftum" – and have faid it as a thing never contradifted, and in latin

too, if he had not, on enquiry, found that it was really fo': – Thefe added circumftances are alone enough to prove that Jerom did not copy his account of this traniaftion from Eufebius. But a much ftronger proof of it may be obtained by comparing their reports with each other. Eufebius, in his E. II., fays – Se *auro: nams TiGtfiu*

o *tiryf& a&yxywt x&i m Xpiriav&v ooyMtros, iwtuesv ns tfura 'ffitws, re irfo: rtti avyxX-mot* txoitoXoywaro *irifi ns tis Xftfo iHTtus – ns* Si fu

To *K. yfvyfi.3. ra favftv, a auros Qatarot* tij'"'?'0'3-'6

r, us Tifrviatot ifti. – And Jerom, in his L. P., fays – Pilato de Chriftianorum dogmate ad Tiberium referente Tiberius retulit ad Senatum, ut inter caetera facra reciperetur – Verum, &c. – ejfaftly as we quoted before.

This oppofite behaviour then of the roman Senate, and of Tiberius, with regard to believers, appears to have been univerfally believed by Chriflians in very early days – and moreover to have been by no one contradifted. No appeal was ever made to the prefumed filence of roman or jevvifh hiftorians concerning it. And it appears, that it would have been but to little ufe to make fuch appeal, for the writings of Philo and Jofephus, of Suetonius and Tacitus, when rightly underftood, are alone fufficient to eftablifh the credibility of the fa& notwithftanding all their care to avoid even the appearance of having noticed it, fo prevaricating are the accounts which they have given of what happened in the latter part of the reign of Tiberius.

Jerom, we perceive, fays, that the Chriftians *only* were ordered to quit Rome – that is, furely, believing Jews and believing Romans. – *The Senate, u. c.* 783, *expelled believers at Jews, %*e.

And the jewifh and roman writers fay that the Jews *alont,* or, as Jofe- phus fays – *nm to lalxnvn* – were, two or three years after Chrift had been preached in that city, expelled. Were then all the Jews, believers and unbelievers, and all the roman converts to the faith, expelled about the fame time ? – If fo, muft not Rome have been almoft left defolate ? – But by whom were they expelled ? – If the Jews were, as Philo and the Evangelifts fay, very much attached to Caefar – that is, to Tiberius, and Tiberius was, as Chriftian writers fay, the patron of Chriftians, in fpite too of the Senate, is it at all likely that he would have expelled either of them ? – Unlefs they difagreed fo much that it was abfolutely neceflary ? – Did they then difagree about any religious point fo much as to render the interference of Tiberius neceflary?

If the Senate would not admit Chrift to be God, and gave this reafon for their refufal – becaufe Tiberius had previoufly acknowledged him to be fo, was it not an encouragement for unbelievers, efpecially Jews, to accufe believers of worfhipping an unlawful Deity ? And if the Senate encouraged fuch accufers may they not have expelled Chriftians as foon as they difcovered them to be fuch ? – That is, merely for deifying Chrift ? – And may not this have provoked Tiberius to publifh his edift threatening periculum, or death, to the accufers of Chriftians ? – But why, if the Senate did not put Chriftians to death, mould Tiberius have threatened to put their accufers to death? That the Senate did not punifh fuch offenders with death, we know, but though the Senate may not have done it, yet why may not the Jews be fuppofed to have ftoned jewifh believers, if not their pro- felytes, as blafphemers of God ? – Or, rather to have fent fuch to Jerafalem to be tried and ftoned for that offence ? – If, as Luke fays, the Sanhedrin was permitted to fend to ftrange cities for Chriftians, in order to try them for blafphemy, and to ftone them, why may they *The Senate, u. c. 783, expelled believers as Jews, 8$c.*

not have alfo fent to Rome for fuch offenders? – And if the Sanhedrin did claim this privilege why may not Tiberius, on that account, have thought proper to threaten death to Jews for putting jewifh believers to death as blafphemers of God ? – And why may not this ferve to explain the reafon of the million of the 4,000 jewifh libertines to Sardinia? – This, at leaft, we know, that the perfecution of blafphemers, by Paul, lafted but a very Ihort time, and then for ever ceafed, but why, we know not.

SECTION 17

V
CHAPTER XVII.

Who were accusers? – When did they begin to accuse ? – - How long did they continue their practice? – By whom were they encouraged ? – By whom, and when, were they suppressed ?

Who were the accused? – Of what were they accused? – Before whom were they accused? – To what punishment were they liable?

VV E read in the work of no writer but in thofe of the two Senecas, Suetonius, Tacitus, and Dion, of accufers being permitted to difturb the peace of a city for any confiderable length of time, without being informed why they were permitted to do it. Thofe writers tell us that, in the reign of Tiberius, and in that only, and in a no inconfiderablft part of it, (that is, as Tacitus feems to fay, iv. 32, 33, from the tcth year of his reign – or, rather, as he fays, iv. 69, from the I4th, till, as Dion fays, 58, 631, D., a little after the death of Sejanus – of, perhaps, as Dion again fays, 58, 634, E., till the t9th – for then, he there fays, Tiberius, in one day, put all the principal accufers to death,) the calamities which this fet of Taraxipolides in-

Accusers -who, S$c. ? – Accused -who, S$c. V

flifted on the people of Rome were worfe than thofe occafioned by any civil war. Now as Tiberius was, during all that period, refiding at Capreae, and as he is faid, by one, to have been then the worfe for age, and by others, to have been, during the firft three or four years of it, wafted with grief, and again, by others, to have refigned the management of public affairs to Sejanus, by whom he was, as Dion fays, 58, p. 623, B., kept in ignorance of every thing done at Rome, and as he is faid, by Dion, to have, at lud, put all the principal ac- cufers to death, in one day, why may we not, all this confidered, fup- pofe that thofe accufers were encouraged, not by Tiberius, but by Sejanus ? – Does not Seneca fen. appear to give us reafon to think fo, by faying, Confol ad Mar. c. 22, that Sejanus was the enfetter of them ? – And docs not Dion too appear to give us ftill greater reafon to think fo, by fpeaking, 58, p. 631, C., of the keennefs with which Tiberius, after the death of Sejanus, profecuted *Sejanic* accufations? – Of this we, however, may be fure, that accufers could not, during the refidence of Tiberius at Capreae, have difturbed the peace of Rome fo very much, and, fo long, unlefs they had been permitted fo to do, either by Sejanus, or, by the Senate; by Sejanus principally no doubt, as we are informed by Dion, 58, p. 622, B., that the Senate were fo completely fubfervient to him as to worfhip him. – Now if thofe accufers were encouraged by Sejanus, and by the Senate, may they not, as Sejanus is, by feveral writers, faid to have entered into a confpiracy, with rnoft of the Senate, againfl his fovereign, be fuppofed to have been encouraged to carry on fotne defign hoftile to the fovereignty of Tiberius – efpecially, as Tiberius is faid, both by-Tacitus, iv. 71, 74, vi. 2, and by Dion, L 58, p. 627, A., 630, A., to have been afraid, during all the time thofe accufers were permitted to prowr", of appearing at Rome, and in the Senate? – Of this, however, we hope to be able to inform ourfelves as we proceed.

Accusers who, $c. ?-Accuscd 'who, S$c. ?

Of all cotemporary writers, it is not a little remarkable, that the two Senecas only take notice of thofe accufers, and their extreme maleficence. All the reft – viz- – Paterculus, V. Maximus, Agrippa, Philo, and Clemens of Rome are entirely filent on the fubjeft. Indeed three of thofe writers – viz – V. Maximus, Agrippa, and Philo feem, as we fhall come to fee prefently, not to have been aware that the peace of Rome was, at any time in the reign of Tiberius, efpecially from the 14th to the 18th, fo much difturbed. And though the other two feem to have acknowledged, as well as the two Senecas, that it was, by fome means, difturbed – and in the I4th, or before the 16th – yet they do not fay1 that it was difturbed by accufers. One of thofe two – viz – Clemens, fays, that the difturbance happened in the 14th, and that Tiberius, from that time, inftead of encouraging accufers to difturb the peace of any one, ordered the *maleficent* to be fearched for, in order to put them to death, firft at Rome, and afterwards in every province – Caefar in urbe Roma, et per provincias maleficos inquiri juffit ac perimi; ex quibus multi jam perempti funt. R. x. 55. And the other – viz – Paterculus, that it ended before the end of the i6th. – But let us hear what each of thofe cotemporaries fays of the peace of Rome during the reign of Tiberius – and, for the purpofe of comparing their feveral reports with that of each'other. – From Romans, Jews, and Chriftians we may hope to be able to get at fomething like the truth.

Paterculus fays, ii. 126, where he enumerates the various bleffings which the Romans had been enjoying under Tiberius, till the i6th of his reign – revocata in forum fides, *fubmota e foro feditio,* ambitio campo, *difcordia curia.* – And what are we to underftand by all this ? When, before the i6th of the reign of Tiberius, had faith been expel-

. *Accusers who, $c. ? – . Accused who, $c. ?*

led from the forum ? – And why ? – When, before the fame year, had any fedition taken place in the forum ? – And why ? – When did the difcord in the Senate, here mentioned, happen, and why ? – Did this difcord happen at the fame time as the fedition in the forum? – Whenever thofe diflentions may have happened, and whatever may have been the occafion of them, who, but Tiberius, by the inftrumen- tality of Sejanus, can, by this writer's report, have put an end to them? After having faid this to Vinicius, the then conful, Paterculus immediately fubjoins – Quando pax hetior? Diffufa pax *Augufta* per omnes terrarum orbis angulos. And did fuch an univerfal peace fucceed thofe difturbances – and, in the i6th of Tiberius? – How long did it laft?

V. Maximus feems to corroborate this evidence of Paterculus, concerning the peace which took place in the i6th of Tiberius, by what he fays, ix. n, where he is fpeaking of the confequences of the fall of Sejanus – Itaque flat pax, valent leges, fincerus privati ac publici officii tenor fervatur.

Agrifipa, who was intimate with Drufus, the fon of Tiberius, as long as he lived, and afterwards lived at Capreae, with Tiberius, fays nothing of this vile praftice – on the contrary, he, though he was 5m- prifoned by Tiberius, reprefents his government, even to his kinfman Caius, when he was afraid to appear in his prefence, as having been uniformly beneficial to mankind at large, and to the Jews above any other people.

Phllo fays, in F. p. 758, F., that Tiberius was ever ready to punifli any of his foreign magiflrates for oppreffion. And, Leg. p. 769, B., that he enjoyed, to the end of his reign, fuch a peace as was never known before. And though he fays of him, p. 785, F., that he liften- ed to the accufations of Sejanus againft the Jews of Rome, fo much as to confent to the expulfion of them from thence – yet he alfo fays,

Accusers who, 8$c. ? – Accused who, Sfc. *?*

that he, immediately after the fall of his prime minifter, wrote to all his foreign praefefts, commanding them to ufe the Jews, *fa few ex- cepted)* in their feveral departments, kindly. And again, in F. p. 748, D., he fays, that the people of Egypt, who were under the more immediate care of the emperor, were during the laft five or fix years of his reign, unufually happy. It was not till the 8th month after the death of Tiberius that this profound peace was difturbed, when, as he fays, in F. p. 749, F., a certain defcription of people, whom he calls *Taraxipolidei,* or city plagues, and who feem to have been very like thofe accufers about whom we are enquiring, difturbed the peace of the Jews of Alexandria, but under what pretence, it is not a little remarkable, he does not fay.

Seneca fen. in his Confol. ad Marc. c. 19, (which Confol. it may not be amifs to obferve, he wrote three years after the death of her father Cremutius Cordus, who, as Tacitus fays, iv. 34, died early u. c. 778, and therefore in the beginning of u. c. 781 – in the I4th of Tiberius, or, a little before the execution of Sabinus – and about a year before the death of Livia) fays to her – nulla publica clades nulla privata confpicitur – which feems to intimate that, in the beginning of the 14th of Tiberius, all things remained in a ftate of tranquillity – and, he had before, c. 15, clafled Tiberius with the greateft of all great and moft eminently virtuous men. But Seneca alfo fays, a little after, in the fame work, c. 22, what looks a little like a plain contra- diftion of the paflage juft adverted to – viz – that Sejanus ufed to encourage informers againft *every body,* by feeding them, for his own purpofe, *with human blood* – Subfcriptio, et acerrimi canes, quos ille, *utjlbi uni* manfuetos, *omnibus* feros haberet, *fangu'me humano* pafcebat, circumlatrare etiam hominem, et ilium imparatum *inci/iiiwt.*-And, a*Accusers who,* Sfe.? – *Accused who, %c.?*

little after this, he feems to fay, that Sejanus was the original enfetter pf accufers – Accufatores Sejano auftore, &c. – Now if Seneca be cor- reft in what he here fays of accufers, does it not feern that Sejanus, and not Tiberius, *began,* u. c. 778, to encourage them?

Again, in another work of this writer, Contr. Superft., he fays, that the ufage of a certain namelefs people whom he reprefents as the moft wicked of all wicked people, had, at a particular time, fo far prevailed, that it had, after having encountered much oppofition, obtained reception in all countries – the conquered having been enabled to give laws to the conquerors. – " Cum *interim* ufque eo fcel'eratiffimae gentis confuetudo convaluit, ut per *omnesjam* terras recepta fit: vifti vifto- ribus leges dedere." – Now to what nation can he, who died a year or two before Tiberius, be fuppofed to have alluded ? – Of all nations then being, which is the moft likely to have been confidered by him as the moft wicked of all others ? – And as having had a ufage not adopted by any other people ? – We do not read, in the work of any roman writer, of any *nation* which was, in the days of the elder Seneca, confidered as being eminently wicked, nor as having any cuftom or ufage which the reft of mankind confidered as being eminently objeftionable – and which it wimed to impofe on the reft of the world, contrary to their inclination. Does not Philo fay, de vita, M. p. 508, C. D., how little regard all the world had for the religious inftitutions of each other ? – Of the difciples of Jefus Chrift, who, when compo- fed of various people, were, for a few years, ftill called Jews, and afterwards Chriftians – we read, in Tacitus, A. xv. 44, that they were univerfally hated for their flagitious praftices – that is, as Athenagoras and others fay, for their atheifm, their horrid feafts, their adulteries, and their compotationsr-and, we alfo read, in the fame paflage of*Accusers who,* fife. ? – *4ccused who, $c. ?*

t Dion, 1. 37, p. 37. Suetonius, T. 23.

Tacitus, that they had embraced a *mo/2 deflruflive fuperjiition,* and that they, at firft – in praefens – endeavored to obtain admiffion into Rome, and were then repulfed, and then – dein – as he fays, L 73, in fpite of all oppofition, eftablifhed themfelves in that city. May not Seneca then, by the moft wicked of all nations, have meant Chriflians? Does not his fon give us reafon to fuppofe, by what he fays, Ep. 108, that he is likely to have meant Chriftians ? – He there fays, that his father diffuaded him from abftaining any longer from the ufe of animal food, though after a year's trial, in compliance with a certain fuper- ftition, he had found it beneficial to him – this fuperftition, he fays, was introduced into Rome, in the reign of Tiberius, and a little before the facred rites of other nations were agitated. This fuperflition, fubjoins he, my father, though he did not fear the *calumny* which was attached to it, hated as a fpecies of philofophy, and therefore requefted me to return to my former mode of living. And does not Seneca, by fpeak- ing of the conqueft of this moft wicked of all people, allude to fome- thing befides their fubjugation ? – For what people had not then been conquered by the Romans? – And how could Chriftians be faid to have been then conquered, unlefs by having been, as Suetonius fays, iii. 36, together with the Jews and Egyptians, expelled as fimilar feftaries? – Now if Suetonius did mean that the Jews, Egyptians, and the like fe&s, were, as being Chriftians, expelled from Rome, then, we find, they were, as Tacitus fays, reprefled, or, as Seneca fays, fubdued. – And Lipfius, we find, thinks, that Seneca as evidently here means Chriftians. Indeed what other clafs of feftaries, befides the Chriftian, were faid to have been, of all men, the moft wicked – or, could be faid to have had fo much prevalence over the whole world, as to impofe on them any obnbxious cuftom? Could the Jews, or any other people, be faid to have been, after the year 774, at war with the Romans – *Accusers"who, S$c.?* – *Accused -who, $c.?*

and could they, or any other people, be faid, after that time, to have conquered their conquerors. – Tacitus, we find, fays, A. xv. 44, with regard to the Jews – Sub Tiberio quies.

The Chriftians then feem to be covertly complained of by Seneca the elder, as having been, in the reign of Tiberius, conquered – or, as Tacitus fays, of their execrable fuperftition, repreffed – or, as Suetonius fays, expelled from Rome. Now if Chnicians were expelled from Rome as Jews, &c. how fhould we fuppofe that any one was known to be of that perfuafion but by accufers ?

Seneca jun. fays, de B. iii. 26, that the rage of accufers among the Roman citizens was, at one time in the reign of Tiberius, frequent and almoft public – that is, we prefume, common – and, not only frequent and public, or common, but even worfe than any civil war – Sub T. C. accufandi frequens et paene publica rabies. Excipiebatur ebriorum fermo, fimplicitas jocantium. But in what year of Tiberius this rage for accufing commenced – by whom thofe accufers of *drunkards* and *jefters* were fet on – whether they accufed them only of words fpoken – and, before what tribunal they accufed them, this writer does not fay. – But he, we find, fays, and to our no little aftonimment, that thofe drunkards and jefters were indifcriminately condemned *to death* for it. What! Drunkards condemned to death for uttering a few incoherent expreffions, and by that greateft of all drunkards Biberius Caldius Mero! Who made Pifo, for his protrafted compotations, the praefeft of Syria! And an obfcure perfon, for a fimilar feat, a quaeftor, and in preference to other noble candidates! And fuch perfons too for only fpeaking! Seneca, iurely, cannot have had the conference to expeft us to believe this. – And why, as the cuftom of accufing was fo very common, were

Who ever heard of the oratorical powers of drunken men – or, of the simplicity of jesters.'

Accusers who, S$c. ? – Accused who, 8$c. ?

drunkards and jefters only the objefts of their accufations? – Of this rage of accufers he immediately fubjoins an example. – Paul, fays he, a praetorian, had a ring with an image of Tiberius in relief, with this ring on his finger he happened one day to be dining with a party, in which there was one Maro, a notorious accufer. Paul being intoxicated, was fo imprudent as to put his hand, with the ring on it, to a certain neceffary utenfil: which Maro inftantly noticed as an aft of impiety to Tiberius. That Maro did fo the fervant of Paul fufpefted, and contrived to take the ring from the hand of his mafter without being perceived by any one, and to keep it till the affair was heard, when he denied that his mafter had been fo impious, and produced the ring as a proof. – Ccenabat Paulus preetorius, &c. – This ftory, it fhould be obferved, Seneca appears to relate as an inflance of the frequency and the publicity of the rage with which accufers worried, to the almoft extirpation of the Roman people, *drunkards* and *jejiers,* for *words* by them fpoken. But is it really what he would have us to believe it is ? – Was Paul accufed of fermonizing when drunk ? – Was he not, *whenfjfuechlifs,* accufed of impiety to Tiberius? – And did not his flave inftantly contrive to prove him innocent of this charge ? – and, at the expence of proving him infenfibly drunk ? – But how happened it that he thought of profecuting any one for this offence – at leaft, after the year 778? – Did the reft of his fort too profecute for this offence ? – Did they not know that Tiberius had, in that year, publicly, in the Senate, protefted againft the praftice of erefting temples to any man ? – Did they not know that he had then, by the account of Suetonius, iii. 26, forbidden any one to ereft any ftatue or image to himfelf, without his permiffion, which he would never, but on this exprefs condition, grant – that it fhould not be confidered as facred, but only as ornamental ? – How then could Maro think of bringing a

How happened it that Maro, so notorious an accuser, w. is admitted to be of this party?

Accusers who, $c. ? – Accused who, S$c. ?

charge of fuch a nature againft an infenfibly drunken man, and of citing all the company to fupport his evidence ? – Were they too ignorant of this prohibition ?

But when does he fay Rome was fo violently agitated by accufers r That it could not have been fo agitated in or *before* the t6th year of Tiberius we are aflured by Paterculus and feveral other cotemporary writers. And that it could not have been fo much difturbed by them *lefore* the nth Tacitus allures us, iv. 32, where he complains that nothing worth the attention of an hiftorian had then occurred ; – that the peace of the city was then not difturbed – or, at leaft, but a little – that the face of things appeared unruffled. – Nobis in arto et inglorious labor, &c. Immota quippe aut modice laceffita pax, moeftae Urbis res, et princeps proferendi imperii incuriofus erat. Non tamen fine ufu fuerit, introfpicere ilia primo afpeftu levia, ex queis magna- rum faepe rerum motus oriuntur. – In the next chapter – viz – 33, he indeed fpeaks of *continued accufations,* &c. And then, in the two next chapters, 34, 35, he relates the affair of Cremutius Cordus, (which, we have already feen, Seneca, the elder, fpeaks of in his Confol. to Marcia, the daughter of Cordus, in the year 781 ; at which time he obferved to her that fhe had not been terrified by the fight of any calamity private or public.) And then, again, in the next, 36, he fays, that the whole year had been fo conftantly occupied in hearing accufations that, on the feriae Latinae, the prafeft of the city had been obliged to attend to them. In the fame year, fays he, chapter 37, Tiberius refufed to be deified; which refufal feems to have put a ftop, for the prefent, to the praftice of accufers, for, he fays very little of their proceedings, during the two following years. And, we find, that he fays, iv. 69, that they began, in the I4th year, while Tiberius was at Capreae, to rage again *more than ever,* and that they cauſed, by the affair of Sabinus, inconceivably more terror, all over the city, than*Accusers who, 8$c.?* – *Accused txiho, 8$c. ?*

ever. – Non alias magis, &c. – This exceſſive rage of the then ſet of accuſers he ſeems to ſay, 71, did not laſt long – they were ſoon ſupſ- planted by others – Ni mihi deſtinatum foret, ſuum quaeque in annum referre, avebat animus anteire, ſtatimque memorare exitus, quos Lati- nius et Opſus ceterique flagitii ejus repertores habuere, non modo poſt- quam C. Caeſar rerum potitus eſt, ſed incolumi Tiberio: qui ſcelerum miniſtros, ut perverti ab aliis nolebat; ita plerumque fatiatus, et *oblatis in eandem operam recentibus,* veteres et praegraves afflixit: verum, &c. Indeed Tacitus ſays, vi. 30, that Tiberius, in the ıgth year of his reign, puniſhed all accuſers. – Ac tamen accuſatores, ſi facultas incideret, poenis afficiebantur. – From thoſe few remarks adduced from the iv. and vi. books of Tacitus, on this point, it appears pretty clearly that the peace of Rome began to be diſturbed by accuſers, in the nth of Tiberius – that in the 12th and ı3th it was not much diſturbed – that in the I4th it was moſt outrageouſly diſturbed – and that in the ıgth it ceaſed to be diſturbed. Conſequently why mould we not conclude that the rage of accuſers, which Seneca jun. mentions as having taken place in the reign of Tiberius, and which, he ſays, was attended with more dreadful effeſts than any civil war, firſt happened in the I4th of his reign, and that it continued about two years ? – Does not Suetonius, by what he ſays, iii. 37, encourage us ſtill more to draw this concluſion ? – He there ſays, that Tiberius moſt grievouſly ſuppreſſed ſome popular tumults – and, that he not only did ſo, but that he took great care that they mould never more happen – Populares tumultus exortos graviſſime coercuit; et ne orirentur ſedulo cavit. – Of courſe, if he took ſo much care that popular commotions Ihould never happen, thoſe which he ſuppreſſed ſo grievouſly could not have happened after thoſe mentioned in the I4th year, which are mentioned by Clemens of Rome, Recog. i. 10, and by Tacitus, iv. 74.

Eee CHAPTER XVIII,

Tiberius forbad the Jews to stone Jewish believers, but did not forbid them to stone, as usual, other Jews.

reconſidering what was ſaid in the xv. chapter, we may perceive that neither the Evangeliſts, nor Agrippa, nor Philo, nor Joſe- phus accuſe Tiberius of having, in the leaſt, irritated the Jews by any innovation in their religious concerns. And we, on the contrary, perceive that each of thoſe writers teſtifies that he was extremely kind to them, and had a great veneration for the objeſt of their religious worſhip – the Evangeliſts ſay, that he was ſo well diſpoſed towards the Jews, and towards their religion, from the xiv. year of his reign till the end of the xvi. – that the rulers of the Jews, in the xiv., acknowledged him as their only king – and that they, in the two following years, took the liberty of ſending any where for tranſgreſſbrs, even for thoſe who, on the teſtimony of Mofes, acknowledged Jeſus to be the true Meſſiah, and for the purpoſe of impriſoning them, in order to try them for blaſphemy againſt Mofes, and, if guilty, of ſtoning them – and, the reſt of thoſe jewiſh writers ſay that he was very kind to the Jews every where, and very forward to cauſc their mode of

Tiberius forbad the Jews to stone Jewish believers, but, S$c.

worfhip to be refpefted, even till his death. How then is it. that we are told that the Talmud of Jerufalem has recorded a tradition, that Ifrael was deprived of the power of putting any one to death, even one fentenced by Mofes – and, in the 4oth year before the deftruftion of Jerufalem? – that is, in the courfe of the t6th of Tiberius, almoft to a day. Who but Tiberius can be fuppofed to have done it ? – And who, . but a fimpleton, can have thought that he did ? – Efpecially, as he muft have known that Tiberius, at the fame time, permitted the Jews to fend any where out of Judea, not only for tranfgreflbrs of the law, but even for thofe who believed that Jefus was the perfbn foretold by Mofes, and that he was equal with God, and to ftone them to death for it. And yet the two profeflbrs, (efpecially the latter) alluded to in a former chapter, feem to fay, that Tiberius had nothing to dp with it – nor Sejanus, who, as Philo, we find, informs us, in F. p.- 747, ad C. p. 785, fought the deftruftion of the whole nation, but that the procurator for the time being did it himfelf. The laft alluded to, of thofe moft celebrated Theologians, fays, vol. iii. part ii. p. 83 – " If the Sanhedrin *obtained from Marcellus* a privilege which they did " not enjoy under Pilate, they *of courfe,* took the earlieft opportunity " of making ufe of it." – And can thofe two peerlefs profcflbrs have really thought that it was poffible to perfuade us that the roman procurators of Judea had undoubtedly the power of making any alteration in the religious eftablimment of the Jews, efpecially one that was the grand fupport of their hierarchy ? – And that the Jews fubmitted to it without the leaft oppofition, even without appealing to their acknowledged king, who, as Agrippa told Caius, p. 800, B., they were confident would not confent to the infringement of their law by Pilate in any cafe ? – Tt(3tfior B&h tfltXsi *rut vptnfut* xamXffo-flat. – If the power of punifhing capital tranfgreflbrs of the law had been taken away from *Tiberius forbad the Jews to stone Jewish believers, but, %c,*

the Jews by any procurator under Tiberius, with what propriety could Agrippa have ventured to remind his coufin of the fufpenfion of the figurelefs gilt fhields, not in the temple, but in the palace of Herod, at Jerufalem, by Pilate – or, of the remonftrance of four of the king's fons, with others of the royal family, to that governor, on that fub- jeft – or, of the petition which they then threatened to fend to Tiberius, and which, it feems, they afterwards found themfelves obliged to fend to Rome? – Tiberius, added Agrippa, was, on hearing of the tranfaftion, (though Pilate flated he had done it out of refpeft to his fovereign – and, that there was no figure on them,) moft unufually exafperated at the prefumption of his praSfeft to. do a thing which was confidered by the Jews as a profanation of the fanftity of Jerufalem, and inftantly ordered him to remove them. – Or, rather, it may be afked, would Agrippa, if Pilate had afterwards taken frorn the Jews the power of ftoning blafphemers, have thought of obje&ing to the nad projeft of Caius at all ? – What other reply could he have ex- pefted to receive from his imperial kinfman but the following? – Pray yemember how contentedly you, and all your race, bore to be deprived of the power of putting any one to death – a power without which your hierarchy could not have exifted, and, by Pilate ? – Why then is all this oppofitiort made to my, not much more objeftionable, project ? And if Tiberius himfelf had, at any time, deprived the Jews of this fupport of their religion, why did not Caius exprefs his furprize at the totally oppofite behavior of Agrippa, on that emergency, and, on the prefent? – On that occafion, he, fays Jofephus, defired permiffion of Tiberius to pay his vefpefts to him, and confented, as foon as he was afked, to become one of his domeftics – but, on the prefent, he was fo Ihocked, at the profanenefs of the projeft of Caius, that he fainted away, and was, the day following, incapable of feeing that prince. – JJefides, if this privation took place in the t6th year of Tiberius, mufl*Tiberius forbad Hie Jews to stone Jewish believers, but, fyc.*

it Hot have happened about the rime when the perfecution, which followed the murder of Stephen, ceafed? – that is, about the time when the churches had reft ? – Or, a little after Saul was converted – and, before he went up to Jerufalem and preached boldly in the name of the Lord Jefus? – And, laftly, before the converfion of Cornelius, who, Clemens of Rome and Eufebius fay, was converted before the death of Tiberius. – Now in what year of Tiberius or of Rome did that perfecution ceafe ?

In the firft place, we take it for granted, that Paul was converted long before Cornelius was, becaufe his converfion is fpoken of Afts ix. a'nd that of Cornelius in the next chap. – In the mean time, fays Luke, Peter vifited all the churches, and tarried, we know not how long, at Joppa-xr -*nfts.* – Now Cornelius was, as Clemens of Rome and Eufebius inform us, converted long before the death of Tiberius – the former fays, Recog. x. 55, and Epit. cxxxiv., that Cornelius was the bearer of a precept from Tiberius to the praefecl; of Caefarea, on fome extraordinary bufinefs of a public nature – and the latter, Eccl. Hift. ii. 3, places the converfion of Cornelius under Tiberius. Again – - Clemens of Alexandria informs us, Strom, iv. p. 528, B., that Paul, though but a young man, became, immediately after the afceniion, a perfect Chriftian – rio fv *m, an t i Kai o* riauXor xpw'r i$ *ivQius t. tr r,* ra *Kvfttt* a. Xnv *aitititiroct.* – Now as Clemens, we find, alfo fays, i. p. 274, that he obtained his information from his elders, one of whom, and the beft informed, he fays, was an hebrew – avtxafo – of Paleftine, why fhould we not think him entitled to credit on this point ? Eufebius too appears to have been of the fame opinion with Clemens, for, in his Eccl. Hift. ii. i, he fays, that the converfion of Saul followed that of the Eunuch by Philip – xi *tm* Tato K. r. X. – He moreover feems to fay that the converfion of Saul happened before Tiberius proteted*Tiberius fordad the Jews to stone Jewish believers, but,* &c,

Chriftians – for he mentions the former event in the firft chapter, and the latter in the fecond. – With this report of Clemens the Alexandrian, and of Eufebius, we find, that one of the excerpta utiliffima, extra&ed from the chronology of Africanus, &c. and publifhed by Scaliger, feems to agree – Paulas autem Apoftolus poft afcenfionem Domini, et poft paifionem Stephani dierum, in Apoftolatum ordinatur vi. idus Januariis *in confulatu Rubellionis,* poft afcenfionem Salvatoris noftri menfes vii. poft dtes xi. paffionis Stephani, pridie Epiphaniae.

. The perfecution of jewifh believers, which, followed the murder of Stephen, appears then to have been begun about eight months after the crucifixion of our Lord, and in the beginning of u. c. 782 – and, about the fame time, before the beginning of the xvi. year of Tiberius, when, the Talmud of Jerufalem fays, the power of inffifting capital punimments was taken from Ifrael. – Now as the churches of Judea, &c. are faid by Luke, Afts ix. 31, to have had reft, long before the converfion of Cornelius, (for Peter, in the interim, vifited all the churches of Judea, Samaria, and Galilee, and at Joppa remained – *luxtitt nfi. tfxs)* and, as Paul is faid not only to have returned to Damaf- cus, but to have gone up to Jerufalem, and there to have preached boldly in the name of the Lord Jefus, within three years after his converfion, why mould we not conclude that the perfecution of the churches of Judea, &c. muft, in the mean time, have been put a ftop to? – And by whom could it have been done but by Tiberius? – And how could he have done it fo well as by forbidding the Sanhedrin to ftone jewifh Chriftians as blafphemers? – Leaving them to ftone capi- , tal tranfgreflbrs of the law, as ufual, and even to fend to foreign cities, as ufual, for all forts-of tranfgreflbrs of it.

On reconfidering the whole of what has been obferved of this matter, why fhouhj we not fufpeft that Tiberius could not, as we are told the *'Tiberius forbad the Jews to stone Jewish believers, lut,* $c.

Talmud of Jerufalem feems to affirm, have, at any time, taken from the Jews the power of punifhing the tranfgreflbrs of the law of Mofes with death ? – And why, on the other hand, mould we not fufpeft that he, in the i6th year of his reign, took from Ifrael the ufurped power of punifhing their believing brethren with death ? – How other-wife can it be accounted for that the perfecution, vhich followed the murder of Stephen, ceafed ? – And, that Paul, *jfiortly after,* went up to Jerufalem and fpake boldly in the name of the Lord Jefus, and dif- puted with the hellenifts ? – That he went up, *very jJiortly after,* why Ihoukl we not conclude, from what Luke fays in the Afts – viz – that *all* the difciples were afraid of him, and believed not that he was a difciple ? – Does not Clemens R. feem to intimate, that Tiberius did interfere in behalf of jewifh believers, by faying, that he ordered inquifition to be made for the maleficent, all over the provinces, for punifhing them with death ? – that he had already put many to death, and that he fent Cornelius to apprehend Simon, the oppofer of the Apoftles, for the fame purpofe ? – And does not Philo feem to intimate the fame thing, by what he fays, in his Leg , of the conduit of Tiberius towards certain of the Jews, in the provinces, after their ex- pulfion from Rome ? – viz – he there fays, that Tiberius ordered all his cheirotonized hyparchs to comfort the Jews, in their refpe&ive divtrifts, and to punifh a few only who were culpable. – And does he not again feem to intimate the fame thing, by what he fays, in his work againft Flaccus, of the Taraxipolides? – Who were thofe Taraxi- polides? – And why did they appear in the time of the profoundeft peace that was ever known ?

r.

Both Agrippa and Philo then are fo far from giving us any encouragement to believe this tradition, that they, on the contrary, as good as tell us, that it was not thought of in their time. – And what better*Tiberius forbad the Jews to stone Jewish believers, but,* 8$c.

evidence refpefting this affair can be expefted than that of a king of the Jews, who, was ever intimate with the family of Tiberius, and, tut a year or two after, lived with Mm, and that of their own am- baflador to Caius ? – But we are not confined to their teftimony only on this point, for Jofephus too has not only not thought this moft important point not worth noticing – he has alfo, we find, faid enough in his A. and B. to convince us that the Jews would not have fuffered the fundamental law of their religion to be fufpended without a pro- portionate oppofition, if not, that Tiberius could not have thought of treating them fo injurioufly. For befides having mentioned the extreme grief which the Jews fuffered when Pilate introduced the ftan- dards at Jerufalem, and their extreme defperation when Caius had re- folved on having his ftatue erefted, as that of a God, in the temple at Jerufalem; he has alfo mentioned how much they were troubled at the attempt of Pilate to violate the facred treafury. And this concern for their treafury, it fhould be obferved, he feems to fay they manifefted pretty nearly about the time when his predeceflbrs are under- flood to have afTerted this total privation took place. For, immediately after he has related how Pilate introduced the ftandards into Jerufalem, he proceeds, in the next feftion, (l3) to relate this other attempt of that procurator to violate their facred treafury. And again, in the feftion following, (y) he fays, *about the fame time – xam rant rot xatfn* – Jefus performed a thoufand wonderful works. And, laftly, he, in the next feftion, *(It)* proceeds to fay, and *about the fame time –* Iitto *ras auras xpotus –* the Jews of Rome were driven from that city. Now the Jews of Rome were, we have feen, CHAP, xv., expelled in the year 783, or, in the fame year in which the Talmud of Jerufalem fays tradition affirmed that Ifrael was deprived of the. power of inflift- ing capital punimments. Confequently why ftiould we. not conclude*Tiberius forbad the Jews to stone Jewish believers, but, $$c.*

that Pilate feems very likely to have endeavored to annoy the Jews by thole two infringements of their laws about the year 783? – If what Jofephus fays, A. xviii. 5, &., has been rightly underftood, Pilate cannot well be fuppofed to have vexed the Jews thus before the year above fpecified – for if, as the two profeflbrs above alluded to will have it, Tiberius died while Pilate was on his voyage to Rome, and had then, as Jofephus fays, governed Judea ten years, he muft have been made governor of Judea before April 780: and as Jofephus fays that the winter was begun – tnSiao-av sv lffoo-oXtot? – when he introduced the ftandards into Jerufalem, he cannot well be fuppofed to have done it before that year was nearly ended: and, as he alfo fays, that Pilate afterwards began the aqueduft, and, that it was, at leaft, two or three if not four hundred furlongs – that is,- 30 or 40 if aot 50 miles long, the probability of our preceding conclufion will be the more apparent.

Now as Jofephus appears to have placed both of thofe events about the year in which the Talmud of Jerufalem affirms tradition placed the privation in queftion, and the latter of them in that year – and has told us how uneafy the Jews were on each of thofe occafions – and how many lives were loft on the latter – but has not taken the leaft notice of any uneafinefs which this privation caufed; – -what can be plainer than that he knew nothing of this tranfaftion?

Before we proceed to confider any other teftimony of Jofephus on this point, it may not be amifs to obferve that the introduftion of the ftandards into Jerufalem muft, by what Agrippa told Caius of the fuf-

Eusebius says, Eccl. hist. ii. 6, that Pilate was, by the Almighty, permitted to vex the Jews thus, for *thetr havtng put our Lord to death – avtatitt o avru xat* o *Imnttros, opatus atro rut* rLX rft.-a Tfro./D/)wv, *ras Kpra Trxtros* Tb *tQms*

Fff

Tiberius forbad the Jews to stone Jewish believers, but, c.

penfion of the fhields in the palace of Herod, have been two different events; and that Pilate, it may be made to appear, muft have fuf- pended the fhields after he had introduced the ftandards.

Jofephus, befides aflerting that they were ftandards, alfo fays, the image of Caefar was affixed to them. – Agrippa, on the direft contrary, reminded Caius that they were plain *gilt unadornedJhtelds,* with no in- fcription whatever on them befides the names of Tiberius and Pilate. Jofephus tells us that thofe ftandardswere conveyed into the city by night and by ftealth. Agrippa faid that they were dedicated to Caefar, and fufpended in Herod's palace, where Pilate refided – and, of courfe, were intended to remain there. Jofephus fays that the people were fo alarmed at it that they inftantly aflembled, even from diftant parts, and went down to Caefarea to requeft Pilate that he would order them to be removed inftantly – and, that Pilate kept them there, in fufpencc, fix or feven days – and, that he then mounted his tribunal, under a pretence of hearing their complaint, but, inftead of doing fo, he gave a private fignal to his foldiers to furround the multitude, and then ordered them, on pain of being treated as feditious, inftantly to difperfe. that they refufed to difperfe, faying that they would rather be cut in pieces than fee the holy city profaned. Pilate, fays Jofephus, perceiving how invincible the Jews were, inftantly, of his own accord, ordered the ftandards to be removed. Agrippa reminded Caius how the king's fons, and others of the nobility, remonftrated with Pilate, and defired to fee the emperor's precept, which, as he had it not to fhew them, they hinted that they meant to fend to Rome for fatis- faftion on the point, which made Pilate apprehenfive that his other numerous oppreffions would be made known – that they did fend a deputation to Rome, and that Tiberius was, though not eafily irritated, on hearing the charge, very much enraged, and ordered Pilate to remove the obnoxious fhields forthwith. '

ifiberius forbad the Jews to stone Jewish believers, but, fyc.

Now who can think that thofe jewifh writers meant to report the fame tranfaftion ? – And, if they did not, who can help thinking that Agrippa meant to remind Caius of that which happened laft ? – Can any one fuppofe that Pilate prefumed to offer two fuch open acls of violence to the religious notions of the Jews after Tiberius had reprimanded him fo feverely for his having dedicated thofe unwrought Ihields, in the palace of Herod, to himfelf ?

As then the two impious attempts of Pilate, mentioned by Jofephus, appear to have taken place about the time of our Lord's crucifixion, and the latter of the two in 783; that other, mentioned by Agrippa, muft, in all probability, have happened a little after in the fame year, or, in the year when the Talmud of Jerufalem has been underftood to fay, tradition affirmed that Ifrael was deprived of the power of putting any one to death, and, as our cotemporary profeflbrs fuppofe, by Pilate, and in the year too when the perfecution by Saul feems to have ceafed. But as Agrippa, we find, told Caius that the Jews were, at the time, confident that Tiberius would not fuffer the leaft point of their law to be violated, and that he reprimanded Pilate fo feverely for fo triffing an offence, how can we think that he, in the fame year, either deprived them of the fupport of their whole law himfelf or permitted Pilate to do fo ?

Laftly, Jofephus tells us, A. xviii. 5, how civilly Vitellius behaved to the Jews on two or three occafions – when he firft went up to Jerufalem he remitted the tax on fruit, and permitted the chief priefts to keep, as they ufed to do formerly, the facred Hole. – And, again, when he was marching with Herod againfl Aretas, he defifted, at the re- queft of the Jews, from his intention of marching his troops through Judea.

Tiberius forbad the Jews to stone Jewish believers, but, $c.

Inftead then of finding this mod extraordinary privation recorded by every one of the early jewifh writers, we find, to our no little aftonifh- ment, that not one of them has mentioned it. And, we moreover find, that each of them has faid enough to convince us that Tiberius would never allow any *prtvilege* to be taken from the Jews – and that the Jews would have refided any attempt to do it, and above all that of ftoning blafphemers.

18

SECTION 18

CHAPTER XIX.
The rise of Sejanus.

i$lius Sejanus was, fays Tacitus, i. 7, 24, the fon of Sejus Strabo, the chief, as Paterculus fays, ii. 127, of the roman knights, and of a lady of rank, who was related to feveral noble families, one of which was probably the ./Elian. – He had, fays Paterculus, ii. 127, brothers, coufins, and an uncle, of confular dignity. – His maternal uncle's name was, fays Tacitus, iii. 35, 72, Junius Blaefus, who was the laft fubjeft dignified with the title of – Imperator.

Sejus Strabo, the father of Sejanus, was in fo great favor with Auguf- tus that he made him the commander of his guards, which honorable and important ftation he filled when Auguftus died. – After the death of his patron, Strabo followed the example of the confuls in fwear- ing allegiance to Tiberius, who continued him in the fame important office, and afterwards made him the governor of Egypt, when he made Sejanus the commander of the guards.

The rise of Sejanus.

Sejanus, on his entrance into life, was, fays Tacitus, iv. i, a companion of Caius Caefar, the firft hufband of Livilla, and, confequently feems to have been brought up in the court of Auguftus, and to have been born rather early in his reign. – He, as

Jofephus fays, A. xviii. 7, *s.,* was alfo afterwards a companion of Drufus, the fecond hufband of Livilla.

Soon after the acceffion of Tiberius, Sejanus, who was, even then, in great authority under Tiberius, was, fays Tacitus, i. 24, made his father's colleague in the command of the guards, and fent as reftor to Drufus, then about 23 years old, with two praetorian cohorts, to reduce to obedience the legions in Pannonia, under Junius Blaefus.

About the beginning of the 7th year of Tiberius, the daughter of Sejanus was, fays Tacitus, iii. 29, contrafted to a fon of Claudius. – This contract, it feems, muft have been entered into by the parents of the young couple in their childhood – for Tacitus himfelf fays, v. 9, that Ihe was but a girl ten years after – and Suetonius fays, v. 27, that this fame, contrafted fon of Claudius died at Pompeii, being choaked by a pear, which he tofled up in play and endeavored to catch in his mouth. The report of this ftipulated marriage was, as Tacitus fays, heard of with indignation–as tending to debafe the imperial family, and, to inflate the exceffive hope of Sejanus – efpecially by Drufus, as he intimates, iv. 7 – but ftill more, we prefume, by the haughty Agrippina, and her adherents. – But would this contraft have been entered into while the parties were fo very young, and, have been in force for ten years (for fo Dion fays, 1. 58, p. 628, C.,) without the confent of all the principal branches of the imperial family – for inftance – of Tiberius, Antonia, Livia, and Livilla ? – As to its tending to inflate the vanity of Sejanus, how could the profpeft of an alliance with the family of Claudius, in the perfon of a lad, have inflated *his* mind,

The rise of Sejanus.

who, if we may believe Tacitus, probably had, at the time, a much nearer profpeft of being more intimately allied to it in the perfon of Livilla? – Suetonius however tells us that a quite contrary report prevailed – viz – that Sejanus, fo far from being elated at the profpeft of having the fon of Claudius for a fon-in-law, contrived to murder him – and why he mould be thought to have done fo, unlefs it was be- caufe he would not have him for a fon-in-law, no one can fee.

One of the two fons of Sejanus was, fays Tacitus, vi. 30, by the advice of Tiberius – confilio Tiberii – alfo contrafted to a daughter of Lentulus Gaetulicus, a man of confular dignity and commander of the legions in Upper Germany. – Whether this marriage ever took place it does not appear – if it did not, we may conclude from an expreffion which Tacitus ufes in that chapter – viz – unus omnium Sejani affinium incolumis, multaque gratia manfit – that Lentulus Gaetulicus was, by feme means or other, allied to Sejanus.

In the courfe of the year 775 Sejanus diftinguifhed himfelf much by his exertions to fave the city, when it was in great danger by a fire which happened in Pompey's Theatre. – Tiberius highly commended him for his exertions to fave the city – and, the Senate voted him a ftatue in the new building. – About the fame time Junius Blaefus, his uncle, who, about a year before, had been, by the intereft of Sejanus, appointed proconful of Africa, was, by the fame intereft, honoured with a triumph, and, foon after, with the title of – Imperator.

In the beginning of the year following, 776, the 9th of Tiberius, fays Tacitus, iv. I, the command of the pratorian cohorts was en- trufted to Sejanus alone (that is, as Dion, we prefume, feems to fay, 1. 57, p. 616, C., on the promotion of his father to the government of Egypt) – and, at the fame time, praetorian honors were conferred on him by Tiberius – that is, furely, not without the approbation of *The rise of Sejanies.*

Drufus (for Drufus had been before invefted with tribunitial authority, and, as Tacitus fays, iii. 56, had been made equal with his father in public matters) – which honors were never before known to have been conferred on any one of his rank. At the fame time, fays Dion, Tiberius made him one of his twenty privy councillors and his minifter of ftate. This Dion remarks, Tiberius did, becaufe his difpofition was like his own. Now Tiberius, it fhould be obferved, is faid, even by Tacitus, to have been, at the time, the beft and the moft fagacious of princes, and to have employed only men of the moft approved charafters, even though they were but little known – Res fuas Caefar fpeftatiffimo cuique, quibufdam ignotis ex fama mandabat. – And Philo, we find, fays, that no prince knew men better than Tiberius. Can it then be fuppofed that he would have made choice of a bad minifter? – Efpecially after fo long a trial ? – If we may believe Pater- culus, ii. 127, who was intimate both with Tiberius and Sejanus, and who addrefled his hiftory to one of the then confuls, who was about to marry Julia, the daughter of Germanicus, Sejanus was, like his mafter, poflcfled of every excellence. But if we can believe Tacitus, iv. i, he had fcarce one excellence, and moft bad qualities: and though by no means a match for Tiberius in cunning, was able to circumvent him.

No fooner was his commiffion enlarged than he, as Tacitus and Dion fay, (though Suetonius, iii. 37, fays, that Tiberius himfelf did it) propofed to colleft all the praetorian cohorts, difperfed throughout Italy, into one body at Rome.

In the beginning of the loth year of Tiberius, when it was ufual to offer up prayers for the prefervation of the emperor, the chief and other priefts, *who, it feems,* Tacitus, iv. 17, fays, *were mojlly related to Agrifi/una,* prayed fpr the prefervation of Nero and Drufus. This*The rise of Sejanus.*

Tiberius refented highly. And, fays Tacitus, Sejanus took care to inflame his refentment, by obferving that the ftate was divided into two parties, fo oppofite, as to be ready to deftroy each other – that Agrip- pina headed the adverfe party – that it was become neceflary to make an example of one or two of the ringleaders. – Inftabat quippe Sejanus, incufabatque diduftam civitatem, ut civili hello; efle qui fe partium Agrippinas vocent: ac ni refiftatur, fore pluris. Neque aliud glifcentis difcordiae remedium, quam fi unus alterve maxime prompt! fubver- terentur.

But did Sejanus think it at all neceflary to apprife his moft faga- cious mafter, then refiding at Rome, of what concerned his fafety? – If not, why is he here introduced as the reporter of this wonderful dif- covery ? – However, does not this feem to imply that the interceflions of the priefts were fuppofed to have a tendency to promote difaffec- tion? – And, that a fort of confpiracy had been entered into by Agrip- pina with certain leading men of Rome, in favor of Nero and Drufus? – If not that the adverfe party confidered Sejanus as aftive to defeat their defign? – But who, does Tacitus fay, were the chief confpirators with Agrippina ? – And, by what means did they hope to cany their plot into effeft ?

Two of the principals, fays he, were C. Silius and T. Sabinus – the former had commanded feven years in Germany – the latter, lays Dion, was a leading man at Rome – av5jiof *rut trfurw, tv Paw.* – Sofia Galla, the wife of Silius, was, fays Tacitus, ajfo accufed, by Sejanus, of being an accomplice. Silius and his wife were, fays he, tried immediately – T. Sabinus, about three years after. But were thofe the only ones concerned ? – Was not Calpurnius Pifo of the party ? – If we may believe Patfrculus, ii. 130, Silius and Pifo feem to have been the

The rise of Syanus.

chief confpirators, if not the only ones – Primum, ut fcelerata Drufus Libo iniret confilia: deinde, ut Silius et Pifo : quorum alterius dignitatem conflituit, auxit alterius ? – Indeed Tacitus himfelf feems to acknowledge, C. 21, that Pifo was much more likely to have been immediately concerned in the confpiracy than Sabinus, for h$ fays that he was tried immediately after Silius and his wife – npt for his attachment to the family of Germanicus, we may well fuppofe, unlefs he was related to Pifo, the governor of Syria, as he pretends they were, nor by the contrivance of Sejanus, but for having confpared againft Caefar – and, for having gone armed into the Senate-houfe – and on the evidence of Q. Granius. – Prifonem Q. Granius fecreti fermonis incufavit adverfum majeftatem habiti: adjecitque in domo venenurri efle, eumque gladio accinftum introire curiam.

Sejanus then feems to have had nothing to do with the accufation of Pifo, and, if fo, and Pifo was, as Paterculus fays, in a confpiracy with Silius, may we not fufpeft that he did not accufe Silius ?

In the i ith year, fays Tacitus, iv. 39, Sejanus, who, we have feen, was, from his infancy, brought up with the imperial family – and who, three or four years before, had been adv-ifed, by Tiberius, to engage his daughter to a fon of Claudius, the brother of Livilla, was, fays he, importuned by Livilla to fulfill his promife of marrying her. – Sejanus, in compliance with her requeft, prefented a petition to Tiberius to obtain his confent. – Tiberius, fays Tacitus, delicately ftated what might be objefted to the alliance, and referred him to Antonia and Livia, as the perfgns nearer concerned; and concluded, not only with declaring that he would not, at a future time, oppofe the match – but with afifuring him that he would do great things for him. – Their attachment to each other, fays Suetonius, iii. 65, continued till the year in which Sejanus fell, even though they both were, as Dion fays, 1. 58,/

The rise of Sejanus.

p. 637, notorious adulterers – and Livilla, it feems, though at the time not married, with not a few, who were afterwards punifhed for it ?- – Whether they ever were afterwards married we fhall come to enquire prefently.

About a year after, that is, in the t2th of Tiberius, Sejanus demon- iirated his attachment to Tiberius in a moft remarkable manner: by rifquing his own life to fave that of Tiberius, when the roof of the grotto fell on him in Campania, and many of his friends and attendants were wounded. – So high an opinion had Tiberius, fays Tacitus, of this fervice rendered him by Sejanus, that he commiffioned him to contrive the deftruftion of the family of Germanicus, and efpecially of Nero, the next in fucceffion, who, he fays, was, at the time, ftimu- lated by his freedmen and clients to feize the prefent opportunity of (hewing his fpirit, and afiured by them that the people of Rome and the army would fupport him. – But what kind of a recompence was this for having rendered him fo vital a fervice ? – Would it not have been much more acceptable to Sejanus if Tiberius had immediately confented to his marriage with

Livilla ? – and endeavored to obtain the confent of Antonia? – which, it feems, could hardly have been necef- fary, for as fhe was always much attached to Tiberius, and could not but have known that the only daughter of Sejanus was, by the approbation of Tiberius, about to be married to her grandfon Drufus, fhe, no doubt, would have been very glad to reward fuch fervice with fuch an alliance. – Why then fhould Tiberius be faid to have propofed fuch a thing to him as a reward for his important fervice, which could only have tended to deprive him of his pleafanteft profpeft. – Was it at all likely that the dependants of Nero could have attempted to per- fuade him that it was a proper time to oppofe his uncle ?- – or, that he

The rise of Syanus.

would be fupported by the Romans? – If there was the leaft danger of an infurreftion why did Tiberius, who, Tacitus fays, A. iv. 67, ufed to be full of fufpicions at Rome – Manebat quippe fufpicionum et cre- dendi temeritas – leave Rome, and with the commander of his guards? And, above all, why, if the people of Rome were inclined to fide with Nero, did they, when the Amphitheatre at Fidenae fell, and when the buildings on Mount Coelius were burnt, petition Tiberius to alleviate their fufferings?

No fooner had this new office been propofed to Sejanus than he entered on it, not with reluftance, but with zeal, not clandeftinely, but openly; and fet fpies on Nero, and even employed his brother Drufus, and his wife (who, Tacitus feems to fay, iv. 60, was the daughter of Livia or Livilla,) to difclofe his fecrets. – And, a few months after, he fet a military guard over not only him but alfo his mother.

In the beginning of the year 781, fays Tacitus, Titius Sabinus, an illuftrlous knight, who had, more than three years before, been accu- fed of confpiring with Agrippina and others, in favor of Nero and Drufus, was, as Tacitus pretends, imprifoned for continuing ftill his adherence to the family of Germanicus – or, rather for having fuffered himfelf to be decoyed to fpeak honorably of Germanicus and his family, and moft difhonorably of Sejanus, and even difrefpeftfully of Tiberius. – The particulars of his hard cafe, as related by Tacitus, we have had occafion to confider in two foregoing chapters – viz – vii. ix. – But as we, in thofe two chapters, were not fo much concerned about the elucidation of the character of Sejanus, as that of Tiberius, we omitted to notice what other writers had and had not faid of the part which Sejanus took in the accufation. – Let us therefore now attend to what one or two cotemporary writers fay of thfc affair – and alfo what Dion fays of it.

The rise of Sejanus.

Seneca, though he wrote his Confolation to Mama about the very time, and in it accufes Sejanus of having been the caufe of the death of Cordus, for fpeaking too freely of thofe in power, and of feeding his dogs with human blood, to make them more favage towards thofe he hated, has not noticed the fate of this knight. – Pliny, who, we have feen, fays that Sabinus was profecuted – *ex caufa Neronis* – has noticed it, but only for the fake of recording the fidelity of his dog, to the no little aftoniihment of the immenfe number of fpeftators who, regardlefs of the fate of Sabinus, flood obferving its motions. – Dion fays not a word of the attachment of Sabinus to the family of Germanic us, nor of the hoftility of Sejanus to him, nor of his perfecution of him on that account – neither does he fay that Sabinus was accufed of having charged either Sejanus or Tiberius of unjuft feverity towards the family of Germanicus. – He, however, feems to fay, that Sejanus had fome kind of diffike to Sabinus – that thofe fenatorial accufers firft began to calumniate any one in order to pleafe Sejanus – that the circumvented perfons were fure to be punifhed if they faid ever fo little in addition to their calumnies – S, rt xi To *favmroi it i* T x0er, i- xoror *tiirairi* xoX$oiTai. – Such, fays Dion, was the conduct of thofe fenatorial fycophants, not only *towards Sabinus,* the only, as Tacitus fays, remaining adherent of the family of Germanicus, but *towards all other people.*

This is the account which Dion gives of this affair. – How very different is it from that of Tacitus! – Tacitus, we find, fays, that Sabinus was the only perfon circumvented by thofe fenators. – Dion fays that he was far from being the only perfon – that they made a fort of trade of accufing. – Tacitus fays that he was decoyed to the houfe of Latiaris, as being notorioufly attached to the family of Germanicus, and, indeed, as being the only remaining client fo attached. – Dion

The rise of Sejanus.

fays nothing pf his attachment to that family, nor of his contumeltous reproaches of Sejanus and Tiberius.

But where was Sejanus while thofe doings were, by his inftigation, tranfafting at Rome? – If we may believe Tacitus, he was, with Tiberius, at Capreae, and feemingly afraid, as well as Tiberius, to confent to an interview with the Senate, &c.; and fo unable to proteft his few dependants, who were permitted to fee him, that he could not prevent the grievous exit that awaited, them.

In the year 782, fays Tacitus, v. 4, Sejanus was, notwithftanding his being guarded by dogs fed with human blood, clandeftinely attacked by anonymous writers – of this it is not faid that he complained; but of the ill ufage which his patron had received, it is faid that he did complain.

In this and the next year – viz – 782, 783, Dion tells us, 1. 58, that the moft unufual honors were beftowed on him both- by Tiberius and the Senate, &c.

Sejanus then, the commander of the pratorian guards and the privy co-unfellor of Tiberius, was, if we may believe Tacitus, after the death of Livia, infulted, together with Tiberius, by the Senate and by the ' people, both openly and by libels, becaufe, as he would have us to think, Agrippina and Nero were accufed of fomething, not of a capital nature, though, if we may believe Patercujus, ii. 130, of a very dif- honorable nature, committed a long while before the death of Livia. But how does this report agree with that of Paterculus, or with that of Dion? – Paterculus, we find, in the end of the year 783, enumerates the praifes of Tiberius and of his prime minuter, and fpeaks very dif- refpeftfully of the conduct of Agrippina and Nero. – And Dion, we find, fays 1. 58, p. 622, A., that Sejanus, tfhortly if not immediately

The rise of Sejanus.

after the death of Livia, began to be ftill more lifted up – a & *in Km* fiaWvot *vft-n.* – And, a little after, in the fame page, B., he fays, that the Senate decreed that his birth-day fhould be kept, and that an innumerable multitude of ftatues were erefted to him, by the patricians, the knights, all the tribes, and the principal men. – The Senate, fays he, the knights, the tribunes of the people, and the aediles fent deputies to him, as well as to Tiberius, oflered up vows for both, facrificed to both, fwore by their fortunes. – And again he fays, in the next page, 623, C., that deceived and credulous people, in the year 784, erected ftatues of brafs to them, and procured their portraits, and placed gilded chairs of ftate for them in the Theatre – and, that thte Senate decreed that their confulfhip fhould be continued for five years – that their body ihould go in proceffion to meet them whenever they Ihould enter the city – and that they ihould facrifice to them alike. – Surely then there appears to be a no little difference between the report of Tacitus and thofe of Paterculus and Dion.

The laft obfervable thing that Tacitus fays of Sejanus is that he was, at laft, the fon-in-law of Tiberius – Non enim Sejanum Vulfinienfem, fed Claudia e et Juliae domus partem, quas adfmitate occupaverat, *tuum Cafar generum* tui confulatus focium, tua officia in republica capef- fentem colebamus. A. vi. 8.

On a review of all that has been faid concerning the rife of Sejanus it appears that he was a companion of Caius – that is, of the grandfon of Auguftus, of the fon-in-law of Tiberius, and of the firft hufband of Livilla – that he was a great favorite both with Auguftus and with Tiberius, and, as Dion fays, 1. 57, p. 616, D., becaufe he was, in, difpofition, like Tiberius – that he was the reftor of Drufus, whofe widdw, Livilla, he, juft before his own fall, married, by the confent of Tiberius, obtained foon after the death of Drufus. – As then Sejanus

The rise of Sejanus.

was, at laft, married to Li villa, by the confent of Tiberius, and, no doubt, of Antonia, her mother – let us next proceed to obferve whether what Tacitus fays of the murder of Drufus be fp credible as he would have us to believe; and, whether any or all of the three perfons, Sejanus, Livilla, and Tiberius, faid to have been concerned in it, were really fo or not.

19

SECTION 19

CHAPTER XX.
Drusus whether poisoned?
is, by Tacitus, iv. 8, faid to have been *long* ill – per *omnes* valetudinis ejus dies. – Indeed it appears, by what he fays of him, iii. 49, that his death had been more than a year before – that is, in the end of that in which he and his father were confuls, generally expefted – and by Suetonius, iii. 62, to have been thought, even by Tiberius, to have died of intemperance – what reafon then have we to think that he died of poifon ? – Had it been fufpefted, at the time, would not an enquiry have been made ? – The caufe of the death of Germanicus, who was not invefted with tribunitial authority, we are told, was, on the return of Pifo, moft carefully inveftigated by the Senate. Why then, if there was the leaft reafon to fufpeft that Drufus had died by the fame means, did not the Senate, who had, but the fecond year before, as Tacitus and Dion fay, put C. Lutorius to death for only compofing an epitaph on him – and who, but the year before, decreed him all and the moft unufual marks of honor – who, as Taci-
Hhh
, *Drusus whether poisoned?*
tus fays, iv. 6, ftill retained the privilege of difcuffing public and the more important private matters, and who, as Tacitus alfo fays, iv. 9, decreed him many more funeral

honors than they had decreed to Ger- manicus, make a fimilar invedigation? – But, fays Tacitus, iv. 10, there was, *at the fame ttme,* a report that Tiberius himfelf adminiftred the poifon – and confequently, it muft have been, at that time, believed that he was poifoned – fed non qmiferim *eorumdem temporum* rumorem adeo validum, ut nondum exolefcat, &c. – But does this pretended rumour agree with what Suetonius fays, iii. 52 ? – he there fays, that people of all parts fent addrefles to Tiberius condoling with him on the lofs of his only fon; and, that the people of Ilium were fo tardy in prefenting their addrefs, that Tiberius pleafantly replied to it that he alfo was forry for their lofs of Heftor.

That Drufus then was poifoned why fhould we be expefted to believe ? – Tacitus and others, however, fay, that he was poifoned. – Tacitus alfo fays that Sejanus, after he was employed as prime-minifter, contrived to get it done – that he did it, in hope of having the fole direftion of public bufinefs – and that he firft feduced and debauched Livilla – and that he then, though married himfelf, promifed her marriage, and a mare in the fovereignty – ad conjugii fpem, cqnfortium regni, et necem mariti pellexit – if me would only affift him in poifon- ing her own hufband, and coufin, by whom fhe had three children. Suetonius, however, feems pretty clearly to differ from Tacitus – he feems to aflert, iii. 55, that Sejanus was not employed till after the death of Drufus – for he there fays of him, that he was employed not only to circumvent the fons of Germanicus, but to fecure the fuccef- fion for the fon of Drufus – nepotemque fuum ex Drufo filium natu- ralem ad fucceffionem imperil confirmaret. – Now if Sejanus was really employed for this purpofe, muft he not have been employed after the detah of Drufus. – Why then does Tacitus tell us that he was mads

Drusus whether poisoned?

prime-minifter before the death of Drufus? – But, admitting that Tacitus is right, if Drufus was then fo very ill, of what ltfe was it to think of poifoning him – befides, is it at all credible that Sejanus would, as foon as he had been made prime-minifter, have made fuch a propofal? And, at a time too when he was, in all probability, employed, becaufe Drufus was unable to attend to the affairs of the ftate? – Or that Livilla would have confented to it ? – Was he indeed fur'e that he mould, by murdering Drufus, fecure to himfelf the fucceffion ? – If fo, why does Tacitus fay, in the beginning of this fame chapter – Ceterum plena Caefarum domus – nepotes adulti, &c.; – and again, chapter 12, that he afterwards thought it neceflary to fet afide the fons of Germanicus – quorum non dubia fucceffio ? – Could Sejaaus have thought that Livilla, the wife of the heir apparent Drufus, the mother of the next in fucceffion, and the aunt of Nero, Drufus, and Caius, would have exchanged her profpeft of fucceeding to the empire by a legal claim, for one which was likely to be difputed? – and, at the expence of injuring the claims of her own fon, and that of her brother's fons? – or, as Tacitus himfelf exprefles it in the fequel of the fame chapterr-ut pro honeftis et pnefentibus, flagitiofa et incerta expcftaret – and at a time too when Tiberius had done every thing praifeworthy, and nothing to offend the people – and Sejanus was but recently employed?

Tacitus afterwards fays, in the fame chapter, that Sejanus, before the death Jf Drufus, if not before his illicit connexion with Livilla, turned his wife Apicata, by whom he had three children, out of doors – and, that he did it, in order to avoid giving

Livilla any fufpicion – pellit domo Apicatam, ex qua tres liberos genuerat, *ne pelllci fuf/tefla- rctur.* – How then could fhe be fuppofed to have known any thing of the fuppofed murder of Drufus? – efpecially as it appears, by what he*Drusus whether poisoned?*

fays in the end of the fame chapter, iv. 3 – viz – Sed magnitude fad- noris metum, prolationes, diverfa interdum confilia adferebat – that the murder was not perpetrated till fome time after her cruel extrufion took place ? – Now after he had faid this, who would have expefted that he would have faid that Apicata alone difcovered the whole tranf- aftion ? – And yet, we find, he does fay fo, chapter 11 – Ordo alioqui fceleris per Apicatam Sejani proditus, tormentis Eudemi et Lygdi pate- faftus eft. – And, ftrange to fay, fhe did not make the murder known immediately, but, as he fays, chap. 8, after an interval of eight years – id Drufo datum per Lygdum fpadonem, ut ofto poft annos cognitura eft. – But, admitting that fhe was let into the fecret, what reafon could. flte have had for concealing this moft atrocious deed from Tiberius, while he was the bed of princes, for Tacitus himfelf fays, that Tiberius continued fuch till the death of Drufus – Quee cunfta reti-

nebat, donee morte Drufi verterentur: nam dum fuperfuit, manfere – and for informing him of it when he had ceafed to be a very good prince and delighted in nothing but cruelty ? – And when he had no longer an opportunity of exercifing his cruelty on the principal perpetrators of fo foul a murder? – If we may believe Dion, 1. 58, p. 628, D., fhe did it in order to be revenged on Tiberius for the lofs of her own children, all three of whom, as V. Maximus, we have feen, fays, were, together with their father, without authority from Tiberius, trod to death by the enraged populace – or rather, perhaps, as, Tacitus, we have feen, fays, two were permitted to furvive, till the rage of the populace had fubfided, and were then, by a decree of the Senate, put "lo death. – Why then, as Tiberius appears to have given no order for the execution of her children, fhould Apicata be faid to have made the difcovery out of revenge to him? – If fhe was at all aftuated by revenge why did fhe not make the difcovery while the perpetrators of the murder were ftill living? – efpecially if they were fo notorioufly in-

Drusus whether poisoned?

famous, as Djion reprefents them to have been; – at 1. 58, p. 623, A., he fays, of him, that he promifed marriage to all the married ladies of Rome – and, at p. 637, A., of her, that fhe, no doubt, while the wife of Drufus, committed adultery not only with Sejanus, but with Scaurus, and with many other men, who, he alfo fays, were, ten years after the death of Drufus, punifhed for it.

In fhort – that Apicata fhould, of all others, be alone in poffeffion of the fecret is what nobody will believe – and, that fhe kept the fecret, under ail tliofe circumftances, for eight years, is what nobody can believe.

This is the report which Tacitus and Dion have recorded as the only authentic one. – But though this is delivered by Tacitus as the only written one that had reached his time, yet it appears, by what he afterwards fays, chapter 10, that it was not the only one – he there fays, that, *at the fame ttme,* another report prevailed – and that though no writer, however adverfe – infenfus – to Tiberius, had noticed it, it was fo much credited by the vulgar, that it had reached his time. – It is this – that Sejanus having preconcerted the matter with Livilla, perfuaded Tiberius that Drufus had invited him to a banquet for the purpofe of murdering him – that Lygdus, his eunuch, was ordered to mix the poifon in the firft cup called for – that Tiberius, thus ap- prifed, ordered the cup to be delivered to his foil – -that Drufus, to avoid fufpicion, drank it.

But could it have been poffible for Sejanus, who, Tacitus acknowledges, was not a match for Tiberius in canning, to have perfuaded, fo eafily, the moft fagacious of princes, that his only child, then in the laft ftage of debility, meant to invite him to a banquet merely tb poifon him ? – Or would Tiberius, who, as Tacitus himfelf allows, was, at the time, only about to begin to be a bad prince, and, but theJDrwsus *whether poisoned?*

year before, recommended his fon to the Senate as a proper perfon to be invefted with the tribunitial authority, have liftened, as Tacitus himfelf obferves, to fo abfurd a ftory concerning his only child ? – And if he would, would he have precipitately put him to death ? – If it had been thought, at the time, that he had been inftigated, by any one, to be the ram caufe of the death of his only child, would all the different ftates have fent addrefles of condolence to him on the occa- fion? – Or would they, if they had heard that fome other perfon or perfons had done it, have prefented fuch addrefles without expreffing their abhorrence of the crime, and of the author? – This evidence alone of Suetonius is fufficient to render the credibility of this vulgar report not a little queftionable. – But in his 6tft and 62d chapters he gives a much more direft refutation of it – 6tft, he fays, that Tiberius was, after the deftruftion of Sejanus, the mrvfr. cruel – and, chap. 6zV that after he was informed by what means his fon had been murdered he was ftill more cruel – that he fpent whole days in the enquiry – that he put every one to the torture who were charged with being concerned in it – and, among the reft, an unfortunate Rhodian friend, who happened . to call on him by invitation at the nick of time. – Butv after all that has been faid of this traditionary report, the other account which Tacitus gives of this matter, on the authority of former writers – viz – that it was, eight years after, difcovered that Sejanus and Livilla were the perpetrators of it, is, though he does not feem to have been aware of it, a direct refutation of at leaft the continuance of it. – For if Tiberius, eight years after, tormented Lygdus and Eude- mus, on the information of Apicata – and, as Suetonius fays, fpent many days together in the enquiry, and fpared nobody, not even an innocent friend, how could any perfon, after all that, have any longer thought that he himfelf was guilty of it ? – And yet Tacitus himfelf devotes a chapter to prove the tradition unfounded – thereby expofing

Drusus whether poisoned?

the dimnefs of his own fagacity – and, confequently difpofing people to queftion the credibility of his other report. – For if it was, at the time, commonly thought at Rome that Tiberius himfelf had poifoned his fon, how muft they have been furprifed to hear that Sejanus and Livilla had done it ? – and interefted to know how the difcovery was made ? And when they were told that Apicata was privy to the whole affair, would they not have been more aftonifhed, and ftill more fo that fhe mould, under fuch ufage, have concealed it fo long ? – and when they were alfo told that me had not difclofed the affair to any neighbour, but to Tiberius himfelf, at Capreae – and, as Dion fays, 1. 58, p. 628, D., by a letter, would they not be inquifitive to know by what means fhe contrived to fend it ? – And above all, when they were informed, as Dion alfo fays, that fhe did it by way 'of revenging the lofs of her children, who had been killed by thofe very people and by the Senate, and that me had-deftroyed herfelf immediately, would they not have been inclined to pity her as infane? – And if the roman people thought fo of her, would not the moft fagacious Tiberius? – Is this then a flory fit to be recorded by an impartial hiftorian ? – Is it not rather fuch an one as none but the calumniating fcriblers, mentioned by Tacitus, iv. n, would have noticed?

Having now difcovered that it would be abfurd to fuppofe that fuch a report could have prevailed after the torturing of Lygdus, &c. and the innocent Rhodian. – Let us next proceed to enquire how far it is likely that it could have prevailed prior to the difcovery.

Paterculus, we find, obferved to *tyL*. Vinicius how Tiberius grieved for the lofs of his only fon. – Ut ad majora tranfcendam quanquam et hoec ille duxit maxima: quid ut juvenes *amhteret* filios? quid ut nepo- tem ex DrufoySw? Dolenda adhuc retulimus: veniendum ad erubef- cenda eft, ficc. – Now if Tiberius had, in the i6th year of hiy reign,*Drusus whether poisoned ?*

been thought to have been acceflary to the death of his only fon, would Paterculus have written thus to M. Vinicius, who probably was, at the time, about to form a family connexion with Julia the daughter of Germanicus?

Jofephus alfo fays, A. xxiii. 7, ., how much Tiberius felt for the lofs of his only fon. He gives us to underftand that he was, for fome time, inconfolable on that account. He tells us that he could not fuffer any of his intimates in his fight – that Agrippa, the moft intimate, was, on that account, obliged to leave Italy ; – and again – 5 – Jofephus fays, how heartily he welcomed Agrippa, on his return to Puteoli, to Capreae, as the acquaintance of his fon.

Suetonius, in feveral places, fays enough to convince us that he cither never heard of this report or confidered it as too abfurd to be noticed – chap. 39, he fays – Sed orbatus utroque filio: quorum Germanicus in Syria, Drufus Romae obierat: feceflum Campaniae petiit: – chap. 52, he fays, that Tiberius did not love Drufus with a fatherly affeftion, and why – becaufe he was difpleafed at his vicious conduft – Alterius vitiis infenfus – chap. 54, that he was deprived of his children by death – deftitutus morte liberorum – chap. 55, he fays, that Tiberius employed Sejanus in order to fecure the fucceffion for his grandfon – nepotemque-fuum ex Drufo filium naturalem ad fuccef- fionem Imperii confirmaret. He alfo fays, 62, that he thought Drufus died by a diforder caufed by intemperance, and that when, at laft, he was informed that he died by poifon, and that Sejanus and Liyilla, then both dead, had adminiftered it to him, he put every perfon fuf- pefted to have been an accomplice to the torture, and, by chance, an unfufpefted Rhodian vifitor, who happened . to come in while the in-

Dion says, 1. 57, p. 6)8, B., *xau Tv tflt, xn xxt povu xAt ynina vtn, XtlTU.*

Drusus uhether poisoned?

quiry was on foot. Confequently, it appears, by this evidence of Suetonius, that Tiberius was never fufpefted to have been the caufe of the death of his own fon.

Dion too fays, 1. 57, p. 610, D., that Tiberius ufed frequently to reprove Drufus, both publicly and privately, for his petulance and cruelty – and, that he once faid to him – you Ihall not do fo, young man, as long as I live, nor, if I can prevent it, after I am gone – and though he acknowledges, p. 618, A. B., that Tiberius was, by fome, thought to have been the voluntary caufe of the death of his only fon – and, becaufe he feems to have taken fo little notice of it. But, continues Dion, that he was fo I cannot believe – *twrot* Ttij-os *o* Xoyoi – becaufe he behaved in the fame manner towards every one of his departed friends – becaufe he loved exceedingly his only fon – and becaufe he punifhed feverely all thofe who were afterwards found to have been concerned in the murder – fome immediately, fome afterward – *res pn ivQvr, rus* St *pirot roivra*

Indeed that Tiberius fhould, in the 65th year of his age and the *gth* of his reign, when, as Tacitus fays, he began to be no longer a very excellent prince – and ftill gave, as Tacitus further fays, chapter u, proofs of his impartial adminiftration of juftice, and was, as he alfo fays, fo dilatory in punifhing all other offences, have been fo precipitate as to poifon his only fon, who had never offended him – infita denique etiam-in extraneos cunftatione et mora, adverfum unicum, et nullius ante flagitii compertum uteretur – and but a few months after he had obtained for him the tribunitial authority, is what nobody, as Tacitus acknowledges, iv. n, can fuppofe.

But what proof have we that Livilla was known to have been concerned in the murder of her hufband ? – Had fhe been proved an ac-

Drusus whether poisoned?

ceflary, may we not expeft to find fome mark of infamy fixed on her memory ? – as, we find, Tacitus fays, A. xi. 38, the Senate afterwards affixed on that of the infamous Meflalina ? – Juvitque oblivionem ejus fenatus, cenfendo nomen et effigies privatis ac publicis locis derno- vendas.

In the beginning of the year after the death of Sejanus – that is, about two or three months after his death, fays Tacitus, vi. 2, the Senate made fome very fevere refleftions on the effigies and memory of Livilia, as if her flagitious praftices had lately been detefted, and had not for a long while been punifhed – At Romae principio anni, quafi recens cognitis Liviae flagitiis, ac non pridem etiam punitis, atro- ces fententiae dicebantur in effigies ac m'emoriam ejus. – By this it appears that Livilia died not long before, but whether before or after the death of Sejanus it is not faid – (certainly before the death of Apl- cata, and, if Dion's report be true, before thofe of the two furviving children of Sejanus,) and, that when fhe died the ufual refpefts were paid to her memory, as if fhe was neither fufpefted of the death of Drufus, nor of thofe numerous adulteries for which fo many, as Dion fays, were afterwards punifhed. Soon after, indeed, her fcandalous praftices and her murder was known – yet they do not appear to have been noticed by Tiberius, though fo exafperated againft all her accomplices, for he ftill permitted her effigies to remain. But though Tiberius did not notice her infamous conduft, yet the Senate, it feems, did. And why ? – Djd they attempt to prove the illegitimacy of the young Tiberius ? – And for the purpofe of excluding him from the fucceffion ? – For it feems her flagitious praftices had been cornrriitted a long while before, and fhe was not married long enough to Sejanus to have had any iflue by him. But whatever they may have thought of the legitimacy of the young Tiberius, yet Tiberius himfelf, it feems, both by what Suetonius, iii. 55, and Tacitus, vi. 46, fay, had no doubt

Drusus whether poisoned?

of it. For Suetonius there ſays that he did not make choice of Sejanus as his miniſter becauſe he liked him, but becauſe he meant to uſe him as his tool to circumvent the family of Germanicus, and to ſecure the ſucceſſion for Tiberius, the ſon of Livilla – and Tacitus, ſpeaking of his grandſon and grandſon by adoption, ſays – of whom the ſon of Drufus, was by blood and natural affeſtion nearer, though ſtill a lad – quorum Drufo genitus, ſanguine et caritate propior, ſed nondum pubertatem ingreſſus – and in the ſequel, he ſays, of Tiberius, that he embraced his grandſon, and, with a flood of tears, ſaid to Caius – thou wilt murder my dear child – and another will murder thee – Occides hunc tu, inquit, et te alius.

20

SECTION 20

CHAPTER XXI.
Of the cause of the fall of Sejanus.

V MAXIMUS, who wrote within fix years after the fall of Sejanus, and dedicated his work to Tiberius, informs us, ix. u, that Sejanus had formed a plot to feize the reins of government. – Tu videlicet efferatz barbariae immanitate truculentior habenas R. imperil, quas princeps parenfque nofter falutari dextra continet, capere potu- ifti ? – He alfo fays that he intended to caufe fuch diftrefs *at Rome,* in particular, as had never been experienced in that city – that all the Gods were interefted in the difcovery of it – that Tiberius, *by divine monition,* forefaw – divino confilio providet – the danger which threatened his moft excellent fervices all the world over. And he alfo adds, that it was no fooner known at Rome, that Tiberius had detefted the perfidy of the treacherous minifter of the author and defence of their fafety, than all ranks of people, in that city, immediately flew to crufh him. And, laftly, that they trod not only on him, but on his whole family. V. Maximus alfo adds, that no fooner was Sejanus dead, than the fame happy ftate of public affairs was again reftored – Itaque flat pax, valent leges, fineerus privati ac publici officii tenor fervatur

Of the cause of the fall of Sejanus.

This is the account which V. Maximus, an eye witnefs of the tran$ aftion, gave, in a work dedicated to Tiberius himfelf, of the fall of this prime-minifter. An account which plainly intimates that Sejanus meant to affume power which belonged to Tiberius, that Maximus thought the Gods were concerned in the difcovery – that the people of Rome ought to be very thankful for it – that they confidered Tiberius as the beft of princes, if not that they were much prejudiced againft Sejanus – and which feems to intimate that he fell, not by a formal procefs, but under the fury of an enraged populace, and that none fell with him but his own children – and therefore feems to exculpate Tiberius, who was then at Capreae, from the imputation that he contrived the deftruftion of his family.

Seneca, another writer who lived at the time, fays – de tranq. vitae cap. n – that the Senate arrefted him – that, *on the fame day,* the people tore him to pieces – that *the Gads were witnefles* – and that *thefe was not enough of ht:n left for the hangman to draw through the jlreets.* – Quo die ilium fenatus deduxerat, populus in frufta divifit, in quem quicquid congeri poterat, *dtt* hominefque contulerant, ex eo nihil fuperfuit quod carnifex traheret, &c.

The account of Seneca, we find, pretty nearly agrees with that of V. Maximus.

Let us next hear what Philo, a jewifh cotemporary, fays of the death of this prime-minifter.

Philo, in his account of his Leg. to Caius, p. 785, F., fays, that Sejanus had, with much contrivance, formed a plot to introduce fome new fcheme or *impofition* – *mtx Zstams to-xeuufet mv tmQso-m.* – *And* how does he fay Sejanus hoped to effeft this deep laid plot ? – fcil – by ac- cufing the Jews of Rome falfely, as he fays – and by feeking the de*Of the cause of the fall of Sejanus.*

ftruftion of *that nation* – To *eQvos* – that is, as he fays in the beginning of his work againft Flaccus, the *whole* nation – *avptnw* To *cQms.* – And why did he feek the deftruftion of the Jews ? – Becaufe he was perfuaded that they would be *the only or chtef pratefiors of the emperor when his life was in danger by the difaffefled.* And this, it feems, by what Philo had immediately before faid, the Jews would, in all probability, have become – for he there not only fays that the people every where, even *thofe not well afefled to the yews, were not in hajle to ajfift any one in the heretical abolitton of their legal rites* – *tva$us* ttjot *mt xuQxtfeo-w tms rut itttixtxM* Vo/ai/awv v/porexi-fo-flt – he alfo fays that the fame indulgence was continued under Tiberius, though they of Italy were in commotion when Sejanus contrived the impofition. If then the Jews had, as Philo fays, been always tolerated by Tiberius in the exercife of their religious fingularities, (and that they were fo both Agrippa and Tacitus fay,) no wonder that they were fo much attached to Tiberius – and, that Sejanus was fo much afraid of them.

This is pretty nearly the fum of what Philo offers on this myfterious point. By which it appears that Sejanus meditated a revolution or impofition of fome kind – and that he, by way of accomplifhing his pur- pofe, thought it neceflary to deftroy not the Jews of Rome only, but the *whole nation* of the Jews, (which, Philo himfelf allows, was then not only tolerated but refpefted every where,) beginning with thofe of Rome and Italy, as being better affefted to Tiberius than any other people, even than Romans.

Under what pretence he hoped to obtain permiffion of his fovereign, who, it feems, was ever fond of the Jews and of their religion, to do it, Philo does not fay.

Having now heard what thofe three cotemporaries fay of the caufe of the fall of Sejanus – let us attend to what four or five later writers fay of it. – And firft let us hear what Jofephus fays of it.

Of the cause of the fall of Syanus.

Jofephus affirms, A. xviii. 7, *s.*, that Sejanus entered into a great confpiracy againft his fovereign, whom he reprefents, 7, *Q.*, as a fort of minor prophet – or, a foreteller of future events – fw/SaXw *yaf ptya-* Xtu *o-vrms ex aunt wtn* Ztnav8 – he alfo fays that moft of the *fenators andfreedmen* confpired with him – and that the army was corrupted –

xjst Tnv (3aXtK 0i TroAXot xzt Toiv *atn.* *vQt(ut -rrfotnQctrv, xt To rfatnwTtxAv StfipQafro.*

This confpiracy, he adds, Antonia, the mother of Livilla, difcovered. And in the next chapter – viz – 8, *ft.,* Jofephus alfo fays, that Herod, the tetrarch of Galilee, was, by Agrippa, accufed to Caius, of having been privy to the plot of Sejanus. – Laftly, he fays, B. ii. 9, *.,* that Agrippa had before gone to Tiberius to accufe Herod, of, no doubt, difaifeftion, and that Tiberius paid no attention to him. Indeed fo far does he, by what Jofephus fays, A., feem to have been from believing any report of this kind, that he, in the year following, fent Vitellius to affift Herod againft Arctas.

Jofephus then, we find, is another witnefs that Sejanus confpired againft Tiberius – and with moft of the fenators and freedmen, or libertines. He alfo fays, that the army in general were corrupted. But that the Jews were then remarkably attached to Tiberius, and, that they were, on that account, at the inftigation of Sejanus, e::pelled from Rome, he does not fay. On the contrary, he feems to fay, that thofe of Galilee were fo hoftile to Tiberius as to have fided with Sejanus. Befides he does not feem to agree with Philo as to the time when they were expelled, by introducing his account of it immediately after that of the death of our Lord. In the 3d §. he gives an account of the death and revival of our Lord, and the 4th §. he begins with thofe words – *Km wo rac auras yftas* – and ends with xaTa Tartv j0iovov – where he propofes to fpeak of the expulfion of his countrymen. Moreover, he fays, that the confuls not only fent 4,000 enlifted, and therefore*Of the cause of the fall of Sejanus.*

libertine Jews, *to* Sardinia, an imperial province – but that they punifhed others for refilfing, in obedience to Mofes, to enlift. Now the confuls, in the beginning of the year in which Sejanus perifhed, were Tiberius and Sejanus, and their fuffefti, when he fell, were Regu- lus and Trio, of whom the former was, as Tacitus and Dion fay, in the intereft of Tiberius, and the . latter in the intereft of Sejanus. – Laftly, in his account of the expulfion of the Jews, he neither intimates that the confpiracy of Sejanus then took place – nor, in his account of the confpiracy of Sejanus, does he intimate that Sejanus had any thing to do with the expulfion of the Jews – on the contrary, he fays, that Saturninus, a confular man, complained to Tiberius of the mifconduft of three or four vagabond Jews, who pretended to be ' Rabbies, towards Fulvia, his wife, who, it feems, was a profelyte, and by that means only procured the expulfion of all the Jews from Rome.

Jofephus then, we find, appears to have contradifted all his prede- ceflbrs not a little – the two Roman writers, by faying, that Antonia difcovered the confpiracy – and his own countryman, in every other particular.

Let us next hear what Juvenal fays was the caufe of his fall.

Juvenal, who it may not be amifs to obferve, appears to have been born within a very few years after the death of Tiberius, in his xth fatire, fpeaks of the vaft power and of the unexpected fall of Sejanus. His fall he feems to attribute to treafonable praftices, for he fpeaks of him as the enemy of Caefar – Caefaris hoftem – and as having fought the extinftion of the fecure old age of the prince – fi oppreffa foret fecura feneftus Principis. He alfo defcribes the very different behavior of the Roman populace towards him, juft before and after it took place. Juft before his fall, he fays, every body worfhipped him, but

Of the cause of the fall of Sejanus.

no fooner was he executed, and his *body drawn by the executioner,* than all rejoiced at it, and haftened to infult his dead body, *as it lay in the bank of the Tybcr,* and even without knowing the caufe of his fall – for, at v. 68, &c. he reprefents an inhabitant of Rome as expreffing the inveteracy of his diflike to him while living," and as queftioning his neighbour concerning the caufe &c. of his unexpefted death – and, at v. 71, he reprefents the neighbour as incapable of giving him any other fatisfaftory information on the point, but that a long epiftle had arrived from the fecure emperor, furrounded by a fet ot Chaldeans at Capreae.

By this teftimony of Juvenal it appears that he took it for granted, though it was not publicly known at Rome a little after he fell what was the nature of his offence, that it was of a treafonable nature – that it was underftood at Rome that a prolix epiftle of Tiberius to the Senate was the caufe of his death – and, that his body, after having been dragged by the executioner through the ftreets of Rome, lay on the bank of the Tyber, where it was infulted by the populace. By this it alfo appears that Tiberius would not take any flep againft Sejanus before he had apprifed the Senate of his mifconduft.

Juvenal afterwards adds – Perituros audio multos – by which he feems to intimate that Sejanus fell alone. He alfo feems to fay that the people were almoft afraid to converfe with each other on the fub-

jeft.

Hi fcrmones

Tune de Scjano: fecreta hxc murmura vu'gi. Let us now hear what Suetonius fays of this affair.

He affirms, iii. 65, that Sejanus, who, he fays, was one of the twenty privy counfellors of Tiberius, had entered into a confpiracy

Kkk

Of the cause of the fall of Sejanus.

with *others* to effeft a revolution. Who thofe accomplices were – and, by what means he intended to accomplifh his nefarious purpofe, Suetonius'does not fay here. But, hi his life of Caius, chap. 30, he feems to fay that moft of the Senate were privy to it – for he there fays that Caius ufed often to inveigh againft all the fenators alike, as having been the clients of Sejanus, and the accufers of his mother and brethren – Saepe in cunftos pariter fenatores, ut Sejani clientes, aut – matris ac fratrum fuorum delatores inveſtus eſt. And, in the life of Vitel- lius, chapter 2, he ſays, that P. Vitellius, after he had diſcharged the praetorſhip, was apprehended as a conſpirator with Sejanus. The time when Tiberius ſuſpected him, he ſays, was juſt after the death of Livia, and juſt before his own laſt conſulate – for Tiberius, he ſays, ſaw that his birth-day was kept publicly – and Dion ſays, l. 58, p. 622, A., that the Senate, after the death of Livia, made a decree for that purpoſe. And the time when he began to contrive his deſtruction (for ſuch, it ſeems, was the power of his miniſter, and ſuch his own dread of tumults, that he could not do it ſpeedily) was juſt before his laſt conſulate. The manner in which he accompliſhed his deſtruction he proceeds next to deſcribe, and prefaces it with this obſervation – viz – that he did not do it by any princely means, but by craft and ſubtilty – aſtu magis ac dolo, quam principis majeſtate – for, firſt, he, ſubjoins Suetonius, diffident and apprehenſive of tumults as he was, inſtead of ſeizing him, diſmiſſed him from Capreae to Rome, where moſt of the other conſpirators, it ſeems, were – and, in order to make him his colleague in the conſulſhip. Having ſucceeded in this, he next gave him cauſe to hope to be allied to the royal family, (as, by the account of Tacitus, iv. 40, he had done ſeveral years, before,) which alliance, appears, by what Tacitus ſays, vi. 8, of the ſpeech of M. Terentius to the Senate, when he was accuſed of having been intimate with Sejanus, actually took place – Non enim Sejanum Vulſinienſem, ſed Clau-

Of the cauſe of the fall of Sejanus.

diae et Juliae domus partem, quas adfinitate occupaverat, *tuum Catſar gencrum,* tui conſulatus ſocium, tua officia in republics, capeſſentem colebamus – he alſo gave him reaſon to expect the tribunitial authority. And after having done all this, he unexpectedly criminated him in a paltry wretched epiſtle to that very Senate, who, as Cains uſed often to ſay, were all the creatures of Sejanus – and who, as Joſephus ſays, ware moſtly conſpirators with him – who, as Tacitus ſays, conſidered him as the only way to preferment – and who, as Dion ſays, had made a decree that his birth-day ſhould be publicly kept, and had been in the habit of paying him all ſorts of honors, not excepting even divine. And in the ſame epiſtle, he, adds Suetonius, deſired the fathers to ſend one of the conſuls, and without naming him, (hough Regulus only was his friend,) with a guard to conduct him, a ſolitary old man, into their preſence, when, at the very time, he had, ſays Suetonius, made preparations for quiting the country, and had uſed means to procure the earlieſt information concerning the ſucceſs of his epiſtle.

By this account of Suetonius, it appears that Sejanus, after the death of Livia, meditated, with certain leading men of Rome, a revolution – that Tiberius ſuſpected it while Sejanus was at Capreae with him – that is, juſt before they were colleagues in the conſulſhip – that Tiberius, crafty and fearful as he was, did not detain him at Capreae, but diſmiſſed him to Rome – that he then firſt made him his conſul, and then again gave him reaſon to expect to be allied to the imperial family, and to be inveſted with the tribunitial authority, and, if we may believe Tacitus, actually fulfilled his intimation by making him his ſon-in-law – that he did not attempt to deſtroy him till nearly eight months after he ſuſpected him, for Sejanus was not put to death till the middle of October, at which time Trio and Regulus were conſuls he then did It, not by his imperial power, but by writing to the *Of the cauſe of the fall of Sejanus.*

Senate, who, Suetonius himfelf, as well as others, acknowledges, were moftly the adherents of Sejanus. And, laftly, that Tiberius, diffident, fearful of tumults, ready to leave the country, and unwilling to leave Capreae, as he was, (for, he fays, he did not move out of the village in which he refided for nine months after,) with much craftinefs and fubtilty, requefted to be conduftedi- by one of the confuls and a guard of foldiers, from Caprex to the Senate-houfe. f

Suetonius, it mould be obferved, had before, chapter 48, faid that the praetorian guards remained all the while firmly attached to Tiberius, and that he handfomely rewarded them for their fidelity – praeter- quam fingula millia denariorum praetorianis, quod fe Sejano non ac- commodaflent. He alfo fays, immediately after, in the fame chapter, that he rewarded the legions in Syria for having refufed to ereft the ftandard of Sejanus. And, to his account of the manner in which he accomplifhed the deflruftion of Sejanus, he has fubjoined what looks like a proof that moft, if not all the legions of Italy, were firmly attached to him – Aptatis etiam navibus ad quafcunque legiones medi- tabatur fugam. If then Tiberius was fo well ferved by his life-guards, and by moft of the legions both in Italy and out of it, and was fo fearful of tumults, and fo apprehenfive about the refult, as to think of flying himfelf, and of leaving Drufus to difpute the fovereignty with his new uncle Sejanus, why mould he be fuppofed to have afted fo imprudently as to fend Sejanus to Rome ? – And then to have heaped

Verum et oppress! conjuratione Sejani, nihilo securior aut constantior, per novem proximos menses non egressus est villa quae vocatur Jovis.

t Tiberius tamen ludibria seriis permiscere solitus egit gratias benevolenlias patrum: sed quos omitti posse? quos deligi? se'inperne eosdem an subtnde alios? et honoribus perfunctos, an juvenes? privates an e majisl. rat. ibus? quam deinde speciem fore, sumentium in limine curia: gladios? neque sibt vitarn tanti, si armis tegenda foret. T. Ann. vi. 2.

Of the cause of the fall of Sejanus.

luch honors on him ? – Or, to have criminated him to the Senate, by an epiftle ? – Or, to have requefted the Senate to fend a guard to conduft his aged felf from Capreae to the Senate ?

Such is the unfatisfaftory account which Suetonius has given of this affair.

Let us now hear what Tacitus fays of it:

The account which Tacitus gave in his v. book, where he treats of the tranfaftions of the year in which Tiberius and Sejanus were con- fuls, of the caufe of the fall of Sejanus, is unfortunately loft – but though this is loft, yet he appears to have faid enough in his iv. v. and vi. books to convince us that Sejanus was accufed of confpiring either againft the ftate, or againft his fovereign. But of whatever he was accufed, it feems, by what he fays, A. iv. I, *his fall was as detrimental to the welfare of Rome as his proffierity had been* – cujus pari exitio floruit, ceciditque.

In the iv. 3, he fays of him, that he, to make way for his treacherous defign, contrived, nine years before, the death of Drufus – and that he enticed Livilla, the wife of Drufus and the daughter of Anto- nia, by the hope of becoming his wife and a partner of the fovereignty, to fecond his murderous defign – ad conjugii fpem, confortium regni, et necem mariti impulit. And though Tacitus would have it thought that Sejanus murdered Drufus to fecure the government, yet he fays, iv. 59, that he gave the rrioft unqueftionable proof of his regard for Tiberius, by faving his life at the hazard of his own. But what? – Could Sejanus have thought, that Livilla, the wife of the heir-apparent Drufus, the mother of the twin fons, and the aunt of Drufus, Nero, and Caius, would have exchanged her great profpeft of becoming the mother of the emperor for fb difhonorable a mode of proceeding-or,

Of the cause of the fall of Syanus.

as Tacitus fays, iv. 3 – ut pro honeftis et praefentibus, flagitiofa ct in- certa expeftaret – rand at the expence of injuring the claims of her own fons and that of her nephews? – This, if we may believe Tacitus, he did – but could not make good his promife, becaufe Tiberius would not give his confent. And though he was, as Tacitus fays, iv. 39, mad for women; and Livilla too, as he fays, iv. 29, committed adultery in her widowhood; and though he had, as he alfo fays, perfuaded Tiberius to retire from the fatigues of government to Capreae, under an expeftation that he mould have the aged monarch in his power, yet he never made the leaft attempt to cut him off for four or five years.

In the v. 8, Tacitus fays, that P. Vitellius, the paymafter of the forces, was, before the expiration of the year in which Sejanus fufrer- ed, accufed, *before the Senate,* of having not only encouraged revolutionary projefts – or, as Suetonius fays, vii. 2, of having been a con- ipirator with Sejanus – inter Sejani confcios – but of having embezzled the military treafure, and even of having applied it to fupport innovation. If he was guilty of peculation it might be eafily made to appear, and he deferved to be duly punifhed for it. And if he applied the public money to the worft of purpofes he deferved to be fevejely punimed. What then was his punifhment ? – He was, fay both Tacitus and Suetonius, placed m the cuftody *of his brother!* But was the Senate the proper body to take cognizance of this offence r – =Of infi- diae in republican! – they, no doubt, were. But were they fo of matters relating to the military ? – Does not Tacitus fay, vi. 3, that Tiberius was violently angry with Junius Gallic for making, in the beginning of the year following, a motion refpefting a new privilege for the difcharged life-guards, and imperioufly demanding of him, as if prefent – quid illi cum militibus – and as acding like a fatellite of Sejanus ?

Of the cause of the fall of Sejanus.

In the 9th, he fays, that the Senate, after the death of Sejanus, and when the popular fury had fubfided, and moft people were fatisfied, proceeded againft the *rejl of* his children – placitum pofthac ut in reli- quos Sejani liberos adverteretur. Now as he had before apprifed us, 5v. 3, that Sejanus had three children only by Apicata, one nly can have been put to death with Sejanus. .

In the nth chapter, he fays, that the two confuls, Regulus and Trio, who had been at variance a long while, became, before the end of the year in which Sejanus fell, publicly hoftile. Trio, in the Senate houfe, reflefted on Regulus for having been backward in oppofing the tools of Sejanus – ut fegnem Regulum ad opprimendos Sejani minif- tros. Regulus repelled the charge, and accufed Trio of having been an accomplice in the confpiracy – ut noxium conjurationis.

In the vi. book, he informs us how the effefts of Sejanus were dif- pofed of; and then, in feveral places, of the trials of thofe who had been either his aflbciates or accomplices; and then, in one or two, of the puniihments of fome of them.

In chapter 2, he informs us that the effefts of Sejanus had originally been depofited in the treafury – that Tiberius had caufed them to be taken from thence as confifcated – and that, a month or two after the death of Sejanus, a ftrong party in the Senate contended that the forfeited effe&s ought to be returned to the treafury – et bona Sejani ab- lata aerario, ut in fifcum cogerentur tanquam referret.

Chapter 8, he reprefents M. Terentius, who was accufed, before the Senate, of intimacy with Sejanus, as making a diftinftion between thofe who had been privy to his *recent* plot – and thofe. who had only fought his patronage – and as exculpating the latter, by the obferva- tion that Tiberius had himfelf, in a manner, fanftioned the praftice,

Of the cause of the fall of Sejanus.

by the very great honors which he had conferred on him – viz – by firft making him joint commander with his father of the life-guards – then praefeft both of the city and the army – then his colleague in the confulfhip – and, laftly, by permitting him to become, by marriage, a part of both the Claudian and Julian families, and his own fon-in-law – and even his deputy in the management of public bufinefs. And again he reprefents him as making the fame diftinftion in the conclu- fion of his fpeech as he had before made – viz – let plots againft the ftate, or againft the life of the emperor, be punifhed as they ought, but as for fociety with any friend of Caefar let it not be blamed.

Chapter 9, he fays, that the fathers were all unanimous in acquit. ting him – and, moreover, that they were alfo unanimous in fenten- cing his accufers, for this and other things, *either to be put to death or to be banijtied,*

In the i gth chapter, he fays, that Tiberius, in the courfe of the year following – viz – the fecond after the death of Sejanus, ordered all thofe that were imprifoned for aflbciating with Sejanus to be put to death – irritatufque fuppliciis cunftos qui carcere attinebantur ac- *cufati focietatis* cum Sejano, necari jubet. Of whom, it feems, by what follows, there was no fmall number of *every* fex, age, and condition. Jacuit immenfa ftrages: *omnis* fexus, omnis aetas; inluftres, ignobiles, &c. But were people of both fexes, of every age and of ignoble condition, admitted to be *conffurattrs* with Sejanus? – Or, were they merely *officiates* with him ? – If they were partifans in the confpiracy could Sejanus have contrived to keep his treafonable purpofe a fecret? – Would he have thought that women and boys, and people of no rank or charafter, would be fit to be entrufted with fo important a fecret ?

If so many persons were conspirators with Sejanus, how is it that V. M. and S. tell us that the people tore him in pieces ?

Of the cause of the fall of Sejanus.

Or, rather, would he, after having been fo exceedingly faftidious as Tacitus reprefents him to have been, iv. 74, in the year 14, have con- defcended, in the year 17, when he had been exalted to the acme of his wifhes, and Tiberius was nearly in the Both year of his age, to aflbciate with fuch perfons? – And if they were not confpirators, but only humble expeftants, why were they, after the acquittal of Terentius, and the condemnation of his accufers to deaths and to banrfh- nients, detained in prifon ? – And, the year after, barbaroufly murdered for it – and by Tiberius ? – Did he not fpare this fame Terentius ? – Did he not approve the decree of the Senate concerning the fentence of the accufers? – And was he not greatly applauded for it? – And not only for that, but for having ordered all the accufers to be put to death in one day ? – Dion, we know, fpeaking of the accufation of this fame Terentius, and of the fentence pronounced on him, and them,

by the Senate, fays, 1. 58, p. 633, D ojr *nal o Tt&fios* iwyxare&ro, *xai tvi mra* /xE *tmntn*. – And of the carnage which Tiberius caufed to ba made immediately after the death of Sejanus, he fays – " but amidft all this fo great cruelty, he (Tiberius) feemed to be porTefled of fame *philanthropy – tllol-e -n xai QAadfuwiuo-Ka-Qai."* – And wherein ? – fcil – In fparing Caffianus, Luciiw Sejanus, the praetor, (who, he obfervcs, had caufed the infirmity of his age to be expofed both on the ftage and in the ftreets of Rome,) and Marcus Terentius. And again, fpeaking of the accufers of Terentius and of the fentence pronounced on them by the Senate, he fays – *aai o Ti&fios mtxanQen o-fim* – for which, fubjoins he, he was applauded – *at tin raru* /xsv *imnm* – and, continues he, he was much more applauded, for having caufed all the foremoft accufers to be put to death in one day – /xjs- *on Tus iirionrorams rut*

7as itimiyofi3. i ir(s/Eiv airo9asi sv /xj ii/'. tfa *sxtr.'ait* – to which CXCCUtioH Tacitus feems to allude vi. 30.

i- 1.11

Of the cause of the fall of Sejanus.

Chapter 23, Tacitus fays, as Suetonius alfo does, that Tiberius gav? . Macro orders that if Sejanus mould have recourfe to arms, he mould liberate Drufus, the nephew of his wife Livilla, and fet him over the people.

Laflly, chap. 30, Tacitus fays, that Lentulus Gaetulicus, the commander of the army in Upper Germany, was, about the beginning of the 22d year of Tiberius, accufed by Albudius, (one of the accufersof Livilla,) his once legionary prefeft and paft aedile, of having formed a family connexion with Sejanus. To this charge he is faid to hav4 replied by letter to Tiberius, pretty nearly as Terentius did to the Senate. The refult, fays Tacitus, was, that Tiberius took no notice of it, but continued on the fame terms of intimacy with him as before, vand even banifhed Albudins from the city.

The fum of what we learn, from detached paflages of Tacitus, concerning the fall of Sejanus, feems to be nearly this – that Sejanus, after he had put away his wife, by whom he had three children, perfuaded Livilla, the fifter of Germanicus, and the wife of Drufus, the prince regent, to be an acceflary to the death of her hufband, in hope of marrying Sejanus, and of partaking with him, in the government – that he, four years after, at the rifque of his own life, preferved that of Tiberius – that he, by the confent of Tiberius, eight years after, and juft before his fall, married her – that he was then poflefled of all power, and Tiberius in his 74th year – that he was thought to have contrived the death of Tiberius – that he, though intolerably proud, confpired with all forts of perfons for that purpofe – -that he was put to death for it, with one of his children, but whether with or without trial he does not fay – that two of his children were, before the end of the year, alfo put to death for it – that none of his accomplices, if he had any, were put to death with him – that the chief of his accom*Of the cause of the fall of Sejanus.* plices was not punifhed – that his effefts were firft depofited in the treafury and then confifcated – that, in the fecond year after, an im- menfe number of perfons, of all forts, were put to death for it – and, laftly, that L. Gaetulicus was, four years after, charged with having betrothed his daughter to a fon of Sejanus.

Having now collefted all that Tacitus fays of the offence of Sejanus, for which he fell, let us next proceed to obferve whether he fays Livilla was an accomplice with him in it.

If Livilla was, as Tacitus fays, induced, by the hope of marrying Sejanus and of fbaring the government with him, to affift in the murder of the heir-apparent, may we not expeft that fhe was alfo concerned in this plot againft her aged uncle and father-in-law ? – Of her having been concerned Jn it Tacitus (though he fays, vi. 2, that fhe died about the fame time,) does not fay. Indeed, by his filence concerning the difpofition of her property, and his report concerning that of Sejanus, (for had fhe confpired with Sejanus would not her property have been confifcated as well as his ?) may we not almoft conclude that fhe knew nothing of his defign ? – But we are not confined to negative proof, for it appears by what he there fays of her – viz – that effigies of her were dill exifting – that fhe could not have been concerned in it – for furely no effigies of her would have been permitted to remain, if fhe had been put to death for high-treafon. It alfo appears that certain mal-praftices, in which fhe had been engaged, had been difcovered fince her death, and that, as fhe could not be then punifhed for thofe practices, fevere reflexions were made on thofe*Of the cause of the fall of Sejanus.*

Query – May not this Lentulus have been the same persen as Dion speaks of as having been a conspirator with Sejanus – r *at$Ksvo-xu. wis* – against Tiberius ?

effigies which were intended to perpetuate her memory. What thofe mal-pracHces were, which came to light after her death, may be col- lefted from what he again fays of her vi. 29 – viz – that Mamercus Scaurus was, more than two years after, charged with having committed adultery with her, and with having frequented, with her too, no doubt, the facred rites of the Magi. Though of adultery, with any one, before the death of her hufband Drufus, Tiberius himfelf, by the report of Tacitus, iv. and vi. 46, clearly acquitted her. Now if thefe were her only offences fhe appears to have had nothing to do with the treafon of Sejanus.

But does it not appear ftill more evident that me was no way concerned in it, by what Jofephus and Dion fay of her mother Antonia, and Suetonius of her brother Claudius? – The two firft mentioned fay that Antonia difcovered the treachery of Sejanus, and the laft, that Claudius was deputed by the knights to congratulate on the occafion *r* But of this more hereafter.

Dion, who fays, p. 628, that Apicata, indignant at feeing the bodies of her children, whom, he fays, Tiberius had caufed to be put to death, firft informed him that his fon had been poifoned by Sejanus and Livilla, it may not be amifs to obferve, alfo fays, in the fame page, that Livilla was alive after the difcovery of the murder – that Tiberius, who, as Suetonius fays, iii. 62, would afterwards fpare nobody, and was convinced that his grandfon was illegitimate, would have forgiven her, but that Antonia, her own mother, who, 33 V. Maximus and others fay, was a moft exemplary woman, oppofed it. Dion further fays of Livilla, that fhe ftarved herfelf.

Let us, in the laft place, hear what Dion fays of the greatnefs and fall of Sejanus.

Of the cause of the fall of Sejanus.

Of the vaft power of Sejanus, Dion fays, 1. 57, p. 617, C., that the confuls and – soyi/xoi – eminent men, ufed, before the death of Drufus, to wait on him, at day-break, and then ufed to lay before him the petitions which they meant to prefent to Tiberius for themfelves – and, to communicate with him the common things about which Tiberius *ought* to give refponfes. And again, in the fame page, he fays, that Sejanus, not content with all this power, determined on the death of Drufus, in hope that he mould get the entire control of his aged fire. So great indeed, he fays, 1. 57, p. 619, B., was his power, that Cremutius Cordus was compelled to lay hands on himfelf merely be- caufe *he had offended him – an ru ttixna* wfou-txpso-ri. – Tacitus fays, iv. I4 that two of his clients accufed Cordus. And, 1. 58, p. 622, A., he fays, that even the Senate, after the death of Livia, made a decree that his birth-day fhould be kept – and that they and all the reft of the Romans erefted an unufual number of ftatues to him – that they fent deputies to him as well as to Tiberius – that they offered up vows for his profperity as well as for Tiberius – and that they facrificed to both, and fwore by their fortunes.

All this Dion fays of the omnipotence of Sejanus, as if it was obtained by univerfal confent.

Again, 1. 58, p. 623, B., he fays, that Tiberius knowing – /taflwv – that the *Senate and others* looked up to Sejanus as emperor, and down upon himfelf as nobody, was afraid that they would make him emperor – and then goes on to fay that Sejanus entirely won over to him *all the body guards,* and *tnoft of the fenators,* and that he, moreover, had the addrefs fo to pleafe thofe about Tiberius, as to bring himfelf acquainted with every thing faid or done at Capreae, and to keep Tiberius, though, as both Tacitus, iv. i, xi. 3, and Suetonius fays, an overmatch for him in craftinefs, in ignorance of every thing done at Rome.

Of the cause of the fall of Sejanus.

And what flep does he fay Tiberius then took ? – fcil – He, notwith- ftanding he was afraid the Senate would make him emperor, made him conful, and called him the partaker of his cares, and, in his letters to the Senate and to the people, " my Sejanus." – Wherefore, continues he, the deceived and believers – *attraraiam xat vtnvnns –* affixed every where tables of brafs infcribed with their joint names, and placed in the Theatres gilded chairs of ftate for both of them. The Senate too, he fays, decreed them a quinquennial confulate, and offered facrifices to the ftatues of Sejanus as well as to thofe of Tiberius, though, as Dion himfelf had previoufly faid, he had before publifhed an edift forbidding any one to worfhip him.

Dion next goes on to fay, that Sejanus, notwithftanding all this affeftation of popularity, caufed *many of the nobles* to be put to death, and among them Caius Rufus Geminius, by accufing him of *impiety to Tiberius* before the Senate – an offence, of which, he had before faid himfelf, Tiberius took np notice. Rufus, fays he, was tried for it, and, before fentence was pafled, retired to his own houfe, and when the quaeftor arrived to tell him his doom, he deftroyed himfelf. Publia Prifca, the wife of Rufus, fays he, was alfo accufed before the Senate of fomething, and by Sejanus, no doubt, though he had, as Dion elfe- where obferves, promifed marriage to all the married ladies of Rome. The refult was that fhe too deftroyed herfelf, and in the very Senate-houfe.

In the next page – viz – 1. 58, p. 623, E., Dion fays, that Sejanus was fo great in his own conceit and in the plenitude of his power that he appeared like an autocrat, while Tiberius appeared like the governor of an infignificant ifland – that he was even attended by the body guards – *$o(it$ofot* – when he went to the Capitol. And, in the next page, 1. 58, 624, D., he fays, that the overdoers – *xaratofsts* – even fwore by

Of the cause of the fall of Sejanus.

his fortune – rv -*n rvst avru xaraxoftis- tipwTaM* – and addrefled him not only as colleague-to Tiberius in the confulfhip, but as his equal in all

power.

Having thus defcribed his power as increafing till the year when he

was conful, and as being then unlimited, Dion next proceeds to de- fcribe his rapid fall. He fays, p. 624, D., that if any God had, in the beginning of the year in which Tiberius and Sejanus were confuls, foretold what was to happen before the end of that year, nobody would have believed it. Early in that year, continues Dion, Tiberius, who (and it deferves to be particularly noticed as being rather contra- diftory to what he had before faid in the page immediately preceding B.) *could not be ke/it in ignorance of any thing about him* – *Ti&fws Se tyeoti* ; xE Ss *en rm xar avrot* – perceiving in what eftimation his minifter was held by the people, determined to cut him off. But if, as Dion himfelf fays, he had caufed him to be fo efteemed, why mould he have determined to cut him off for being fo efteemed? – And how could he have hoped to accomplifh his purpofe ? – In. the fame page, E., he fays, that Tiberius being aware that he could not venture to do it openly, contrived to do it in fuch a manner as aftonifhed every body, not excepting Sejanus. And then, in the remainder of the fame page, he proceeds to point out the fteps which Tiberius took in order to leflen the public opinion of the great power of his confular colleague, and which, he fays., were effeftual. The popular opinion of his potentiality being thus leflened, it was, fhortly, after, confiderably more fo, by obferving a prodigy or two, which happened to certain ftatues of Sejanus, which were the objefts of adoration.

, Suetonius says, iii. 65, that Tiberius, before he entered his v. consulate, koew tint Sejauus was meditating a revolution.

Of the-cause of the fall of Sejanus,

Tiberius having, in confequence of what he had obferved, taken thofe fteps, and being confident of the affiftance of the Senate (though it was, as both Jofephus and Dion fay, devoted, by favors, received, to Sejanus) and of the people, aflailed him – /a9v *ravra o* Ti$fpof, *M.*

Qatfavttrots us xm n 5r/ov *xat rnu* sXnt *ffvfitfiutas tctv, nrlftfwtt avru –*

p. 626, B. C. – And how did he contrive to do it? – Did he fend an officer with a company of armed men to fecure him in his own houfer Far, very far from it. – For though Laco, the captain of the night watch, met him, *as foon as it "was day,* on the way to the Senate, yet he, fays Dion, did not apprehend him, but permitted him to take, as ufual, his feat among his friends in the Senate. How then did Tiberius contrive the matter? – Why he, in the plenitude of his power and of his infidioufnefs, wrote a tedious unconnefted epiftle to thofe very fathers, who were unanimous in deifying and almoft in confpiring with him, in which he fometimes commended him, fometimes criminated him, though his co-partner in divinity, but of what Dion does not fay – no doubt, of fome myfterious offence; for, notwithftanding he was confident of the co-operation of the Senate and the people, he was iifraid to write, in plain terms, of his execution, *left there JJtould be it*

tumult on that account – aunxfvs yaf ivrroQxtfnt avrov o TtGtftos a trfotntaa. ty. an ax efaXtro, *aMC* or/ fpo$uflD *pn rafnrt -nt tx rara ytmfatt* – but, as Dton

wifely obferves, that he ought to be confined. Towards the end of it, fays Dion, he alfo obferved that they ought to proceed againft two fenators the friends of Sejanus. And without faying for what offence, Enough to have alarmed all the other confpirators, and to have made them think of their own fafety.

It is remarkable that Dion has not told *us* the names of those two friends of Sejanus, nor what they had done to offend the emperor. – Of r. Ia-sus, the uncle of Sejanus, whom Tiberius afterwards deprived of the priest-hood, Tacttus, we know, says, v. 7 – in Blxsum tnulla foedaque ineusuvit

Of the cause of the fall of Sejanus.

After fome of the multifarious contents of this incoherent epiftle had been read, continues Dion, the friends of Sejanus, who fat near him, began to defert him, and the praetors and tribunes of the people to furround him to prevent his efcape, and making an infurreftion. – And no fooner was the whole epiftle read, than the whole body of the Senate, *who had but juft before joined in adoring him, and moft of whom were then in con/piracy with him, without knowing that he was accufed of any thing f. tedfic, with one confent, began to utter exclamations and malcdiflions.* The Seriate then, fays Dion, perceiving that none of the guards were near to proteft him, and, *in order to gratify the people,* tmmediately, without a trial and without fuffering him to fpeak for him- felf, proceeded to condemn him, and Regulus, with the reft of the magiftrates, condufted him to prifon. On the way the commonalty vociferated, on account of thofe that had, by his means, perifhed – oxvi – and mocked him for thofe things which he had hoped –

But what ? – Did the Senate, loaded as they had been by him with favors, and confpirators as moft of them were with him, and without knowing what Tiberius had to fay againft him, indeed manifeft fo much rancour towards him? – And did they, in compliance with the whim of the people, commit him, without any fpecific accufation, to prifon, and as already condemned,? – And did they, if they fuppofed that Tiberius meant to accufe him of a defign againft the government, commit him alone ? – That they did commit any other with him, Dion does not fay, though he fays, that Tiberius, towards the end of the epiftle, obferved, that two fenators, who were his intimates, *ought* to

be tmprifoned – 5yo *re @favras rut* otKftiVfV-'v *0i xoat&Qnvxt xat* tt pfsfat *ytttr-* v. – Vnd does it not appear, by this treatment of Sejanus, Mram

Of the cause of the fall of Sejanus.

that the Senate was moft obfequious to the will of Tiberius, and that the common- alty of Rome were, without underftanding the nature of the alledged offence, much exafperated againft Sejanus, and, if for revolutionary praftices, does it not prove that they muft have been well pieafed with the government of Tiberius? – Indeed can we fuppofe that they would have approved of fuch praftices as long as a fon ofGermanicus was alive? – Does not Dion himfelf fay, p. 625, E., that Tiberius, by making Caius a prieft and by fhewing figns of inclination to make him his fucceflbr, alarmed Sejanus ? – Do not Suetonius and Tacitus fay that Tiberius gave orders, in cafe Sejanus fhould caufe an infurreftion, to liberate Drufus ? – Does not Tacitus tell us that a counterfeit Drufus met with, at the very fame time, fupport in moft places, and expefted the fame even in Italy ?

Hitherto, it feems, the Senate had proceeded not only without evidence but without hearing any thing in defence of the culprit. – And what did they do next? – Quickly after – *vnfot* a *mtAu* – they fentenced him to be put to death: for which, fays Dion, 1. 59, p. 652, A., Caius, in a laudatory fpeech on Tiberius, reproached them. – But had not Tiberius, feveral years before, decreed that no one mould be put to death within ten days after his condemnation ? – No matter for that. The populace, without knowing that he had committed any offence, dragged his body through the ftreets three days: and the Senate, not content with having proceeded fo precipitately in the execution of Sejanus, condemned and executed his children alfo, even a girl betrothed to a fon of Claudius; and, as V. Maximus fays, the populace trod them alfo under foot. But, fays Dion, 1. 58, p. 633, A., Tiberius, who does not appear, even by what Dion himfelf fays, to have given any order for the trial 06 Sejanus, and certainly not for his execution, and does appear to have hinted that two only of his fenatorial relatives fhould be taken into cuftody, then (785) fpared certain others*Of the cause of the fall of Sejanus.*

though related to hltn – Tots Se teturo /v . *xt xtxv* nva/v, xiro/ TaJ Zi:tv-D

uxctatLatn. – Now if, as Dion fays, Tiberius had not given any order for the trial of his prime-minifter, nor any for his execution, and if, as Dion alfo fays, he only hinted that no more than two of his fena- torial relatives ought to be taken into cuftpdy, with what propriety could Dion have fatd that Tiberius, in the year following, fpared his relatives ? – who were thofe relatives ? – That his wife deftroyed her- felf, foon after the fall of Sejanus, Dion himfelf fays; – that the reft of his children were deftroyed, by the Senate, before the end of the year, Tacitus, we find, fays; – that his uncle, Blaefus, though accufed, by. Tiberius, of many and fcandalous things, when Sejanus fell, was continued in the prieft-hooi two years after, Tacitus alfo fays; – thatL. Sejanus, the praetor, was alfo fpared, even though he had, but the year after his brother had been fo unjuftly and fo cruelly ufed, been fo unaccountably indifcreet as to expofe publicly, not the moral or religious enormities of his prince, but a fingle perfonal defett, natural to moft men of his age, Dion moreover teftifies.

But though we find thofe relatives only mentioned as fpared, may not his very aged father have been then alive ? – and alfo fpared ? – if not honored with an office of the greateft truft ? – We know that he was, not many years before, alive, and the governor of Egypt, and of his death we have not any account, neither have we of his return from his prefefture. Let us then not think it ufelefs to endeavour to get fome information on this point, becaufe, if it can be made to appear that his father was alfo fpared, it may help us to form a little more decifive opinion whether Tiberius is likely to have cauied Sejanus to be put to death – and, for having been guilty of treachery towards himfelf.

Of the cause of the fall of Sejanus.

But, the learned will be ready to afk, how can any one expeƈt to obtain any information on this point? – Not improbably, by confider- ing whether Strabo, the geographer, may not have been the praefeƈt of Egypt. If it fhould appear that he prefided over that country, he, we prefume, muft have prefided over it after the cities of Afia had been re-built, and, feemingly, after the year 780 – that is, in the latter part not only of his own life but in that of the life of Tiberius alfo – for, we know, that he, in the laft book, gives a geographical defcription of Egypt, and, in the courfe of it, frequently calls that country, in a certain fenfe, *our country:* and we alfo know that he muft have written that book, no one knows how long after the cities of Afia were rebuilt – that is, as we have already feen, CHAP, xvi, after 780. Why then, if it can be made to appear that Strabo, the geographer, did, in all probability, govern that country, may we not prefume that he may have been no other than the father of Sejanus ? – If we may, and can make it appear that he governed Egypt when Sejanus fell, we may hope alfo to be allowed to make this conclufion- – viz – that what Dion fays of Sejanus' intention to innovate, and, of the confequent deftruc- tion of his whole family is, to fay the leaft, a little more queftionable: for if his own father, the prafeft of Egypt, does not appear to haie confpired with him, how can he be thought to have had any defign on the fovereignty ?

Strabo, we find, was, by his own account, xii. p. 336, born in the city Amafea, the metropolis of a Roman province of that name, between Pontus and Cappadocia, and his maternal uncle Moaphernes was, as he himfelf alfo fays, xi. p. 343, the governor of Colchis, under Mithridates. – Of the city Amafea he fpeaks *as our 'city.* – In his early years he appears to have removed to Rome, and to have refided fo long there as to think it not indecorous to call it and its dependenciis

Of the cause of the fall of Sejanus.

our territories – for inftance, fpeaking, iii. p. 116, of the inhabitants of Cadiz, he fays, that they, though by no means a great people, covered *our fea* and *the exterior* with many and large fhips – *Ovm yaf*

na-it 0i av$fts, 0i rx irtia xai imyia tiamwpia fAotres, tis ri Tw xaQ' tipac

6a. *Xixrrm,* xa *tis T, iv sxns,* – And he, we find, notwithftanding he thus claims a fhare in the property both of his native city and the Roman feas, &c. afterwards, in the laft book of his work, where he is fpeaking of Egypt and of the contiguous countries, much more frequently claims a fhare in the property of the former – a fingular liberty, it muft be confefled, for a Roman to take with an exclufively imperial province, if he had not been the praefeft of it; and what is ftill more ' remarkable than either of the former things noticed, he, not far from the beginning of that book, fpeaks of the Ethiopians, of his own times, as leading a paftoral life, for this and one or two other reafons – viz – becaufe they are far from *us,* that is, furely, from *us Egyptians,* of whom he is principally fpeaking, and with whofe cuftoms, &c. he is comparing thofe of the Ethiopians, as may be thought to appear a little more clearly by the fubjoined remark – the Egyptians, on the contrary, are more civilized.

Why then fhould we not conclude that Strabo, the geographer, is likely to have governed Egypt, and, that he is likely to have been the father of Sejanus ?

But, admitting that he is likely to have been fo, how will it be made to appear that he furvived his fon ?

To this we will reply, that we hope to make it appear that he did furvive his fon – firft, by what he fays, book xvi, of thofe Chaldeans who were, by the reft, undervalued, becaufe they ftudied genethlia. logy – fecondly, by what he afterwards fays, in the fame book, of the conquefts made by the Jews after they came under the control of *Of the cause of the fall of Sejanus.*

fupcrftitious governors – next, by what he fays, in the xviith, of the inattention paid by his cotempbraries to the oracle of Jupiter Ammon, and, to oracles in general – then, by what he fays of the name of the queen of the Ethiopians *in his time* – of the Ethiopians worfhipping an immortal and a mortal God, and of fome of them denying the exift- ence of God – and, laftly, by what he fays of *the hterefy* of the Cyre- nians.

Firft, he fays, of certain Chaldeans that they were, by the reft of their countrymen, undervalued, for ftudying genethlialogy – a diftinc- tion which he has not made, book i. p. 16, where he fays how much the Chaldeans in general, or *Mjgi*, were, for their learning, honored. That thofe Chaldeans, or Magi, were confulted at Rome, from the days of Horace to thofe of Juvenal, appears by what the former fays in his ode to Leuconoe, and, by what the latter fays in his vi. fatire. That they were more confulted, in the reign of Tiberius, than even the ancient oracles, may be inferred from what Juvenalt and Tacitus fay. J That they were, a little before his death, patronized by Tiberius, and that he ftudied their favorite fcience and was a great proficient in it, Juvenal, Jofephus, and Tacitus fay.

Secondly, he fays, of the Jews, 1. xvi. p. 524, that the feparatifts, from them difturbed the peace of their own and of the neighbouring countries, and that partifans of thofe in power among them wafted other countries, particularly Syria and Phoenicia – οι sv *yuf*

Tt)v %wfav *fK. atxst, xxt avrvt xat* rt)v *yttntoxrott, 0i* St of/ATTfxTTotref *rols* xxflrfwaot rx aXXorla, *xat ins Zvflas xarfrftQotro, xatt Tns (fiotvtxns* 7roXXxt. –

Now what does he mean by thofe feparatifts ? – When did they leave*Of the cause of the fall of Sejanus.*

Strabo says, p. 509, that Seleucns was one of the Chaldean al οΧοyot – and Seleucus, Suetooius says, vii. 4, was a genethlialogist, or mathematician.

t S. Ti. 557, &c. + Tacitus, ii. 27.

the Jews and lay wafte not only Judea but the country furronnding it? When did thofe agents of thofe in power lay wafte Syria and much of Phoenicia? – When did any party of Jews lay wafte their own country and the furroundingr – When did any coadjutors of thofe in power upfet Syria and much of Phoenicia? – If by this he did not mean to allude to the difturbances caufed by the numerous arrefts, in Judea and in all the furrounding countries, of believers as tranfgreflbrs of the law of Mofes, what can he have meant ?

Strabo next remarks, xvii. p. 559, of the oracle at Ammon, and of oracles in general, how much they were, in his time, difregarded – to all I have faid of Ammon I have this to add – that both it and divination in general, and places for that purpofe, were more in repute formerly. Now they are much neglefted, the Romans being contented with the refponfes of the Sibyl, &c. – riou S' *ttfvxons wtft ra Apltams, roo-urot* etwv *ftvoptQx, on nts af%fuott* fu&tov Sjv sv *riftZ* ""' " *fuam. n* xafloXs, *x. xt* T Jlft)fta!v vtu Se oX/ywf/at *natrsfft troKkn, rut Pulit. a!tat afxtsftutut ruts a'ts , xatt Tois* Tt/ffnv/xo'f *Qtovfotrlots, tn* Tt *irffvxput, xxt oftiQttas,* v. *fulotng xatt To* tv *AptJ. uu ff%itin Ti txttentrat* j$fns"n/ir, *trfonftt* Jt

Strabo then informs us that the name of the queen of Ethiopia, who reigned in his time, was Candace – and, that fhe was of a maf- culine mind – and, that Ihe had but one eye. – He alfo adds that the Ethiopians worfhipped two Gods, an immortal and a mortal – and, that fome of them denied the exiftence of any God – which, we find, the early Chriftians were faid to have denied, if not to have worfhipped a man.

In what repute the responses of the Sibyl were with the Romans, in the reign of Tiberius, any one may form an opinion from what , Petronius Arbiter represents Agamemnon (Tiberius) to have declared – viz – Nam Sibyllam qui- dem Cumis ego ipse oculis meis vidi in ampulla pendere; et cum illi pueri dice- rent 2t$vM, *n Qesu* respondebat ilia

Of the cause of the fall ofSejanus.

Laftly, Strabo fays of the Cyrenians that they held an haerefy, which Anniceris was, in his time, defirous of reftifying – *ai Ammpis, a* SoxJv

E7r.-iv, fflit7j T KrpiivioHttiv *eiifsyiti xai irapayaytiv ar r avrns m Amxtfim.* –

But who ever heard of any haerefy before the publication of Chriftian- ity? – And who does not know that men of Cyrene are faid to have been fome of the firft publifhers of it ? – And fo early as the beginning of the year 782 ?

Now if all or any of thofe feveral things above noticed, as mentioned by Strabo in his two laft books, be fuppofed to have a reference to the firft publifhing of Chriftianity, why may we not conclude that Strabo was no other than Iberus, mentioned by Dion, as the predeceflbr of Flaccus in the year 785; however we feem to have reafon enough to conclude that the father of Sejanus furvived his fon, and was, at his death, entrufted with the command of Egypt.

If then with Sejanus neither his wife, nor two of his three children, nor his father, nor his brother, nor his uncle fell, why are we told that all his family fell with him; – and if, when he fell, his father, his brother, and his uncle were permitted to continue in offices of the greateft truft, why mould we think that Sejanus was put to death for revolutionary projefts ?

After Sejanus and one or two of his children had been put to death, not by the order of Tiberius, but by the tumultuary proceeding of the Senate, and, as Dion, we have feen, fays, to gratify the people of Rome, that city was, no doubt, as V. Maximus fays, foon quiet. – Far, very far from it. Dion informs us that much confufion ftill pervaded it – flofuCW *re* TroXur *n -m iroXit a-vmn-)$y* – that the populace proceeded to murder not only thofe who had *been pojjejj'ed of /tower under Sejanus* but alfo thofe who *had behaved injultingly under him* – o 7p

Pliny,, in his N. H. xxviii. 2, which he entities – An sit in medendo ver- bonnu aliqua is. &c.: seems lo complain of insults by sneezing – and, to say

Of the cause of the fall of Sejanus.

ct its na rui /y itxfa ra Swata SyEflsvrw *nai* S' Okitov *oGfiymrcw nxfl-*

yufa, tQonot. – The foldiers too, (notwithftanding Tiberius had, as Dion fays, given exprefs orders to the magiftrates and commanders to pre- ferve the peace,) indignant at finding themfelves fufpefted of attachment to Sejanus by the fubftitution of' night watches more in the confidence of the emperor- – ? d *m avroxfarofos irtf!t* – became incendiaries and depredators. – If fuch outrages were, notwithftanding the exprefs orders of Tiberius to the magiftrates of Rome to preferve the peace, permitted to prevail, how could Tacitus have faid, vi. 10, of Pifo, the U. P., that his chief praife was for having been wonderfully difcreet in the ufe of his power when the people were difpofed to be infubor- dinate ? – fed praecipua ex eo gloria, quod praefeftus urbi recens, con- tinuam poteftatem et infolentia parendi graviorem, mire temperavit. – But what were the Senate doing in the mean time? – Inftead of paying the leaft attention to it they decreed a ftatue to *Liberty-* to be fet up in the Forum, and ordered, what was never done, on fuch an occafion, before, that the day, on whidi Sejanus fell, fhould be annually celebrated, as a feftival, by all perfons in office, and by all'priefts, and by horfe races, and by the exhibitions of the fights of wild beafts – that they, being perfuaded that the Gods had infatuated him, in contempt of his memory, inftituted new rites to the Gods. – And, what fome perhaps may think rather more remarkable, they even ordered that

that Tiberius encouraged the practice, by taking with him, in his carriage, that most dismal of mortals. – Whence this insulting practice originated, and who this most dismal wretcfi was, we leave Theologians to divine.

+ Pighius tells us that there is the following monumental inscription at In- Icrumma, which he supposes was engraven on this occasion – Saluti perpelua e Angustx, Liberia!ique perpctuie P. R. – Providcntiie Ti: Caesaris Augusli, *nut! ail o-ternitateat romtmi nominis,* sublato hoste perniciosissimo.

Nnn

Of the cause of the fall of Sejanus. neither exceffive honors fhould be paid to any one, nor oaths made *by*

any one but the emperor – xaii /ajiti ripa; p$i uwtfoyxBi SiSoo-8asj, *fam* Tbs *ofKus eir' xj. Xn Titos, irtot ra avroxfarofor iroittir6a!.*

But does not the Senate, by fo doing, appear to have been not only inattentive to the prevailing anarchy, but even encouragers of it ? – And to have been clearly hoftile, not only to Sejanus, but to Tiberius as well? – By erefting a ftatue to Liberty in the Forum, they appear to have encouraged anarchy. – By voluntarily ordering the day on which Sejanus perifhed to be annually a day of rejoicing, they appear to have been enemies to Sejanus. – And by decreeing that no exceffive honors fhould be paid to any one, or oaths taken *by* any but the emperor, they appear to have afted not only moft ridiculoufly (for Tiberius ever defpifed fuch honor and fuch a mode of fwearing) but moft infultingly – as indeed they feem to have acknowledged, only a few months after, by unanimoufly approving the fpeech of Terentius, in the courfe of which he faid – Non eft noftrum aeftimare, quem fuper caeteros et quibus de caufis extollas. T. vi. 8. 9.

Sejanus then was, we find, by the report of Dion, moft extravagantly honored, even as an autocrat, by Tiberius, the Senate, and the people, efpecially by the married ladies of Rome, the katakoreis, the deceived, and the believers, till within a few days of his fall. – And Tiberius was, by the report of the fame writer, confidered, by the Romans, as little more than the autocrat of Capreae. – That Sejanus put many of the nobles to death, he alfo fays, but for what crime, he, to our furprife, does not fay. – That he profecuted Fufius, the jeering conful of his aged fovereign, *for impiety to him,* the year before he fell, he, to our greater furprife, fays. – That Fufius, and perhaps his wife, killed themfelves, on that account, he, to our ftill greater furprife,

rrti Tu etfut opoa-ai – to swear *by* the sacred victims.
Of the cause of the fall of Sejanus.

afferts. – - And, notwithftanding he fays all this, he, to our much greater furprife, fays, that he intended to feize the government. – That the emperor's letter accufed him of any attempt, or even defign, to injure or moleft his perfon, or to leflen his prerogative, he does not fay. – It faid nothing of his death, and perhaps not of his imprifonment,. without a fair trial. – And yet no fooner was it known that Tiberius did not uniformly fpeak of him in his ufual tone, than all his fenato- rial friends and dependents began to defert him, and the confuls, one of whom was his friend, to pleafe the people who knew nothing that had been dorie, conducted him publicly to prifon, and apparently without a military guard. – The populace, moft of whom had con- fpired with him, feeing him thus difgraced, without knowing the rea- fon, infulted him and all his ftatues in the moft outrageous manner. – Not long after, he was, *by a decree of the Senate,* (moft of whom he, it feems, had obliged) and apparently without any order from Tiberius, executed, and his body expofed for three days to the infults of the populace, and then thrown into the Tyber, – All his children were, by a decree of the Senate, then deftroyed, not excepting a girl be trothed to Claudius. Dion, it fhould be obferved, does not fay that any political innovators fuffered with him, (neither does V. Maximus) neither does he fay (as V. Maximus and Juvenal do) that order and public tranquillity were foon eftablifhed; – on the contrary, he fays, that the moft terrible confequences enfued – that the very guards, as well as the populace, committed every kind of outrage – and that, fhe Senate, though Tiberius had ordered the magiftrates to preferve the public peace, feemed to pay no attention to it – that they were overjoyed at the fall of Sejanus, and apparently inclined to trench on

V. M. says to cause a general massacre at Homo.
Of the cause of the fall of Sejanus.

the prerogatives of Tiberius, and even to infult him – and that Tiberius, *under the pretence of Sejanic accufations,* put many to death, and caufed many to put themfelves to death.

By the teftimony of thofe feven or eight writers then, three of whom were cotempo- raries with Tiberius, and two born foon after his death, Sejanus was, in the beginning of the tSth year, accufed, by Tiberius, of fomething – but whether of meditating fome kind of political innovation it does not appear. – Tacitus affirms that it was againft the fecurity and life of Tiberius – and that perfons of all ranks and ages, fenators and foldiers, men and women, were concerned iij it. Jofe- phus fays nearly the fame. Dion too fays that the married women were efpecially concerned in it. – At the time when Sejanus thought of executing this plot, the imperious Agrippina and her forts Drufus and Caius, in favour of whom, and againft Sejanus, the populace of Rome had already declared, were ftill alive. – Confequently, it would be of no ufc to crufh Tiberius in his retreat, unlefs Rome was at firft fecured. – But the Jews, of whom there were fwarms at Rome, were, fays Philo, much attached to Tiberius. – To make way for the execution of his plot, Sejanus thought it neceflary to perfuade Tiberius to expel them from Rome – though under what pretence he does not fay.

Sejanus then having, as Philo fays, on fome pretence or other, prevailed on Tiberius and the Senate to expel the Jews from Rome, for fear they would oppofe his long meditated plot, next *intended,* as V. Maximus fays, *to majjacre all the reft of the inhabitants,* though they were moftly, *effucially the married women,* in his interert – and not a few of them fwore, as Dion fays, even by his fortune. – But, in the mean time, fays V. Maximus, this long meditated plot was, by *the divine providence* and by the forefight of Tiberius, who was ftill at*Of the cause of the fall of Sejanus.*

Capreae with his Chaldean aflbciates, happily difcovered. – This dif- covery, it mould obferved, feems, according to V. Maximus, Philo, and Dion, to have been made after the confulate of Tiberius, and not as Suetonius fays, before. – Tiberius no fooner found out what his minifter intended to do, than he confidered with himfelf how to de- ftroy him – and finding that he could not do it, with fafety, in an open manner, he devifed a method that aftonifhed Sejanus and all his party. The ftep which he took was this – he, every now and then, wrote letters to Sejanus and the Senate, in which he gave different accounts of himfelf – and fome times commended Sejanus and his aflociates, fometimes found fault with them – which method of proceeding dif- concerted Sejanus, who, though he had fpies at Capreae, yet he never once thought of having recourfe to arms. – At laft Tiberius fent, by Macro, a very long and incoherent letter to the Senate, towards the clofe of which he faid that two fenators, the intimates of Sejanus, ought to be punifhed; and, laft of all, that Sejanus, ought to be confined. The two fenators feem to have been the two Blsefi, one of whom was the uncle of Sejanus, the other Pontifex Maximus. – As foon as it was only fuppofed that Tiberius had intimated a defire that Sejanus mould be imprifoned, all his adherents and creatures, even Trio, leTt him, and the other conful and other ftate officers furrounded him, and, without permitting him to fpeak for himfelf, condufted him to prifon, and all ranks of people, molt of whom were concerned in his confpiracy, without waiting for the formalities of a trial, flew, early as it then was, to crufh the enemy of their defender and proteftor of their peace, together with *all his family,* excepting Livilla, his brother Lucius the praetor, and his uncle Blaefus, and perhaps his father. – All this was, as Juvenal and Dion fay, effefted by the laft letter of Tiberius to the Senate, in which he, fays Dion, only, now and then, blamed*Of the cause of the fall of Sejanus.*

Sojanus and intimated that he ought to be imprifoned, but faid nothing of the imprifonment of any other, nor of his death. – No writer, it mould be obferved, fays that any other confpirator was imprifoned with him – nor, that any other, befides his own family, fell with him – neither does any one fay that any of his confpirators abfconded. – V. Maximus fays that the people trod him to death. – Seneca fays that they tore him in pieces – that there was not enough of him left for the hangman to drag through the ftreets of the city. – Juvenal fays that the hangman did drag his *body* through the city – and that it lay on the banks of the Tyber, where the people, to mew their allegiance to Tiberius, went and trod on it. – V. Maximus fays that no fooner was Sejanus put to death than tranquillity was reftored. – Juvenal feems to fay that the people were totally unconcerned about the matter – But how different is this from that of Tacitus and Dion. – Tacitus fays that his fall was as injurious to the inhabitants of Rome as his continuance in power had been – that a fort of contention arofe between the Senate and Tiberius concerning the difpofal of his effects – that his adherents were profecuted and executed continually for feveral years after. – Dion, we find, fays, that the greateft anarchy enfued – that the commonalty proceeded to murder thofe who had in- fulted under Sejanus – that the foldiers became incendiaries and depredators – that the Senate took no notice of all this infubordination, but rejoiced at his death – that they immediately decreed that his fall fhould annually be celebrated by the priefts and by new rites to the Gods – and that they decreed one or two other things highly offenfive to Tiberius – and, that Tiberius, *under a pretence of Sejanic accufations,* put many to death, and caufed others to put themfelves to death – *TtGtftos trpoQaffn rix Zwcuat tyx. npatra votno-xpsns, vous Tnxvv enruMvt res* x. r. X.

Of the cause of the fall of Sejanus.

On a review of all that has been faid concerning the caufe *of his fall,* what do we perceive befides obfcurities, improbabilities, contradictions,, and even glaring abfurdities? – Had the report of any of thofe hiftorians been fatisfactory, would Juvenal, who was born before any of thofe who were not cotemporaries with Sejanus, have reprefented the people of Rome as afking fuch queftions concerning it ? – and ac- quiefcing in the fuggeftion that the fole caufe of it was a letter of the emperor to the Senate, the contents of which were never known.

After all that has been faid of the caufe of the fall of Sejanus, it may not be amifs to obferve two things: the firft is – that if there was, as Seneca fays, and P. Arbiter alfo feys, a civil war at Rome, and in, the end of 783 and beginning of 784, why did not Sejanus then feize the opportunity to effect his purpofe ? – efpecially as all claffes were well affected to him ? – The other is – that V. Paterculus, who fpeaks moft highly both of Tiberius and of him the year before he fell, and of the then univerfal tranquillity of the Roman empire, is himfelf, thc'jgh a great favorite of Tiberius, fuppofed to have fallen a victim to his attachment to Sejanus. – Now if two fuch fubjects, who had been indebted to Tiberius for all their preferment, confpired againft him, can we wonder that he ordered them to be executed ? – Or rather can we fuppofe that two fuch favorites (one of whom had publicly acknowledged how much they were both obliged to him) would, in the time of the greateft tranquillity, have confpired againft their fovereign? Paterculus, we know, in the laft chapter of his work, ufes an expreffion which has puzzled annotators – fome think he fpeaks of com- plaints made to the Gods of fome God or Gods, but may he not by this have alluded to the introduction of fome new Deity ? – And he, we alfo know, promifes, in the end of that chapter, to conclude with a petition. – What then is that petition ? – It is that which occurs in

Of the cause of the fall of Sejanus.

the work of Seneca, de Benif. 1. 4, c. 7 – or, that which V. Acidalius notices – and which he prefaces with a fort of acknowledgement that the author of nature had different appellations, and that Vinicius was at liberty to addrefs him by what name he pleafed ! CHAPTER XXII.

When and why did Agrippa leave Italy ?

9J OSEPHUS inforrns us, A. xviii. 7, ., that Agrippa was obliged to leave Italy on account of the vaft debt which he had contrafted, moft of which, he fays, he had expended *on thefreedmen of Cafar.* – But what he had to do with the freedmen of Caefar, Jofephus has omitted to inform us, at leaft in plain terms – he only feems to hint, and very obfcurely, that Agrippa hoped that fome projeft of theirs would fucceed – E?.7nSj *irf!-sus ns avrut,* – To this very incomprehenfible reafon our hiftorian, in the end of the fame feftion, has fubjoined another, as an auxiliary to that above ftaed – viz – that Agrippa had been one of the moft intimate companions of Drufus, and that, as Tiberius could not bear the fight of any of his fon's favorites, he found it neceflary not only to leave Rome but Italy, and to retire to his own country. But is this other any way likely to have been the fmallefl part of the true caufe of his quitting Rome and Italy too, at any time ? – What fay Seneca, Tacitus, and Suetonius of the manner in which Tiberius bore

Ooo

When and wliy did Agrippa leave Italy ?

the lofs of his only fon? – Seneca, in his Confolation to Marcia, then almoft difconfolate for the lofs of her fon, chap. 15, propofes to her, before the death of Livia, Tiberius, as the moft remarkable pattern of fortitude under the lofs of his deareft fon. – He fays, that he fpoke bis dear fon's funeral oration, and that, when all Rome was quite overcome with grief for the lofs of that promifing prince, Tiberius was alone unmoved. – Tacitus fupports the evidence of Seneca on this point, he fays, iv. 10, that he did not relax his concern for the public welfare – that he had recourfe to public bufinefs as his folace – that he adminiftered juftice, and attended to the complaints of the provinces as ufual. – Sed Tiberius nihil intermifla rerum cura, negotia pro folatiis accipiens, jus civium, preces fociorum traftabat. Suetonius too confirms this teftimony, he fays, iii. 52, that Tiberius made this reply to the people of Ilium, who were a little too , tardy in addreffing him on the occafion – that he was very forry for their lofs of Hector.

Now as thofe three writers bear fuch unanimous teftimony as to the noble conduft of Tiberius, on this airlifting occafion, why fhould we fuffer ourfelves to be perfuaded by Jofephus that he could not endure the fight of Agrippa, becaufe he had been one of the more intimate companions of his only fon? – And why, ifjthat had really been true, fhould we fuffer ourfelves to be perfuaded that Agrippa would have thought it at all neceflary to leave Italy? – efpecially if Tiberius had, before he did it, left Rome? – And why mould we not fufpeft that Jofephus muft have had fome very finifter view for endeavoring to impofe a falfe opinion, in this cafe, on our credulity ?

As we feem to have fo great an appearance of reafon for fufpe&ing Jofephus of a defign to impofe on our credulity in this affair, let us proceed to examine what he fays further, with a degree of caution fuited to our fufpicions.

When and tvhy did Agrippa leave Italy ?

Though he feems inclined to perfuade us, in the firft feftion of this 7th chapter, that Agrippa went from Italy foon after the death of Drufus – that is, either in the year 776 or foon after it, yet who will deny that he feems to fay enough in the very next feftion to convince us that that prince did not reach Judea till after the marriage of his uncle and fifter, which, we fuppofe, happened in the year 780. – But whether he went from Rome and Italy1 to avoid his creditors, or to avoid injuring the feelings of Tiberius, it appears, both by what Jofe- phus fays in the fifth feftion of this fame 7th chapter, and from what he again fays in his B. ii. 9, S. *t. t* that he, not many years after, returned thither again – for he, in this fame chapter, fays that he returned before the death of Pifo – that is, as Tacitus and Dion fay, before the end of the year 785 – and, in his B. ii. 9, &., he, having faid that Pilate rifled the facred treafury, alfo fays, in the next ?., that Agrippa, in the interim – Kv *rxm* – went to Rome for the purpofe of accufing (not Pilate obferve, but) his uncle, the tetrarch of Galilee, of fome- thing. – In Italy he now appears to have remained, in the family of Tiberius, till the death of that monarch, as the tutor of his grandfon. But regardlefs of the patronage of that moft benevolent monarch, he, fays Jofephus, inftead of fhewing his gratitude to his benefaftor, and his concern for the only child of his friend Drufus, paid his court to Caius, and wifhedTiberius dead, and his own darlingCaius his fucceflbr.

As then Agrippa, by the account of Jofephus, feems to have lavim- ed fuch an immenfe fum of money on the freedmen of Caefar, and *in hope that their projefl would fucceed,* and to have left Judea for fome other reafon befides the fear of aggravating the grief of Tiberius, and afterwards to have been fo ungrateful to his beft friend, and fo bafe towards the furviving child of his departed companion, how are we to be fure that he was not the inftigator of the libertines?

SECTION 21

CHAPTER XXIII.
Was Peter at Rome in the days of Tiberius ?
  W E have feen that the faith of Chrift appears to have been received at Rome in the year 781, that is, nearly ten years before the death of Tiberius, and that, though much oppofition was at firft made to the reception of it by unbelievers, Jews, and Romans, thofe who received it were, during the remainder of his reign, permitted, under his patronage, to profefs it without moleftation. And we feem to have reafon to think that it was, very fhortly after, received in almoft all the provinces – for Clemens of Rome informs us that Tiberius caufed inquifition to be made, throughout all the provinces, for the maleficent, (of whom Simon, it feems, was one,) in order to put them to death – and, immediately after the fall of Sejanus, ordered all his cheirotonized hyparchs, in the provinces, to be favorable to thofe Jews only who behaved peaceably. – Indeed Eufebius as good as tells us, Eccl. hift. ii. 2. fin. and 3. init., that the example which Tiberius, by becoming obedient to the faith, fet, was, in a fhort time, followed by
  Was Peter at Home in the days of Tiberius f
    all the world. – At leaft we have reafon to think that churches or focieties of Chriftians were, in the courfe of his reign, eftablifhed in moft great cities – for inftance – in Antioch, in Alexandria, in Edefla, in Adiabene, if not in countries ftill

more remote from Judea – viz – in Parthia, Mefopotamia, Arabia, India, Ethiopia, Libya, and Cyrene, of which province Crete, fays Strabo, xviii, was a part. – About the end of his reign 10,000 perfons were, fays Clemens of Rome, Recog. x. 71, in the fhort fpace of feven days, converted, at Antioch alone, to the faith, on which occafion Theophilus, the molt eminent perfon there, converted his palace into a church.

Now how were thofe various focieties of Chriftians governed during thofe ten years ?

We do not read, in the new teftament, that any one of the twelve Apoftles attempted to preach the gofpel to Gentiles before Peter went, at the fpecial command of God, to Cornelius, which, by all accounts, happened feven years after the afcenfion, or, u. c. 788, at which time the other Apoftles demanded of him the reafon why he took fo extraordinary a ftep, and Peter thought it neceflary to enter into a formal juftification of his conduit in that affair. – Neither do we read, in any part of the new teftament, that any of the Apoftles left Judea, for the purpofe of preaching to Gentiles, till the murder of James, who appears to have been put to death after the difciples were firft called Chriftians at Antioch, which event, as John, of that city, tells as, happened in the loth after the afcenfion, or rather, if, as Eufebius fays, Eccl. hift. ii. 9, James fuffered after Claudius began to reign, he appears, by what Luke and Jofephus fay, to have fuffered before the feaft of unleavened bread in the 3d of Claudius, and therefore in the 13th or 14th after the afcenfion; for Luke fays that he was put to

Was Peter at Rome in the days of Tiberius?

death before that feaft, and, feemingly, in the fame year that Agrippa died; and Jofephus fays that Agrippa died in the 7th of his reign.

As then we cannot find the leaft encouragement in the Afts to think that any of the twelve Apoftles left Judea, for the purpofe of preaph- ing to Gentiles, before the death of James – that is, according to Eufe- bius, before the I3th or i4th year after the afcenfion, and confequently not any encouragement to think that Peter was at Rome in the reign of Tiberius; let us proceed to enquire whether any early ecclefiaftical writer appears to authorife us to think that Peter may have been at Rome in the reign of that monarch.

Clemens of Rome, in his Recog. Homil. and G. P., mentions Petqr as having op- pofed the preaching of Simon, the forcerer, at feveral places near Judea, and efpecially at Antioch, but he no where feys that he was at Rome in the reign of Tiberius. – Juft before his martyrdom he mentions him, chapter 144 of the laft mentioned work, as having appointed himfelf bifhop of that city.

. Papias, it has been thought, has mentioned Peter as having been at Rome, becaufe he fays that Mark wrote what Peter preached, and Mark, Eufebius tells us, ii. 14, wrote his gofpel at Rpme, as Peter preached it, – But though Papias may be fuppqfed to have faid fo, yet he does not fay that Peter was at Rome *in the reign of Tiberius.*

By what Luke and Joseph us say of the employment of Agrippa, at Caesa- rea, whom he was, by the people, supposed a God, it appears that he was celebrating the llth quinquennial in commemoration of the building of that city by Herod – for a Greek chronologist informs us that it was compleated in the first year of the 192d olympiad, or u. c. 742. OA – P0B. A. *Kawraptix* St/w- rwvoi *wo* HfwSa *enteiuQy.* Bus. Chron. Can. p. 266, says the same. – See Chron $yn. y. 385.

Was Peter at Rome in the days of Tiberius?

Eufebius, indeed, who fays, in his Chronology, A. n. p. 62, 1. 26, that Cyrenius was, in the year 33 of Herod, fent to tax Judea – and, that our Lord was, as we alfo fay, born in that fame year, f fays alfo, in that fame page, 1. 53, that he was baptifed in the 15th of Tiberius, and that he fuffered in the i8th year. – Eufebius furthermore fays, p. 64, 1. 47, that Peter went, after he had founded a church at Antioch, in the 4oth year of the incarnation, (which, by his own previous account concerning the year in which our Lord was born, p. 62, 1. 26, muft have been the 2Oth of Tiberius, and therefore, if, as fome fup- pofe, Cornelius was not converted within feven years after the afcenfion, the year *before* Cornelius was converted) to Rome to preach the gofpel there. – But does Eufebius appear to have been always of the fame opinion? – If he does, why has he told us, Eccl. hift. ii. 14, 15, of the effeft of Peter's preaching at Rome in the reign of Claudius ? – Why has he, on the authority of Apollonius, of Hierapolis, recorded, Eccl. hift. v. 8, p. 126, C., the following tradition? – and, without the leaft animadverfion on the fingularity of it? – viz – that our Lord, after his refurrection, commanded the twelve *not'to* depart from Judea till the expiration of twelve years, which twelve years expired in the year*Was Peter at Rome in the days of Tiberius?*

of Rome 793, or the third of CaiUS – EW Se *us sx irapa$uo-cus ro*

Ev *ru* Xy Ercj HpwSs *Kvfvivios ma* Tb atyxXrs /3rX? s EWomo-aro *rut afiut xai rut*

f E *ru avTu* (Xy) Iiio-Sr Xfiroi o *Qmsyfut tv* BflXtE/i *rys* The same, thing he also says Chron. Can. p. 186.–See Epit. Chron. p. 67.

I Ev *rt i aury yQy o Xjxt'- Atriofiav rtit trZit apiQpos, ram ru avru* Etei, *HpuSa* St Xy, *Kvpywos x. r. X. sv $i rZ avTu trti* IHZOT2 o *Qsos ypuiv, n* Bd. Et/ *ymSirai,* – Chron. Syn. p. 390.

Query – Wrhat say the Syrian Christians in India of the year in which our lord was born ?

. – Can Eufebius have thought this tradition handed to him by an immediate fucceflbr of an intimate of the Apoftles of no account? – Did he not know that Clemens, of Alexandria, a cotemporary of Apollonius, has recorded the fame tradition, and, as obtained, through Hebrews. – He fays, Strom, vi. p. 636, 7, E /xs a T/j *d&ntn, ra ia-pm*

fj. trx'ij!.3. i, Six ra 0vo/jtror *p. a iriftvin iiri* psy"D3tov, *&fina-mTai aura at axpriai ftirx S. ixx ivn tl-sQtre tis* Tov *xi-.-it. ot,* (/. d *ns tiny ax mvyx. im.* – This, it fhould be obferved, Clemens gives as the report of Peter, for he prefaces it with the following remark – $ Tsto *Qvo-m a ritrfos tipwtiai m* r. – Now as the Apoftles are faid, by thofe very re-

Scil – of Papias – How it happens that the works of this most learned and niost venerable Apostolic bishop are no longer apparent is unaccountable, but still more unaccountable that our modern recondite Theologians consider him as a mere mitred ninny. Had they paid due attention to the evidence of Afri- canus, Eusebius, Jerom, Andrew bishop of Ctesarea, Photius, and the Alexandrine Chron. concerning him, they would have discovered, that instead of having been what they 'unjustly suppose, he was among the first Apostolic presbyters, and *not* inferior, as a writer, to either Ignatius, Polycarp, or Clemens of Rome.

Eusebius says of him, Eccl. hist, iii, that he emigrated from Judea, with Quadratus (who was a hearer of the Apostles) and many others, to preach the gospel – that he was, in the reigfl of Trajan, bishop of Hierapolis – that he was *anf Tx iratra foyivrar-s xai rys yfatyns ti$yiMit* – that he was one of the Apostolic three who published a written record of the true Apostolic doctrine – that he was the only Apostolic presbyter that attested the authenticity of the gospels by Matthew and Mark, and that of the revelation to John. – And in his Chron. A. II. he says, that Papias was, with Polycarp, a hearer of John *the Theologian.*

Jerom says, in Cat., that he was a hearer of John *the Apostle* – the companion of Polycarp – and, the instructor of Irena; us. – And, epistle to Luc., a Spaniard, that his voluminous works were so *elegantly* written, that he was afraid to undertake to translate them.

Andrew of C., who lived about A. D. 500, quotes his work.

Lastly – M. Aurelius thought him so great a pillar of the church that he caused him to be put to death.

Was Peter at Rome in the days of Tiberius ?

fpeftable early Chriftian writers, to have been commanded by their Lord, after his refurreftion, not to go to the Gentiles till the expiration of twelve years, does not this feem to imply that they did not, till the end of that period, leave Jerufalem for the purpofe of preaching to the Gentiles ?

In fhort – as Tiberius is faid, by Tacitus, to have left Rome in the year 779 for the purpofe of dedicating churches, and in the year 780 to have finifhed that pious work – as he is alfo faid, by him, to have deprived, in the year 788, the Blaefi of the prieft-hood, and to have given it to others – as he is faid, by Philo, to have had certain hyparchs cheirotonized – and as he is faid, by Pliny, to have been fond of taking with him that moft gloomy of mortals in his chariot, to the great annoyance of ihe Romans. – and, laftly, as it appears that Peter was not at Rome in his reign, why mould we not conclude that fome other Apoftle ordained the firft preachers in Italy ?

Ppp CHAPTER XXIV.

A recapitulation of what early "writers say of Tiberius, and of his conduct towards Christians,

j HAT the Romans, and all the people fubjeft to them, excepting only the Jews, were, notwithftanding Tiberius had, as Tacitus, Suetonius, and Dion fay, then caufed his fon-in-law, his adopted fon, and his only fon to be murdered, difpofed, fo late as the year 778, to worfhip him, with his mother and the Senate, Tacitus himfelf informs us. – That Tiberius, in that year, objefted to the praftice, as impious in man and derogatory from the honor of the Gods. – That he, ever after, ufed, in his private converfation, to fpeak moft contemptuoufly of the worfhip of man, the fame writer alfo fays. – That fome perfons, notwithflanding his objection to fuch a mode of honoring him, continued, ever after, to worfhip him, and, that many were, till the end of his reign, perfecuted for not worfhipping him, even by the Senate, is faid, not only by the fame writer, but by Seneca and Dion. – That he was, till he went to Capreae, that is, till he was nearly 70 years of age, accounted a favorite with the Gods, is plain from what the fame writer alfo fays of the means by which the fire on Mount Coelius was

A recapitulation of what early "writers say of Tiberius, $c.

commonly thought to have been extinguifhed. – That he was, till that time, accounted a moft admirable prince, is plain, from what Suetonius fays of the importunity of the people to fee him immediately after the Amphitheatre at Fidenae, when crowded with two or three myriads of fpeftators, fell and buried moft of them in its ruins – and that he really was, at that late period, fo good a prince, is alfo plain, from what the fame writer fays of his readinefs, though at the . time overcome with grief, to comply with their requeft, on that occafion, and of his extreme condefcenfion to every body while there. – That he was, for his beneficence on thofe two occafions, thanked both by the Senate and the people, Tacitus affures us. – That he was, till near the end of the fame year, (780) confidered, by the Senate, as the only fuffuge from exifting evils, that is, the evils caufed by accufers, Tacitus alfo aflures us. – That he was, ftill later in that year, fufpicious and remarkable for *a* temerity of believing, and that Sejanus increafed it, he

complains. – That the Senate was, in the beginning of the year 781, fo fubmiffive to his will, and fo hoftile to the family of Germanicus, as to condemn Sabinus, the only remaining adherent of that family, unjuftly, he alfo complains. – That Tiberius, at the fame time, complained that his life was in danger, he furthermore fays. – That a motion was made, in the Senate, by Gallus, to requeft Tiberius to explain the caufe of his fears, in order to have them removed; – that Sejanus objefted to the motion on the fcore that the dilatory prince did not choofe to have the ground of his apprehenfions known, he alfo fays. – That the Senate, in the fame year, fought to conciliate his alienated affeftion by the moft prepofterous devices, he furthermore fays. – That they, again and again, petitioned him to indulge them with an interview, but to no purpofe. – That they, finding all other expedients unavailable, came to the refolution of proceeding, together

*A recapitulation of what early writers say of Tiberius, %*c.

with the knights and commonalty, to the coaft of Campania, in order to intreat him to grant them an interview. – That he would not, even then, confent to be feen. – That Sejanus did condefcend to fee a few of them, who were, foon after, on their return, made to fuffer a grievous exit for it, Tacitus moreover teftifies, but without attempting to account for this myfterious ftrangenefs. – That his mother, who had, for feveral years before, been, with him and the Senate, worfhipped, and who knew that coeleftes religiones had been decreed to Auguftus, defired him, a littsle before her death, (which happened early in the year 782,) to objeft to her confecration or immortalization, or, apo- theoofis, for a certain reafon; Tiberius himfelf, who, for fome reafon, abftained from attending her funeral, faid – that her reafon could not, as Tacitus fays, have been *left* coeleftial religion mould be decreed, any one may perceive by what has been juft faid – that her reafon is more likely to have been *unlefs* coeleftial religion fhould, at the fame time, be decreed, is, we think, not improbable. – That very foon after his mother was buried much oppofition was made, both by the Senate and by the people, to fome meafure propofed, to the Senate, by Tiberius, relative to Agrippina and her fon Nero, is, we alfo find, faid by Tacitus. – That both he and Sejanus were, in the Senate, publicly afperfed, and even by one of the confuls, is, we find, alfo faid. – That Sejanus then complained of the infubordination of the people j – and, that Tiberius then alfo complained that his imperial authority had been publicly evaded by the finefle of one fenator, and that he then publifhed an edict reprimanding the populace, he moreover informs us. – That Tiberius and Sejanus were, in the year following, on the beft of terms, Paterculus aflures us. – That they were, in the fecond year following, colleagues in the confulfhip, we know. – That Tibe-

If, as Petronius Arbiter says, Cæsar complained that he was driven from Rome, how could any one expect th§t he should attend his mother's funeral ?

A recapitulation of what early writers say of Tiberius, c.

rius then ufed, in his letters to the Senate, to ftyle him, *the-partner of hh cares,* Dion and others fay. – That the mifinformed and *believing* wirKwmr then erected ftatues of brafs, with infcriptions on them, to both Tiberias and Sejanus, and placed gilded chairs of ftate, for both of them, in the Theatre, and, that the Senate, at the fame time, decreed that their confulfhip fhould be quinquennial, that a procef- fion fhould go to meet them as often as they fhould enter Rome, and, that they facrificed to both alike, Dion alfo fays. – That Sejanus was, in the courfe of that fame year, permitted to marry Livilla, Tacitus clearly feems to fay. – That he was, before the end of that fame year, put to death, nobody doubts. – That Tiberius was accufed of having been the caufe of it, we know. – But why he is fuppofed to have done it, nobody knew, even in the days of Juvenal. – That he procured it to be done by fending a long unintelligible epiflle to the Senate, in which he faid nothing of his execution, though he, as Dion afterwards faid, had given orders to the magiftrates of Rome to prevent tumults, Dion moreover fays. – That the Senate, *perceiving that nyie of the guards were near to /iroteſl him, and in order to gratify the /lopulaae,* immediately, without a trial and without fuffering him to fpeak for him- felf, condemned him, and, the fame day, proceeded (in defiance of the decree forbidding fuch precipitate executions,) to execute him, Dion furthermore fays. – That the Senate decreed alfo that his children fhould be put to death, and that Livilla is alfo faid to have been, about the fame time, put to death, Dion alfo teftifies; but whether fhe was executed by the order of Tiberius, or by that of her own mother, Dion could not fay. – That a tumult enfued in the city, notwithftand- ing Tiberius had given orders to the magiftrates to preferve the peace,

Who those misguided and believing persons were, Dion, it is observable, does not say j he, however, says, that they were not more inclined to treat Tiberius and Sejanus with respect than the Senate.

A recapitulation of what early writers say df Tiberius, c.

he alfo fays. – That the people murdered the partifans of Sejanus. – That the life-guards alfo became mutinous, not becaufe their commander and his frierfds had been killed, but becaufe night centinels, *more in the faith –* tjr *writ – of the emperor,* had been appointed, and not only mutinous, but depredators and incendiaries, Dion alfo fays. – That the Senate too difagreed much among themfelves, and that thofe among them, who had been the adherents of Sejanus, were in great trepidation and overcome by fear, as well they *who had accufed others,* as they *-who had borne tejlimony again/1 them,* left they mould come under a fufpicion of having been the caufe of the death of thofe accufed perfons, not to gratify Tiberius, but Sejanus. – That a few, not of this number, hoped that Tiberius would be more merciful, for they thought that what had pafled was occafioned entirely by Sejanus, and, that' *Tiberius had nothing to do with it, and that he might perhaps have been ignorant of the whole affair, if not compelled* *to a$l the part which he had in it.* – That private perfons, almoft to a man, were of the fame opinion. – That the Senate unanimoufly decreed that nobody fhould mourn the fallen mifcreant, that the effigies of Liberty mould be fet up in the Forum. – That the day on which he fell fhould, by all perfons in office and by *all the 'priejls,* be kept as a feftival. – That it mould be annually celebrated by horfe-races, and by the exhibitions of the fights of wild beafts, and *ty the four colleges of priejls,* not ex- cepting the fociety of thofe lately inftituted to Auguflus. – That they, in contempt of his memory, *injlituted new rites to the Gods.* – That they believed the Gods had infatuated him. – That they ordered that no one fhould fwear by any other than by the emperor. – That the Senate decreed all this *tojhew tbeir delegation of Sejanus,* Dion fays. – That they alfo, at -the fame time, decreed feveral things *in token of their approbation of Tiberius* – viz – that he fhould, from henceforth, be faluted with the title of father of his country – that his birth-day

A recapitulation of what early 'writers say of Tiberius, %c.

mould be celebrated with ten horfe-races, and, with a fenatorial banquet, the fame writer likewife fays.

After the fall of Sejanus, Dion proceeds to mention the following occurrences:

That Tiberius, on hearing of his fate, rejoiced, as might be ex- pefled. – That the Senate again fent a deputation to Tiberius, confift- ing of perfons of all ranks. – That he again would not permit them to fee him. – That he would not permit even Regulus, the conful, who, as Dion fays, was his loyal fupporter, to fee him, though he went, on purpofe, with a party of armed men, to conduft him, as he is faid to have requefted, fafe to Rome. – That many of the friends and relations of Sejanus were, after his fall, alfo put to death, and that many others, who had before been acquitted, were again tried and put to death. – That fenators and knights, men and women, were put in the fame prifon, and, if they furvived the rigour of their confinement, praecipitated from the Tarpeian rock. – That Tiberius was defirous to have every thing forgotten. – That he would permit Sejanus to be mourned, though the Senate would not. – That he was, in the following year, 785, ftill fo much in fear of. the Senate, that he would not venture among them. – That Lucius Sejanus dared, notwithftanding the fate of his brother the year before, to infult him, and that he took no notice of it. – That the Senate was, in the year 786, entirely fubfervient to his will. – All this, Dion fays, happened in lefs than two years after the death of Sejanus.

Of Tiberius, while at Capreae, Suetonius aflerts the following particulars :

Tacitus says that Tiberius found no fault at all with Sejanus; and, at the same time, found the greatest with the Blaesi, on whom he hail conferred the pontificate, and whom he, *v.* c. 789, dispossessed of that office, and gave it *to others.*

A recapitulation of -what early writers say of Tiberius, Sgc.

That he, foon after his philanthropic vifit to Fidenae, when he was nearly 70 years of age, became a monitor of unnatural luft and of favage cruelty – that he drank human blood, as he formerly ufed to drink wine – that he, while at Capreae, caufed a civil war at Rome. – That many perfons of all ranks, even condemned criminals, notwith- ftanding the machinations of fpies and accufers, took the liberty of ex- pofing him, for his fuppofed deteftable vices, in the moft public manner, if not to his face. – That he paid no attention to thofe multifarious accufations, but calmly faid – Oderint dum probent. – That he, who, in 784, expelled the Jews, &c. for praftifing profane rites, was, a little before his death, negligent about the Gods and religion, and a fatalift; and that the people of Rome, after his death, execrated hira as impious.

Jofephus, on the contrary, fays, that he, at the fame time, prayed to the Gods of his country to be direfted in the choice of a fucceflbr, and to fome one God above the reft. – Agrippa, who had fpent much time with him, fays, that he was, during all his reign, *a dally "worJJtiJi- fer of the moft htgh God.* – And this he ventured to aflert to his own enraged patron and kinfman Caius, even when he dared not to appear in his prefence. – V. Maximus gives us to underftand that he confider- ed him as being fo notorioufly the patron and encourager of morality and religion, that he, after the fall of Sejanus, prefumed to addrefs him as fuch. – Juvenal, who, had he been fo notorioufly vicious and irreligious, would not have omitted to expofe him for being fo, only fays, that he aflbciated much, at the fame time, with Chaldeans. – And of Chaldeans, Strabo fays, that they were, excepting only thofe who ftudied genethlialogy, men of the higheft reputation for fcience, efpecially Seleucus.

Let us then attend to fome other particulars whch Tacitus affirms of Tiberius.

A recapitulation of what early writers say of Tiberius, %c.

That a moft grievous deftruftion crept, by the no little artifice of Tiberius, into Rome, he fays, but of what nature it was, from whence it proceeded, and when it fo crept into Rome, he does not fay, though, if we miftake him not, he promifes to let us know, in the cafe of two rornan knights, how it happened, and, feems to hint, that it was of a religious nature. Now if it was of a religious nature, and fo defttuc- tiVe, could it, confidering what has been juft faid, have been faid to

V.

have crept in, by the artifice of Tiberius, before the 13th year of his reign? – That this moft grievous deftruftion, though fuffered to creep into Rome, after the 13th of Tiberius, by his no little artifice, was, by fome means or other, foon after reprefled, he alfo fays, but by whom it was reprefled he has taken care not to fay. – That it again fucceeded in finding a reception at Rome, but not irreptitioufly, it, on the contrary, blazed out and confumed every thing. – That Chriftian- ity, which he alfo calls a deftruftive fuperftition, was, for the prefent, by fome means, alfo reprefled, he likewife fays, but when, and where, and by whom, he omits to fay; – that it again broke out, not only in Judea, but in the city itfelf, he moreover affirms. – That accufers began their trade in the 13th year of Tiberius, and that he then dif- couraged them. – That they, in the I4th year, prowled moft furioufly and caufed indefcribable terror at Rome, but to what defcription of the inhabitants he does not fay. – That the internus pavot happened in the fame year, but where the caufe of it originated, how it found admiffion into Rome, and of what nature it was, and how long it continued, this writer has, according to his cuftom, taken care not to fay.

Let us now then attend to what the two Senecas fay – and, firft, to what the younger fays:

If Tiberius was really so impertous, as this writer would have us to believe, what necessity was there for him to use so tuuch artifice to procure the entrance of any thing into Rome ?

A recapitulation of what early writers say of Tiberius, 2$c.

That the rites of foreign nations were, in the reign of Tiberias, he- fore the death of Seneca the elder, and while the younger was juft entering on manhood, agitated by the Senate, the younger himfelf fays. That a certain fuperftition, which confifted chiefly in abftaining from certain forts of animal food, attracted, at the fame time, the attention of the Fathers, he alfo feems to fay. – That even fome of the Romans, of eminence, followed this *new ffiecies of philofophy,* and himfelf, among the reft, he alfo admits. – That it excited fome fprt of calumny, he alfo admits. – That accufers were, in the reign of Tiberius, fuffered to difturb the peace of Rome, worfe than any civil war, f he alfo acknowledges. – That the things whereof they accufed people were of a religious nature, why iliould we not, from the example which he immediately adduces, conclude, though he would have it to be un- derftpod that it was only for difhonoring an image of Tiberius.

Seneca the elder fays, in his work on fuperftition, that the practice of that moft wicked of all people has acquired fuch an afcendancy that it has, even now, obtained a reception all over the world – the conquered have given laws to their conquerors. – That he fpeaks, in the fame work, of the jewifh facraments, Auguftin informs us.

Let us now attend to what Petronius Arbiter fays :

In the beginning of his Satyricon, he fays, that Fabricius Vejento, in the days of Tiberius, publimed a work, which he entitled, de reli- gionis erroribus. – That he, in that work, detefted certain myfteries, he prefumes. – That thofe myfteries were, in his own days, publifhedv-4 *recapitulation of what early writers say of Tiberius,* Sfc.

He says, Cons, ad Jlrlv. – Apicius in ea urbe, ex qua aliquando *philosophi,* velut corruptores juventutis, abire jussi sunt. – Now what does be mean by this ? – When were *philosophers,* as corrupters of youth, ordered to leave the city?

t That those accusers must have been encouraged by Tiberius is undeniable, if he, as Suetonius says, was the cause of that civil war.

boldly, and with a *deceitful fury of vaticination,* and *by Jiriejls,* he aflerts. He alfo fays that Eumolpus prefaced his poem on the civil war with this moft unexpected confeffion, that nobody could expect to fucceed in the attempt, unlefs he was plenus litteris – that he then affigned the following reafon for it – viz – that tranfaftions, which had far better be recorded by an hiftorian, were not to be the fubject of verfe, but that a free fpirit was to be hurried, with precipitation, through intricacies and the *minifieries of the Gods,* and a fabulous diftortion of fen- tences, that it may rather appear to be the *vaticination of an infuriated mind,* than the faithful exhibition *of a religious oration* attefted by wit- nefles. – He then proceeds to recite the poem, in the courfe of which, after having fpoken *repeatedly of drinking blood,* the compofer fays, that in the winter of the year when the *Gemini were confuls* a civil war, not lefs dreadful in its effects than that caufed by Sylla, commenced at Rome. – That this civil war was kindled, not, as is always the cafe, by thofe who were impatient of government, but *by Cefar himfelf,* whom he reprefents as folemnly protefting that he had been compelled to engage in it, *becaufe he had been driven from the feat of hh government.* – The refult of this civil war, he fays, was, , that the inhabitants of Rome thought it preferable, in the fpring of the year 783, (when, we fuppofe, the Chriftians were expelled,) to defert that city, by all manner of ways. – Laftly, that Tryphaena was one of the emigrants, Petronius himfelf feems to intimate.

et us then hear what Paterculus fays:

Pc fays, with apparent aftonifhment, that Tiberius was, in the year 783, making a levy, which caufed not the leaft uneafinefs. – He then immediately appears to demand how he could help it, if complaints were made concerning the Gods. – And, laftly, he addreffes a prayer to the Deity, as though he was in doubt by what name he fhould call him.

A recapitulation of what early writers say of Tiberius, $e.

– The teftimony of V. Maximus next deferves a little attention.

This writer, long after Tiberius had difclaimed any pretenfion to divinity, acknowledged, even to him, and *with the mojl profound rt- f/tcff,* his divinity, and obferves that it *it,* not like that of the reft of the Gods collefted by opinion, but charafterifed by a *prefent faith.*

In the laft place, let us attend to what Pliny has faid of the interdiction of magic ceremonies under Tiberius.

This writer fays that the praftice of immolating a man was fo common, in the Roman empire, in the reign of Tiberius, that it was, by the devotees who followed that praftice, accounted a moft falubrious thing to feed on the flefh of fuch viftims – but to what Deity they were facrificed he, it is rather remarkable, omits to fay – that this inhuman praftice was, through the Cyprians, derived from Mofes, he feems to intimate – that it was, by the Senate, in the reign of Tiberius, prohibited, he, with feeming exultation, informs us. – That any other ceremony of the fame Deity was, at the fame time, prohibited, he has omitted to fay. – That they obtained inconceivable applaufe for it, he has taken care not to omit.

In the laft place let us hear what Philo fays:

This writer fays that a certain defcription of people, whom he names Taraxipolides, diflurbed the peace of citizens and efpecially that of the jews of Alexandria, a little before Tiberius died, and that, when lie died, a moft unufually profound peace pervaded every part of the world.

Let us now then proceed to obferve what ecclefiaftical writers fay of the year in which our Lord was born, of that in which he fuffered, and of the difturbances that attended the firft preaching of the gpfpel, not only in Judea, but in almoft every other place.-

A recapitulation of what early writers say of Tiberius, %c.

That bur Lord was born in the 33d year of Herod, Eufebius, we find, fays, in his Chronology, p. 62. – That the 33d of Herod coin- cided with the year of Rome 747, the preceding fynopfis manifefts. – . That he was, when 30 years of age, baptized, Luke informs us. – That the 30th year of our Lord coincided with the year of Rome 777, or, with the loth of the monarchy of Tiberius, and' not, as Eufebius fays, with the 15th, the preceding fynopfis alfo evinces. – That Tiberius was colleague, in authority of every kind, to Auguftus five years, we have proved. – That Luke, by faying that the 30th year of our Lord happened in the 15th of Tiberius, muft therefore have meant to fay that Tiberius began to reign five years before the death of Auguftus, is evident. – That in the year 778, when our Lord began his miniftry, the 46th year of the temple had elapfed, Jofephus has made it appear by what he fays, B. i. 21 – viz – that the rebuilding of the temple commenced in the 15th year of Herod. – That our Lord's miniftry lafted three years, we hope to prove, in a fubfequent treatife, on the chronology of the new teftament. – That our Lord fuffered in the year 781 feveral authors appear to have attefted. – That the pafchal full-moon happened that year on a Friday, we are told. – That he was expefted to appear in the laft jubilee, we are alfo told. – That the laft jubilee, before the deftruftion of Jerufalem, ended in the 13th of Tiberius, we hope to prove alfo in the propofed treatife. – That the gofpel was preached at Rome in the courfe of the fummer after our Lord fuffered

Eusebius, F. ccl. hist. i. last chapter, says, that it appeared by the records in the archives of Edessa, which he copied *verbatim,* that Thaddcus went *to* Edessa in the year 340 – that is (according to the computation of the Edesse- nes, who began their aera with the first year of Seleucus – or, the first year of the 117th olympaid,) in the first year of the 202d olytnpaid, in which year Christ ascended.

The excerpta utilissima, adduced by Scaliger, as taken from the first book of Eusebius' chronology and from the works of others, say – Paulus in aposto- latum ordinatur iu cousulatu Rubellionis.

A recapitulation of what early writers say of Tiberius, c.
Clemens of Rome informs us. – That fierce oppofition was then made to it, he alfo informs us. – That it was, by the Jews, continued feve- ral years after, and on account of certain meats, Paul fays. – That Tiberius was, before Paul fent him an account of it, apprifed of all that had happened in Judea by Pilate, he himfelf told that prince. – That his attention was then occupied by fome difturbances in Spain, he alfo told him – That he had, before he received the letter from Abgarus, referred the confideration of admitting the worfhip of Chrift to the Senate, he moreover told him. – That the Senate refufed to comply with his propofal, he confefled to him. – That it expelled Chriftians, as being Jews, from Rome, we are told. – That he then threatened death to the accufers of Chriftians, he informed him. – That he made inquifition, not only at Rome, but in all the provinces, for the maleficent, in order to punifh them with death, Clemens of Rome likewife informs us. – That the jewifh libertines were the firft who o'ppofed the faith of Chrift, Luke aflures us. – That they did fo, and thereby caufed Stephen to be ftoned, as a blafphemer, about the end of the year in which our Lord fuffered, may be eafily made to appear by what ecclefiaftical writers fay. – That Agrippa impoverifhed him felf, by profafe largitions, to certain libertines, In hope that fome projeft of theirs would fucceed, Jofephus informs us. – That 4,000 of them were fent to Sardinia, and many others punifhed for not enlift- ing, he alfo informs us. – That the former were Taraxipolides, and the latter believers, why mould we doubt? – That the Sanhedrin, in the year 782, fent to ftrange cities – that is, cities in other countries, for tranfgreflbrs of the law of Mofes, and even for the believers in Chrift, as being fuch, Luke informs us. – That many of thofe believers in

Chrift werei as tranfgreflbrs of the law of Mofes, ftoned to death, Paul, who was employed to do it, informs us. – Tht the cuftom of ftoning Chriftians, as blafphemers, was continued for the fpace of two years,

A recapitulation of what early writers say of Tiberius, $c.

we learn from what Paul told the Galatians. – That this perfecution of believers, by the Sanhedrin, was, about a year or two after, by fome hitherto unknown means, caufed to ceafe, and, that Paul went, about a year after, up to Jerufalem, and there preached Chrift, in the face of thofe who had commiffioned him to perfecute others for the fame offence, we are aflured both by himfelf and by his travelling companion Luke. – That Ifrael was deprived of the privilege of putting a certain fet of perlbns to death in the 40th year before the deftruftion of Jerufalem – that is, in the t6th year of the monarchy of Tiberius, the Talmud of Jerufalem informs us. – That this privation made not the leaft commotion among the Jews, even of Judea, all hiftorians grant. That the Jews were, till late in the year 784, more attached to Tiberius than any other people, Philo, we find, aflures us.

22

SECTION 22

N
, 2 T, IV 77 1
Condition.

J. F the premifes be right who will deny that the following con- clufions may be drawn from them? – viz – That the fcoffers at revealed religion are incomparably greater fools than they have hitherto been thought. – That Unitarians are rather more fo. – That the firft Pope was an arch-impoftor, and the greater part of the firft general council a fet of knaves or fools. – That the Catholic claims are the claims of dangerous haeretics.

THEWMANS. PBINTEBS. EIETEH,

:/' ."
"?